The Scottish Pioneers of
Upper Canada, 1784–1855

The Scottish Pioneers of

NATURAL HERITAGE BOOKS
TORONTO

Upper Canada, 1784–1855

Glengarry and Beyond

LUCILLE H. CAMPEY

Published by Natural Heritage / Natural History Inc.
PO Box 95, Station O, Toronto, Ontario M4A 2M8
www.naturalheritagebooks.com

Cover illustration: Detail of painting by Owen Staples, 1912, of the oldest log house in Peel County. The cottage was built about 1842 on lot 19, second Concession in Caledon Township. Many Argyll settlers came to the Caledon area from the mid-1820s. *Courtesy of Toronto Reference Library, J. Ross Robertson Collection JRR 304. Back cover:* View northeast from the south side of Loch Tay, Perthshire, towards Kenmore. Large numbers of Scots emigrated to Upper Canada from this and other parts of the Breadalbane estate. *Photograph by Geoff Campey.*

Design by Blanche Hamill, Norton Hamill Design
Edited by Jane Gibson
The text in this book was set in a typeface named Granjon

Printed and bound in Canada by Hignell Book Printing

Library and Archives Canada Cataloguing in Publication

Campey, Lucille H.
The Scottish pioneers of Upper Canada, 1784–1855 : Glengarry and beyond / Lucille H. Campey.

Includes bibliographical references and index.
ISBN 1-897045-01-8

1. Scots – Ontario – History. 2. Ontario – Emigration and immigration – History. 3. Scotland – Emigration and immigration – History. 4. Ships – Scotland – Passenger lists. 5. Ships – Canada – Passenger lists. 6. Passenger ships – Scotland – Registers. 7. Passenger ships – Canada – Registers. 8. Ontario – Genealogy. I. Title.

Canada Council for the Arts   Conseil des Arts du Canada   Canada   ONTARIO ARTS COUNCIL CONSEIL DES ARTS DE L'ONTARIO

Natural Heritage / Natural History Inc. acknowledges the financial support of the Canada Council for the Arts and the Ontario Arts Council for our publishing program. We acknowledge the support of the Government of Ontario through the Ontario Media Development Corporation's Ontario Book Initiative. We also acknowledge the financial support of the Government of Canada through the Book Publishing Industry Development Program (BPIDP) and the Association for the Export of Canadian Books.

To Geoff

Contents

Tables & Figures

Tables

Figures

Acknowledgements

I am indebted to many people. In particular I wish to thank the staff at the National Library of Scotland, the National Archives of Scotland, the Library and Archives Canada, the Special Collections Department of the Toronto Reference Library and the Aberdeen University Library for their kind help with my various requests. I thank Barb Thornton of Wallaceburg for sending me a letter which was written by one of the original Baldoon settlers. I am also very grateful to the many people who have assisted me in obtaining illustrations. I thank David Roberts of the Paisley Museum and Art Galleries for his help in locating material relating to Paisley's early handloom weavers. I am grateful to Susan McNichol, Curator of Perth Museum, for the photograph which she located of the Lanark & Renfrew Heritage Pipe Band and for providing me with other excellent material. I also thank Karen Wagner of the Wellington County Museum and Archives, Dawn Owen at the Macdonald Stewart Art Centre in Guelph, Jessica Yack at the Grey County Archives in Owen Sound, Theresa Regnier at the University of Western Ontario Archives in London, Adam Hollard at the Woodstock Museum National Historic Site, Rev. Fred Hagle and David Jenkins of Knox United Church in Ayr, Evan Morton of The Tweed Heritage Centre, Dan Conlin of the Maritime Museum of the Atlantic in Halifax Nova Scotia, John Edwards at the Aberdeen Maritime Museum and Paul Johnson of the National Archives of England at Kew, London, England.

Anyone who glances through the secondary sources in my bibliography will notice the many books which have been published by Natural Heritage. This publishing house is making a considerable contribution to the recording of Ontario's history and cultural heritage. I am extremely pleased to be one of their authors and to be in such good company.

I wish finally to record my thanks to my dear friend Jean Lucas for her comments on my initial manuscript. Most of all I wish to pay tribute to my husband Geoff for his guidance, practical help and loving support. A tower of strength at all times, he is a constant source of inspiration and encouragement.

Preface

Ontario's Scottish pioneers are the subject of this book. While a great deal has been written about the individual settlements which were founded by Scots, no overview of the total picture has ever been attempted. This is surprising in light of the considerable long-term achievements of the province's Scottish colonizers.

This book gathers together a large body of material, from both primary and secondary sources, and considers the nature, direction and impact of the emigrant flows from Scotland to Upper Canada (Ontario). As ever, it is the very first arrivals who should command our greatest attention and respect. They were the Glengarry Highlanders whose settlements began to take shape from the mid-1780s. Their actions spearheaded the significant tide of emigration from Scotland which occurred over the next seven decades. This study pieces together the various strands of the story as some 100,000 Scots headed for Upper Canada. Why did Upper Canada hold such appeal to Scots? How did the emigration process actually work? Where did Scots settle? Why did the Glengarry settlements have such a major impact? And what happened to the Scottish traditions which were brought over by the early pioneers?

These are some of the questions which I have attempted to answer in this book. I have considered the various social and economic developments in Scotland which caused people to leave. I have also looked at the factors which attracted Scots to Upper Canada. The regional patterns of emigration from Scotland became apparent when I delved into the shipping records. Very few passenger lists survive but, by making use of customs records and newspaper shipping reports, it has been possible to estimate passenger numbers. They reveal the individual emigrant streams which developed from various parts of Scotland as the zeal to emigrate took hold.

A recurring theme of this book is the predominance of Scots amongst the earliest immigrant arrivals. The greater cost and difficulty of reaching Upper Canada, compared with the Maritime provinces, meant that some form of organization and support had to be given to the early groups who chose to emigrate. This support was provided by government, wealthy proprietors, settlement managers such as Thomas Talbot, and later on, by the Canada Company. However, in the earliest stages of colonization this support came mainly from government, which preferentially selected Scots for assisted emigration schemes.

Two other recurring themes are the importance placed by Scots on their religion and culture. Scots often emigrated in large groups and follow-on emigration usually occurred from the areas of Scotland which had fostered the original settlements. Highly distinctive Scottish communities were the result. The Presbyterian clergymen, sent out from Scotland, were a valued religious and cultural lifeline. Their visit reports, describing the progress being made by various communities in forming congregations and building churches, give an added dimension to our understanding of pioneer life. Some clergymen had a tough time coping with the free and easy ways of the New World and their frustration is evident in their reports, which they never expected would be made public.

This study traces the progress of the many Lowland and Highland communities which developed in Upper Canada. Because they were Gaelic-speaking, Highlanders were far more visible than Lowlanders. They sought isolated locations where they could continue to practise their traditions and customs, often to the consternation of other people who criticized their clannishness. Lowlanders were more easily assimilated into mixed communities, but Highlanders remained apart from the rest of society. However, when Gaelic began its decline in the late nineteenth century, Highland culture would soon fade away with it. Because Gaelic was primarily a spoken language, little has been recorded. So, although symbols of Highland culture live on in the province, they are vestiges of a Highland past which has largely been lost.

For me, one of the abiding images of this study is that of the Scot, with axe in hand, hacking his way through large swathes of the province. As some of the province's earliest pioneers they were expected to play a vital role as defenders of territory. And Scots were always at the cutting edge of each new frontier as colonization began its westward and northward spread.

Scots have contributed greatly to Ontario's sense of identity. However, it is easy to see them today as just one of the province's many ethnic groups. After all, in 1961 they represented only 13 per cent of the population. And yet, they were a founding people who had an enormous influence on the province's early development. Most of all they should be remembered for their outstanding successes which could not have been envisaged, given their humble origins.

Abbreviations

ACA	Aberdeen City Archives
AH	*Aberdeen Herald*
AJ	*Aberdeen Journal*
AO	Archives of Ontario
AR	*Acadian Recorder*
AU	Aberdeen University
DC	*Dundee Courier*
DCA	Dundee City Archives
DCB	*Dictionary of Canadian Biography*
DGC	*Dumfries and Galloway Courier*
DPC	*Dundee, Perth and Cupar Advertiser*
DT	*Dumfries Times*
DWJ	*Dumfries Weekly Journal*
EA	*Edinburgh Advertiser*
EC	*Elgin Courant*
GA	*Greenock Advertiser*
GC	*Glasgow Chronicle*
GH	*Glasgow Herald*
GSP	*Glasgow Saturday Post*
IA	*Inverness Advertiser*
IC	*Inverness Courier*
IJ	*Inverness Journal*

JJ	*John O'Groat Journal*
KM	*Kelso Mail*
LAC	Library and Archives Canada
LSR	*Lloyd's Shipping Register*
MG	*Montreal Gazette*
MT	*Montreal Telegraph*
NAS	National Archives of Scotland
NLS	National Library of Scotland
PA	*Paisley Advertiser*
PC	*Perthshire Courier*
PEIG	*P.E.I. Gazette*
PRO	Public Record Office
PP	*Parliamentary Papers*
QG	*Quebec Gazette*
QM	*Quebec Mercury*
SM	*Scots Magazine*
SRA	Strathclyde Regional Archives

The Scottish Pioneers of
Upper Canada, 1784–1855

One

THE VULNERABLE COLONY

It is with regret I have heard persons of distinguished judgement and information give way to the opinion, that all our colonies on the continent of America, and particularly the Canadas, must inevitably fall, at no distant period of time, under the dominion of the United States.[1]

O NTARIO OWES A GREAT DEAL TO its early Scottish pioneers. In the early 1800s, when the 5th Earl of Selkirk warned of its vulnerability to the Americans, Upper Canada, as it was then known, had an uncertain future. "The danger to be apprehended," Selkirk warned, "is not merely from an invading military force, but much more from the disposition of the colonists themselves, the republican principles of some, and the lukewarm affection of others."[2] Its settlers, who were mainly of American origin, had doubtful allegiance to Britain. As a result, Britain's hold over Upper Canada was very precarious. Henry Addington, the then British Prime Minister, actually went on record as saying that, "the British government had so slender a hold on the province" of Upper Canada that he could not encourage any of "the King's loyal subjects" to emigrate there.[3] Upper Canada's situation could not have been bleaker. It faced being invaded by its big neighbour to the south and, because Britain was preoccupied with costly and lengthy wars with France, little attention and few resources were being devoted to its defence needs. However there was one glimmer of hope.

Highland Scots had been trickling into what was then the old province of Quebec from as early as 1784. The first group came as Loyalists from the United States following Britain's defeat in the American War of Independence. Being mainly the families of ex-servicemen, they had been relocated at public expense to an area just to the west of the French seigneuries. When Quebec became divided into Upper and Lower Canada from 1791, this area would be on the eastern extremity of Upper Canada, making it one of the most important defensive locations in the province. Their success would initiate a major influx of Highlanders, producing the remarkable Glengarry communities whose name commemorates the Inverness-shire origins of the first settlers. Their culture and Gaelic language set them apart from the rest of the population and, being fiercely loyal to the British Crown, they would play an invaluable role in safeguarding Upper Canada as British-held territory.

These Highlanders were some of Upper Canada's earliest immigrants. Even though Britain had controlled the St. Lawrence region since 1763, following the close of the Seven Years War, she had made little effort to colonize it. Compared with the Maritime provinces which were much closer, Upper Canada was exceedingly difficult and expensive for immigrants to reach.[4] Loyalists had been brought to the province in 1784 for the specific reason of bolstering particularly vulnerable border areas. As a preliminary step to achieving this, it had been necessary to remove the Native Peoples from their lands.[5] Whereas in the Maritime provinces this policy had led to much bloodshed, it was carried through in the Canadas with little disturbance.[6]

Having achieved its objective of moving this first group of Highlanders into their new location on the St. Lawrence River, the government could not have anticipated the impact this would have back in Scotland. Relocating Highland families from the United States to Upper Canada was all that had been intended. But, their fellow countrymen rushed forward in droves to join them. The follow-on emigration from Inverness-shire was a most unwelcome development for the government, and it did everything in its power to stop the exodus, but it was unstoppable.

Various publications at the time reflected the increasing alarm felt by Highland landlords over the loss of tenants from their estates. An anonymous commentator believed that 4,000 people had left the lands "belonging to MacDonnel of Glengarry" between 1784 and 1803, all having emigrated to Upper Canada.[7] Judging from the number of transatlantic passengers reported in newspaper shipping reports, passenger lists and the Scottish customs records, it would seem that this figure has a ring of truth.[8] However, when one considers the overall population of Upper Canada which had reached 71,000 by 1806, these Highlander numbers seem miniscule.[9] Yet, the fact remains that they were among the few settlers which Upper Canada could rely upon at the time to defend its interests.

Thomas Douglas, the fifth Earl of Selkirk (1771–1820). This is a photograph of a portrait of Selkirk which is believed to have been painted by Sir Henry Raeburn. *Courtesy of the Toronto Reference Library, J. Ross Robertson Collection MTL 2840.*

The Highland exodus was partly a reaction to the large-scale clearances which were taking place to make way for sheep farms, "but this is not the only cause; the high rents demanded by landlords, the increase of population and the flattering accounts received from friends in America do also contribute to the evil."[10] While most prominent Scots opposed emigration, Lord Selkirk grasped its inevitability and personally sought to direct pioneer settlements. He argued that emigration provided an escape route for dispossessed Highlanders while bringing much needed colonizers to British America. Emigration's particular appeal to Highlanders was that it enabled them to perpetuate their Old World lifestyles while, at the same time, giving them the benefits of the New World – especially the prospect of land ownership.

Through his book, *Observations on the Present state of the Highlands*, which was published in 1805, Selkirk turned public opinion his way. And he would live to see his policies being pursued with great vigour by the very landlords who had previously tried to halt emigration. However, his book's importance went far beyond the great emigration debate.

Selkirk's book also presented a coherent strategy for relocating Scots to British America. The success that had already been achieved two years earlier, by his Belfast settlers in Prince Edward Island, gave added weight to the feasibility of his ideas.[11] He was the first eminent Scot to actually

Lt. Col. John Graves Simcoe. He was Lieutenant-Governor of Upper Canada from 1792 to 1799. After his death in 1806, he was buried in the grounds of the family chapel at Wolford in Devon. The chapel is being maintained in perpetuity by the Ontario Heritage Foundation as a place of worship. There is also a monument dedicated to Simcoe in Exeter Cathedral together with an Ontario provincial plaque, which marks the site of the house in the Cathedral Close where Simcoe once lived. The artist was J.W.L. Forster. *Courtesy of Library and Archives Canada C-008111.*

consider colonization from the settlers' point of view when no one else at the time came close to understanding the issues involved. The government's colonization policies relied more on wishful thinking than any master plan. It was hoped that the granting of land to wealthy proprietors, would stimulate them to recruit settlers but in reality few did. Land speculators had a field day while ordinary settlers were left with a bureaucratic muddle.

The large American population in Upper Canada, which was causing such anxiety, can be attributed to actions taken by Lt. Col. John Graves Simcoe, Upper Canada's first Lieutenant Governor. Out of a desperate need for settlers he had actively encouraged Americans to settle in Upper Canada, believing that they could be won back to their previous allegiance to Britain, but it was a vain hope. The values of the mother country had little resonance in pioneer society and, in any case, most Americans were disinterested in the prospect of being brought back into the British fold. Simcoe never understood the democratic ideals which were brewing at the time and instead lived out his fantasy world of a feudal Britain reincarnated in Upper Canada.

Under Simcoe's policies, large grants of Crown land were made to privileged individuals while the Crown and Clergy Reserves set aside even further acreages to the British Establishment. Neither measure advanced the cause of ordinary settlers one iota. In fact, they made matters considerably worse. Vast tracts of land were put beyond their reach. Such vestiges of old-world patronage were resented by settlers and were totally inconsistent with the egalitarian society which they were seeking to create.[12] Left at the mercy of the government's capricious and partisan land policies, most settlers took the only step open to them. They seized their land by squatting.[13] The Crown Reserves, the Clergy Reserves, Crown land, Indian land and privately-held land were all theirs for the taking and it was by squatting that much of Upper Canada came to be settled.

The expected American invasion did materialize in 1812, but it was successfully repulsed by 1814, primarily because of Britain's superior naval power. While Britain eventually secured control over the upper Great Lakes, this was only achieved after several setbacks and victory was by no means a foregone conclusion.[14] Scots were prominent in the militia raised before and during the conflict, with the most conspicuous of the militia units being the Glengarry Light Infantry Fencible Regiment.[15] Having been impressed by Glengarry's contribution in the war, Lt. Col. Edward Baynes wrote to General Sir George Prevost, who masterminded Britain's defence strategy, stating that had it not been for the loyal Scots of Glengarry and those living nearby, Upper Canada would have been taken by the Americans as much by peaceful penetration as by war.[16] And Glengarry men would serve once again with distinction during the Upper Canada Rebellions of 1837–38.[17]

The War of 1812–14 left Upper Canada with a clearer sense of identity and a strong determination to halt any further American influxes. That lesson had been learned. And by this time Lord Bathurst, Secretary of State for the Colonies, had also come to see the wisdom of Selkirk's thinking. Emigration did have its advantages. He hatched a plan in 1815 to replicate what had been achieved in establishing the Glengarry Scots. Using public funds as an inducement, he brought a large contingent of Scots to Upper Canada – this time to the Rideau Valley. Situated just to the west of Glengarry County, their settlements would help to form the government's second line of defence between the St. Lawrence and Ottawa rivers. Three years later, a similar scheme brought even more Scots from Perthshire to the Rideau Valley.

Meanwhile, the Scottish-born author and social reformer, Robert Gourlay, added his voice to the growing colonization debate. Arriving in Upper Canada in the summer of 1817, he visited the fledgling Rideau Valley settlements. While he approved of this initiative, he became highly critical of the government's dysfunctional land policies and advocated that the Crown Reserves should be sold. His proposal fell on deaf ears, but it would be one of the key principles behind the founding of the Canada Company in 1826. Gourlay, himself, had very little influence. His fiery temper made him a loose cannon and after several attempts at silencing him, he was eventually put in jail. He later returned to Scotland.[18]

Even more Scots were brought to the Rideau Valley in 1820–21 as a result of further government-sponsored schemes, but, by this stage, emigrants were having to raise some of the funds for their relocation themselves. Those who came in this later influx were principally destitute weavers from the cotton districts near Glasgow and Paisley. As a result of these various schemes, a total of 4,000 Scots were assisted to emigrate to Upper Canada. However, when considered in the context of the whole population, which at the time stood at around 155,000, their numbers seem tiny.[19]

The Scottish influx to Upper Canada only reached sizeable proportions after 1815, when Scotland became gripped in an economic depression, following the ending of the Napoleonic Wars. The influx was at its height between 1830 and 1855, but even then it only accounted for eleven per cent of the total immigration from Britain.[20] Scots quickly lost ground numerically to the Irish and English. They ranked first before 1825, then were second to the Irish until 1830, but after this they were also outnumbered by the English.[21] Thus, while Scots played a vital role in safeguarding early settlement footholds, their numbers were never very large.[22] It was their early arrival and not their overall numbers which made them so important.[23]

Henry Bathurst, 3rd Earl, who was Secretary of State for the Colonies, 1812 to 1827. *Courtesy of Library and Archives Canada C-100707.*

Although its good land and climate made Upper Canada highly desirable to emigrants, it was relatively late in acquiring settlers, principally because of the large distances which had to be covered in reaching the interior. The first wave of

Highlanders, who founded the early Glengarry settlements, generally had sufficient funds to pay their own way, although some groups needed assistance to get to their final destinations and to see them through their first winter. Those Scots who followed in the subsidized schemes of 1815, 1818 and 1820–21, included many desperately poor people who could not have emigrated without help. And, in spite of the repeated pressure which the government came under to assist other destitute Scots to emigrate, these schemes were never repeated. Thus, from the mid-1820s onwards, emigration has to be seen as an option which was only open to people of relative means. Only those Scots who could pay the higher

Portrait of Robert Gourlay. His major accomplishment was in writing the *Statistical Account of Upper Canada*, published in 1822. *Courtesy of the Toronto Reference Library, J. Ross Robertson Collection, MTL1861.*

travel costs associated with getting to Upper Canada could contemplate emigration. The one exception was the landlord-assisted emigration which occurred during the infamous Highland Clearances of the late 1840s and early 1850s, but, even in these instances, relatively little government aid was forthcoming.

Inland travel at the time was both gruelling and expensive and, coming as it did after a long sea voyage, it was an added ordeal. Emigrants took steamers from Quebec to Montreal and, because stretches of the St Lawrence River beyond Montreal were impassable, they had to transfer to large Durham boats which were dragged up river to Prescott.[24] Those going on to the western peninsula could go from Prescott by steamer up the St. Lawrence to Lake Ontario, travelling on to Hamilton where they disembarked:

> The Durham Boats were a slow means of conveyance. It took a fortnight to make the trip from Montreal to Hamilton. At the various rapids all the passengers, except the infirm or sick had to get out and walk up the shore, the men carrying the smaller children. The [Durham] boats were then drawn by ropes or pushed with poles against the stream.[25]

Timber depot near Quebec. Scottish merchants in Quebec were major beneficiaries of Quebec's important timber trade. By 1810, some 75% of the value of goods exported from Quebec came from lumber and timber products. From *Canadian Scenery Illustrated*, from drawings by W.H. Bartlett; the literary department by N.P. Willis, London, 1842. *Courtesy of Library and Archives Canada F5018 W5 1842.*

The final destination was then usually reached by wagon. A trip to the western limit of the province, a distance of 800 miles, might cost as much as £14 to £15 and, when the costs of provisions and accommodation are added, the overall cost for a family could be as much as £300.[26] It was a considerable outlay.

However, following improvements in inland routes and the lowering of Atlantic fares from 1830, Upper Canada's further distances became less of a hurdle. An important development was the growth in shipping which resulted from Quebec's burgeoning timber trade. Ships were sent from Scotland to collect timber cargoes and, rather than travel empty, they often took emigrants in their holds. Shipowners built up regular shipping services based on a two-way trade in timber and people. Competition brought down fares and emigrants thus had regular and affordable Atlantic crossings. Upper Canada's popularity rose sharply with these transport improvements, and it soon became the preferred destination of most British emigrants, including most Scots.[27]

While the timber trade had immense importance in the Maritime provinces, where it actually shaped settlement patterns, it had far less impact on settlement in western Upper Canada. The first settlers found fertile land, but there was little outlet for their timber produce.[28] Transporting timber through a vast land-locked area to get it to Quebec for export proved impractical and thus western Upper Canada (the peninsula bounded on the south by Lake Erie, on the west and north by Lake Huron/Georgian Bay and on the east by Lake Ontario) had only a negligible trade with Britain. Potash and pearl ashes, which could be shipped more economically, had a market in Britain, but not the timber itself.

Thus, while the shores of rivers and lakes were cleared to create settlements, little or no gain was necessarily expected initially from the sale of felled timber. The first settlers had little opportunity to sell their timber beyond their local markets. An important and lucrative timber trade with the United States would eventually develop, but this would have to await the arrival of steam-towing and the railways.[29] In the initial stages of land clearance farming was the emigrant's main concern. However, the situation was quite different in eastern Upper Canada, where there were two distinct export routes for timber, one along the St Lawrence and the other along the Ottawa River. The Ottawa Valley had large areas which could not easily support farming and here, timber was cut, not as a by-product of land clearance but as a product in its own right. Timber rafts regularly scudded down the Ottawa River to the St. Lawrence and on to Quebec to be loaded onto ocean-going ships.[30] The Ottawa Valley had a major timber trade, although, here also, it had little impact on the process of settlement.

Despite their domination of the early colonization phase in eastern Upper Canada, Scots were soon overtaken by Irish emigrants. One of the reasons for this was the greater Irish attachment to their early communities than was the case with the Scots. While Irish settlers continued to pour into the Rideau Valley region, Scots increasingly looked further afield for their settlement sites. In this respect they were very different from the Irish.[31] Scots were to be found at the edge of each new frontier as the spread of settlement moved westward and northward. Scots were scattered far and wide in the central parts of Upper Canada but, as they moved west, they came together in substantial numbers in Ontario, York and Simcoe counties. By the 1820s they were clearing areas to the north and west of York (Toronto). Included in their numbers were Argyll settlers, especially people from the island of Islay, who would attract followers over many decades.

While many Scots settled in remote locations around Lake Simcoe, others opted for the more populated areas to be found further to the west. Lowlanders, from Aberdeenshire and Dumfriesshire, and Highlanders, from Sutherland and Perthshire, ended up being near neighbours in the heart of the western peninsula. Being some of the earliest arrivals in the region, they each acquired a sufficient quantity of wilderness to enable them to expand as distinct communities. Scots were amongst the first to colonize the southwestern extremity of the province, and they would become particularly prominent in Elgin and Middlesex counties. Argyll settlers were once again extremely well-represented – so much so that when the Governor General visited St. Thomas in 1881, he commented that he had never before seen so many Argyll people – not even in Scotland. And once the Canada Company's Huron Tract, which fronted on Lake Huron, was opened up to settlers, it also became a magnet for Scots. Roman Catholics from South Uist would colonize its western extremity and turn it into a major Scottish enclave. In fact, such was the appeal of the western peninsula that it soon generated a major east to west migration of Scots.

Highlanders from Sutherland, who had originally settled in Nova Scotia, came west in the early 1830s and founded the very important Zorra settlement in Oxford County. Areas of the Huron Tract also acquired Scots from Nova Scotia at this time as did the London district in the Thames Valley. A decade later the Huron Tract attracted yet more Scottish settlers – this time from the Rideau Valley. Cape Breton Scots, who arrived from the early 1850s, mainly went to Bruce County. Originating as they did from the Western Isles, they opted for this more remote location because it enabled them to combine farming with fishing, as they had been able to do in Cape Breton.

The northward progression of colonization only reached Bruce and Grey counties in the 1840s. Being at the edge of the frontier once again, Scots came in large numbers as land became available for settlement. While Presbyterians from the island of Lewis chose Bruce County, Roman Catholics from South Uist were drawn to Grey County. Both counties also attracted a great many Lowlanders as well as Argyll settlers – principally from the islands of Mull, Tiree and Iona.

Meanwhile, Perthshire settlers had no special allegiance to any part of the province. Having founded a number of communities in eastern

Upper Canada by the early 1820s, they then went on to colonize areas of Middlesex County, and a decade later were ensconced in Ontario and Simcoe counties as well as in Wellington and Perth counties further west. Thus, subsequent settlers, wishing to join a Perthshire community, had a truly amazing choice of locations stretching across the entire province.

The Scots who came to Upper Canada were generally well-organized. There were influential men like Adam Fergusson, the Perthshire-born landowner who founded Fergus, and William Dickson, the Dumfriesshire-born merchant and lawyer who founded the Dumfries communities. They stimulated interest in emigration in their part of Scotland and gave practical help to their followers. John Galt, the well-known Scottish novelist, gave the Canada Company added appeal to Scots when he became its first superintendent. And when he assisted the unfortunate group of Scots who came to Guelph, after their abortive attempt to found a settlement in Venezuela, he fell out with the Canada Company directors for showing undue generosity to his fellow Scots. However, the prize for strong leadership must surely go to Thomas Talbot. Combining the mannerisms of a British lord with the domineering tendencies of a military officer, he was a particularly unlovable character. But his supervisory skills were superb. He managed the colonization of those areas in the Thames Valley and along the north shore of Lake Erie, which proved so attractive to Scots. Although they loathed him, he was an important factor in their eventual success and prosperity.

Of course, religion was important to Scots. Father Alexander Macdonell, the first Roman Catholic Bishop of Upper Canada, represented the interests of the Glengarry settlers with great flair and rose to considerable public prominence. Men like the Reverend William Bell, Perth's first Presbyterian Minister, served his congregation for forty years. By bringing Presbyterianism to scattered communities in the Rideau Valley, he helped to reinforce Scottish values and traditions. Belonging to a Canadian Presbyterian sect, not the established Kirk, he was very much his own man. While he had a loyal following, the various Presbyterian missionaries, sent out by the Established Church of Scotland, were often far less well-received. They stood no chance at all within Highland areas unless they spoke Gaelic. But, irrespective of this, many of them were simply not in tune with the people. When Reverend Peter MacNaughton visited the Highland communities in Thorah and Eldon in Ontario

County, he found them "to be as rugged as the rocks they had left in Scotland" and likened them to "wild beasts."[32] And what was even worse, they boasted "of their equality, independence and liberty."[33] Mac-Naughton had demanded subservience, but it was not forthcoming.

It is widely believed that most emigrant Scots were forced to leave their country and that those who emigrated were always destitute and helpless. While some of them were indeed very poor, few Scots were forced to emigrate. In fact, the first wave of emigrants were subjected to quite the opposite pressures. Before 1815 the Scottish ruling classes actually did everything in their power to stop people from emigrating. It was only when the Scottish economy declined, with the ending of the Napoleonic Wars, that attitudes changed. Afterwards, emigration increasingly came to be regarded as a cure-all for the nation's social ills. Highland landlords, who had formerly fought to retain their tenants, swung around in favour of emigration. With the passing of the 1845 Poor Law Amendment Act, which made landlords legally responsible for their poor tenants, landlords had an added incentive to get rid of their unwanted tenantry.

Highland emigration, with its connotation of forced clearances, continues to evoke strong passions on both sides of the Atlantic. Some Highlanders were forced to emigrate, particularly during the dark days of the Highland Famine years from 1846 to 1856, but these were very much the exception. In any case, more Lowlanders actually emigrated to Upper Canada than did Highlanders. Poverty and lack of prospects in Scotland stimulated emigration but they were not the only factors. Scots were also strongly motivated by a desire to succeed as pioneer farmers. "A respectable body of passengers" was how Archibald Buchanan, the Quebec Immigration Agent, often described Scottish arrivals.[34] A good many came with substantial funds and, according to Buchanan, most Scots arrived "in good circumstances."[35]

The Scots who emigrated to Upper Canada were not pitiful down-and-outs. They were positively motivated people who sought to benefit from the better quality of life which Upper Canada offered. It had the best farming opportunities of any province in British America. That is why Scots came in such great numbers. They quickly adapted to New World conditions and were some of the province's most successful pioneers. It is their phenomenal success which should linger in the mind – not the traumas of the Highland Clearances.

The Glengarry settlers excelled as pioneers, even though they arrived without the requisite practical skills. "They had no experience as lumbermen. They had been dwellers by the sea and it is probable that few of them hade ever even cut down so much as a sapling. Their first handling of the axe was clumsy and ineffective."[36] The secret of their success was their ability to cope with isolation and extreme hardship. Later on, when Highlanders colonized large stretches of Middlesex County, they would become known for "their stalwart physique and power of endurance…. They were gifted with strong intellects and keen powers of observation."[37] The Glengarry pioneers would demonstrate these qualities as they spearheaded the Scottish influx to Upper Canada.

Two

THE GLENGARRY
SETTLEMENTS

"Go not to Glengarry if you be not a Highlander."[1]

GLENGARRY'S CLOSE-KNIT HIGHLAND COMMUNITIES impressed John MacTaggart when he visited Upper Canada in 1826. Twenty years later the picture was much the same. Glengarry's inhabitants spoke "nothing but Gaelic" and consequently, "there is scarcely a stranger among them."[2] When MacTaggart came to Glengarry County he saw a Scottish population which had, in fact, been growing in size over some forty-two years. Their undoubted success in attracting waves of followers was plain to see. Predictably they became closed communities where Highland customs could be practised "unaltered, unadulterated and unsullied."[3] In the book which he eventually wrote, MacTaggart advised emigrants to follow the Glengarry example, "Set yourselves down near those who have led such a life as yourself and whose wants are similar to your own."[4] This was what these Highlanders had done. They had banded together and created their own distinctive communities in this one district in eastern Upper Canada.

Most of the Glengarry County settlers had originated from Inverness-shire (Figure 1). The majority came from the vast Glengarry estate which stretched westward from the Great Glen along Glen Garry and Loch Quoich to the peninsula of Knoydart and North Morar, a distance of some forty miles. The adjoining Lochiel estate, extending from Loch

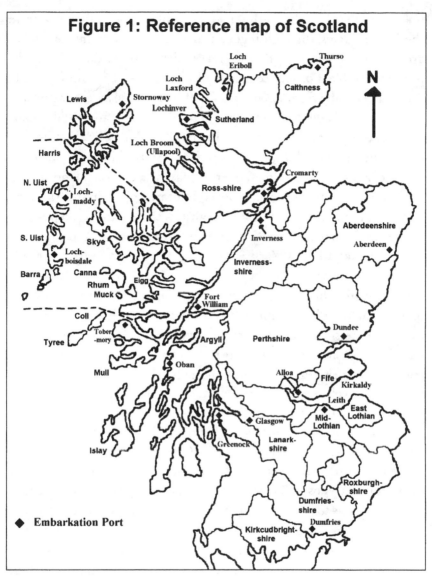

Figure 1: Reference map of Scotland

◆ **Embarkation Port**

Eil to Loch Arkaig, also lost people to Upper Canada as did Glenelg, lying to the north of Knoydart, and Glen Moriston to the north of Glen Garry (Figure 2). The first group of emigrants arrived in 1784, although they had come from New York State, not Scotland as might have been expected. They had arrived in the major Loyalist influx from the United States, which followed Britain's defeat in the American War of Independence in 1783.

Fearing that British North America would be open to attack from the United States, the British government had given grants of land to around 40,000 Loyalist settlers in areas which were considered to be the most vulnerable. For servicemen, land was granted according to rank, ranging generally from 1,000 acres for officers to 100 acres for privates. Civilians usually got 100 acres for each head of family and 50 additional acres for every person belonging to the family.[5] This policy brought settlers with military skills, who were loyal to Britain, to particularly exposed areas along coastlines, river frontages, lakes and inland boundaries. While most people were moved to coastal areas in the Maritime colonies, around 1,500 New York Loyalists were sent to the old province of Quebec.[6] They included a good many Inverness-shire people who had emigrated to New York State in 1773, just two years before the American War had begun.

Complaining of the high rents and the "hardships and oppressions of different kinds" being imposed by their landlords, just over four hundred Inverness-shire people left for New York.[7] Sailing on the *Pearl* from Fort William in 1773 these emigrants had originated from districts within the Glengarry estate (especially Glen Garry itself) and Glen Moriston as well as from Urquhart and Strathglass, further to the east.[8] Leading them had been four influential tacksmen. Three were Macdonell brothers – John of Leek, Allan of Collachie and Alexander of Aberchalder, who owned land in the eastern end of the Glengarry estate, while the fourth was a cousin – John Macdonell of Scotus (known as Spanish John) whose land was to the west, in Knoydart.[9] The tacksmen too had reasons to be aggrieved over their conditions.[10] The more productive farming methods which were being introduced at the time had caused Duncan McDonell, their Clan Chief, to withdraw their favourable leases. Also to make matters worse their social standing was set to decline.[11] Their response was to emigrate and when they did, these four tacksmen took many of the Glengarry estate tenants with them.

The Glengarry emigrants of 1773 had been attracted to New York by the colonizing efforts of other Highlanders who had arrived before them. Some had settled in the area as a result of the free land grants which had been given to ex-servicemen from Highland regiments at the end of the Seven Years War (1756–63).[12] By 1770 New York had a substantial Highland presence and it could offer excellent farming

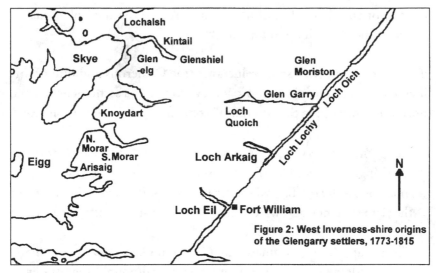

Figure 2: West Inverness-shire origins of the Glengarry settlers, 1773-1815

opportunities. By seeking out Sir William Johnson, the most prominent landowner in Upper New York, the Macdonell tacksmen obtained a large tract of land on the north shore of the Mohawk River above the village of Johnstown. Most of the emigrant families were able to settle together in compact groups thus creating a small Highland colony in this district of New York.[13]

The Glengarry Highlanders, being accomplished and seasoned soldiers, took up arms on the British side in 1775 when fighting broke out in the American War of Independence. This they did despite the bloody and savage defeat which Highlanders had suffered at the Battle of Culloden in 1745. A desire to preserve their clan and country links outweighed any resentment they may have felt toward their old enemy. They put themselves under the command of Sir John Johnson, William's son, who by then had acquired his father's land.[14] Then, after fighting in various campaigns as members of the King's Royal Regiment of New York, they fled north with their families after the war ended in 1783.[15] As she prepared to leave, Nancy Jean Cameron, wife of John, could see the problems which lay ahead:

We expect the journey to be long and hard and cannot tell how many weeks we will be on the road. We have four horses and John has made our big wagon as comfortable as he can. Through the forests we must trust to Indian guides. Many of Scotch origin will form the band of travellers. The children little realise the days of hardship before them and long to start off.[16]

Thus it was that, with some reluctance, the Camerons and other families left "this beautiful Mohawk Valley" to found a settlement "on the northern shore of the St. Lawrence" some fifty miles from Montreal:

> Our grandparents little thought when they sought this new land, after the risings of Prince Charlie, that a flitting would be our fate but, we must follow the old flag wherever it takes us. It is again the march of the Cameron men and wives and children must tread the hard road.[17]

The group, having originated mainly from Glengarry, would name the new settlement after their Scottish estate, although, regrettably, it would "lack the mountains" of their homeland.[18] In time it would become one of Upper Canada's best known and arguably most successful early settlements.[19]

The government had, in fact, allocated two regions to the New York Loyalists. Land was granted by regiment and having served with the First Battalion of the King's Royal Regiment, the Scottish Loyalists were allocated their land along the north shore of the Upper St. Lawrence River immediately to the west of the French seigneuries.[20] Meanwhile men of the Second Battalion of the King's Royal Regiment and Major Jessup's Rangers obtained their land in the township block which lay further to the west, between Cataraqui (Kingston) on Lake Ontario and the Bay of Quinte region (Figure 3). As a result of these land allocations, Loyalist Scots would become concentrated in the first township block, in what would become Glengarry County.

In addition to having many Catholic and Presbyterian Highlanders, the First Battalion of the King's Royal Regiment of New York, also included Calvinist and Lutheran Germans, and Anglican English among its former members. By common consent they all agreed to settle together but in separate territories, according to ethnic group and religion. The Highlanders occupied the two most easterly townships of Lancaster and Charlottenburg while the German and English settlers went to the townships of Cornwall and Osnabruck in Stormont County and Williamsburg in Dundas County (Figure 4).[21] Other Highlanders

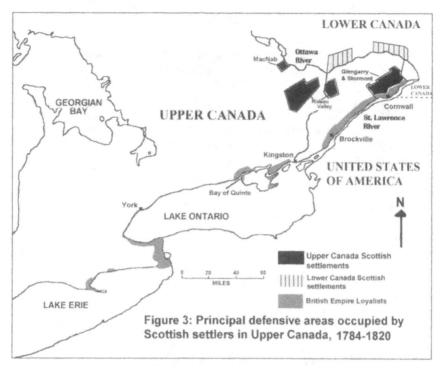

Figure 3: Principal defensive areas occupied by Scottish settlers in Upper Canada, 1784-1820

who had served in the Royal Highland Emigrants Regiment (the 84th) and with John Butler's Rangers, were also granted land in Lancaster and Charlottenburg as well as in the neighbouring township of Cornwall.[22] Thus it was that large numbers of Highlanders came to be concentrated in Glengarry County at the eastern extremity of Upper Canada. Having a boundary with Lower Canada to the east and a boundary with the United States to the south, this was one of the most important defensive locations in the whole of Upper Canada.

Sudden rent rises, the increasing introduction of sheep farms and the favourable news filtering back to Scotland from North America brought a further influx of Inverness-shire emigrants to Upper Canada. Only months after the Glengarry Loyalists had taken up their lands, many more Scots were already on their way to join them. Led by Allan Macdonell, a prominent Glengarry tenant, some two hundred people from Glen Garry and one hundred from Glen Moriston left Scotland in June 1785.[23] The large Roman Catholic contingent was accompanied by their priest, Father Roderick Macdonell, whose father, John Macdonell of Leek, had been one of the tacksmen leaders of the *Pearl* emigrants of 1773. Having taken seventeen weeks to cross the Atlantic, the onset of

Table 1

Victualling list for the 1785 group of Glengarry settlers. They left Scotland in 1785 and arrived in Glengarry, by way of New York and Albany, in 1786.

Names	Men	Women	Males above 10	Females above 10	Males under 10	Females under 10	Total[1]
John Grant	1		3	4		1	8 1/2
Don'd McDonald	1	1	4	1	2		8
John McIntyre	1	1					2
Angus McDonald	1	1	2	4			8
Alex'r McDonald	1	1	1	1	1	1	5
Alex'r Frazer	1	1	1	1		2	5
Don. McDonald	1	1		1			3
John McDonald	1	1			2		3
Allan McDonald	1	1		1			3
Angus McDonald	1	1					2
Alex'r McDonald	1						1
Ranald McDonald	1	1	2		1	1	5
Duncan Kennedy	1	1	1	1	1	1	5
Angus McDonald	1	1					2
Angus McDonald	1	1	1		2		4
William McQueen	1						1
John McDonald	1	1			1		2 1/2
Angus McDonald	1	1			2		3
John McIntosh	1	1		2	2		5
John McDonald	1	1					2
Don'd McDonald	1	1				1	2 1/2
Don'd McMillan	1	1	1		1	1	4
Arch'd McDonald	1	1			2	1	3 1/2
Philip McDonald	1	2	2		2		6
Angus McDonald	1	1					2
John Kennedy	1	1	1	5			8
Henny McDonald		1	1	1		3	4 1/2
Angus McDonald	1	1			1	2	3 1/2
Dougall McDonald	1	1		3			5
Iver McTavish		1	1				2
Annie McTavish		1		1		1	2 1/2
Angus McDonald	1	1	3	1	1		6 1/2
Katheryn McDonald	1					1	
Isabella Chisholm		1					1
Allan McDonald	1	1	1	1			4
Collin Fraser	1	1					2
Totals	31	33	24	23	20	15	133 1/2

[1] Each child below 10 years is counted as 1/2 person in computing the total.
Source: LAC RG 19 Vol. 4447 No. 14.

winter forced them to land at Philadelphia where they had to wait until the following year before making their way to Upper Canada via New York and Albany. Requiring assistance with food supplies during this period, the names of roughly half the initial group of 300 came to be recorded in a provisioning list which was produced in 1786.[24] Predictably they were mainly MacDonalds (Table 1).

Others followed in 1786. Just over five hundred people, mainly Roman Catholics, sailed on the *Macdonald* to Quebec from Knoydart on the 29th of June.[25] Writing many years later, Iain Liath Macdonald, one of the passengers, described the scene as the ship left Knoydart:

It was on Sunday morning / that we sailed from land / In the big three masted ship / with our parish priest with us / He made the fervent prayer / to the King of the Elements to protect us / And to the Angel, St. Raphael / To bring us safely to land.[26]

Once again evictions to make way for advancing sheep farms in the Glengarry estate holdings in Knoydart had been a major factor in the exodus. The group's spiritual leader had been Father Alexander McDonell from Scotus (Knoydart) while Lieutenant Angus McDonell had taken charge of the shipping arrangements.[27] Announcing the ship's arrival in September, the *Quebec Mercury* claimed that the *Macdonald* had come with "nearly the whole of a parish in the north of Scotland."[28] Alarmed by this large influx of impoverished people, colonial officials doubted whether the "infant settlement" of Glengarry could cope with them over the winter.[29] However, judging by their readiness to grant financial aid, it would seem that these Highlanders were a welcome addition to the local population. Brigadier General Henry Hope, who was in overall charge of the Loyalist settlements, decided "to adopt every measure in my power to save them from want."[30] They were to be furnished "with bateaux from Lachine to the settlements" and, "in order to provide for their support until next year's harvest, a supply of provisions ...will be advanced to them."[31]

Four concessions in Lancaster and Charlottenburg townships were surveyed, in the spring of 1787, for these latest arrivals.[32] A compact area, some eleven miles long and five miles wide was set aside, comprising the 5th to 8th concessions of Lancaster and the adjacent 7th to

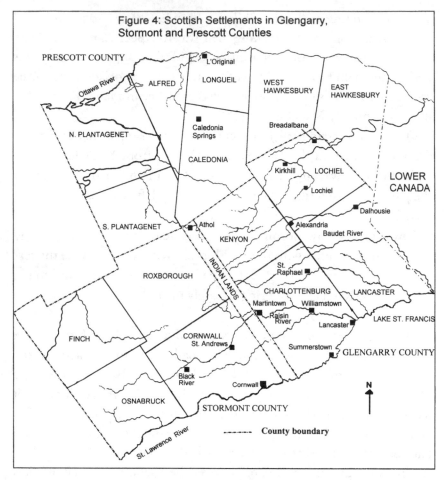

Figure 4: Scottish Settlements in Glengarry, Stormont and Prescott Counties

9th concessions of Charlottenburg.[33] A Highland settlement was duly formed and, gaining inspiration once more from St. Raphael, it was named after him.[34] Meanwhile, the continuing influx of Scottish settlers progressed northward in both townships. The two very large townships of Charlottenburg and Lancaster were eventually subdivided. The southern sections retained the names of Charlottenburg and Lancaster while the northern sections became the additional townships of Kenyon and Lochiel (Figure 4).[35] By 1791 Glengarry County would have 1,285 inhabitants, representing some 13 per cent of the total Upper Canada population.[36]

Advancing sheep farms, rising rents and the continuing success of the early pioneer settlements stimulated the exodus even further. The *British Queen* brought eighty-seven people, who originated from eight

A pioneer view of Kenyon Township in Glengarry County. A
sketch by Rev. Jacques Frederic Doudiet, a Swiss Presbyterian,
dated September 12, 1846. *Courtesy of Library and Archives
Canada C-127635.*

separate Inverness-shire districts, to Quebec in 1790.[37] This time the
Glengarry estate only contributed a minority of the settlers. The largest
single group came from the Clanranald lands in the island of Eigg, which
provided thirty of the eighty-seven passengers. However, the exodus
from the Clanranald estates had been much more extensive than this.
In addition to the emigrants who sailed on the *British Queen* to Quebec
in 1790, there were also 328 Clanranald tenants from Moidart, South
Morar, Eigg and South Uist who were taken on the *Jane* and *Lucy* to
Prince Edward Island (then the Island of St. John).[38]

Having arrived at Quebec in November 1790, with little money, the
British Queen emigrants needed assistance to survive their first winter.
Miles Macdonell, the son of Spanish John, who had organized the crossing, petitioned the governor of Quebec on their behalf. The colonial
government responded by supplying bateaux to transport the emigrants
from Quebec to the Glengarry County settlements while Montreal merchants gave further aid in the form of food.[39] Most of the them settled
together in Lochiel township (then part of Lancaster) at a site, just north
of present-day Alexandria, which is still remembered as the Eigg Road.

Hundreds more people emigrated from the Western Isles in 1791, but
they all went to Prince Edward Island and Nova Scotia.[40] However, more
contingents from mainland Inverness-shire arrived in Upper Canada over
the following three years. Led by Alexander Macdonell of Greenfield, a

second cousin of the Glengarry chief, and Alexander McMillan of Glenpean, a tacksman's son, some "40 Highland families" from the Glengarry estate sailed to Quebec on the *Unity* in July, 1792.[41] On their arrival in September in Glengarry County, they too were allocated land in Lochiel Township. Meanwhile the long-established settlers, whose communities were primarily concentrated along the River Raisin, were progressing well. When Lieutenant Governor Simcoe and his wife visited eastern Upper Canada in June of that same year they were taken to Glengarry House, one of the first stone houses to be built in Upper Canada:

> At a small Inn on the Pointe au Baudet we found the principal inhabitants of...Glengarry – Highlanders in their national dress. They came to meet the Governor, who landed to speak to them. They proceeded in their boat, a piper with them, towards Glengarry House, Mr [Col. John] McDonell's [house], where the gentlemen went.[42]

A year later one hundred and fifty Glenelg emigrants, led by their tacksman Kenneth MacLeod, sailed to Quebec on the *Argyle*.[43] Plagued by severe storms halfway across the Atlantic, the *Argyle* had to return to Greenock for repairs. Transferring to a second vessel, they once again encountered a heavy storm. After their ship had lost her upper masts and sails, they were forced to return a second time to Scotland to transfer to yet another vessel. In their third attempt they actually crossed the Atlantic but, upon reaching Prince Edward Island in early winter, they experienced a severe snowstorm and had to take refuge there.[44]

Once the *Argyle* landed safely on the island, Captain Alexander, Kenneth MacLeod's son, organized accommodation for his passengers and arranged for them to be taken to Quebec six months later. The schooner *Simon Gallon* arrived in early June 1794, with "115 men, women and children" while the *John,* a second schooner, came with a further "42 men, women and children" a week later.[45] From Quebec "they were accommodated on the King's boats with a passage to the Rivière Aux Raisin in this province. From thence they proceeded overland to what was then called North Lancaster, now Lochiel, and the settlers, or rather the heads of families, having obtained a grant each of 200 acres of land all settled down on their respective lots."[46] Yet again, they took up residence as a group and created a settlement which later became known as Kirkhill. And some forty-four years later, these settlers would be described as "a thriving and numerous body in their own persons and in that of their descendants."[47]

Emigration from Scotland reached new peaks, but it declined sharply with the onset of the war between Britain and France in 1793.[48] Then with the resumption of a temporary peace in 1801, a rapid growth in emigration, particularly from the Highlands and Islands, was once again experienced. Lamenting this increasing exodus, influential people in Scotland did everything in their power to halt it. They regarded emigration as a threat, arguing that it would deprive the nation of people who would otherwise be in its workforce or serve in its armed forces. But people emigrated in spite of the barriers placed in their way.

Knoydart had already lost a third of its population to British North America by 1801 and the losses were set to continue.[49] Glenelg had also contributed large numbers of people to the emigration movement. "To such an extent has this prevailed that America too rejoices in a Glenelg with a population at least equal to that which the parent parish still possesses."[50] A report, written in 1801–04, grieved over the loss of "1,000 from the greater and most respectable part of the tenantry of Glengarry with some from Glen Moriston and Strathglass," who had already emigrated in 1773.[51] The emigration fever, which so concerned the Scottish ruling classes, had gained ground to such an extent that, by 1806, it was difficult to find a single parish in west Inverness-shire which had not contributed large numbers of people to the exodus.[52] According to a contemporary commentator, the number of people who left the Highlands in the period from 1801 to 1803 "may be moderately calculated at 4,000 and 20,000 more...are capable of doing so."[53]

Word of the intended departure of several hundred Highlanders from Fort William first reached the Committee of the Highland Society of Edinburgh in June 1802. Colin Campbell, a Greenock Customs official, had written to the committee warning them that a number of ships were being "fitted out" at Greenock, Port Glasgow and Saltcoats "for the purpose of taking out emigrants."[54] By this time the Society's campaign to halt the exodus from the Highlands was in full swing. Information was being collected to provide ammunition for new passenger regulations, which would ultimately restrict the numbers able to emigrate.[55] But within days of Campbell writing his letter, four ships were already heading for

Fort William to collect some 1,100 west Inverness-shire emigrants to take them to Quebec.[56] Just under half, 552 people, were to be accommodated on three ships – the *Helen* of Irvine, the *Jean* of Irvine and the *Friends of John Saltcoats* while the remainder would sail on the 308-ton *Neptune* from Loch Nevis, just to the south of Fort William.[57]

The *Helen, Jean* and *Friends* had been chartered by Archibald McMillan of Murlaggan, a prominent Lochiel tacksman.[58] Believing that he and his fellow Highlanders faced a bleak future in Scotland, McMillan decided to emigrate, bringing with him large numbers of the tenantry from both the Glengarry and Lochiel estates. Eventually these emigrants would become known as the "Lochaber emigrants," taking their name from the Highland region from which they had come.[59] It seems that conditions on board ship had been particularly good as a result of the strenuous efforts made by McMillan to ensure that his group would have a smooth crossing. Certainly the *Helen* and *Jean* are known to have top quality A1 ratings from Lloyds of London and McMillan had specified relatively spacious passenger accommodation berths "of six feet by six feet."[60] He had also advanced the entire costs of the Atlantic crossings which amounted to over £1,861.[61]

However, the *Neptune* passengers probably travelled in far less comfort. Originating mainly from the west coast districts of North Morar, Knoydart, Glenelg, Kintail and Lochalsh, they had no prosperous benefactor to assist them (Figure 2). But it seems they were fortunate in having Captain William Boyd who provided "his care during a passage of nine weeks."[62] Arriving in a destitute state, the emigrants required financial support to see them through the rest of their journey to Upper Canada. Some sixty local people raised just over £103 for them, with substantial donations being made by the owner of *Neptune* and General Peter Hunter, the Lieutenant Governor of Upper Canada.[63] By contrast, those emigrants in McMillan's group, who had sailed on the *Helen* and *Jean,* had a fight on their hands to claim back their surplus food rations. With McMillan's help, their case was brought before Justices of the Peace in Montreal who ruled that any food rations not consumed during the crossings belonged to the emigrants and not to the ship captains.[64] While McMillan remained behind in Montreal to see to his business affairs, most of the emigrants in his group journeyed upriver to Glengarry County, reaching their destination in October 1802.[65]

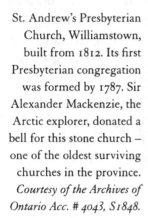

St. Andrew's Presbyterian
Church, Williamstown,
built from 1812. Its first
Presbyterian congregation
was formed by 1787. Sir
Alexander Mackenzie, the
Arctic explorer, donated a
bell for this stone church –
one of the oldest surviving
churches in the province.
Courtesy of the Archives of
Ontario Acc. # 4043, S1848.

By this time several villages and hamlets had taken shape. A Roman
Catholic church, known as the "Blue Chapel" had been established in
St. Raphael by 1786.[66] Also, the Presbyterian congregations at nearby
Williamstown and Martintown, situated on the banks of the Raisin River,
had each acquired their first wooden church by the early 1800s.[67] However, according to Lord Selkirk who visited the area in 1803, Reverend
John Bethune, the Williamstown minister, had "but a small congregation in comparison to the priest," Father Alexander Macdonell (Scotus)
who ministered to the Roman Catholics.[68] Although "Lancaster township was on the first survey condemned as useless" because of its many
swamps, the village of Lancaster, located to the south of Williamstown
on the Raisin River, was progressing well. By 1796 its inhabitants had
built their first Presbyterian wooden church.[69] Meanwhile Presbyterians in Lochiel Township had to wait until 1818 before they could acquire
their first wooden frame church which was erected at Kirkhill.[70]

By 1802 it was no longer possible for emigrants to settle in large compact groups in the way their predecessors had done because, by this time,
much of the land in Glengarry County had already been allocated.

Although Crown land in other districts was available on easy terms, it was rejected. Refusing to be separated from their friends and family in Glengarry, the 1802 arrivals acquired small scattered tracts of unclaimed land in the immediate area, while some rented land on the Crown and Clergy Reserves.[71] Archibald McMillan, however, had his own solution to the problem of land scarcity. Having taken up residence in Montreal he was barred from acquiring land in Upper Canada, but Lower Canada's land was readily accessible. After contacting the emigrants whom he had brought out, he applied for an extensive tract of wilderness land on the north side of the Ottawa River.[72] In his application, which was successful, he claimed to have the backing of seventy-five people who had travelled to Quebec in 1802.[73]

Having acquired land in Grenville Township (Argenteuil County), Suffolk Township (later renamed Lochaber) and Templeton Township (both in Papineau County), McMillan hoped to build up a considerable Highland settlement in Lower Canada but his plans met with little support.[74] Most of the 1802 arrivals rejected his Lower Canada land holdings, favouring Glengarry where they could settle close to their relatives and friends.[75] Thus even though Highlanders "were pouring down every day in most astonishing numbers," few of them wanted to settle on McMillan's land:

> Our countrymen have a great aversion to going on new land. They are afraid to encounter fresh difficulties and they live among their friends [in Glengarry] formerly settled in the country who encourage them as they find them useful in clearing their land without considering that they are losing time for a bare subsistence.[76]

McMillan decided to move to his fledgling Lower Canada settlement in 1806, hoping that by doing so he might have greater success in persuading other Highlanders to join him. "I mean to set the example myself, having come to a resolution to reside among them, considering that step as most effectual to forward the settlement." Once there he could more readily deal with the "opposition made by the Gentlemen of the Upper Province whose interest is to put a stop to the progress of a Scotch settlement in the Lower Province."[77] Competition from Upper Canada Scots, who sought to attract all Highland newcomers to their localities was a serious enough obstacle but, in addition to this, McMillan also had to contend with bureaucratic delays in gaining access to his land. But, even so, by 1807 he claimed that "50 to 60" Gaelic-speaking settlers were on their way to his settlements.[78] It would appear that such numbers actually did arrive in Montreal, but they came two years later. Originating from Perthshire, some sixty people left Dundee in 1809 with "20 bagpipes and nearly as many fiddles."[79]

However, few Highlanders took up McMillan's land holdings and, in time, he would lose many of his initial recruits to the Glengarry communities on the opposite side of the Ottawa River.[80] And, as Glengarry County filled up, new arrivals took up land in the adjoining Stormont County, especially in Cornwall and Finch townships (Figure 4).[81] As it soon became clear to McMillan that he could make profits far more readily from lumbering than from farming, he devoted much of his time to the timber trade. Nevertheless, some of his settlers did remain in Lower Canada. The many Grenville and Lochaber farms which were still owned in 1879 by families of that name, are a lingering testimony to McMillan's modest success in attracting Scots to these townships.[82]

The Roman Catholic priest and future bishop, Alexander Macdonell, also played an important role in encouraging Highlanders to emigrate, but unlike McMillan, his efforts were concentrated entirely in Upper Canada. Like Lord Selkirk, he was motivated by humanitarian concerns, believing that emigration offered the best escape route for the many Highlanders who faced persistent poverty and an uncertain future. According to those who knew him, "his stature was immense and his frame Herculean." Being six feet four inches in height, he was a commanding figure who was "above all, a born leader of men."[83]

In 1792, when evictions to make way for sheep farms were becoming more frequent, Father Macdonell took it upon himself to find jobs for dispossessed Highlanders in the cotton mills of Glasgow. When they lost their jobs in the economic depression which followed a year later, he then persuaded the British government that these same Highlanders should be formed into the Glengarry Fencibles Regiment. He later became its first chaplain.[84]

When the regiment was disbanded in 1802, Father Macdonell sought government support to have its former members relocated to Upper Canada, but obstacles were placed in his way at every turn. He travelled to London for a meeting with Prime Minister Henry Addington, but he

Portrait of Rt. Rev. Alexander Macdonell. Born in Glen Garry, Scotland, in 1762, he was the first Roman Catholic Bishop of Upper Canada. He emigrated to Glengarry County in 1804 and settled at St. Raphael. He was the first Catholic chaplain in the British Army since the Reformation and he achieved considerable public prominence in Upper Canada. The town of Alexandria is named after him. The artist was M.A. Shee. *Courtesy of Library and Archives Canada C-140071.*

was advised that "the British government had so slender a hold on the province of Upper Canada that he [Addington] could not think himself justified in giving encouragement to the King's loyal subjects to emigrate to that colony."[85] Trinidad was apparently a much more attractive option. Turning down an offer of free transport, free land and cash to purchase slaves, as well as other offers of land in the Maritime colonies, and coming under pressure from government worthies to see "the folly of his undertaking" and abandon his emigration proposals, Father Macdonell still pressed on.[86] He was adamant that, by going to Upper Canada, his men would achieve "the double purpose of forming an internal defence and settling the county."[87] But although eventually he obtained his land grant from Lord Hobart, Secretary of State for the Colonies, the planned colonization venture never took place.[88]

According to Father Macdonell, "the Scottish landlords combined to keep their people at home."[89] The landlords had been instrumental in the passing of the new Passenger Act of 1803 which took effect just when he was looking for willing recruits. The new legislation, which required shippers to provide emigrants with more generous food and space allocations, caused a dramatic rise in fares. Far fewer people could afford to emigrate and with the onset of the Napoleonic Wars, that same year, the Highland exodus to North America was reduced to a trickle.[90] Although twenty-five veterans of the Glengarry Fencibles Regiment did manage to get to Glengarry County shortly after 1803, this was a far cry from the large group emigration scheme which Father Macdonell had first envisaged.[91] Father Macdonell eventually travelled by himself to Glengarry in October 1804 and settled at St. Raphael.

Irrespective of any fare rises, the long distance to Upper Canada made it a prohibitively expensive destination for most ex-soldiers. Being of modest means, Father Macdonell had insufficient resources for recruiting them as settlers. On the other hand, the wealthy Lord Selkirk was making great strides in finding Highlanders for his Baldoon settlement in Dover Township (Kent County) at the western end of Upper Canada.[92] Since they shared similar views on emigration, it was inevitable that both men would meet.

Selkirk could see that Father Macdonell wanted to assist Highlanders to emigrate, and offered him the sum of £2000 to come to Sault Ste. Marie (formerly Falls of St. Mary) to help manage his planned colonization venture. Its location between lakes Superior and Huron had appealed to Selkirk because of its strategic position in relation to the American border.[93] However Father Macdonell declined, being "apprehensive that emigrants settling themselves in so remote a region would meet with insuperable difficulties."[94] He also had concerns over the damage which Selkirk's scheme might inflict on the North West Company, especially since "several of the principal members of that company were his particular friends."[95] In any case, the Sault Ste. Marie scheme never actually came to fruition. Rising public concerns over the numbers of Highlanders who were expected to emigrate caused the government to withdraw its support, and ultimately Selkirk had to make the best of a much smaller land holding at Baldoon.

The Baldoon site appealed to Lord Selkirk because of its proximity to the American border. He shared Father Macdonell's concerns over the large numbers of Americans who were taking up residence in Upper Canada. Selkirk sought to thwart this "contagion of Republican principles" by relocating loyal civilians, at his own expense, into border areas such as Baldoon, where they could act as a barrier to American influences and encroachment."[96] He recognized that in order to entice emigrant Scots to such remote locations, he had to offer an attractive relocation package which included interest free loans and cheap land. The British government certainly had no intention of following Selkirk's example. Its policy was to spend as little money as possible in promoting colonization and to give only grudging support to proprietors like Selkirk. Irrespective of any concerns it had on the need to promote population growth in Upper Canada, its hands were tied by the strongly anti-emigration stance of the Scottish ruling classes. However, when American soldiers actually invaded Upper Canada in 1812, the government realized that its laissez-faire policy was simply not going to work. Unless steps were taken to improve Upper Canada's defensive capability, there was a real risk that it would be lost to the Americans.

Defending Upper Canada's long borders with armed forces was impractical and prohibitively expensive. The crucial need was to bring civilians, who would be loyal to Britain, to those certain key areas, which were considered most vulnerable to attack. The only settlers whose loyalty could be guaranteed in the vitally important area between Kingston and Montreal were the Scots of Glengarry and Stormont counties. Building on this initial Scottish nucleus, the government decided to create a second defensive line, once again using civilian Scots. The inducements were considerable. They were to have free transport, free provisions and free land. The scheme had an air of desperation and even panic about, it but it did produce the expected response. In 1815, just as the Napoleonic Wars were ending, hundreds of Scots would be making their way to the so-called Perth military settlement in Lanark County.

Three

THE PERTH
MILITARY SETTLEMENT

*At two in the morning the embarkation commenced amidst hurry, noise
and confusion. Soon after three the steamboat taking the schooner in
tow passed down the river amidst the shouts of thousands who lined the
shore bidding Adieu to their departing friends. The scene to many of the
emigrants was the most affecting they had ever witnessed...* [1]

THE PEOPLE ON BOARD THE schooner which slowly made its
way down the River Clyde from Glasgow on June 24, 1815, were
bidding a final farewell to their native land. They were on their
way to Greenock to board a ship which would take them on to Quebec
and their new life in Upper Canada. Seven hundred people, almost all
Scots, had agreed to take part in the British government's scheme of
assisted emigration. Under this plan, intended to promote emigration
specifically to Upper Canada, the government was supplying free passages and provisions and in addition, giving each family a land grant
of 100 acres. An added bonus was the provision of a church minister
and schoolteacher on a government salary. Such inducements had
attracted people from most parts of Scotland and many, having con-
gregated at Glasgow, now awaited their embarkation.

After some delay, the *Atlas* set sail on the 11th of July with her 242 passengers. The *Dorothy* followed a day later with 194 Highlanders, the *Eliza*
left on the 14th of July with 123 passengers, while the *Baltic Merchant* left

on the 3rd of August with 140 passengers.[2] All four ships departed from Greenock. To minimize its costs, the government had provided troop carriers. As a result, the emigrants had to endure spartan and cramped accommodation on what turned out to be very lengthy crossings.[3] "Their provisions were ample in quantity, being the same as for the troops when on board, but the quality of the bread and beef did not please them...the rum however was good as well as the pork, pease and oatmeal and made some amends for the deficiency of other articles."[4] In a final touch of irony, government officials had to sidestep the terms of the 1803 Passenger Act, initially passed to restrict emigration, in order that the emigrants could carry "with them their tools and certain articles of furniture together with their arms."[5]

Mainly farmers and labourers, the emigrants originated from both the Highlands and Lowlands. The Highland response was concentrated in just a few parishes while Lowlanders had emigrated in small groups. Just under one hundred people were from the parishes of Callander and Killin in Perthshire, while Knoydart and Glenelg in west Inverness-shire contributed nearly 200 emigrants.[6] Most Lowland counties supplied emigrants but the majority were concentrated in the southwest, particularly in Lanarkshire and Ayrshire. In all, there were around 350 Lowlanders and an equal number of Highlanders. The original intention was that both groups would take up their land allotments in the new settlements being established in the Rideau Valley, but the Highlanders insisted on settling near to their friends and relatives in Glengarry County. Thus, the 1815 assisted emigration scheme did not go entirely to plan.

The government's purpose in subsidizing emigration was to place people who would be loyal to its interests in strategically important areas of Upper Canada. Some progress had been made in 1784 with the relocation of Loyalists from the United States. They had been concentrated in three regions – along the St. Lawrence River close to the eastern boundary with Lower Canada, on Lake Ontario between Kingston and the Bay of Quinte and along the Niagara River. However, in spite of the good land and climate which Upper Canada had to offer, this Loyalist influx attracted only a modest follow-on emigration from Britain. Upper Canada's principal drawback was its inland location, making it far costlier to reach than the Maritime colonies. They had initially been the favoured choice of most Scottish immigrants who dominated the

The lock at Davis Mill, looking towards Kingston, 1840. This
lock is one of forty-seven locks along the Rideau Canal. Built to
provide a secure route between Upper and Lower Canada, the
canal was a great feat of engineering. The artist was Thomas
Burrowes. *Courtesy of the Archives of Ontario C 1-0-0-0-48.*

late eighteenth century influx from Britain.[7]

However, when the Americans actually invaded Upper Canada in
1812, the government realized that it had to take steps to bolster its
defences or risk losing the colony. With only the width of the St. Lawrence
as protection against attack along the stretch from Montreal to Kingston,
there was an urgent need to establish a second line of defence along the
Rideau Valley between the St. Lawrence and Ottawa rivers (Figure 3).
This would provide an alternative route between Upper and Lower
Canada in the event of the Americans seizing control of the St. Lawrence.
The intention was to form "a good population between the two rivers
[St. Lawrence and Ottawa] with a view to establishing a communication with Upper Canada distinct from that of the River St. Lawrence."[8]
It was a two-fold plan. New settlements were to be created and, as an
extra defensive measure, an internal waterway would be built, linking
Kingston with Bytown (later renamed Ottawa). Loyal settlers, consisting of both civilians and demobilized soldiers, would provide a civilian
resistance to invasion and would be on hand to protect the planned waterway. This policy produced the Lanark County military settlements and
the Rideau Canal, which was completed in 1832.[9]

Having decided to find its recruits for its 1815 scheme from Scotland,
the government published advertisements in several Scottish newspapers.
Predictably, they attracted considerable interest.[10] All regions of Scotland
were feeling the initial effects of the severe economic depression, which

SETTLERS

IN

CANADA.

APPLICANTS in and about Glasgow, and in the West Country, will take notice, That the Commissioner in the Agency for Government will be at the George Inn, George's Square on Wednesday Morning the 19th day of April, and will remain but for a few days. He will there receive Recommendations and Certificates, which must be precisely in the terms mentioned in the Conditions of the 22d February last, and the Explanation of 24th March, which were published for some weeks at these periods in all the Newspapers in Scotland, and sent to every Clergyman. He will also receive the Deposit Money, viz. L. 16 for persons above sixteen years of age, and Two Guineas for Wives, &c. In the meantime, much trouble and correspondence will be saved if they will forward, without delay, to this office, their Certificates and Deposit, in Cash, or Bank or Bankers Bills indorsed ; as all this must necessarily be arranged sometime before their Embarkation, and to prevent disappointment in cases where Applicants may be rejected.

Copies of the Advertisements may be had at Mr Duncan's, Printer to the University, Morrison's Court, Glasgow, or here.

The Requisites for Certificates are as follow :

1st. General Good Character.

Applicants who, from misfortunes, have failed in their Circumstances, must bring a regular Discharge from their Creditors, or satisfactory evidence of a fair surrender or compromise; otherwise they will not be suffered to embark. And for the purpose of detecting any Imposition in this respect, the List of Applicants and Settlers is open for inspection. Nor will any Individual, or any of his Family, be permitted to proceed, who are known to be engaged in defrauding the Revenue by illicit Distillation or otherwise.

2d. Occupation or Trade.

3d. Former Occupation, if changed.

4th. Whether Married, Unmarried, or Widower.

5th. The number of Children, &c. who accompany them, distinguishing Male and Female.

6th. The Ages of all.

Recourse must be had to Parish Registers for Proof of Marriages and Births; or where this cannot be obtained, other satisfactory Evidence. Application may be made for this purpose to Magistrates, Clergymen, Dissenting Pastors, Elders of the Parish, Schoolmasters, or other respectable Persons, with a reference to Persons here or at Glasgow, when necessary.

Embarkation.

No Notice to this Date has yet been received from the Transport Board, who provide Vessels, of their being ready in the Clyde. The time of Embarkation, already published, is in April, and to proceed to Quebec as soon after as Circumstances will permit. Notice will be given in the Newspapers whenever their arrival is known here, and that they are ready to receive the Settlers. The Ports of Embarkation are Port-Glasgow or Greenock. Those who proceed from Glasgow or the Eastward and Neighbourhood, will be accommodated, free of Expense, with small Vessels, down the River.

The hours of attendance are from 9 to 11 in the Morning, and from 6 to 9 in the Evening. For those coming from the country from 2 to 4, afternoon.

Edinburgh, April 7th, 1815.
Abercrombey Place.

"Settlers in Canada" poster, April 7, 1815, printed in Edinburgh. The 699 emigrants who signed up for the scheme paid a total of £3,110.46 in deposits. *Courtesy of The National Archives, Kew, London, UK ref: CO42/165 p. 134.*

followed the Napoleonic Wars. Highlanders had long shown a particular zeal for emigration and as their economic prospects worsened they flocked in their thousands to sign up for the scheme. However, the many thousands who applied dwindled to a few hundred when it was realized that a hefty deposit was required.

Unlike the assisted emigration schemes of later years, this one was geared to well-resourced people.[11] To qualify, families had to provide certificates of good character and pay a refundable £16 deposit for each male of sixteen years and over, and two guineas for a married woman.[12] If they could pay their deposits, each family would get free transport, 100 acres of land and various food rations and farm implements. Thus, the government's aim was to attract people who could have afforded to pay their relocation costs in the first place. The deposits ensured that no paupers would be selected and they also provided a strong incentive for settlers to stay in Upper Canada. Anyone drifting across the border to the United States in search of better opportunities would forfeit their deposits.[13] However, those who remained in Upper Canada would have their money returned.

By a strange quirk of fate, the man chosen to act as agent for the government in locating settlers for the 1815 emigration scheme was John Campbell.[14] Having been a law agent for Lord Macdonald, he had been closely associated with the Highland Society of Edinburgh's campaign to restrict emigration through the passing of the 1803 Passenger Act. Now he was dispensing public money in the hope of facilitating it. He had become a convert to Lord Selkirk's long-held view that emigration offered a practical remedy to the poor and destitute while providing British America with much-needed colonizers. In fact, Selkirk's way of thinking was being increasingly supported by Scottish lairds. Having opposed Selkirk's pro-emigration stance initially, Campbell was now in full agreement with it:

Lord Selkirk's book upon the subject of emigration and of the population in the Highlands contains many principles and remarks which are well-founded and which have been evinced since that publication...His book was received at the time with some prejudice and excited considerable opposition. But it has been found that it contains much of truth in it.[15]

Campbell certainly shared Selkirk's preference for Highlanders, believing that "the habits and character of the Highlander afford a much better and more stable security and pledge than persons selected from the low counties of England or Scotland."[16] However, he soon found them to be tough negotiators. Typical were the twenty-nine families from Fort Augustus, Inverness-shire, who claimed that they had insufficient time to raise "the sums of money mentioned in the advertisement appearing in newspapers on 22nd February."[17] Most of the family heads were ex-soldiers and as such were ideal candidates for the scheme. However the deposits were mandatory and all but one family withdrew from the scheme (Table 2).[18] Four hundred people from Skye were "making it a condition" that ships called for them in Skye.[19] They, like most Highlanders and Islanders, objected to having to pay the extra costs of getting to Glasgow. Realizing that he would lose many recruits by not complying with this and similar requests, Campbell sought government backing, but his recommendation that government ships should call at Highland ports was rejected.[20] However, while the deposits and the extra costs involved in getting to the Clyde were serious obstacles, they were not the principal stumbling block.

If he had not realized it from the start, John Campbell would soon discover that kinship ties and a landscape reminiscent of home were far more important to Highlanders than any economic benefits which he could bestow. Even with his offer of a subsidized crossing, John Campbell was never going to make much headway in the Highlands and Islands. While this region had already lost many people to British America, the exodus had gone principally to Prince Edward Island, Nova Scotia and Cape Breton. People living in the Western Isles and most parts of the Highlands had shown little interest in going to Upper Canada since those wishing to emigrate preferred to settle in the Maritimes, where they could join communities which had been founded by their own kinsfolk.[21]

These kinship ties explain why it was that people from Inverness-shire and Perthshire enrolled in such large numbers in the government's assisted emigration scheme. Inverness-shire contributed seventy-six emigrants from Knoydart and one hundred and fifteen from Glenelg, while Perthshire supplied forty-one emigrants from Callander and fifty-three from Killin.[22] What was significant about these areas was the region's earlier links with Upper Canada. Knoydart and Glenelg had been losing a good many people to the Glengarry settlements in Upper Canada from

Table 2

Fort Augustus petitioners wishing to emigrate to Upper Canada, 1815. Petition of March 11, 1815.

Names	Wives	Male children Above 16 years	Below 16 years	Female children Above 16 years	Below 16 years	Remarks
Alex'r McDonald	1		1		2	Labourer, Private, Volunteer Corps
Duncan McDonell	1		2		1	Late Serg't GBF Labourer
Mary McPhee	1					Widow woman
Ewen Kennedy	1		5		1	Late Serg't GBF Labourer
John McDonell	1		1		1	Late soldier Volunteer Corps
Angus McDonell	1				4	Late Soldier GBF Taylor {tailor}
Wm McKinnon	1	1	1	1	2	Weaver
Alex'r McDonell	1	1		1		Late soldier GBF
Ronald McDonald	1		1		4	Late soldier GBF, shoemaker
Edward Fraser	1		1		1	Private, Horse Artillery, shoemaker
Alex'r McDonald	1		1		1	Perthshire Militia, shoemaker
Donald McDonald	1		3		2	Labourer
Donald Fraser		1	3			Labourer
Ewan Gillies	1				2	Late Private GBF
Arch'd McDonell	1	2	1			Late Sergeant (2 sons in Ayr & Renfrew Militia)
Alex'r McDonald	1		1		6	Late Soldier GBF
Kenneth Ferguson	1		4		2	Labourer
John Hall						Presently at his education
Arch'd Fraser						Labourer
William McKay	1				2	Labourer
Alex'r McMillan	1		1			Private, Fraser Fencible
John McDonell	1	3	3		2	Shepherd
Donald McDonald	1	1			1	Shepherd
Alex'r Robertson	1	2	4		1	Gard'ner & a late Military man
Alex'r McDonell						Labourer & a late Military man

Names	Wives	Male children Above 16 years	Male children Below 16 years	Female children Above 16 years	Female children Below 16 years	Remarks
Arch'd McDonell	1	1	1	1	1	Late soldier, Grant's Fencibles, Mason
Totals	22	12	35	3	36	

General Total 133 persons young and old.

signed since this was furnished

Widow Kennedy	1	1	1	2	2	
John Kennedy	1		2	1	3	Taylor [tailor]
Ronald Cameron	1		2	1		Shepherd

Source: PRO CO 42/165, 307.

---

the late eighteenth century. News of their success had clearly spread to the nearby parishes of Callander and Killin in Perthshire.[23] It probably came as no surprise to John Campbell to learn that the 1815 groups would emigrate to Upper Canada as long as they could go to Glengarry County where they had family and friends in established communities. Their acceptance of the government scheme was thus conditional on being allowed "the indulgence of settling among their countrymen."[24] Highlanders had taken the subsidies on offer but they had rejected the new township locations. The Rideau Valley settlements, would consequently, get their primary intake of people initially from Lowland Scotland.[25]

Having arrived in September, the three hundred and fifty Highlanders had to spend their first winter in barracks in Cornwall and Lancaster before being allocated their land (Figure 4).[26] As previously, land was assigned to allow distinct communities to settle together. The Knoydart, Glenelg and Perthshire emigrants obtained their land in different concessions of Lochiel Township in Glengarry County while the Glenelg settlers also acquired land in the adjacent township of West Hawkesbury in Prescott County.[27] Having strong Baptist and Congregational affiliations, the Perthshire emigrants soon established a flourishing Baptist congregation at a place near the northern boundary of Lochiel which they named Breadalbane, in honour of their Perthshire roots. They met initially in each others' homes until a log church was built in 1835.[28] Meanwhile Reverend John McLaurin, from Breadalbane in Scotland, became

Mr. McKillican's house in Breadalbane, Glengarry County. Pencil and crayon sketch by Rev. Jacques Frederic Doudiet, drawn on June 19, 1845. *Courtesy of Library and Archives Canada C-127644.*

Lochiel's first Presbyterian minister in 1820. At St. Columba Church erected in Kirkhill, he administered communion for the first time on the October 6, 1822. "The weather was exceedingly fine and a great number attended on this occasion, some of whom came forty miles."[29]

Beginning with high hopes of attracting thousands, the government ended up with only around three hundred and fifty people, mainly Lowlanders, for its Rideau Valley settlements.[30] A list of letters, received by the Colonial Office early in 1815 from Lowlanders wishing to emigrate to Upper Canada, reveals the diversity of their home locations.[31] Families were applying in twos and threes from almost every county in the south of Scotland, although the predominant response was coming from the west side of the country. But, as was the case with the Highlanders, these people had reservations about moving to the Rideau Valley. They were concerned about its more remote, inland location and felt they could do better for themselves by moving west of Kingston:

> The crops in the Rideau are subject to hurts from early frosts; the lands are badly watered for cattle, at an immense distance from the St Lawrence and [there is] no water conveyance for their wood and produce.[32]

However, having less clout than the Highlanders who successfully negotiated a relocation package to Glengarry, the Lowlanders had to comply with the government's wishes. Arriving late in the season, they

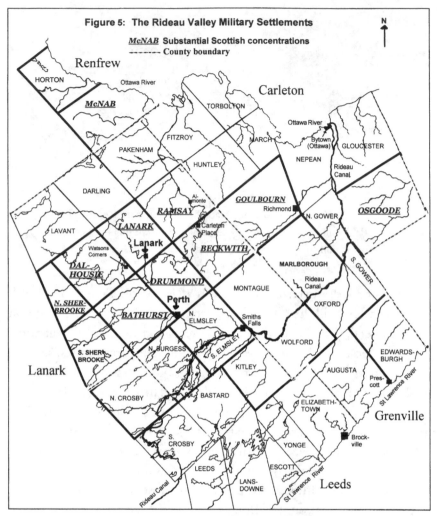

Figure 5: The Rideau Valley Military Settlements

lived in temporary accommodation at Kingston, Brockville and Cornwall until the authorities were in a position to grant them their land in the new Lanark County townships.

Ex-soldiers were also heading to the Rideau Valley at this time. Having served in the Napoleonic Wars and the War of 1812–14, large numbers of discharged soldiers faced bleak economic prospects in Britain. The government's offer of a free passage and free land in the military settlements of Upper Canada was an attractive alternative to returning home.[33] Although most of the veterans who came to the military settlements were British, they included men from Switzerland, Germany, Hungary, Italy, Poland and Russia.[34]

Bureaucratic muddle and squabbles led to considerable delays in choosing the actual settlement sites. Wishing to establish compact settlements, the government was forced to abandon its plan of settling emigrants along the Rideau waterway system since much of the land in this region had been lost to absentee landlords. Choosing the area to the north of the Rideau River and lakes as the next best alternative, the government obtained a large tract of wilderness land by treaty early in 1816 from the resident Algonkian First Nation, and immediately began the process of surveying and allotting land to settlers.[35]

After an arduous journey to the site through dense forests, the first waves of civilian and soldier settlers obtained their land in the three newly surveyed townships of Bathurst, Drummond and Beckwith.[36] Their communities developed initially along the so-called Scotch Line, which ran between Bathurst and Burgess townships (Figure 5).[37] Perth, by the River Tay,[38] in the southeast corner of Drummond, became the administrative centre for Bathurst and Drummond, while the new town of Richmond (founded in 1818) performed a similar function for Beckwith and a fourth township, (Goulbourn in Carleton County), which by then had been opened up to settlers. Both Beckwith and Goulbourn suffered from rocky and swampy conditions which hampered progress, but in the other areas, where good land was available, successful communities soon took shape and prospered.[39]

Perth on the River Tay, 1828, Thomas Burrowes, artist. *Courtesy of the Archives of Ontario C 1-0-0-0-22.*

Reverend William Bell (1780–1857) was Perth's first Presbyterian minister. He served his congregation from the moment he arrived in 1817 until his death 40 years later. He founded temperance societies, Sunday schools and Bible classes and helped to form Presbyterian congregations in Beckwith and Lanark townships, Smiths Falls and Richmond. This photograph was taken in 1848. *Courtesy of the Perth Museum, Perth, Ontario.*

Pioneer life in a military settlement had its difficulties. The early waves of emigrants had the advantages of subsidies and food rations and could rely on the organization and direction provided by the half-pay military officers, who managed the settlements. However, militarily important sites do not necessarily have good land. Moreover, the restrictions of military rule ran counter to the rough and tumble of pioneer life. Independent spirits like John Holliday, the schoolmaster from Dumfriesshire, objected to being managed constantly by others.[40] He had been one of the ringleaders of the earlier attempt made by twenty-six settlers to break free and move to a better location west of Kingston, but this had failed. Labelling him a troublemaker, the military administrators dealt with his so-called "insubordination" by withholding his schoolmaster's pay. But, in spite of his problems Holliday remained and established one of the Scotch Line's earliest homesteads.[41]

The Reverend William Bell, Perth's first Presbyterian minister who arrived in 1817, was much better suited to the constraints of a military regime.[42] Despite protests from his wife, Bell accepted the government's offer of a land grant and a £100 per year salary to serve as minister to the Scottish settlers in Perth.[43] He preached on the first Sunday after his arrival, renting "the large upper room of an Inn" and by the second Sunday had opened a Sunday school "with five children only."[44] Preferring him to John Holliday, the military officials readily accepted Bell's proposal to run a school in Perth, which came with an additional annual salary of £50. He required unquestioning obedience to his teachings, railed against the moral and social evils of his day and truly was "a man austere."[45]

When Robert Gourlay first visited the Bathurst and Drummond settlements in July 1817, only thirteen months after their commencement, he met some twenty-four of the Scotch Line settlers, one of whom was John Holliday, the schoolmaster. They all declared themselves to be "well-satisfied."[46] The settlers had been required to wait more than a year for their land but by the time of Gourlay's visit, they had built their houses and by June 1818, had cleared an average of ten acres. Six settlers came from Lanarkshire, four from Perthshire, four from Edinburgh, three from Ayrshire, two from Angus, two from Dumfriesshire, one from Morayshire, one from Berwickshire and one from Yorkshire in England (Table 3).[47]

Table 3

The Scottish settlement at Perth, Upper Canada, 1818.

Name	Geographical Origins of Settlers	Original Professions of Settlers
Peter McPherson	Callander (Perthshire)	Farm grieve
William McPherson	Callander	his son
James McLaren	Callander	Weaver
James Taylor	Carnwath (Lanarkshire)	Dyer & clothier
John Simpson	Rothes (Morayshire)	Shoe maker
James Miller	West Kilbride (Ayrshire)	Ship master
Hugh McKay	Glasgow (Lanarkshire)	Weaver
William Spalding	Dundee (Angus)	Mason [Wife & 1 child left at home]
William Rutherford	Dundee	Millwright
John Hay	St Vigeans (Angus)	Farm labourer
Thomas MacLean	Dunscore (Dumfriesshire)	Mason
Archibald Morrison	Glasgow (Lanarkshire)	Ship carpenter
John Holliday	Hutton (Dumfriesshire)	Schoolmaster
Alexander McFarlane	Kilbirnie (Ayrshire)	Farmer
James McDonald	New Greyfriars (Edinburgh)	Whitesmith
John Ferguson	Callander (Perthshire)	Farmer
John Flood	Glasgow (Lanarkshire)	Weaver
William McGillevry	Glasgow (Lanarkshire)	Farmer
John Brash	Glasgow (Lanarkshire)	Farm Labourer
Ann Holderness	Yorkshire	Widow of Wm Holderness
John Miller	Coldingham (Berwickshire)	Farm Labourer
William Old	Canongate (Edinburgh)	Shop Keeper
Francis Allan	Corstophine (Edinburgh)	Clerk in property tax
Thomas Cuddie	Corstophine (Edinburgh)	Gardener

Totals: 24 heads of household, 15 wives and 74 children.
Averages: No. of acres chopped 10 2/3 acres; cleared 9 1/2 acres

Source: Robert Gourlay, *Statistical Account of Upper Canada*, Vol. I, 524-6.

It was no accident then that William Spalding and William Rutherford (both from Dundee), William Old, Francis Allan and Thomas Cuddie, (all from Edinburgh), and Peter and William McPherson, together with James McLaren, (all from Perthshire), were immediate neighbours. Small groups had clearly been allocated land in clusters to enable their members to settle together. Gourlay found some of them to be "doing well" and others "unpromising."[48] However, by 1824 the Reverend Bell was in no doubt about the merits of the Perth military settlement, "No place in Canada presents a more agreeable residence for British emigrants." By then it had streets, "regularly laid out crossing each other at angles," along which were about one hundred buildings, "some of them finished in an elegant and commodious manner."[49]

Meanwhile, John Campbell had been inundated by enquiries soon after the 1815 group had left for Upper Canada. People wanted to know "whether the government intends to hold out the same encouragement for 1816 and would consent to send vessels to the north and west Islands." Apparently Lord Selkirk and others were "busily employed in the north collecting emigrants."[50] In Campbell's view, government support was needed to stop people from "going with private adventurers."[51] Lord Bathurst rejected this advice, and instructed Campbell to issue public notices stressing that it was no longer government policy "to provide for the conveyance of any further numbers of Scots to North America."[52] All future transport needs were to be met by "ships in the timber trade."[53] That summer saw the beginning of a two-way trade in timber and emigrants between Quebec and Scotland's major ports which was to last over many decades.

However, even though emigrants now had to be self-sufficient, they continued to request government help. Having learned that their ship, the *John and Samuel* of Liverpool, was going to be delayed until August, seventeen families from Duirinish parish in Skye, petitioned Lord Bathurst in the summer of 1816 for food and accommodation. Bathurst asked the Treasury for funds to help them pay for the cost of their sea crossings and food rations for three months but was refused.[54] However his recommendation to Sir John Sherbrooke, the Governor of Upper Canada, that they be given aid to help them survive their first winter was accepted.[55] Most of them settled in Glengarry County.[56] This was also the likely destination of the two hundred and forty or so people who arrived at Quebec from Fort William in 1817–18 (Appendix II).

They would have included many west Inverness-shire emigrants who had strong family links with this one part of Upper Canada.

Although it no longer provided an assistance scheme, the government continued to offer free land in the Rideau Valley. This in itself fostered a steady influx of emigrants from Scotland. The *Caledonia, Greenfield, Lady of the Lake* and *Fame*, each arrived at Quebec from Greenock in 1816 with from twenty to thirty people who were heading for Lanark County.[57] By the following year much larger groups were arriving. The *Harmony* from Greenock, the *Prompt* of Bo'ness and *John* of Bo'ness, both sailing from Leith, each carried well over one hundred passengers. Ship after ship was taking fresh reinforcements to the military settlements.[58] No doubt the government's previous generosity had given people grounds for hope that they too might receive some assistance. And newspaper shipping advertisements sometimes fed these expectations by hinting at "indulgences from the Government" or "the encouragement by government" which awaited emigrants on their arrival.[59] It was a confusing time for emigrants since in 1817 the government changed its mind once again and offered yet another assistance scheme.

When four hundred and fifty tenants who lived on the Earl of Breadalbane's estate in Perthshire expressed a desire to emigrate, the government stepped in with an assistance package which was similar to the one offered in 1815. The scheme, which was not advertised generally, required settlers to provide a £10 deposit, which the government would later repay.[60] Coming "from a circuit of thirty miles around Loch Tay," these people were ready to leave their homes in Dull, Killin, Comrie, Kenmore and Balquhidder.[61] Learning that the Breadalbane tenants were organizing a petition, John Campbell, the Earl's man of business, alerted Lord Bathurst to these developments:

I feel it is a duty that I owe to my noble Friend and client, Lord Breadalbane, and especially in his absence on the continent to communicate to Earl Bathurst my sentiments on the subject. The distress of the Highlands of Scotland from the low price of cattle...is so well known...It is not Lord Breadalbane's case only, but that of every landed proprietor in the Highlands...He has bent his mind to this subject and the improvement of his land...His lordship's character and humane disposition are so well known...nothing is dearer to his heart than his tenants.[62]

Loch Tay in Breadalbane, Perthshire. This view is from the south, looking towards Glen Lochay. *Photograph by Geoff Campey.*

Campbell stressed that it was not the Earl's wrong-doing which had made "minds somewhat afloat on the subject" of emigrating. His tenants were being lured "by news of the good treatment of a few neighbours who went to America under the encouragement of government in 1815."[63] However, the fact was that major clearances had occurred on the estate to make way for sheep farms.[64] High rents were a strong bone of contention and Campbell's claim that tenants would "sit down quiet at home" once they learned of the "abatements they are to be allowed on their rents" was quite laughable.[65] When he visited the estate, John McDermid, a writer in Edinburgh, found that many tenants had been "reduced to such an extreme state of poverty as to be unable to procure but one scanty meal per day."[66] Their minds were made up to emigrate. Campbell's portrayal of an Earl reluctant to lose his tenantry may have been true, but his tenants did not wish to remain. They were desperate to find a better life in Upper Canada. The government came forward with an assistance scheme while the emigrants raised the required deposit money, which amounted to £1,234. Just over 100 families set sail from Greenock in 1818 on three ships provided by the government – the *Curlew* with 205 passengers, the *Sophia* of Ayr with 106 and the *Jane* of Sunderland with 131 passengers.[67]

A key element of this negotiation was that all emigrants had to move to the Rideau Valley military settlements. They were allocated land in Beckwith and Goulbourn townships in Lanark County and in Osgoode Township in Carleton County (Figure 5).[68] The Beckwith and Goulbourn settlers probably had difficulty in finding good land, but the prospects of the Osgoode settlers were much better. By 1828 they were reported to be doing "well in America and are anxious that their friends in this country would follow them."[69] However, some members of the 1818 group did not go to Upper Canada. Having become discouraged by the immediate prospects open to them, "they proceeded without delay to Montreal," and headed for Cape Breton where they had families. Apparently because of dense fog, their ship's captain lost his way and they landed at Prince Edward Island by mistake. Arriving "in a deplorable state of poverty," they remained on the Island and are believed to have settled at Seven Mile Bay.[70]

As early as 1817 the government could feel satisfied that the Rideau Valley settlements were taking shape. By then the Perth military settlement had acquired a population of just under 1,900. At this stage discharged soldiers and their families outnumbered civilians by more than two to one.[71] Ex-soldiers continued to get assisted sea crossings, but civilians had to find their own funds. Thus the imbalance was set to continue, but only for a short while.

Predictably, the 1815 and 1818 schemes sparked off a huge demand throughout Scotland for further publicly-aided emigration, but this was not forthcoming. Letters home proclaiming the good opportunities to be had in farming helped to stimulate the growing zeal for emigration, but the high cost of actually getting to Upper Canada continued to be an insurmountable barrier for most people. However, in the southwest Lowlands of Scotland, where a severe economic depression and changing work practices had created dire economic conditions, new forces were at work. Large numbers of unemployed craftsmen realized that, by acting collectively, they could obtain sufficient funds to pay for their relocation costs. Forming themselves into emigration societies, they would soon be arriving in Lanark County in their thousands.

Four

THE LANARK
MILITARY SETTLEMENT

*It is nothing uncommon to see a poor Glasgow weaver, who came
along with scarcely a stitch to cover his nakedness, strutting between
the stumps of his trees as pompous as an Edinburgh magistrate.*[1]

B Y THE EARLY 1820S UPPER Canada's Lanark County was rapidly living up to its name. Thousands of people from the
Lanarkshire and Renfrewshire textile districts in Scotland were
pouring into the county. The introduction of power looms and the
growing influx of poorly paid migrant workers to the Clyde region
had created catastrophic conditions for handloom weavers. Having
been faced with very low wage rates or redundancy, many of them
emigrated. Acting collectively by forming themselves into emigration
societies, whole communities raised money to fund their resettlement
costs. Local businessmen and landowners made charitable donations
while the government provided some financial assistance and free land
in the Rideau Valley. Because of its strategic defence location, this was
the one region of Upper Canada where the government was particularly anxious to encourage loyal Scots. In all, nearly three thousand
people were assisted to emigrate in 1820 and 1821. Taking up land in
the four townships of Lanark, Dalhousie, North Sherbrooke and Ramsay, they founded the so-called Lanark settlement lying to the north
of Perth (Figure 5).

Weaver working at his loom. *Courtesy of Renfrewshire Council, Paisley Museum and Art Galleries.*

As self-employed craftsmen, it is hardly surprising that so many hand-loom weavers chose to emigrate. Over the previous fifteen years their earnings had fallen from 25s. a week to 5s. Their status and self-esteem as artisans had once been considerable.[2] Now, they were working night and day for a pittance and their families were starving.[3] All that redundant weavers could look forward to in Scotland was a life of drudgery and subservience in a factory or in some other poorly paid job outside their trade.[4] But, by emigrating they could become landowners in Upper Canada and win economic independence for themselves. Emigrating in very large numbers in 1820–21, they made the transition from skilled artisan to farmer with surprising ease, and quickly prospered.

The principal hurdle which destitute weavers had to overcome was the high entry cost of getting to Upper Canada. Even the basic steerage fare to cross the Atlantic, of up to £6 for adults, would have seemed a considerable sum, but added to this were the additional costs of the onward journey from Quebec to the Rideau Valley as well as the initial provisioning requirements which, taken together, could amount to around £22 per person.[5] Individuals had no hope of raising such sums but, by forming themselves into groups, weavers could apply far greater pressure on the government to provide funding. Most handloom weavers belonged to Friendly Societies which collected subscriptions and paid out funds to members when they were ill, injured or had to pay funeral expenses.[6] By a clever adaptation of this co-operative principle, weavers transformed their Friendly Societies into emigration societies. However, whereas Friendly Societies could function entirely on the yearly subscriptions of a few shillings collected from their members, emigration societies needed thousands of pounds to finance their costs. Realizing that they could not rely solely on internally raised subscriptions, they sought financial help from the government. While the societies failed to get as much assistance as they would have liked, the government was eventually persuaded to provide free land in the Rideau Valley military settlements, as well as sizeable loans and help with their transport costs.

The first petitions for help were received by the Colonial Office in March 1819. Robert Brown, who came from Rutherglen, near Glasgow, wanted funds to emigrate, being unable to subsist on "the muslin weaving" which "is at present so bad and wages so low."[7] William Granger, a calico printer, made a similar request on behalf of sixty Glaswegian families. Although most of the breadwinners were weavers, they did include the occasional sawyer, wright, mason and cooper, as well as other tradesmen.[8] Not meeting with any success, they turned to more high-profile measures. Three months later, at a public meeting held in Glasgow, thousands of unemployed weavers petitioned the authorities "for the necessary means of transporting all those of the trade who may be disposed to emigrate to the British settlements in North America."[9] Meanwhile weavers from Bridgeton in southeast Glasgow were "forming into a society," believing that emigration was "the only means of alleviating their distress."[10] Their society was the first of many.

The government's initial response to the increasing deluge of petitions was to offer assisted emigration – not to Upper Canada but to the Cape of Good Hope in Africa. Because of the Clyde region's participation in the assisted emigration scheme of 1815 to the Rideau Valley, Glasgow and Paisley weavers had strong community ties with Upper Canada. They had some idea of what to expect there, but Africa was an unknown quantity. "When we ask for bread you give us stone the poor weavers may well say."[11] Africa was firmly rejected. By this time the economic situation had deteriorated even further, heightening fears of civil unrest.[12] In September, a public meeting held in Paisley and attended by between 12,000 and 18,000 people, ended in a riot and, in April 1820, posters inciting people to revolt appeared suddenly in Glasgow and Paisley as well as in their neighbouring towns and villages. Troops were called out to deal with the insurgents in what turned out to be an abortive uprising.[13]

It was against this background of a shared fear of imminent insurrection that the government acquiesced. That same month local businessmen and landowners formed the Glasgow Committee on Emigration. Government backing for assistance was obtained a month later when Lord Archibald Hamilton, the Whig M.P. for Lanarkshire, and Kirkman Finlay, a prominent local businessman and Tory M.P. for Malmesbury, who led the Committee, presented the weavers' case before the House of Commons. A package was agreed upon, entitling emigration society members to free transportation from Quebec to Upper Canada, seed corn and implements, a 100-acre grant of land and loans which had to be repaid within ten years. However, society members would have to pay for their sea crossings. Crucial to their success in doing this were the private donations which were channelled through the Glasgow Committee on Emigration.[14] Robert Brown, the Duke of Hamilton's factor, acted as the conduit between the Glasgow Committee and the individual emigration societies. Once funding was available, Robert Lamond, the Committee Secretary, took charge of the shipping arrangements.

Robert Brown's involvement seems surprising given his vicious attacks against Lord Selkirk's proposals some fifteen years earlier.[15] Like John

Weavers' Flag, supporting Lord Grey's Reform Act of 1831. Many weavers were involved in political protest and campaigned for electoral reform. *Courtesy of Renfrewshire Council, Paisley Museum and Art Galleries.*

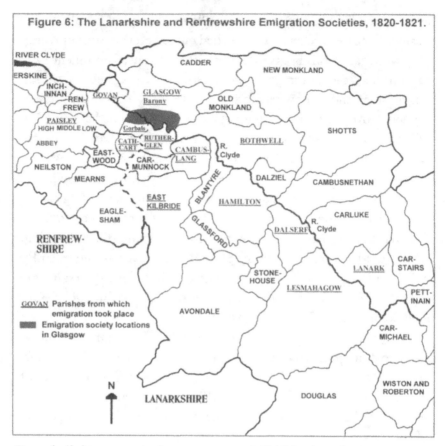

Figure 6: The Lanarkshire and Renfrewshire Emigration Societies, 1820-1821.

Campbell, he too was a late convert to Selkirk's view that emigration, if properly planned, could offer destitute people a welcome escape from their poverty. In fact, the growing economic crisis had completely transformed public opinion. Far from being an unwelcome force which had to be curtailed, emigration was being increasingly lauded as the ideal means of dealing with the nation's surplus population. Charitable one-off donations to assist people to emigrate were far preferable to any longer term schemes which might be devised locally to ameliorate poverty. Thus, the ruling classes and the poverty-stricken weavers had a common interest in promoting the advantages of assisted emigration. The emigration societies besieged the Colonial Office with requests to be included in the scheme while, two months after its formation, the Glasgow Committee had secured a sufficient number of private donations from landowners, merchants and local councils to enable the first contingent of weavers to leave Greenock for Quebec.[16]

A total of 1,100 people from five Lanarkshire emigration societies — the Bridgeton Transatlantic, Abercrombie, Bridgeton Canadian, Anderston and Rutherglen and Lesmahagow had presented a joint petition to the Colonial Office.[17] Most of the others were from single groups. However, because the total funds raised in 1820 only provided for eight hundred places, each society had to prune its lists, done by requiring its members to draw lots. In this way, one hundred and seventy-seven people were able to sail in the *Commerce* of Greenock in June, while a further one hundred and seventy-six people, who were members of the Abercrombie, Bridgeton Transatlantic and Muslin Street emigration societies left the following month in the *Broke*. Both groups originated principally from southeast Glasgow. That same month the *Prompt* of Bo'Ness also left for Quebec with three hundred and seventy people, including twenty-eight Lesmahagow families (Figure 6).[18] Members of the Highland and Lowland Associated and Union Emigration Society of the Gorbals in south Glasgow were among those who had to remain behind until sufficient funds could be raised.[19] Likewise the thirty-eight families from the Anderston and Rutherglen Emigration Society had to wait until the following year when they were able to depart on the *Margaret* from Grangemouth.[20]

Because the government's terms were initially only made available to petitioners from Lanarkshire, their societies had proliferated. By 1821 Lanarkshire had thirty-one emigration societies, Renfrewshire had three and there was one each in Clackmannanshire, Stirlingshire, west Lothian and Dunbartonshire (Table 4).[21] However, faced with a petition from Paisley weavers, which was presented by John Maxwell, a member of Parliament for Renfrewshire, the government relented and extended its scheme to other areas of southwest Scotland from the Spring of 1821. In 1830, there were seventeen Renfrewshire emigration societies. By this time the total number of societies had grown to just over one hundred, all but three of them being Scottish.[22] Just over half were based in Glasgow, taking their names from the parish, street or neighbourhood in which their members lived. Their geographical distribution reveals the extent to which the exodus was concentrated in the industrial communities which lined the banks of the River Clyde. Weaving districts, like Calton, Bridgeton, Mile-End, Anderston and the Gorbals in Glasgow and those in Paisley, were to lose considerable numbers to the growing exodus to Upper Canada.

Table 4

Scottish Emigration Societies, 1820–21

Glasgow Emigration Societies
Abercrombie (Friendly), Calton
Abercrombie Street
Barrowfield and Anderston (near Bridgeton)
Barrowfield Road, Calton
Bridgeton Canadian
Bridgeton Transatlantic Social Union
Brownfield and Anderston
Camlachie
Glasgow Canadian Emigration (Mutual Cooperation Society) Mile End
Glasgow Junior Wrights Society for Emigration
Glasgow Loyal Agricultural Society
Glasgow Trongate
Glasgow Union
Glasgow Union, Hutchison Street
Glasgow Wright's Society for Emigration
Highland and Lowland (Gorbals)
Kirkman Finlay
Muslin Street Society, Bridgeton
North Albion
Spring Bank (two)
St. John's Parish, Calton

Other Lanarkshire Emigration Societies
Anderston and Rutherglen
Cambuslang Canadian
Govan
Hamilton
Kirkfield Bank (Bothwell parish)
Lanark
Lesmahagow Canadian
Rutherglen Union
Strathhaven and Kilbride (East Kilbride parish)
Wishawton (Dalserf parish)

Renfrewshire Emigration Societies
Cathcart
Paisley Townhead
Parkhead (Paisley)

Other Emigration Societies
Alloa (Clackmannanshire)
Balfron (Stirlingshire)
Hopetown Bathgate (West Lothian)
Milton (Dumbartonshire)

View of Paisley in 1825. The first signs of prosperity brought about by the shawl trade can be seen in this engraving. *Courtesy of Renfrewshire Council, Paisley Museum and Art Galleries.*

The eight hundred or so weavers who managed to obtain places in the 1820 government scheme were allocated land in Lanark and Dalhousie townships.[23] However, the 1820 influx from Scotland was probably far greater since a proportion of the 1,300 Scots who are known to have sailed that year from Greenock to Quebec, completely unaided, almost certainly went to live in the Rideau Valley military settlements (Appendix II).[24] And the influx was set to continue. Beset by further petitions, the government agreed to extend its scheme for another year. In 1821, some 1,883 individuals were assisted to emigrate to the townships of North Sherbrooke and Ramsay.[25] Yet again it had been necessary for emigration society members to draw lots since the demand far outstripped the available places. The successful ones left Greenock in one of four ships: the *Earl of Buckinghamshire* with 607 people (7 emigration societies); the *George Canning* with 490 (11 societies); the *Commerce* of Greenock with 422 (9 societies) and the *David* of London with 364 (9 societies).[26] Setting sail on the 19th of May, the *David* was the last to leave:

She was towed out by a steam-boat and immediately proceeded to sea with a fair wind under very favourable auspices. The *David* was left by the owner and friends of the passengers about two miles below the Cloch Light-house at six o'clock p.m. with three hearty cheers from the passengers and crew which were immediately returned from the boat and repeated from the ship; a general smile of satisfaction closed this parting scene.[27]

Thus, a total of around 2,700 people from Lanarkshire and Renfrewshire had been assisted to emigrate to the Rideau Valley settlements in 1820 and 1821.[28] Encouraged by the favourable reports which filtered back to Scotland, many more would follow. John Climie advised people, "to get into a Society as I did, for it is very expensive coming from Quebec to this place and maintaining a family until a crop is got off the land. Indeed, there are a good deal of hardships to overcome before obtaining the prize; such as selling our articles for half-nothing – leaving our country and friends we held so dear – crossing the Atlantic."[29] William Gourley was "very uneasy to know how all the poor people" back in Scotland "got through the winter [of 1821]. I wish that many of them were here, for they would be able to make themselves comfortable in a short time. Let our friends know that they would do well by taking land."[30] William Miller told his father that he "never thought such a country was here and I wish that I had been some years sooner. You may tell my friends that they need not come here but for farming; no tradesman is hardly wanted at all."[31]

It soon became abundantly clear that far from deploring the loss of their trades most weavers welcomed the opportunity to become farmers:

> I never was so happy in my life. We have no desire to return to Glasgow to stop there, for we would have to pay a heavy rent and here we have none: in Glasgow I had to labour sixteen or eighteen hours a day and could only earn about six or seven shillings a week – here, I can, by labouring about half that time, earn more than I need. There I was confined to a damp shop – but here I enjoy fresh air.[32]

The majority of weavers had a rural background. Very often they had parents or grandparents who had moved from the country to the industrial towns and cities in the west of Scotland in search of better pay and conditions.[33] Thus despite initial fears on the part of the government that their seeming unfamiliarity with farming would cause them to fail, weavers made the transition to farming with remarkable ease:

> a Glasgow weaver, although not bred to spade and pick axe...makes a much better settler, can build a neat little house for his family and learn to chop with great celerity, so that in a short time nobody should suppose that he had been bred amongst bobbins and shuttles.[34]

One weaver was "very well pleased to handle the axe instead of the shuttle and would not for a good deal give up my present for my past employment. I had to struggle here for a year or two. I had to do so always at home."[35] Glowing accounts of their success abounded. The *Glasgow Courier* thought it "would be endless to enumerate all the examples that occur."[36] Yet it was careful to point out to its readers the scale of the adjustment which weavers had to make. They were exchanging their sedentary manual jobs in a town or city for a life of hard physical labour in a wilderness:

The native of this country goes upon new lands without emotion; but to the emigrant it is at first terrific to place himself in the midst of a wood – the trees heavy; not a ray of sunshine able to penetrate; no neighbours, perhaps within several miles, and only an axe in his hand – he is ready to despair. But he has only to persevere a very short time, and apply his strength judiciously and in a few months he will equal a native in felling trees and clearing lands.[37]

By 1822 sizeable Scottish communities had become established in the Lanark County military settlements. Perth, the town centre for Bathurst and Drummond townships, had nearly 4,700 inhabitants, Richmond, the centre for Goulbourn and Beckwith, had a population of 1,800, while Lanark, which encompassed the four townships of North Sherbrooke, Dalhousie, Lanark and Ramsay, had just over 3000 inhabitants.[38] Although people of many nationalities would have been included in these figures, Scots predominated.

Within four years of settling in Dalhousie Township, Peter Munro could boast to a friend in Scotland that in his "last harvest I had in 140 bushels of potatoes, besides grain of all sorts. We had difficulties, but now they are almost over...I have got a large house built, 20 feet by 30 feet and a barn, 20 feet by 40 feet."[39] Andrew Angus, living in Lanark Township, also wrote home with optimistic reports: "Some that left Scotland with nothing have now got from 12 to 18 head of cattle, besides sheep and hogs."[40] However, Duncan Campbell and Peter McLaren disagreed in their assessment of Perth. Campbell, one of the 1815 arrivals, complained of the poverty he had suffered in Perth, but McLaren, a fellow-Scot, chastised him and accused him of spreading negative and false reports.[41] It would seem that McLaren's more positive view was closer to the truth. When John MacDonald, author of *Narrative of a Voyage to Quebec and Journey thence to New Lanark in Upper Canada*, came to the area he wrote glumly and with great foreboding about the problems which lay ahead for settlers. But even he had to admit that "Perth is a thriving place."[42] Visiting the "many farms of those emigrants who came out last year [in 1820] and viewing their crops" he concluded that "they have generally a great deal of potatoes set with Indian corn or maize, and some have wheat and barley."[43]

By and large, Scottish communities were able to establish stable and successful settlements in Lanark County in spite of the varying qualities of the land which it had to offer.[44] Progress in Lanark and Dalhousie townships had been particularly difficult. By 1835 "Dalhousie with a physical soil more barren than much of our native Scotland," was said to have "already reached what...must long be the maximum of its population as the emigration is from it, not toward it."[45] Lanark Township also had its share of stony land and useless swamps. Had the land in both townships been better "the greater number of them now would have been as comfortable as settlers in the interior of Canada...But much of the country round here is good for nothing, a mere heap of rocks and

Residence and farm of Peter McLaren, Perth. The building still stands and is used as a bed and breakfast. Taken from *Historical Atlas of Lanark & Renfrew Counties, Ontario, 1880–1881. Courtesy of the Perth Museum, Perth, Ontario.*

stones. Many of the original settlers have been obliged to desert it and it is thought that many more must follow their example, so soon as their lots are cleared of the wood which is valuable for pot ashes."[46] Bathurst and Drummond townships also had sizeable areas considered unsuitable for cultivation.

However, in spite of having to cope with patches of poor land, Scots in their widely dispersed communities were making good progress by the early 1830s:

> "The first establishment, fostered by government, was made in 1815 by British emigrants chiefly from Scotland, many of whom are now heads of excellent farms, possess comfortable habitations and reap the fruits of their perseverance and industry...
>
> ...but its relative situation with the surrounding country and canal make it the natural entrepot of settlements in the Saint Lawrence and those of the Ottawa River and promises to contribute to its rapid aggrandisement and prosperity independently of the advantages it derives from being seated in the midst of a fertile and luxuriant tract of country."[47]

Ramsay, "settled almost entirely by emigrants from the west of Scotland," was apparently "considered the most fertile township in the neighbourhood." In 1832, its inhabitants were in "easy circumstances and are taking measures to procure a minister from the Church of Scotland."[48] When William Bell visited Lanark in 1821, he observed "a stone church," which had been built "with money collected from Scotland."[49] However, "though there is a church at Lanark capable of containing a congregation of 400 and costing above £300 currency there is no stated Minister there and if there was it would be altogether impracticable for the people of this township to attend."[50] The problem was that the church "which stands at one corner of the township" could not serve the needs of the widely scattered congregation.[51] It had no resident minister and insufficient places of worship. By 1832 Smiths Falls, on the Rideau Canal in Goulbourn Township, had become yet another Scottish stronghold, while Beckwith Scots had "built a neat, stone church and were putting the roof on it."[52] However, in spite of these signs of progress, life was a constant struggle for the early settlers:

Not a grist mill, saw mill, factory, store, shop, post office school, horse, chimney, stove nor even a chair could be found in Beckwith…The first year men carried flour and provisions on their backs from Perth and Brockville. Families subsisted for months on scanty flour. Their homes were shanties, chinked between the logs with wood and mud, often without a window, cold in winter, stifling in summer – uninviting always.[53]

The Rideau Valley acquired its first group of Irish settlers two years before the large Scottish influx of 1820–21. Led by Richard Talbot, some fifteen Protestant families from Tipperary, came to settle in the Richmond military settlement in Carleton County.[54] Arriving in 1818, they had been assisted to emigrate by the government as were the five hundred and sixty-eight Irish Catholics who arrived in the Pakenham and Ramsay townships of Lanark County in 1823.[55] Peter Robinson, brother of Upper Canada's Attorney-General, John Beverley Robinson, organized this second venture.[56] Renewing the offer two years later, the government assisted a further 2,069 Irish immigrants. However, Presbyterian Scots and Irish Catholics could not live together peacefully and, following a riot in Ramsay Township, it was decided that the much larger 1825 group would need to be located in a different range of townships. Most of them settled in Peterborough County.[57]

As the 1842 Census would later reveal, people of Scottish ancestry occupied a much higher proportion of the good land in Bathurst and Drummond, the first two townships in Lanark County to be surveyed and settled, than did the Irish. In fact, most of the poor land in these townships was held almost exclusively by Irish settlers.[58] The crucial factor was that, being the earliest arrivals, Scots were able to obtain the best available land:

> Many of them who arrived first got the best lots as they had the first choice, and if not pleased with it when viewing, Colonel Marshall still indulged them with more tickets for other lots until they were satisfied…Those who come first, study very naturally to obtain the most eligible situations and have of the consequence the best chance of good lots…the inferior or worse lots are left to those who follow.[59]

In addition to having access to the best land, the Scots, having emigrated in groups, also had the advantage of being able to settle together with their families and friends. Whole communities were effectively transplanted from the Clyde region to Upper Canada. Sometimes the inhabitants of a street – like Abercrombie Street in Glasgow, which formed four different emigration societies, moved *en bloc* to the Rideau Valley townships.[60] When Alexander Watt came to Dalhousie Township, he reported that "all of our Society were settled in the course of four days. There are 20 of us settled in the 1st line or road, between the 1st and 2nd concession and 12 of us on the 2nd line or road between the 2nd and 3rd concession."[61] Having been neighbours in Glasgow, they were now neighbours in the Rideau Valley. This pattern was repeated again and again. Although their farms were scattered far and wide, they lived in distinct, self-contained communities.

Arthur Stocks' letter home provides us with a detailed overview of the community which Paisley emigration society members had forged for themselves in North Sherbrooke:

We are very well off for Neighbours. Robert Twaddle from [Paisley] Parkhead is our nearest, it is not a quarter of a mile from us [to] their clearance...our two families will have a clearance of 22 acres. Ebenezer Wilson is about a quarter of a mile from us and his clearance and Robert Twaddle's are mett all to a few yards; these two lies North west of us. Ebenezer has 7 or 8 acres already cleared and about two months ago his son, David, came here from Nova Scotia and is handy at cutting down the trees.... Duncan McDugal and Daniel Ritchie, Archibald McDugal, Josiah Davies, James Nisbet, John Porter, Alexander Young, Robert Simm, David Wilie, James and Robert Smith, Thomas Hall, Anthony McBride, James Esson, James Gilmour, and son, Captain Eliott and George Watson are all around us within two miles distance of us and a little further lies three Brown Lee lads and a Crawford, Duncan and Archibald Campbell, Ewen Creeliey, William Cristelaw and many more too tedious to mention. So you see we have many neighbours and they are all agreeable and very helpful to each other. David Wilson says that the land here is much better and easier cleared than when he was in Nova Scotia.[62]

Table 5

The North Sherbrooke Scots, 1825–42

Lot Nos	I	II	III
		Concession Nos	
5	William Christelaw		
6	[Owen Crawley]	Archibald Campbell	
7		[Duncan Campbell]	
8	Alex'r Young & [John Porter]		
9		[Robert Sym]	
10	James Nisbit & Josias Davies	Robert Smith	
11	Duncan & Archibald McDugal	Arthur Stocks	David Wylie
12	Ebeneezer Wilson & [Daniel Ritchie]	Robert & [Thomas] Twaddle	
13	Anthony McBride & Jas. Easson	James Smith & Thos Hall	
14		James Gilmour	

[ ] Denotes settler who was named in Arthur Stocks' 1825 letter, but who was gone by 1842.

Sources: NAS GD 1/814/5/3: Arthur Stocks letter to his brother in Paisley, Dec. 10, 1825; LAC M-5505: Monthly Nominal Returns of emigrants, 1815–22; Ontario Genealogical Society, 1842 *Census Returns for Lanark County* (Kingston, 1992).

And having been allocated this land in 1822, they kept it. Arthur Stocks and many of his neighbours still owned farms at these same locations some twenty years later in spite of North Sherbrooke's reputation for poor land. The distinctive cluster of holdings owned by the Paisley weavers which lay between lot numbers 5 and 14 in the first three concessions, was still very much in evidence by the time of the *1842 Census* (Table 5).[63] They were typical of most settlers. Overall, nearly all of the 569 heads of families who were known to have occupied lots in 1820–21 were still residing at their original locations in 1829. Five years later seventy-one per cent of them could still be found at these same places.[64] However, the growing inducements which western Upper Canada could offer eventually caused people to leave the area. From the 1840s onwards, many Scots moved to the Huron Tract to take advantage of its far better land which was being sold on easy terms by the Canada Company.

The policy of subsidized emigration to stimulate the colonization of Upper Canada's vulnerable areas had been very expensive and was never repeated. Following the 1815 scheme, the only one to offer free sea crossings, the government had to issue public notices stating that no further free passages would be forthcoming. However, expectations had been raised and the Colonial Office continued to be inundated with requests from emigrants wishing to have their transport costs paid. When the government offered a reduced scheme of assistance in 1820–21, it was careful to exclude the cost of sea crossings. But even after that it continued to be besieged by requests to pay transport costs and to provide further assistance schemes. A Glasgow group, "believing that emigration in one shape or form will become inevitable," sought assistance in 1822 for 1,800 individuals who were members of thirteen emigration societies.[65] One hundred Argyll families requested "a small grant of land and small pecuniary help from H.M. Government similar to what is given to families in Lanarkshire and Renfrewshire only they would be satisfied with a smaller sum."[66] In 1825, the "near relations of some of the settlers in the townships of Lanark and Ramsay" who lived in Glasgow requested government help.[67] And Archibald MacNiven, the principal emigration agent for the northwest Highlands and Western Isles, petitioned on behalf of "many distressed families" after "hearing that your Lordship [Lord Bathurst] encouraged lists to be made and signed by poor people in certain districts of the Highlands."[68] However, there were no lists and all such requests were rejected.

The emigration societies had sprouted up at a time when the government had to contend with great disquiet in the Clyde textile districts. Whole communities were coming forward asking for help. The emigration societies were a heaven-sent mechanism for channelling funds and organizing departures, and the government grasped them with both hands. By oiling the wheels of emigration, the government bought its way out of an impending social crisis.[69] However, even though government help was made available, it was never going to be enough to cope with the overall demand. When the government scheme of 1820–21 was in full swing, Robert Lamond had observed that "such is the desire to emigrate, that…double the number of persons would have embarked, if the means of transportation had been afforded.[70] Even so, when the threat of civil unrest receded, as it had by 1821, the Glasgow Committee saw no justification in continuing with the scheme and advised the government that it had served its purpose. Although weavers continued to protest about their miserable conditions and prospects, the government declined to help them to emigrate. From henceforth, emigrants would have to find the funds for their relocation costs themselves.

The government's policy of encouraging emigrant Scots to settle in the militarily vulnerable regions in eastern Upper Canada had worked. Because most of the initial Scottish influx to the province had been directed towards these districts, they would be the ones to attract follow-on emigration in the years which followed. In spite of the withdrawal of public funds the zeal for emigration grew. The rapid growth in the St Lawrence timber trade brought affordable and regular sea crossings within the grasp of the average emigrant. Now, as news filtered back to Scotland of the good farming opportunities to be had in eastern Upper Canada, Scots financed their own departures on timber ships and made their way to the fledgling communities which had been established by their family and friends.

Five

THE CONTINUING INFLUX
TO EASTERN UPPER CANADA

The old settlers are in general comfortably lodged, though not
in the style that the Americans of the same standing would be...
Their accommodations appear poor compared to the American
and English settlers but they are a wonderful advance from
the hovels of Glen Garry [Scotland].[1]

LORD SELKIRK WAS NOT OVERLY IMPRESSED with the Glengarry settlements, when he visited them in 1803, some twenty years after
the first foundations had been laid. Had they not succumbed
to the Highlander practice "of living all together" which gave them
less opportunity "of learning the modes of carrying on work, adapted
to the country," he felt that they might have made more progress in
their colonization endeavours.[2] The author, John Howison, who visited the place nearly twenty years later, could barely conceal his loathing
of them just for being Highlanders. According to him "their mode of
life" was "dirty, ignorant and obstinate...Few of the settlers have more
than 60 or 70 acres cleared and the generality is only 30 or 40 acres."[3]
His "high expectations" had been dashed and before him was a settlement "not in a flourishing state."[4] Its inhabitants seemed "too
un-ambitious to profit by the advantages of their condition. A very
great majority of houses are built of logs and contain only one apart-
ment."[5] However, as Selkirk pointed out, although their first houses

had been crudely built, they were far better than the hovels they left behind in Scotland.

While Selkirk had noticed that "the young men, who have come over as children are as expert as any at the axe," he may not have appreciated the importance of the timber trade to Glengarry's economic well-being.[6] Because of the "advanced prices of lumber and potash,"[7] most of Glengarry's adult men divided their time between clearing the forests and farming. Father Macdonell had little time for axe skills and admonished his parishioners for neglecting their "agriculture and the raising of grain."[8] But they were simply following their entrepreneurial instincts. When Dr. Thomas Rolph, who later became the official emigration agent for Upper and Lower Canada, visited Glengarry in the 1830s, he too was critical of its inhabitants for "allowing their lands to be neglected," having been "induced by the greater wages to engage in lumbering."[9] But he also had to admit that this activity had contributed to their "considerable wealth and independence."[10] The 1841 Emigration Select Committee would learn from him that Glengarry had the highest proportion of freeholders of any other county in Upper Canada, "The circumstance of their polling in such numbers [freeholder numbers] is a test of their comfortable and prosperous condition."[11] The Hon. Christopher Hagerman, one of the "Justices of the Queen's Bench" in Upper Canada, would also comment favourably on Glengarry, "Many of them have excellent farms and are possessed of considerable wealth and live in comfort and independence on their own property...their patience and industry have been fully rewarded."[12] So, in spite of its relatively disappointing appearance, Glengarry enjoyed above-average prosperity.

As has already been noted, Glengarry had its beginnings in 1785–86 when, with the ending of the American War of Independence, it acquired just over 800 Highlanders who mainly originated from west Inverness-shire. This one region of Scotland continued to supply Glengarry with a steady stream of new emigrants over many decades. During the early 1790s and, in 1802, over 1,600 people arrived in Glengarry County from various Inverness-shire locations – especially Glen Garry, Glenelg, Glen Moriston, Knoydart, Morar, and from Kintail and Eigg. They had been followed in 1815 by an additional 350 Highlanders who originated from both Inverness-shire and Perthshire.[13] However, although there was this later intake of Perthshire emigrants, Glengarry's dominant links would remain with west Inverness-shire.

With the ending of the Napoleonic Wars in 1815, the Scottish economy had gone into a sharp decline. Glowing reports of the opportunities to be had in Glengarry became a powerful inducement to the many Highlanders, living in west Inverness-shire and nearby Wester Ross, who wished to escape from their poverty. However, most of them lacked the means to finance their relocation costs. Donald MacCrummer, a Skye merchant knew of "several hundred people in Glenelg, Glenshiel, Kintail, Lochalsh and Loch Carron who, "deploring of being able any longer to live in comfort in the land which has produced the kilted heroes of Waterloo," planned to emigrate.[14] He wanted to arrange ships for them but they could not afford the cost of their fares which were around £6 to £7. Similarly, John McRa of Lochalsh, a shipowner, had dealings with a "few hundred poor people" from Wester Ross who longed to emigrate but because of "their extreme poverty" could not afford to pay for their passages.[15] John McMillan from Kintail pleaded with the Colonial Office for help to be given to the twenty or thirty families from Wester Ross, who wanted to join friends already settled in Upper Canada.[16] But it was to no avail. Countless numbers wanted to emigrate, but it was an option only open to those people who could afford to finance their own transport.

However, in spite of the economic constraints and difficulties of the post-war period, there were still some self-financing Highlanders who could afford the fares to Quebec. In 1817–18, two ships, the *Ardgour* of Fort William and the *Waterloo* of Fort William, each carried around 100 emigrants from Fort William to Quebec. It is highly likely that both groups were heading for Glengarry since Fort William was the prime embarkation port for west Inverness-shire and Wester Ross emigrants. The eighty-seven Lochaber emigrants, who sailed from Oban to Quebec on the *Speculation* a year later, were also probably intending to join Lochaber compatriots who had previously settled in Glengarry.[17] However, in addition to having raised sufficient funds for their sea crossings, these emigrants also had to face the further hurdle of locating land. As a result of the large Scottish influx of the late eighteenth and early nineteenth centuries, there was little vacant land left in Glengarry County. New arrivals would have to find land in the nearby townships, such as in Finch and Roxborough (Stormont County) or Caledonia and West

Hawkesbury (Prescott County).[18] Thus with the continuing influx, land acquisition was becoming increasingly difficult and people were being forced to settle some distance away from the original communities which had been established by the first arrivals.

A group of Highlanders who arrived in 1817, probably on the *Ardgour* of Fort William, thought they had found a suitable tract of land. They had taken out leases on the "Indian Lands," a small strip measuring about 1.9 miles wide and 25 miles long, sandwiched between the Glengarry County townships on the east and the Stormont townships on the west (Figure 4). Renting their holdings directly from the St. Regis Iroquois, they soon came to realize that, "besides their yearly rents," they were going to have to pay "the sum of ten pounds for every 160 acres."[19] Claiming that they had failed to fully understand the terms of their agreement "from their ignorance of any language but the Gaelic," thirty-six family heads petitioned Sir Peregrine Maitland, Lieutenant Governor of Upper Canada, in 1821 for help in extricating themselves from their contracts.[20] It is not clear whether they were able to acquire land on more favourable terms, but it would take another 25 years or so before the "Indian Lands" came into the possession of the Crown.[21]

One hundred and forty-five families (around 440 people) from Inverness-shire took a more cautious approach than this first group when planning their emigration. They would only emigrate if "a proper place could be found to form a settlement adjacent to that part in which some of their friends were located." Ronald McDonald travelled to Upper Canada in 1821 on their behalf and, having found a desirable situation, "being a gore situated between the townships of Kenyon, Alfred, Plantagenet, Roxborough and the Indian lands which is contiguous to Glengarry, where many of the friends of the parties who are desirous of accompanying your petitioner are now settled," he submitted a formal application for land.[22] He wanted 1,000 acres of land for himself, "as remuneration for collecting the different parties" and requested 100 acres "for such of the males as are desirous of joining your petitioner in the proposed undertaking who have attained the age of twenty-one years." And finding "old barracks" at the mouth of Black River, he recommended their use as a temporary residence for the group during their first year. McDonald also requested public funds to cover the group's costs "in conveying the parties from Quebec to the intended place of

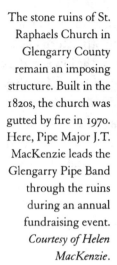

The stone ruins of St. Raphaels Church in Glengarry County remain an imposing structure. Built in the 1820s, the church was gutted by fire in 1970. Here, Pipe Major J.T. MacKenzie leads the Glengarry Pipe Band through the ruins during an annual fundraising event. *Courtesy of Helen MacKenzie.*

settlement" as well as help "with provisions for the first year after their arrival." However requests of this nature were always rejected, although the group may well have obtained their chosen tract of land.[23] Some Inverness-shire people were almost certainly among the one hundred and twenty-seven emigrants who sailed in the following year from Fort William to Quebec.[24] The likelihood is that they proceeded to the Glengarry area to settle close to their compatriots.

By this time Charlottenburg Township had emerged as the most compactly settled of the Glengarry townships, with population centres at Martintown, Williamstown and Lancaster on the Raisin River, at Summerstown on Lake St. Francis and at St. Raphael in the centre of the township (Figure 4). With a population of 3,000 in 1822, it was said to be "so entirely confined to Scottish settlers it seldom attracts other strangers."[25] Having five churches, twelve schools, twelve stores, eighteen taverns and six gristmills, it was clearly prospering. In 1846, it would be described as "the most settled township in the Eastern District...the principal part of whom are Scotch."[26] A Roman Catholic chapel had been in place at St. Raphael since 1786,[27] while Presbyterian churches had been erected soon after this at Martintown, Williamstown, Lancaster and Summerstown.[28] By 1825 Martintown, which was "situated in the centre of a flourishing Scotch Settlement,...having a handsome Manse and Glebe of about 12 acres of excellent land," was looking for a resident minister.[29] Having visited the place, Reverend John Burns advised that a minister stood no chance at all unless he could speak Gaelic. He had "to be able to officiate in Gaelic one-half of the day as that language is generally spoken by the lower orders of the old settlers...and he must be able to deliver his discourses as they are generally averse to reading."[30] And even though Lancaster's Presbyterian congregation consisted of "a mixture of Highlanders, Lowlanders, English and Dutch...," its minister, Reverend Alexander MacNaughton, was adamant that "one Gaelic missionary" was needed to speak "from our own pulpits."[31]

Meanwhile, Reverend John McLaurin, who presided over a widely scattered Presbyterian congregation in Lochiel, was also attending to worshippers in Prescott County:

My congregation is numerous and spread over a large tract of country. I preached first at three different places; at Lochiel to about 500 hearers; at Longueil [Prescott County] 16 miles from Lochiel, to about 200 hearers...and occasionally at several other Scotch settlements in my neighbourhood...

For the last 2 years I preached every third Sunday at Lochiel, which is 20 miles distant from my present place of residence at Hawkesbury [Prescott County]...You will, perhaps, have a better notion of my congregation when I tell you that the first year when I administered the Sacrament at Lochiel there were 275 communicants; the second year 400. Almost all my congregation are old settlers and are considered wealthy. I may add that the people consider me an excellent preacher, and that I am very popular with them....[32]

By 1839 the Presbytery of Glengarry had expanded in size to encompass eleven churches which were spread across Glengarry County itself and its neighbouring counties.[33] The "Indian Lands" congregation, having grown to 1,100, was looking for a minister of its own, while the combined congregation of Côte St. George (in Lower Canada) and Roebuck Mills in Lancaster Township were "some 800 strong."[34] The townships of Finch and Osnabrook (Stormont County) were "one of the most promising localities in the Synod." The Osnabrook congregation was already organized, having "been for many years under the pastoral charge of Mr. Lyle of the United Synod, but they have grown quite tired of him [and want] an able minister of our Church."[35] Meanwhile, Roman Catholics had built a stone church at St. Andrew's (Stormont County) by 1803, but Presbyterians in Cornwall (Stormont County) where "the greater part of the settlers are Scotch, but a few English and German are intermixed," had to wait until 1827 before their congregation was formally organized.[36]

Glengarry continued to attract emigrants throughout the 1820s from Glen Garry, Glen Moriston, Knoydart, Moidart, Lochiel and Glenelg in West Inverness-shire and from Kintail and Glenshiel in Wester Ross but not in any great numbers. A Kintail merchant described the distressed state of two to three hundred families from Kintail, Glenshiel and Lochalsh who were asking for government help to emigrate, while some 500 people, mainly from Glen Garry, made a similar request in 1826, blaming their plight on "the introduction of the sheep system."[37] However, no government aid was forthcoming.

With the better land prospects available in western Upper Canada from the 1830s, Glengarry's appeal waned although it did occasionally acquire large groups even at this time. Having arrived at Quebec in August 1836, "A considerable number of Scotch families" were heading for "the Glengarry settlement where many of them have their friends: they have the appearance of studious, industrious settlers, and all are possessed of means."[38] And, when the Potato Famine hit the Highlands, in the period from 1846 to 1855, Glengarry once again experienced another substantial influx of Scots. Large-scale depopulation followed in the wake of the famine and with this crisis came a large increase in emigration, some of which was compulsory, and most of which was landlord-assisted. Those Highlanders who were driven primarily by the desire to settle close to people who shared their customs and traditions, would have been attracted to Glengarry. With its many long-established Highland communities, it was an obvious choice.

Acquiring funds from the Highland Destitution Committee, James Baillie, a wealthy Bristol merchant and banker, made arrangements in 1849 to assist three hundred and forty-one of his Glenelg tenants to emigrate to Upper Canada. Having petitioned him for assistance to emigrate, the tenants pledged themselves "to remove at whatever time of the ensuing season we may receive notice"(Table 6).[39] Sailing on the *Liskeard* of Liverpool, probably from Glenelg, they were "not only provided with a free passage to this port [Quebec] but furnished, in addition, with full means for their inland transport to their respective destinations."[40] Some three hundred and eleven of them were proceeding to Glengarry. William Lillingston, a London businessman, assisted 300 of his Lochalsh tenants to emigrate in 1849, although it is not clear whether any of them actually settled in Glengarry (Table 7).[41]

Table 6

Glenelg tenants from James E. Baillie's estate who are to emigrate to Upper Canada in 1849.

No.	Name	No. of Dependents	Location	Occupation
1	John Macrae	5	Bancro	Small Tenant
2	John MacLennan	6	"	Labourer
3	Arch'd MacDonald	8	"	"
4	Donald Chisholm		"	"
5	Donald MacLeod	6	"	"
6	John MacDonald	4	"	"
7	Mary McNeil	5	"	"
8	Malcolm Beton	6	Galder	"
9	Archibald Chisholm	2	"	"
10	Arch'd MacLennan	7	"	"
11	Neil MacIntosh	8	"	"
12	Donald MacLeod	6	"	"
13	Norman McCrimmon	5	"	"
14	Allan McIntosh	4	"	"
15	Kenneth McCrimmon	6	"	"
16	John Campbell	4	"	"
17	Finlay McLennan	3	"	"
18	Donald McConing	3	"	"
19	John McCrimmon	4	"	"
20	Roderick McLean	3	"	"
21	Malcolm McLean	1	"	"
22	Kenneth MacLeod	9	"	"

No.	Name	No. of Dependents	Location	Occupation
23	Alexander Sinclair	9	"	"
24	Alexander MacLeod	7	"	"
25	Neil Beton	1	"	"
26	Peter McCrimmon	7	"	"
27	Donald McLean	4	"	"
28	Arch'd McGilvray	8	"	"
29	Angus McKinnon	7	"	"
30	Roderick Chisholm	6	"	"
31	Malcolm McNeil	8	"	"
32	Donald Fraser	8	Galder	Labourer
33	A. McAskill	1	"	"
34	Donald Robertson	5	"	"
35	Mary McLeod	8	"	Widow
36	Alex. MacPherson	1	"	Labourer
37	Alex. MacDonald	3	"	"
38	Alex. MacDonald	3	"	"
39	Alex. MacPherson	3	"	"
40	Neil Beton	8	Kirkton	Small Tenant
41	Malcolm McNeil	3	"	Labourer
42	Donald Beton	7	"	"
43	Alex. Beton	7	"	"
44	Roderick MacLeod		"	"
45	Alexander MacRae	1	"	"
46	Neil McCrimmon		"	"
47	Roderick MacRae	6	"	"
48	Kenneth Cameron	2	"	"
49	Donald McLeod	6	"	"
50	Kenneth MacRac	9	"	"
51	Finlay MacRae	3	"	"
52	Donald MacRae	3	"	"
53	Alex'r Morrison	5	"	"
54	Donald MacRae	6	"	"
55	Malcolm MacRae	3	"	"
56	Kenneth McConing	5	"	"
57	Alexander Nixon	6	"	"
58	Kenneth McKenzie		"	"
59	Norman MacLeod	6	Corsaig	"
60	Murdo MacLeod	2	"	"
61	Arch. MacLeod	4	"	"
62	Malcolm MacLeod	2	"	"
63	Roderick Conig	7 ·	"	"
64	Roderick McLeod	5	"	"
65	John MacRae	6	"	"
66	Duncan MacRae	7	"	"
67	Neil Beton	3	"	"
68	John McIntosh	6	"	"
69	Alexander MacLeod		Balvraid	"

No.	Name	No. of Dependents	Location	Occupation
70	Duncan MacLeod	7	"	Small Tenant
71	Alex'r McIntyre	8	Cambusbaine	Carpenter
72	Widow McIntosh	2	Cambusbaine	Widow
73	Duncan McGilvray	4	"	Fisherman
74	Donald McGilvray	3	"	"
75	Kenneth McGilvray Snr	1	"	Weaver
76	John McInnes	2	"	Fisherman
77	Duncan McLeod – an old man aged 53 wants to go to a Brother			
78	John McGilvray	4	Cambusbaine	Fisherman
79	Donald Campbell	4	"	"
80	John McGilvray	4	"	"
81	Angus Campbell	6	"	"
82	Roderick Fraser	2	"	"
83	Duncan MacKenzie	6	"	"
84	John McIntosh	3	"	"
85	Ewen MacKenzie	7	"	"
86	Kenneth McGilvray Jnr	6	"	"
87	Kenneth Fraser	2	"	"
88	John McGilvray	9	"	"
89	Widow McGilvray	2	"	Widow
90	Widow MacDonald	5	"	Widow
91	Donald McConig	5	"	Fisherman
92	Norman Mclore	7	"	"
93	John McConig	2	Corran	Labourer
94	Farquhar McCrimmon	3	"	Fisherman
95	Donald Campbell	5	"	"
96	John McConig	2	"	"
97	Donald McConig	1	"	"
98	Widow Campbell	3	"	Widow
99	Andrew Fraser	8	"	Builder
100	Duncan McConig	8	"	Blacksmith
101	Duncan Cameron	4	"	Fisherman
102	Malclom McInnes	1	"	"
103	Ewan Macfie	1	"	"
104	Donald MacRae	6	Invergradden	Labourer
105	John MacRae	5	Bearblach	"
106	Farquhar Campbell	6	Beolery	"
107	Murdo MacLeod	8	Cragemore	"
108	Murdo Campbell	5	Ellarnoch	"
109	Donald Cameron	7	"	"
110	Alex. McLeod	4	"	"
111	Neil McConig	6	Ellarnoch	Labourer
112	Arch'd McLeod	7	Vallesmore	"
113	Arch'd McKillop	5	Bewley	"
115	Mary McNeil or Beaton	1	"	Widow

Source: NAS HD 21/35: This source also lists 10 tenants who are to emigrate to Australia.

Table 7

Recipients of relief in Lochalsh and Plockton, Ross-shire, who intend to emigrate. (n.d.)

Name of District	Residence		Name of Head of Family
Lochalsh	Avernish	1	John Bain MacKenzie
		2	Christopher MacRae
		3	John Big MacKenzie
		4	Farquhar Matheson
		5	John Bain MacRae
		6	Dugald Matheson
		7	John MacRae, Tailor
		8	Duncan Finlayson
		9	John Bain MacLennan
		10	Malcolm MacRae
		11	Donald MacRae
		12	Rory Finlayson
		13	Widow John Bain MacKenzie
		14	Alexander MacRae
		15	John Matheson
		16	Alexander Finlayson
		17	Duncan MacRae
	Aultnason	18	Duncan MacCulloch
		19	Alexander MacRae
	Ardelve	20	Alexander MacRae, Carrier
		21	Duncan Finlayson
		22	Duncan MacRae
		23	Duncan MacKenzie
		24	Kenneth MacKenzie
Plocktown	Drumbuy	25	Angus Cameron
		26	Christopher Matheson
	Erbenaig	27	Finlay Finlayson
		28	John Bain Finlayson
Lochalsh	Muirtown	29	John Finlayson
		30	John MacRae
	Reraig	31	John MacRae
	Canimonie	32	John MacKinnon
	Kulhillan	33	Donald Bain MacRae
	Brandaloch	34	Archy MacRae
		35	Duncan MacRae, Douine
	Auchtertyre	36	John MacRae
	Sallaby	37	Duncan MacRae
Plocktown	Craig	38	Dugald Matheson

Source: NAS H21/53

In the following year, eighty-two of MacDonald of Lochshiel's Moidart tenants sailed on the *George* of Dundee from Oban to Quebec, having been provided with free transport. Arriving in "great destitution," they were given "a free passage to Lancaster, their destination being Glengarry and the Eastern District."[42] One hundred of Mr. Lothian's Glen Garry tenants were also assisted to emigrate in 1851. Sailing on the *Ellen* of Liverpool, they "were proceeding to their friends in Lancaster, Toronto and Hamilton."[43] Having been issued with summonses of removal, tenants on Mrs. Josephine Macdonell's Knoydart estate were left in no doubt about their future prospects.[44] "Those who imagine they will be allowed to remain after this are indulging in a vain hope as the most strident measures will be taken to effect their removal."[45] Borrowing £1,700 under the terms of the Emigration Advances Act, Mrs. Macdonell provided her tenants with assisted passages as far as Montreal.[46] Sailing from Isle-ornsay, Skye, in 1853, on the *Sillery* of Liverpool,some three hundred and twenty-two of them arrived at Quebec. Having the appearance of "a fine healthy body of emigrants," the Quebec immigration agent felt certain that "the increasing demand for labourers of all descriptions throughout the province" would enable them "to do well."[47]

Glengarry was one of two magnets drawing emigrant Scots to eastern Upper Canada. The other one was the Rideau Valley, although it only began to attract settlers from 1815, some thirty years after Glengarry had acquired its first Scots. A severe economic depression in Scotland coupled with the government's assisted emigration scheme produced this second stream of emigrants who were directed to the military settlements in Lanark County (Figure 5). The first arrivals of 1815 were small groups from different parts of the Lowlands, to be followed three years later by a second group of around four hundred and fifty people, entirely from Perthshire.[48] The third and largest contingent, of nearly three thousand people, arrived in 1820–21, having originated mainly from the Clyde weaving districts in southwest Scotland.

Another Perthshire contingent came to the region in 1825, although, unlike the previous Perthshire group, these emigrants received no financial aid from the government. Having taken possession of a large tract of wilderness land in Renfrew County, Archibald McNab, a Perthshire grandee, looked set to fulfil his dream of founding "a transatlantic colony."[49] The township, which he named after himself, had a strategic location on the Ottawa River. Situated just to the north of Lanark County, it would become one of the final links in the chain of military settlements, which the government had been fostering in the Rideau Valley.[50] Under terms authorized by the government, McNab agreed to recruit settlers, take responsibility for their relocation costs and assign to each family head not less than one hundred acres of land. As his reward for furthering the colonization of this area, he would receive 1,200 acres for himself initially, plus a further 3,800 acres later on. With the help of a relative, Dr. Francis Hamilton Buchanan, McNab persuaded some of his former tenants from the Breadalbane estate in Glendochart near Killin to emigrate to Upper Canada.[51] Just over 100 emigrants from his native Perthshire duly set sail from Greenock to Quebec on the *Niagara* on the 19th of April, 1825.[52] McNab, in full Highland dress and accompanied by his piper, met them on their arrival at Montreal. It all seemed so plausible, but the man was a rogue whose sole aim was to restore his family fortunes with the money he collected from his hapless settlers.

McNab had actually fled in disgrace to Upper Canada to escape from his creditors in Scotland, who were threatening to imprison him. Before embarking on the *Niagara,* each head of family had been required to sign a bond agreeing to pay McNab £36 for himself, £10 for his wife and £16 for each child, with interest on the money being payable in money or produce.[53] The emigrants might have believed that a portion of this payment was for the purchase of their land, but it was not. McNab did not actually own the land and so it was not his to sell. His settlers never had any chance of clearing their debts and accumulated formidable arrears. They were locked into a legally binding contract with a man who treated them little better than medieval serfs.[54] Yet, in 1830, in spite of this deplorable situation, McNab was able to entice new arrivals from Islay, whom he met in Montreal, to accept his outrageous terms. They settled at McNab Township as did another large group from Blair Atholl who arrived in 1834.[55] However, McNab's days as a feudal baron finally ended in 1839. The Upper Canada government stepped in and paid McNab the sum of £4,000, which it was felt would cover, with interest, all of his claims against his settlers. They were then given the right to purchase their lands from the Crown. McNab later moved to the Orkney Islands and after falling into debt once again, he retired to a small village in France where he died at the age of 82. Meanwhile McNab Township's population grew to 782 by 1846, at which

Archibald McNab, the last laird of McNab (c.1781–1860). *Courtesy of the Archives of Ontario, Ref: S450.*

time its male inhabitants were said to be "principally engaged in the lumber trade."[56]

McNab had little trouble in attracting his settlers. Favourable reports from Upper Canada had stimulated an enormous desire to emigrate. However, most people at the time were unable to finance their removal costs. The McNab settlers thought they had secured a way out but soon found themselves at the mercy of an unscrupulous proprietor. Rather than taking this route, many people hoped that they might be fortunate enough to obtain funding from the government. The government's earlier policy of subsidized emigration had raised their expectations in spite of repeated pronouncements that funding was no longer available. Alexander McGregor, from Balquhidder, Alexander McLaren from Kenmore, and Donald Dewar from Carie on Loch Rannoch, all tenants living on the Breadalbane estate in Perthshire, were typical of those wishing to emigrate. "As many of the petitioners' relatives are doing well in America and are anxious that their friends in this country [Scotland] would follow them…they have been induced from these considerations to make the present application" for funds.[57]

Help was sought, but it was never granted. Two hundred and thirty-five Stirlingshire petitioners hoped to settle "in the neighbourhood of Perth, Lanark or Little York [Toronto] or somewhere adjacent" while some Edinburgh petitioners simply wanted "the usual allowance of land."[58] Believing that help was at hand, people from the weaving districts in Lanarkshire and Renfrewshire formed themselves into emigration societies and besieged the Colonial Office with petitions. In a single petition sent in 1822, some 1,800 "mechanics, labourers and others residing in Glasgow and its vicinity," who were members of thirteen emigration societies, expressed their wish to settle close to their friends and relatives "in the neighbourhood of New Lanark."[59]

The Colonial Office continued routinely to refuse aid, but, in this climate of growing hardship and frustration, the government was eventually forced to take a closer look at the question of assisted emigration. A Parliamentary Select Committee was appointed in 1826 and 1827, but its very existence boosted the emigration fever in Scotland even further. After considering evidence from the distressed areas of the British Isles, it concluded that public money should be given to aid poor emigrants, provided that it was repaid.[60] However, because of concerns over the high costs of such schemes, the government rejected the Select Committee's advice.[61] The outcome was a devastating blow to the 12,000 Scots, who had sent numerous petitions to the Colonial Office in 1826 and 1827.[62] The large number of Irish workers living in southwest Scotland were considered largely to blame for their plight. The Select Committee recommended that the flow of Irish migrants to the Glasgow area should be stemmed.[63] However, these conclusions brought the Scottish petitioners little comfort. They wanted to emigrate. The emigration societies would have to battle on with limited resources and from henceforth would rely solely on charitable donations.

Having failed to win government support, members of the Paisley Emigration Society proceeded to raise funds from local businessmen. Sufficient money was collected by the Spring of 1828 to enable two hundred and six of their members to depart for Quebec:

Thursday last, the brig *Mary*, with a fair wind, sailed from Greenock with emigrants for Canada, the greater proportion of whom were from this town and neighbourhood, and had been assisted by the Paisley Emigration Society…. The Rev. Patrick Brewster [minister of Paisley Abbey] as Treasurer for the Emigration Committee, went to Greenock and arranged for their passage and provisions. On leaving the port they were all in good spirits.[64]

However, after receiving letters "from some of our townsmen who emigrated in April last to Upper Canada," the *Paisley Advertiser*'s reporting became less sympathetic. Foolhardy emigrants were held up to ridicule:

A considerable number of passengers, anxious to escape from the sufferings inseparable from a sea voyage, contrary to the advice of the

Captain, went on shore. A seasonable breeze having sprung up, the vessel left them, and owing to their destitute state, they were unable to proceed to join it. A number of the inhabitants, commiserating their distressed situation, solicited one of their clergymen to deliver a sermon in their behalf. After a very suitable discourse upon the danger of going down in ships to the great deep, £30 was collected to assist them in proceeding up the St. Lawrence.[65]

But, when Reverend Mr. Brewster intervened to say that it was through his letter of recommendation that the £30 was collected, the newspaper had to retract its rather fanciful story.[66]

The *Advertiser*'s harrowing account of the mishaps and suffering experienced by Paisley Emigration Society members must have attracted widespread interest. There were the sad events surrounding individuals like Norris Hamilton's wife, who was on her way to join her son and grandchildren in Ramsay, Upper Canada. She had died on the roadside within a few miles of reaching her destination "none being present but a young niece. Her friends, having seen her distressed situation, had gone to endeavour to procure some mode of conveyance, but upon their return found that she had breathed her last in the arms of the little girl. – Some of the emigrants were so poor, that when they left Greenock, they had not half a crown in their pocket."[67]

Then there was the unfortunate threesome of John Moore, his wife and Robert Wilson who had to walk the 68-mile distance from Prescott to Brownsvale. "Being obliged by their poverty to abandon their original intention of cultivating land," they sought employment there. "They were almost stung to death by mosquitoes in travelling through the woods and Mrs. Moore in particular was cut in such a shocking manner, they had to stop for two days upon the road; but with the help of God they at length reached Brownsvale, and made an engagement to work at a new woollen factory."[68] This heart-rending saga provides evidence of some poorly resourced and badly organized emigrants, but it does not necessarily give a fully representative picture. Presumably the *Paisley Advertiser* gave prominence to the group's suffering to discourage others from following them. After all, Paisley's economic prospects had considerably improved by this time. However, the exodus from the area would continue, although this was the last large group to leave until the 1840s, when a sharp economic downturn stimulated yet another great surge in emigration to Upper Canada.[69]

It is not clear whether any members of the 1828 Paisley group actually reached the Rideau Valley that year. Those who did would have been greeted by thriving Scottish communities. By 1822 the total population of the Rideau Valley townships amounted to nearly 11,000.[70] William Bell could recall that when he first came to the area in 1817, "the majority of the population consisted of discharged soldiers. This however is not the case now [in 1824]. The number of emigrants has increased while that of the soldiers has decreased."[71] The town of Perth was growing rapidly, having seven merchant's stores, five taverns, four churches and around 100 houses.[72] And the settlers had acquired relative prosperity with well-supplied farms. There were "heavily laden dinner tables, houses packed with Indian corn, pease, wheat and oats...several hams resting in nooks."[73]

Although Scots were the predominant settlers in many of the Rideau Valley townships, Irish settlers were rapidly overtaking them numerically in some parts of the region. Even in the Lanark military settlement, founded entirely by Scots in 1820–21, some twenty per cent of the population were Irish by 1824. The Lanark Presbyterian minister described his congregation as forming "a very heterogeneous mass: having come from different countries – being different in their habits, prejudices, and dispositions – and widely and variously opposed in their religious sentiments and creeds."[74] Dense concentrations of Irish settlers were forming along the Rideau Canal axis, particularly in the townships of March, Goulbourn, Huntley and Marlborough in Carleton County. The initial Irish settlers had received government assistance, coming in 1818 with Richard Talbot's group of Tipperary Protestants or in 1823 with Peter Robinson's contingent who were Roman Catholics from County Cork.[75] Their numbers were further augmented when large numbers of Irish workers who, having been employed in the building of the Rideau Canal during the late 1820s and early 1830s, decided to settle in the area.[76]

Many of Lanark County's first pioneers had been Scottish weavers and, though it seems barely credible, they had been happy to relinquish their trades and became highly successful farmers. Preserving their collective approach to problem solving, they settled as "one neighbourhood" and continued to regard themselves as a distinct society. It was "out of our society [that] we would select our associates and friends."[77] They

William Bell's first Presbyterian Church, Perth. A wooden structure, built in 1819, it was used until the congregation united with
St. Andrews in the 1850s. The church burned down in 1867 and
only the bell survived. *Courtesy of the Perth Museum, Perth, Ontario.*

even preserved their long-established tradition of debating and reading
books. Long hours working over a loom provided much time for con-
templation. For recreation, weavers formed themselves into debating
societies and acquired books. They and their families had no intention
of giving up this aspect of their lives. When he arrived in the early 1820s,
Robert Mason, "though a plain weaver," carried "with him a library for
the use of the emigrants."[78] In fact, all those who had sailed on the *George
Canning* in 1821 were granted special permission to take such "books
which they may have as a private library."[79] Weavers were understandably renowned for their intellectual pursuits and enquiring
minds.[80] Bookish tradesmen though they were, they soon acquired the
practical skills needed to cope with pioneer life.

As Dalhousie Township grew in size, it acquired its own public library,
which was founded in 1828.[81] Developing out of the private libraries
which had been brought over by the emigrant Scots, it would become
one of the first public libraries to be founded in the whole of North America.[82] Thomas Scott, a member of the Lesmahagow Emigration Society,

led the group which eventually raised funds for both a building and a supply of books.[83] The library collection owed much to the "very valuable donations," made in 1828, by the Earl of Dalhousie, then Governor-in-Chief of Upper Canada:

He has become a patron to a Public Library which we have established...and has sent us one hundred Dollars and two boxes of books including a complete set of the Encyclopaedia Britannica as a foundation stone (to use His Lordship's own words)...The Books have not yet reached us, so that I cannot tell you what number of other volumes there may be. I need not tell you...the desire for knowledge appears to be a particular inherent principle in Scotsmen. And though we have expatriated ourselves, and are now obscured in interminable forests in Canada, we are still anxious to keep the intellectual machinery in motion ...[84]

St. Andrew's Hall, a log building with shingles, measured "32 feet by 22 feet within."[85] The planks for the bookcases "were made out of great pine trees from neighbouring hills and manufactured in a sawpit in the forest. Two wooden cases were constructed, each nine feet high and six feet wide by about eighteen inches deep."[86] At the time of its completion in 1832, the library had 500 books:

The reading was always eagerly sought, and the members made long tramps through the woods to procure delights for the coming two months, for issues to readers were made but six times a year. Every Library Day the Hall was crowded from morning till night.[87]

George, 9th Earl of Dalhousie (1770–1838), Governor-in-Chief of Canada 1819–28. Painting by Sir John Watson Gordon, circa 1830, engraved by Thomas Lupton. *Courtesy of Library and Archives Canada C-005958.*

However, interest in the library dwindled by 1880 and soon after this the hall disappeared. A plaque placed at Watson's Corners, west of Lanark, commemorates this historic site.[88]

The region's continuing prosperity owed much to the building of the Rideau Canal, which had opened by 1832. Providing a waterway link between the Ottawa River and Lake Ontario, the canal benefited Perth on the nearby Tay River, as well as Smiths Falls. The latter was now "the centre of an important, populous and rapidly improving district of the county" being "at the junction of four well-settled townships, Elmsley and Kitley [Leeds County], Montague [Lanark County] and Wolford [Grenville County]."[89] Situated "on a grand canal with fine water-powers and fertile country" Smiths Falls offered "the best advantages for trade, manufacture and agriculture. This being a much more recent settlement than most of the others such as Lanark, Ramsay, Perth, Beckwith etc., the settlers are of course more under their first difficulties but these are gradually disappearing as most of them are industrious and intelligent."[90] Although "it is only seven years since this settlement was begun," Smiths Falls "has advanced very rapidly. It had built its first Presbyterian Church by 1834, "which, in the present infant state of the settlement, is a bold undertaking."[91] The church was "a Gothic building and has a very handsome appearance."[92] Meanwhile "in the town of McNab," settlers were "speaking of applying...for a Minister."[93]

Having been prominent in McNab Township, Perthshire immigrants were also making good headway in Osgoode Township (Carleton County).[94] By 1836 Osgoode had more than 50 families "in communion with the Church of Scotland," who were seeking help from their former landlord, the Marquis of Breadalbane, to fund a new church.[95] The port of Dundee suddenly experienced a dramatic rise in emigrant departures, almost certainly reflecting a surge in emigration from Perthshire.[96] Advertisements began appearing in Perthshire newspapers describing ship departures for Quebec as did emigration news reports:

We alluded...last summer to the numerous respectable families, chiefly from Logie Almond and the western districts of this county which have sailed for the British settlements in North America to join several colonies composed for the most part of old friends and neighbours who had several years previously emigrated to these quarters...many families carried out £200 to £300 in cash each.[97]

While many of these Perthshire emigrants were probably heading west to the newer areas being opened up for cultivation, the newspaper's reference to "old friends and neighbours" suggests that a substantial number had gone to join the longer-established Perthshire communities, at Beckwith and Goulbourn (Lanark County) and Lochiel (Glengarry County).

As inland communications improved, more Scots headed for the western peninsula to take advantage of its better land and economic prospects. However, when the handloom weaving districts in the southwest of Scotland were hit by yet another severe economic slump in the early 1840s, Lanark County experienced a further influx of Scots.[98] The Quebec Immigration Agent's reports tell us of the many Scots who intended to settle in the Bathurst District of Upper Canada.[99] Encompassing the Lanark military settlements this region had been attracting people from southwest Scotland since 1815. As was the case with the later Glengarry arrivals, these people had been driven by a desire to settle near their own people. Nearly all were destitute, often having insufficient funds to pay for their onward travel and, as a result, most were dependent on finding immediate work.[100] The Quebec Immigration Agent occasionally grumbled about some Glasgow Emigration Society members who, having arrived penniless, seemed unwilling to work for their onward fares, expecting the government to look after them. But, more frequently, the agent's view was that although very poor, these were intelligent and industrious people.[101]

About three thousand members of the various Glasgow Emigration Societies, which had suddenly sprouted to raise funds for fares and provisioning, arrived in Quebec between 1841 and 1843.[102] They were, on the whole, extremely poor. The Glasgow arrivals of 1842 were in a more destitute condition than any other emigrants from the United Kingdom.[103] The nine hundred people who had sailed to Quebec from Glasgow in 1843 were due to land "without the means to carry themselves further."[104] In spite of their "best exertions," they had not been able to raise sufficient funds. After complaints from the Canadian authorities over "the special burdens" which had been placed on them to assist these emigrants to reach their onward destinations, the Colonial Office wrote to the Lord Provost of Glasgow with a stern rebuke.[105] These were difficult times.

The colonization of eastern Upper Canada by Scots had played a vital role in consolidating Britain's hold over Upper Canada. Much of this colonization was concentrated in the east where the government was particularly keen to build up defensive barriers to ward off a feared invasion from the United States. As previously noted, the late eighteenth and early nineteenth century Glengarry settlers were entirely self-funded and led by people of substance. Even as late as 1841 commentators referred to them as people who "went out with money."[106] Then the lure of government-assisted passages triggered off a huge exodus of impoverished Scots beginning in 1815, setting in train enduring emigrant streams which drew people into the Rideau Valley from the Lanarkshire and Renfrewshire weaving districts of southwest Scotland. By 1871 an amazing eighty-nine per cent of Kenyon's population in Glengarry County would be claiming Scottish ancestry, while the townships of North Sherbrooke, Dalhousie, Lanark, Ramsay, Bathurst, Drummond and Beckwith in Lanark County, Osgoode Township in Carleton County and McNab Township in Renfrew County had become major Scottish strongholds.[107]

However, although Scots continued to predominate in most of Glengarry and Stormont counties and much of Lanark County, the majority of people of Scottish descent by 1871 were to be found in western Upper Canada, not in the east. When the western interior became accessible, Scots had shown a preference for its better land and economic opportunities. Thus, colonization extended further to the west as new areas were surveyed and offered to emigrants. And the region to the north and west of Toronto was set to acquire particularly large concentrations of Scots.

Six

SCOTTISH COLONIZATION
MOVES WEST

*It has pleased God to furnish us with a table in the wilderness
and he hath filled our cup till it overflows.*[1]

IN 1841, WHEN JOHN MILLAR wrote to his brother in Dumfriesshire,
extolling the benefits of Upper Canada, many thousands of Scots
were heading across the Atlantic to North America. The prospect
of becoming a landowner in Upper Canada seemed irresistible to people with a sense of enterprise and sufficient capital to finance their
journeys. Millar and his seven children arrived in the mid-1830s, just
as this great exodus was gaining ground. Settling on the 7th concession
of Edwardsburgh Township near Spencerville in Grenville County, they
joined many other Dumfriesshire families who had already come to live
in this region of eastern Upper Canada.[2] In fact, Edwardsburgh had
long attracted settlers from Scotland. Together with the other townships along the north shore of the Upper St. Lawrence River, it lay within
a region which had been selected by the British government to accommodate Loyalist refugees from the United States. While the Loyalist
influx of the mid-1780s had brought many Scots to Glengarry County,
it had also left Edwardsburgh with some settlers who had been members of the Royal Highland Emigrants Regiment (84th).[3]

The Loyalists were followed by a second large group of mainly Scottish colonists who came to eastern Upper Canada during the seven-year

period from 1815 to 1821. They were mainly concentrated in eight Rideau Valley townships lying to the north of Grenville County.[4] Like the Loyalists before them, they too had most of their relocation costs funded by the government. Other groups, like Archibald McNab's Perthshire settlers who followed in 1825, extended Scottish domination to a ninth township in the Rideau Valley in what became McNab Township in Renfrew County. Also coming to the area around this time were former weavers, all members of the Glasgow Emigration Society, who settled in Grenville County, possibly taking up land near the Scotch Line Road in Oxford Township, lying to the north of Edwardsburg.[5]

Thus, although Edwardsburgh never acquired large concentrations of Scots, it was quite close to many long-established Scottish communities. They were the product of the Loyalist relocations to Glengarry and the government sponsored schemes which brought emigrant Scots to the Rideau Valley. However by the mid-1820s, the government decided that it had done enough to encourage population growth in eastern Upper Canada and withdrew financial aid.[6] When subsidies were provided, emigrants went only to areas designated by the government and formed compact settlements. Left to their own devices, they settled at sites which best suited them and in doing so were likely to become widely dispersed over large areas. The government may have hoped that emigrants would establish well-organized settlements, but its policies actually conspired against this laudable aim. Its land policies, such as they were, promoted everything under the sun except effective colonization. Land speculators thrived but ordinary colonists found it extremely difficult to cope with the many obstacles which were placed in their way.

Settlers had low priority. From the late eighteenth century, the government had been granting huge quantities of land as rewards to favoured individuals. Most recipients sold their land on to speculators, who amassed huge holdings but did nothing to further colonization. The government's policy of allocating Crown and Clergy Reserves meant that millions of acres of land were beyond the reach of ordinary settlers.[7] As a consequence, they had the residue which was often inferior land, and what holdings they could obtain were relatively small and scattered over huge distances. It was a bureaucratic muddle which favoured the rich and privileged while hindering the growth of compact settlements. Thus, apart from those communities which had been formed with the benefit of government funding, settlements were generally spread very thinly.

By 1823 Upper Canada's sparse population of a mere 150,000 was scattered over a 500-mile distance, stretching along the Upper St. Lawrence River, Lake Ontario and Lake Erie.[8] Settlements had been formed initially along river and lake frontages and only limited progress was being made in colonizing the forested areas further inland. While a total of eight million acres had been granted to private individuals, only about 500,000 acres were under cultivation.[9] As a consequence, the settled agricultural landscape of Upper Canada developed very slowly. York (Toronto), "the seat of government for the Upper Province," was still a small town with none of the trappings of a provincial capital city:

> It was a place of considerable importance in the eyes of the inhabitants; to a stranger however, it presents little more than about one hundred wooden houses most of them well built and one or perhaps two of brick. The thread of settlements along the road to this town is slender and frequently interrupted by long tracts of hemlock-swamp and pine-barren.[10]

Thus, although Edwardsburgh Township was long-settled, its population would have been widely dispersed by the time John Millar arrived in the mid-1830s. He probably selected it because it already had colonists who originated from his native Dumfriesshire.[11] His farm in Spencerville was clearly surrounded by various Dumfriesshire neighbours:

> The Douglas women are all well [also] Johnnie's family and George Elliott. I have not seen Walter Carlyle since February but I frequently hear from him and there are a good deal of acquaintances within reach. I saw Gabriel Chambers and Johnston from Branteth, someone of the name of Mundle that came from your side. I think about [the] Craigs and Edward Mundle from Ruthwell [Dumfriesshire] and a great many more that I cannot name.[12]

Edwardsburgh's Dumfriesshire community may have become established soon after 1817. It was from this time that Dumfriesshire began losing many of its people to North America. According to an anonymous letter

Kingston, 1819. From *Canadian Scenery Illustrated,* from drawings by W.H. Bartlett; the literary department by N.P. Willis, London, 1842. *Courtesy of Library and Archives Canada F5018 W5 1842.*

writer of that year, "no fewer than 547 persons have…emigrated from this port of Dumfries alone and we believe considerably more than 100 have sailed from Annan."[13] Attributing the "spirit of emigration" to the Upper Canada assisted emigration scheme of 1815 and to the favourable reports which were sent back to Scotland, he firmly believed that they had gone to a place "where misery is already at its height."[14] But, this view was not shared by his fellow countrymen who headed for Prince Edward Island, Nova Scotia and Upper Canada in ever-increasing numbers.[15] Around one hundred and twenty emigrants sailed from Dumfries to Quebec in 1820, while a further two hundred did the same in 1831 and 1833.[16] However, these arrivals from Dumfries were probably just a small fraction of the total. Although no figures are available, it is likely that most Dumfriesshire emigrants sailed from Maryport, Workington and Whitehaven in north-west England, which, by 1830, were the main emigrant embarkation ports for the west Border region of Scotland (see Appendix II).[17]

Thus, a good many Dumfriesshire emigrants were coming to Upper Canada, but the main attraction was not Grenville County. The western peninsula beckoned. Having acquired an entire township northwest of Hamilton and naming it Dumfries, William Dickson had little difficulty in locating settlers from his native Dumfriesshire.[18] By 1834 its mainly Scottish population had reached nearly 2,000.[19] In selecting Edwardsburgh, John Millar was swimming against the tide. Possibly he was won over by its long-established Dumfriesshire connections.

Looking back over his life in 1852, John Millar wondered why so few Scots had followed his example. More would come "if people from Scotland really knew how much better this place is for a poor man or family, particularly young lads if steady and careful."[20] His son James married "a young woman beyond Perth," whose grandfather "is from Berry Scar in Hutton parish [Dumfriesshire], a John Holliday, sent out by the government to teach a free school in the year of 1815."[21] The granddaughter of the independently-minded Holliday would join this Dumfriesshire community and probably enjoy a prosperous future. In addition to running a farm, James, together with his younger brother and father, established a forge in Spencerville and later became successful merchants.

Kingston's farming and business opportunities also attracted emigrant Scots, although their numbers were relatively small. The Quebec Immigration Agent's reports, throughout the 1840s, mentioned the farmers and tradesmen who intended to settle in Kingston, these were fairly infrequent occurrences. Although a Gaelic newspaper was being printed in Kingston but its primary readership was based further to the east in Glengarry and Stormont counties. It was no doubt sold in Kingston although Highlander numbers there were "not very many."[22] However, Kingston did receive one notable Scottish emigrant in 1841. Delighted with his recent acquisition – a 400-acre farm "situated on the banks of the St. Lawrence and bounded on one side by the road from Montreal to Kingston," Alexander Douglas, from Watten (Caithness) was adamant that "the good folk in Scotland" should know about it.[23] Describing his farm in great detail to the editor of the *John O'Groat Journal*, his published letter must have made his family and friends back in Caithness green with envy:

> The locality in which I have fixed myself [near Kingston] is a beautiful one and I only wish that I had taken possession of it 26 years ago, instead of remaining in rack-rented Scotland. I have got 20 fine Teeswater cows, 50 young cattle, 13 horses, the worst of which would grace a Caithness carriage, two oxen, 31 sheep and a number of swine, with a variety of farm implements…. We live better here than any man in Caithness, be his rank what it may.[24]

Perhaps Alexander Douglas settled in Ernestown Township (Addington County) to the west of Kingston where "the great body of the people

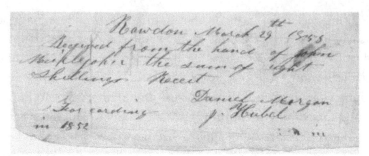

This receipt, made out to John Meiklejohn and dated March 29, 1853, records the sum of eight shillings paid for the carding of wool in 1852. The Meiklejohn family, handloom weavers from Saline (Fife) and Tillycoultry (Clackmannanshire), emigrated to Canada in 1843, settling in Rawdon Township, Hastings County. Early receipts for fulling and carding, plus a woven coverlet in the possession of the Tweed Heritage Centre, confirm that the family continued their trade in their new homeland. *Courtesy of The Tweed Heritage Centre, Tweed, Ontario.*

are Presbyterians."[25] Another possibility was Gananoque, "a village 25 miles east of Kingston" which apparently had "some wealthy and spirited men" among a Presbyterian congregation which numbered around 300 people.[26]

The townships of Cobourg and Colborne (Northumberland County) further to the west along Lake Ontario, had appreciable Scottish populations by the early 1830s. Cobourg had a Presbyterian congregation of 400 which "may be got as soon as they have a place large enough to meet in."[27] Colborne was apparently "a thriving settlement with the people around in easy circumstances."[28] Although they were largely of Scottish descent, most originated from the United States. The congregation had constructed a stone church measuring "50 feet long by 40 feet wide," but they were around £300 "short of the sum necessary to complete the building."[29] Their church named St. Andrew's became one of the oldest surviving Presbyterian churches in Ontario.[30] Peterborough, lying further inland to the north of Cobourg in Monaghan Township, was also reported to have "a large Scotch population" who lived near "a considerable number of Presbyterian Irish," the latter probably originating from the United States.[31] And there were sufficient numbers of Presbyterians living in Otonabee, "a settlement 12 miles from Peterborough," for the congregation to attract a resident Presbyterian minister in 1839.[32]

The adjoining townships of Darlington and Clarke (Durham County) lying along Lake Ontario to the west of Cobourg, had substantial numbers of Presbyterians who were considered worthy of support because of "the improved state" of their settlements.[33] Pickering Township (Ontario County) further to the west had attracted George Barclay, a Baptist minister from Cupar in Fife. Having emigrated in 1816 with his wife and six children, he worked initially as "a teacher of the common school at Newmarket" in York County but came to Pickering a year later. "Being possessed of the means to cultivate and improve" land, he was determined to acquire a farm and eventually purchased 1,000 acres in the 6th and 7th concessions at Brougham (Figure 7).[34]

Reach Township, lying to the north of Pickering, acquired its Perthshire settlers by the early 1830s.[35] Originating from the Breadalbane estate, they petitioned the second Marquis of Breadalbane in 1848 for help in building a church. "If we can plant a gospel ministry...now, when the settlement is young we will inject a character which it may never lose."[36]

This pattern of small groups of Scots taking up land in scattered communities, along and inland of Lake Ontario between Kingston and Toronto, would be repeated many times over. Unlike the east where Scottish colonists dominated entire township blocks, here in the central region they were mere components of ethnically mixed population centres. Substantial Church of Scotland congregations developed by the mid-1830s at Belleville, Colborne, Cobourg, Peterborough, Scarborough and Toronto, but, because of the large Irish intake by this time, Scots

Fairview Farm, Pickering Township. David Lyons Barclay, George Barclay's eldest son, established the farm on lot 15 in Concession 7. *Courtesy of Library and Archives Canada MG25 G272 (the Barclay Family Fonds).*

were unlikely to have been the dominant group.[37] However, this dispersed pattern changes dramatically as we move north and west from Toronto. The Lake Simcoe region in particular attracted many Scots. One of the largest concentrations of Highland Scots was on the eastern side of Lake Simcoe (Figure 7). The adjacent townships of Eldon (Victoria County) Mara, Thorah, Brock and Georgina (Ontario County) all had major Scottish populations. Three other Scottish clusters developed: one at Caledon (Peel County); Esquesing and Nassagaweya (Halton County) west of Toronto; another at King and Vaughan townships (York County) north of Toronto and a third to the west of Lake Simcoe at West Gwillimbury, Innisfil, Essa, Oro and Nottawasaga (Figure 7).[38]

Many of the emigrants Scots who settled in these clusters to the north and west of Toronto originated from the Argyll islands. The general economic depression which set in with the ending of the Napoleonic Wars in 1815 and the collapse of traditional kelp markets by the mid-1820s, had stimulated a growing exodus from the Western Isles.[39] While a great many Islanders emigrated to Cape Breton, substantial numbers of Argyll settlers also came to Upper Canada at this time.[40] The 143 emigrants who sailed on the *Traveller* of Aberdeen in 1819 and the 259 passengers carried by the *Monarch* in 1823 were the first large Hebridean contingents to arrive from Tobermory, and they would be followed by many others.[41] Some Western Isle emigrants may have also boarded ship at Oban at this time.[42] Even more groups emigrated during the 1830s.

Emigrating mainly in large groups, these emigrants would have sought to relocate themselves in Upper Canada as distinctive Highland communities. The townships on the east side of Lake Simcoe and along the Penetanguishene Road, north of Lake Simcoe, had been surveyed by the 1820s and were thus available for settlement.[43] These remote stretches of Upper Canada would have had particular appeal to Gaelic-speaking Scots wishing to preserve their customs and traditions. However, colonists acting on their own would have faced great difficulty in acquiring large tracts of wilderness land. Donald Cameron's timely intervention seems to have provided the catalyst which brought many Argyll settlers to Thorah and Eldon townships. A Highlander, who lived in Lancaster in Glengarry County, he had previously originated from Fort William.

While initially claiming to have land on the St. Lawrence, Cameron would eventually acquire two entire townships near Lake Simcoe.

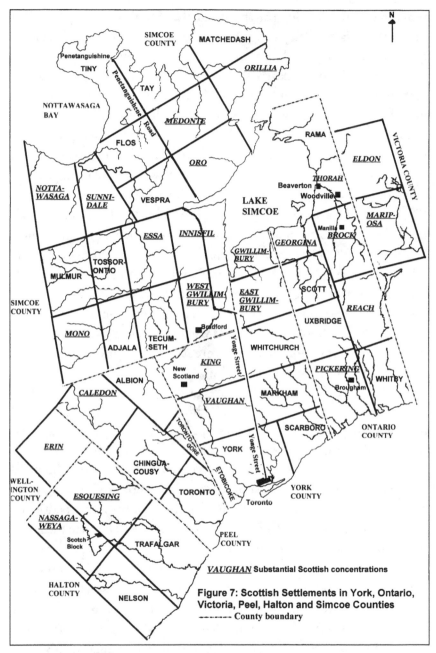

VAUGHAN Substantial Scottish concentrations

Figure 7: Scottish Settlements in York, Ontario, Victoria, Peel, Halton and Simcoe Counties
------- County boundary

Describing himself as "Mr. Donald Cameron from Upper Canada," he advertised, in the January 1823 edition of the *Inverness Journal*, that he had land to offer which was "conveniently situated on the River St. Lawrence." It could be obtained in lots of between 140 to 200 acres "at a quit rent of nearly one penny sterling per acre annually." He also promised loans of up to £18 per family "all paying interest for such advances…Able labourers will receive two shillings and sixpence per day exclusive of their provision."[44] Cameron clearly shared Archibald McNab's aspirations of becoming some sort of feudal landlord in the wilds of Upper Canada, but, like McNab's colonization venture, his also ended in failure.

Cameron had actually begun his involvement with emigrants two years earlier when he launched himself as a shipping agent. Setting up a network of sub-agents throughout the northwest Highlands, he made a determined bid to locate emigrants in Inverness-shire and Argyll.[45] By 1823, having arranged ship crossings for some 690 Highlanders who had sailed from Fort William to Quebec, he diversified his business interests to include land settlement.[46] However, his timing was somewhat askew since the land that he advertised in the *Inverness Journal* had not yet even been requested let alone received. It was only in June of that year, as "we leave the country soon," that Cameron actually made his first enquiries to the Colonial Office.[47] In the meantime, any people who were relying on him for their land were having to work as labourers in various parts of the province.

In 1825, the Upper Canada Executive Council agreed to grant Cameron 1,200 acres of Crown land for himself and, in addition, granted him the newly surveyed townships of Thorah and Eldon on the east side of Lake Simcoe for the use of his settlers.[48] To comply with the terms of his grant Cameron was required to have his settlers established on their holdings by 1827. Claiming that they were experiencing great difficulty in raising the funds to finance their journeys, he petitioned for an extension of time. This he did several times, but by 1829 the Executive Council lost patience with him and launched an investigation. A neighbour visited Eldon and Thorah and concluded that Cameron had exaggerated the number of his settlers and that only a small fraction of the total lots were actually occupied. Cameron was found to be guilty of perjury and was sent to jail. His legal battles dragged on for years.

Cameron's settlers were his staunchest allies throughout this sorry saga. As the years went by they sent six petitions on his behalf, one of them in 1834 was signed by some two hundred and sixty people.[49] In spite of having deceived them over the location of his land, they probably felt that that he had had their interests at heart. Cameron had clearly worked behind the scenes to assist emigrants in their attempts to raise funds. In 1824, he had composed a petition to Lord Bathurst on behalf of fifty families who mainly originated from Kilmalie (Argyll).[50] He may have helped on other occasions.[51] And Eldon and Thorah were both left with large Scottish populations. The 1861 *Census Returns* would reveal that three-quarters of the people in both these townships had Scottish Presbyterian affiliations while the adjoining Township of Mara had a similarly high concentration of Scots.[52]

Vaughan's Presbyterian minister, Reverend Peter MacNaughton, on visiting Eldon and Thorah in 1833, was highly disapproving of their inhabitants:

> The generality of the people of Thorah and Eldon seemed to me to be rugged as the rocks they had left in Scotland and wild as the forests they possess in Canada. They seemed much given to drink, and if I judge from what I witnessed, a few of them are given to fight. Free from the restraints of religion and education they are growing up like wild beasts.[53]

This close-knit Highland community clearly had a mind and will of its own. A Presbyterian missionary who had visited these townships a year earlier discovered that their population "is mostly Highland Scotch who came from North Carolina two years ago and have not yet got over their first difficulties. They may be said to be without roads."[54] These North Carolina migrants would have originated mainly from Argyll.[55] This suggests that Eldon and Thorah must have had some pre-existing Argyll communities which attracted them to this corner of Upper Canada. They were probably Donald Cameron's settlers. More convincing proof of Thorah and Eldon's links with Argyll is provided by the influx which followed. Most Scots who came to the Lake Simcoe region during the 1820s and 1830s originated from the Argyll islands of Tiree, Mull, Iona and Islay.

Tiree emigrants first made their appearance in Brock Township during the 1820s. When the sixth Duke of Argyll requested government help a decade later for those of his tenants who wished to follow, he was careful to point out that they wanted to go "to [Upper] Canada where many of their countrymen are happily settled."[56] According to Reverend

Norman McLeod, the Duke "shed tears over the distress of the Island of Tiree." He remembered the Duke saying, "These people wish to remain. They are devotedly attached to that Island and I cannot think of removing them; they were my fencible men and I love them."[57] Yet they did leave. The 106 passengers, collected by the *Adrian* from Tobermory in 1833, probably included many Tiree emigrants who were on their way to Brock.[58] Its Tiree settlers eventually became concentrated along the 7th concession west of the village of Manilla. After the clearances which followed the severe depression and famine of the 1840s, even greater numbers of Tiree people emigrated but most went to live in Bruce and Grey counties.[59] During this time many of the Tiree arrivals used Brock as a stepping-stone before moving on to their more permanent residences further west.[60] As a consequence there was a good deal of secondary migration from Brock to Bruce and Grey counties during the 1840s and 1850s.[61]

Eldon Township also attracted settlers from Tiree from the 1830s as well as from the Duke of Argyll's other estates in Iona and Mull.[62] However, the largest number of emigrant Scots to come at this time were from Islay. Four ships are known to have brought 762 passengers from Islay to Quebec between 1832 and 1836.[63] There may have been others. Some of the Islay emigrants went to Thorah Township on Lake Simcoe, others went west of Toronto to Caledon (Peel County) and Esquesing (Halton County), while a third group went further north to Nottawasaga on Georgian Bay. Meanwhile, a fourth group, having been lured away by Archibald McNab soon after their arrival in Montreal, had gone to McNab Township, much further to the east in Renfrew County.

Islay settlers augmented the Presbyterian congregation at Thorah, which was itself part of a much larger combined congregation encompassing Georgina, Eldon, Thorah and Mara.[64] Beaverton in Thorah acquired its first stone church by 1840 and its services were for some time conducted in both English and Gaelic.[65] The exodus from Islay continued into the 1840s, especially from the parish of Oa where people received some financial assistance from their landlord.[66] The strong Islay presence in the region would be reflected in the "Argyle" and "Islay" place names which sprouted just to the east of Beaverton. Eldon attracted further Iona and Mull emigrants during the 1850s, many of them having friends and relatives who had previously emigrated in the 1830s.

Two shanties on the Coldwater Road, Orillia Township, Simcoe County, drawn by Titus Hibbert Ware (1810–90), September 1844. *Courtesy of the Toronto Reference Library, J. Ross Robertson Collection T14381.*

However, the largest exodus from Islay occurred in the 1860s. Believing that emigration to Canada was the best escape route for his poverty-stricken tenantry, John Ramsay encouraged entire communities to leave. Assisting them with their relocation costs, he helped some 400 people to emigrate in 1862–63.[67] After visiting them in their new locations in 1870, he became even more convinced of the benefits of emigration:

> I went…to visit the residents from Islay who are located on the banks of Lake Simcoe, Georgian Bay and Lake Huron and what I saw there fully satisfied me that whatever people thought of the fact of people emigrating to Western Canada, I came home with the solid conviction that its was certainly the people who had occasion to be benefited by their removal from the Western Isles. I know I am subjecting myself to the criticism of those who deprecate the removal of a single soul from the Hebrides.[68]

John Ramsay had actually begun his travels in Lower Canada. Journeying west to Toronto from Montreal, he went north to Bell Ewart where he boarded a boat which took him across Lake Simcoe to Beaverton:

> I learned that Lewis emigrants were chiefly settled in the Eastern Townships while the great body of those who had gone from Islay and other parts of Argyll are located in the Province of Ontario, Canada West…Some years since the number who went from my own

estate...was very considerable. In one year I think the number from Islay must have been nearly 400.... There are a great many Islay men in and near Beaverton. [Thorah].[69]

Ramsay also visited "some of the Islay people in Orillia [Simcoe County] and Mariposa [Victoria County] and travelled "for some miles from Woodville [Thorah Township], along a road, the whole of which on both sides was mostly settled by Islay people" (Figure 7).[70]

Large numbers of Highlanders settled to the west of Toronto in the adjoining townships of Caledon (Peel County) Esquesing, Nassagaweya (both Halton County) and Erin (Wellington County). Islay had been losing people to Caledon from the 1830s, and possibly earlier. John Crichton had been one of the first arrivals:

The people who were nearer York [Toronto] used to say to us when we were going to Caledon that we were going out of the world altogether, but now there are settlers going upwards of thirty miles father back than we are, even almost to the shores of Lake Huron.[71]

By 1826 Caledon was reported to be in "a flourishing condition," having eighty families who were "chiefly Presbyterian."[72] The population of Erin "was nearly the same" while the number of families in Esquesing "amounts to several hundreds."[73] Apparently, Nassagaweya was populated primarily by Highlanders "belonging to the Kirk."[74] The so-called "Scotch Block," which straddles Esquesing and Nassagaweya townships near the present-day intersection of the 2nd line and 15th side-road, was probably the site of what was once a major settlement. While Scottish Presbyterians were prominent in all four townships, they were "thinly scattered" and living in "back settlements" and, as a result, their needs were best met by "itinerant preachers."[75]

However, by the 1840s many Islay settlers were being enticed by the even better opportunities to be had in the so-called Huron Tract lying further to the west. Owned by the Canada Company, formed in 1826, this was a vast area in the far reaches of southwest Upper Canada which acquired its first emigrant Scots from the early 1830s. It attracted growing numbers of Scottish emigrants throughout the next decade, both directly from Scotland as well as from other parts of Upper Canada.[76] In

1842, Alexander Fraser from Glengarry claimed that "nearly 500 families from my native Islay" were proceeding directly to the Huron Tract "as the whole host of their relatives and countrymen in the townships of Caledon, Esquesing, Thorah and many other places in the vicinity of Toronto …will repair to the Huron settlements this ensuing autumn and winter"[77] Fraser was going to be supervising the Canada Company's operations in twenty-three townships and so presumably had some knowledge of the numbers of Scots being attracted to this region. If he is to be believed, there was a substantial migration of emigrant Scots during the 1840s from this region to the Huron Tract settlements.

Meanwhile, the area between Toronto and Lake Simcoe had acquired a substantial Scottish population by the early 1830s. A visiting Presbyterian missionary observed that on "the line of a road leading from York directly north to Lake Simcoe" called Yonge Street, both sides of the road were "thickly settled and in various places our countrymen abound" (Figure 7).[78] And as he travelled through Vaughan and King townships, he met more Scots, many of them Highlanders. Vaughan had a Presbyterian church where "about 250 people meet on the Sabbath when there happens to be preaching."[79] King Township "contains a considerable Scotch population though many of the inhabitants are comparably new settlers. There is no church but they have fellowship meetings regularly in a school house." Presumably they founded King Township's "New Scotland," lying at the intersection of the 8th concession and the 16th sideroad.

The congregation in Vaughan were particularly keen "to have a minister who could preach in Gaelic" and "seemed overjoyed" when the Gaelic-speaking Reverend MacNaughton arrived the following year.[80] However, his reaction was anything but joyous:

I cannot speak favourable of either the piety or of the intelligence of the Scotch settlers in Canada. In Canada I have met persons of decided piety, and I have met persons possessed of some knowledge – but the generality of them in sound and useful knowledge are…on a level with the general class of labourers in Scotland. They boast of their equality, of their independence and liberty. I do not know what they mean by equality, independence and liberty. They seem equal in poverty, in ignorance, and in indifference to religion. They seem to think that they depend neither on God nor on Man.[81]

As Reverend MacNaughton had discovered at Thorah and Eldon, he was among people who no longer felt subservient to anyone.

A fourth cluster of emigrant Scots was to be found west of Lake Simcoe. The first arrivals were Scottish colonists from Lord Selkirk's Red River settlement (now Winnipeg) who came to Simcoe County in 1815. The turmoil at Red River, which came to a head in 1815, and the North West Company's offer of land and free passages to Upper Canada had persuaded one hundred and thirty-four people to leave. Most of them had originated from Kildonan Township in Sutherland County.[82] Travelling by canoe with a North West Company escort, they first went to Fort William. Then, having transferred to a fleet of small boats, they crossed Lake Superior and entered Lake Huron. There they split into two groups. The first group went down Lake Huron to Lake St. Clair and on to Lake Erie, to settle at Aldborough and Dunwich townships (Elgin County) on land which belonged to Thomas Talbot.[83] The second group crossed into Georgian Bay, landed at Penetanguishene and waited for land to become available.

Having arrived at Penetanguishene, they travelled by road to Kempenfeldt Bay, then crossed Lake Simcoe to the mouth of the Holland River, where they took up residence in some frontier settlements on Yonge Street. Acquiring their land a short distance southwest of Bradford in West Gwillimbury some four years later, they travelled up the Holland River

Site of the "Auld Kirk," West Gwillimbury. A timber-framed church constructed in 1827 replaced a log church built four years earlier. *Photograph by Geoff Campey.*

to the site and founded the "Scotch Settlement."[84] Included amongst its first colonists were: Donald Sutherland, James Wallace, John Armstrong, Haman and William Sutherland, and James and Roderick MacKay.[85]

Located on the west side of the Holland River, at the southern end of the township, the "Scotch Settlement" acquired its first Presbyterian church in 1823, built on lot 8, on the 6th concession. A log cabin, it was replaced by a small timber-framed church four years later. By this time West Gwillimbury had a substantial Church of Scotland congregation composed of "a good many Highlanders and Presbyterian Irish in tolerably good circumstances."[86] When Reverend Matthew Miller, Presbyterian minister for Ancaster (Wentworth County) paid a visit to West Gwillimbury in 1833, he was struck by the large numbers of Highlanders who still spoke in "their native tongue." Believing that "the charm of their native tongue would be irresistible" to them, he recommended that they be sent "two or three preachers who can speak Gaelic."[87] While he noted that most of these Highlanders had originated from Perthshire and Argyll, Reverend Miller failed to mention the original nucleus of Sutherland families. He was either badly informed or the Sutherlanders may have set up their own independent Presbyterian congregation which he had chosen to ignore. While the settlement prospered, initially, it later became a deserted site with an "Auld Kirk."[88]

Having been surveyed during the 1820s, the area west of Lake Simcoe began attracting its first waves of colonists. Some of the earliest arrivals were Scottish Lowlanders who came to this area in the early 1830s (Figure 7). Having previously emigrated to Dalhousie Township (Lanark County), they moved west and settled in the southeast of Innisfil and in west Essa (Simcoe County).[89] Most of them had originated from Lanarkshire and Renfrewshire and included in their numbers were former Glasgow and Paisley weavers. In 1832, more Lowlanders arrived in Innisfil Township from Dumfriesshire and their followers came in successive waves until 1850.[90] Nearby Oro Township also attracted Scots at this time who were mainly from the island of Islay.[91]

Further to the north, the area to the west of the Penetanguishene Road was also being opened up to settlers. "On account of our principal naval depot for Lakes Erie and Huron being now at Penetanguishene," Lieutenant Colonel Sir Francis Cockburn had advised that "settlements should be established between Lakes Simcoe and Huron in the vicinity of the Penetanguishene Road and extending toward the Nottawasaga River."[92] His advice had clearly been taken. Nottawasaga attracted large numbers of Highlanders from 1832 who mainly originated from Islay. By 1842 Nottawasaga had only a small population of "four hundred and twenty, who are principally Scotch."[93] A few of them later migrated eastwards to nearby Sunnidale, Medonte and Orillia townships.[94] By 1861 around fifty per cent of Nottawasaga's population had Scottish Presbyterian affiliations and nearby Mono Township also had a substantial proportion of Scots.[95]

Thus, while emigrant Scots were scattered far and wide in the central region of Upper Canada, they were to be found in considerable numbers in York, Simcoe and Ontario counties. By far the most predominant group were the settlers from Islay. Seven Upper Canada townships acquired Islay emigrants throughout the 1830s. Arriving as they did without government assistance or a well-heeled proprietor, they were probably unable to find sufficient cheap land in one place for all of their numbers and were, as a result, forced to disperse to a number of townships. However, they did stay roughly together in the sense that most of them settled in this one region to the north and west of Toronto.

Upper Canada was not colonized in strict chronological sequence from east to west as might be expected. The Glengarry communities on the eastern extremity were the first to take shape in the late 1780s; but they were followed in the early 1800s by Scottish settlements situated some 600 miles further to the west, at Elgin and Kent counties on the north side of Lake Erie. Southwestern Upper Canada had attracted the government's attention because of its vulnerability to attack from the United States. As a consequence, the government had granted large tracts of land in the region to proprietors who intended to promote colonization. The best known of these was Lord Selkirk who sponsored the Baldoon colony in Dover Township (Kent County) in 1804. Colonel Thomas Talbot, an Irishman, also came forward at this time. Unlike Selkirk, he played no part in the Scottish emigration controversy, which raged during the early 1800s, and could thus be granted land without antagonizing the many landlords in Scotland who deplored the loss of tenants from their estates. Founder and supervisor of the so-called Talbot Settlement, he would become Upper Canada's foremost colonizer.

Seven

THE LAKE ERIE AND THAMES VALLEY SETTLEMENTS

There is not a place under the sun better than this place [Baldoon].
Any person that intends to come to this country and that can take
£10 sterling to this place he may make a living of it with very little
trouble.... You may tell Ronald, your brother...he would get more
land than was in all Mull for about £10 sterling.[1]

IN SPITE OF THEIR INITIAL difficulties, Lord Selkirk's Baldoon settlers were beginning to make progress by 1806. A malaria outbreak,
claiming many lives, had not dampened John MacDougald's spirit
or belief in the opportunities which lay ahead. So much so that in the
height of the outbreak he wrote to his brother in Mull encouraging him
and others to join the Baldoon settlement in southwestern Upper Canada.
While there had been "a good spell of sickness since we came to this
place, as no doubt you have heard," the settlers "thank God are getting
the better of it now."[2] Having come initially to a waterlogged location
in the northern stretches of Dover Township (Kent County), they moved
a short distance to a better site in Shawnee Township (Lambton County)
afterwards known as Chatham Gore.[3] There, at the forks of Big Bear
Creek they founded Wallaceburg, named after Sir William Wallace the
founder of Scottish nationalism, and prospered. (Figure 8)[4]

The first Baldoon settlers were fifteen Scottish families (102 people),
who mainly originated from the Argyll Islands. Having sailed on the

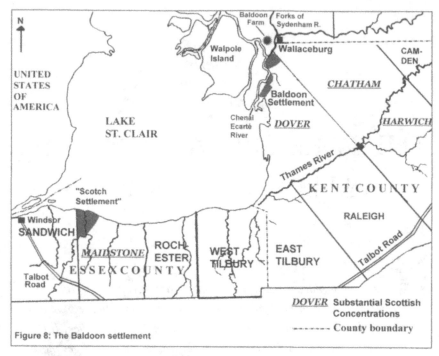

Figure 8: The Baldoon settlement

Oughton from Kirkcudbright in May, 1804, they arrived in Lachine, near Montreal, on 19th of July.[5] They then travelled west to Kingston where their paths crossed with Lord Selkirk. Meeting him on the 5th of August, they made various requests for credit, food provisions, employment and land, which he dealt with on the spot.[6] They then sailed across Lake Ontario and along the Niagara River to Queenston. Travelling by land to a point beyond Niagara Falls where they could safely continue their progress along the Niagara River, they entered Lake Erie and proceeded along its north shore to Amhertsburg. From there they went up the Detroit River to Lake St. Clair, entered the Chenal Ecarté River and finally reached the Baldoon site on September 5, 1804.[7]

The heavy rains which greeted the settlers continued throughout October, destroying most of the crops sown during the summer. Since July there had scarcely been a day on which it had not rained. The sodden ground bred mosquitoes and people soon fell ill with malaria. By November there were 16 deaths, five of them heads of families. To add to their difficulties the settlers had to cope with the dysfunctional Alexander McDonell, Selkirk's site manager and agent. Treating his work at Baldoon as a spare time activity, he failed completely to bring any form of

Portrait of Alexander McDonell (of Collachie) who managed Lord Selkirk's estate. A former tacksman on the Glen Garry estate in Scotland, he emigrated with his family to New York in 1773 and relocated to Glengarry, Upper Canada, just over a decade later, as a Loyalist. *Courtesy of the Toronto Reference Library, J. Ross Robertson Collection JRR896.*

management or direction to the site. He cared little for the settlers or their problems. Baldoon was simply a career move, for which he was completely unsuited. His continued ambition for high office combined with his marriage in 1805, which caused him to settle at York, meant that he spent increasingly less time at Baldoon.[8] When he finally made his first appearance at Baldoon, he gave the order for 14 log houses to be built, summoned up provisions and a doctor from Sandwich (later Windsor) but, by then, the malarial fever had already taken its toll.[9]

Initially, it must have all seemed so perfect. The government had granted Selkirk 1200 acres of lush farmland for himself in Dover Township and, having recruited fifteen families, gave him an additional 200 acres for each of them, thus increasing his total holdings by 3,000 acres. He established a 950-acre private farm while his settlers colonized the nearby river frontages to the south and east of his property.[10] It was stocked with the finest sheep, bred from imported Spanish Merino rams, and had a grand house together with various outhouses, stables and sheds.[11] The settlers were to be the initial workforce, labouring for a fixed number of years according to the terms of indenture contracts agreed with Selkirk.[12] In return for this they obtained free transport to the site and other benefits, including their own land.[13] However, as flooding and disease took their toll, a new site needed to be found. Selkirk ordered McDonell to move the settlers immediately to higher ground, but McDonell repeatedly ignored his instructions.[14] Also, the government compounded the growing sense of crisis by refusing to let Selkirk have the land he sought for the permanent relocation of his settlers. This was a tract of land further to the north at Chatham Gore.[15] Eventually, his settlers took matters into their own hands and acquired this better site for themselves.[16]

Selkirk's settlers had been extremely well chosen. Alexander McDonell never understood or appreciated them. His regular reports back to Selkirk, which were full of unremitting gloom and despair, blamed the settlers for the many mishaps which occurred, while glossing over the confusion and chaos being caused by his own failings and long absences from the place.[17] Yet these settlers were first-class pioneers, being highly adaptable to extreme conditions. Poor people from remote parts of the Western Isles were easily satisfied with the basics of life. As Selkirk predicted, they applied "themselves with vigour to the essential object of clearing their lands."[18] And he had been right to select large families with plenty of teenage sons to take over the family farm from deceased fathers. Eight of the original fifteen heads of family had died by 1809.[19] Their sons enabled the settlement to survive and later prosper. Without them the settlement would have failed.

If Selkirk's contemporaries and many later commentators are to be believed, Baldoon was an unmitigated disaster.[20] But this was not so. As a commercial undertaking, Selkirk's home farm certainly was a dismal failure. Selkirk suffered huge losses on Baldoon Farm, much of it attributable to Alexander McDonell's incompetence. Running costs had spiralled out of control. McDonell's profligacy and mismanagement probably cost Selkirk at least £5000 sterling – some £250,000 in today's money.[21] Selkirk had to sell up and recover what he could. But his colonists surpassed themselves. They persevered against all the odds, remaining immensely loyal both to Baldoon and to their Scottish roots. In doing so they realized Selkirk's aim of establishing a Highland colony in this important border area. With their distinctive culture and traditions, these Gaelic-speaking Highlanders were especially well-placed to resist "the contagion of American influences" which so concerned Selkirk at the time.[22]

Selkirk did achieve his objective although the settlement was far short of the grandiose scheme which had first been envisaged. Situated close to the American border, the Baldoon settlers were Selkirk's civilian army. Baldoon was invaded and pillaged by American soldiers in 1812, and again in 1814. High value goods were looted, including pewter plates, while more than 900 of Selkirk's Merino sheep were stolen and taken across the Detroit River to Fort Detroit. But each time his settlers were

Plaque recording the early history of the Baldoon settlement. It was originally situated at the site of the schoolhouse built in 1824 (corner of Kilbride Road and Bluewater Road) and was later moved to its present location at MacDonald Park, Wallaceburg. *Photograph by Geoff Campey.*

there to pick up the pieces and rebuild their communities.[23] Scots did not flock to Baldoon in large numbers, but those who did became defenders of territory just as Selkirk had intended. They were the first large group from Argyll to reach southwestern Upper Canada and their favourable reports home to family and friends clearly stimulated further emigration. They were the catalyst which spurred the growing Argyll influx from the 1820s. It was Highlanders, principally from Argyll, who dominated the early immigrant stream to southwestern Upper Canada.[24] Settling some distance away from Baldoon, they went mainly to those areas of Elgin and Middlesex counties which were under the control of Thomas Talbot.

Talbot, an aristocrat of Anglo-Irish descent, "was a short and strong-built man, with a ruddy face and an aquiline nose."[25] Adopting the manner of a British lord and having the air "of a military officer of distinction," he was a formidable character.[26] To some he was a gentleman with social graces but most people found him to be domineering, tyrannical, rude and high-handed. He was said to have a "total disregard or rather total ignorance of the feelings of others."[27] During the War of 1812–14, Talbot commanded the 1st Middlesex Militia and supervised the militia regiments in the London district. However, when a force of 500 men came to be mustered at Long Point on Lake Erie to march to the relief of Fort Amherstburg (Malden), there was a mutiny. The men simply refused to march under Col. Thomas Talbot.[28] Unlovable though he was, there was a practical side to his character. Known for his superb supervisory skills, he eventually became Upper Canada's most successful settlement promoter.

Talbot acquired what Selkirk had so passionately desired and failed to get. He commanded colonization operations on a grand scale in border country. While Selkirk led the pro-emigration debate in Scotland and attracted much criticism for his efforts, Talbot concerned himself only with the management of settlements. Based entirely in Upper Canada, he made little effort to locate or recruit settlers but merely accepted, or rejected, those who came to him. And although Talbot was renowned for his eccentricities and "despotic habits," he got results.[29] Realizing the importance of good communications, he spent considerable sums of his own money on the building of roads. He set strict targets for his settlers and produced a string of flourishing settlements. From his command centre, a large log house situated on a cliff above Lake Erie, he masterminded and supervised the agricultural and commercial development of vast regions along the north shore of Lake Erie and in the Thames Valley.

Having served in 1792–94 as Lieutenant Governor Simcoe's private secretary, Talbot had travelled widely throughout Upper Canada. His visits to the north shore of Lake Erie opened his eyes to the region's enormous settlement opportunities. By 1803 he had obtained a field officer's grant of 5,000 acres in Dunwich and Aldborough townships (Elgin County), but settlers were slow to arrive. Understandably, the on-going Napoleonic Wars (1803–15) and the War of 1812–14 with the United States had impeded emigration, but the British exodus grew afterwards and by 1817 Talbot had signed up 840 families.[30] Ignoring the original terms of

Colonel Thomas Talbot's residence at Port Talbot, called
Malahide Castle after his ancestoral home in Ireland. Talbot
lived here on the top of a hill for some 50 years. The painter was
George Russell Dartnell (1799–1878). *Courtesy of Library and
Archives Canada C-013303.*

his grant, he soon extended his superintendence of land settlement to vast
areas outside of his 5,000 acre grant. The provincial government acquiesced and even allowed Talbot to privately allocate land without
registering transfers through the office of the Surveyor General.[31] So Talbot became a law unto himself, eventually acquiring supervisory control
over twenty-nine townships, totalling just over half a million acres, along
Lake Erie and in the Thames Valley.[32] His "Princely domain" extended
more than 130 miles from Long Point in Norfolk County to the Detroit
River and north to the boundary of the Huron Tract.[33]

Talbot had been fortunate in getting good land and wise in antici-
pating that settlers needed to be set clear land clearance goals. Lots were
granted to "persons of wholesome habits and moral character" who were
allowed to select their own locations.[34] He offered each settler a free grant
of 50 acres, conditional on the building of a house and the sowing of 10
acres within three years.[35] The settler had to clear half the width of the
road in front of his lot as well as one hundred feet adjoining it. Talbot's
pencilled notes were the only records kept and only he could understand
them. If settlers met his conditions, they could buy additional land, if not,
they were forced to vacate. When settlers were ousted, he simply erased
their names. Thus his terms were clearly stated and ruthlessly monitored.
By the 1820s his settlers had built a road nearly 300 miles long. In fact,

this was the Talbot Road, linking Sandwich (later Windsor) with Aldborough and Dunwich townships, which had enabled the first large group to actually get to his land in 1816 (Figure 9). These first arrivals were people whom Lord Selkirk had recruited originally for his Red River Colony. Fleeing from the campaign of intimidation and violence which was being pursued by the North West Company in the far northwest, they sought safety and a fresh-start in Dunwich and Aldborough.[36] As events transpired, Selkirk's recruitment and funding of Scottish emigrants actually provided Talbot with some of his first settlers.[37]

The former Red River colonists, who originated from Sutherland, were joined in 1816 by further Highlanders who had previously settled in the "Caledonia Settlement" in the Genesee River area of New York State.[38] Two years later, they were followed by thirty-six Argyll families, mainly Baptists, who originated from Knapdale and mid-Argyll.[39] And a year later even more Argyll settlers are known to have arrived.[40] Donald McArthur, a Baptist preacher from Bute (Argyll) who was living in New York State by 1821, occasionally made visits to Elgin County to conduct baptisms.[41] His appearance provides evidence of a substantial Baptist presence in Elgin County. Judging from the many hundreds of people who sailed from the Argyll port of Oban to Quebec, the Argyll influx had been a major happening.[42] In 1819–20, four ships, the *Harmony*, *Hope* of Greenock, *Betsey* of Greenock and *Duchess* of Richmond together carried seven hundred and sixty-one emigrants from Oban to Quebec.[43] A good proportion of these people were almost certainly Argyll emigrants who were making their way to the Talbot settlement.

Gaelic-speaking Highlanders dominated the growing influx to Aldborough and Dunwich which occurred during the second decade of the nineteenth century. While the new arrivals came principally from Argyll, there was also a Perthshire presence by 1819. Having worked in London Township (Middlesex County) as part of a survey team, a group from the Breadalbane estate had been won over by the good land in the place. "The land is of the finest quality we ever saw; and [the] soil is generally very black and deep, and at the same time intermixed with a small portion of white sand."[44] While most Perthshire emigrants at this time were heading for Glengarry or the Rideau Valley in eastern Upper Canada, these people obtained 100-acre lots in London Township from Thomas Talbot, when their survey work was completed.[45] It is easy to see why they remained in the area. The "wintering of cattle and horses" was a lot cheaper than in the east and good land was easy to find:

> We have had no trouble getting our lands. When we made choice of them, we applied to Col. Talbot and we have 2 years to perform the settlement duties, which is all to our own advantage. Several of our friends are now here and every new settler who has money, or is industrious, can buy provisions from our neighbours on Talbot Road and in Westminster, on the opposite side of the River Thames, to last until they can grow them from their farms.[46]

By 1820 some two hundred and seven Scottish families, who were mainly Highlanders, were living in Aldborough and Dunwich. Having become increasingly exasperated by Talbot's dictatorial ways, their frustration began to surface and a bitter dispute erupted.[47] Talbot had allocated 50-acre lots to a group of them, land which had not yet been granted to him, and then went on to promise additional Crown land near these lots which he was unable to give.[48] The Highlanders were angry with the small size of their holdings and pressed for additional land. The only land which Talbot offered on easy terms was in other townships far removed from the already established Highland communities in Aldborough and Dunwich. Believing they had a right to the extra land, which they had requested, the Highlanders felt that they were being defrauded and became resentful and indignant.[49] During elections for the House of Assembly a short time later, one hundred and fifty Highlanders made a point of marching to the poll "with a piper at their head...to display their independence by voting against Mahlon Burwell and [Colonel John] Bostwick, who were friends of Colonel Talbot."[50] Feelings of outrage would continue over several subsequent generations.

The Highlanders and Colonel Talbot shared a mutual loathing of one another. Talbot called them "a stupid, ignorant, obstinate, and vindictive race."[51] He advised Peter Robinson not to accept them for his colonization ventures as "they make the worst settlers for new roads"[52] and offered similar advice to John Elmsley, who sought settlers for land he had purchased in Westminster Township. He should dispose of his land only to English immigrants and not to Highlanders.[53] However,

Duncan Patterson must have given Highlanders good reason to cheer and certainly gave Talbot good reason to mend his ways:

> The Colonel transacted business in a room in his log cabin; he was curt and at times uncivil to applicants for land. A stalwart Highlander named Duncan Patterson called upon him to enter his name for a fifty acre farm. The Colonel said something that offended Patterson, who by way of punishment put his arms around the Colonel's waist, carried him out and laid him on his back on the lawn where he left him; ever after this incident the Colonel transacted his business with applicants for land through an open window.[54]

In spite of the constant quarrelling, Highlanders continued to flock to the Talbot townships. By 1822 they had 12,000 souls, most of them being either Scottish or American-born.[55] Scots came principally to those townships in which Talbot exercised some control.[56] Aldborough and Dunwich in Elgin County and Ekfrid, Mosa, and Lobo townships in Middlesex County acquired considerable numbers of Highlanders throughout the 1820s, while Westminster and London townships drew their intake from both the Highlands and Lowlands (Figure 9).[57] Aldborough quickly developed into a major Presbyterian stronghold and was one of the earliest Upper Canada districts to be assigned a resident minister, which it achieved through the auspices of the Glasgow Colonial Society.[58] Taking up his duties in 1829, Reverend Alexander Ross found that the congregation had only "a log house, as an apology for a church," although it was about to be replaced by "a suitable church."[59] He remained minister until 1839 when "his overindulgence in alcoholic beverages" caused him to be dismissed.[60]

Thomas Talbot (1771–1853) army officer and settlement promoter. Died at the age of 81 and was buried in the Anglican cemetery at Tyrconnell near Port Talbot. *Courtesy of the Archives of Ontario, Ref: S1362.*

Highlanders in Ekfrid occupied "by far the largest portion of the township" and it later became "one of the finest and most prosperous townships in the county."[61] By 1844–45 they had constructed Knox Presbyterian Church which stood at Strathburn, on the corner of Longwoods Road and the Ekfrid/Mosa township line.[62] Having arrived "when the township was yet nearly all a wilderness," Mosa Highlanders, took possession "of the best land" and had built their first Presbyterian Church by the early 1840s.[63] Even by as late as 1859 Ekfrid and Mosa were places where "the old folk" spoke "little but the Gaelic."[64]

Lobo, "one of the best and most fertile [townships] in the county," had "the greater part of it occupied by Highland pioneers."[65] A substantial number of its Highland inhabitants were Baptists. Their numbers were replenished in 1831 when seventy members of the Baptist congregation at Knapdale emigrated to Lobo.[66] By contrast, London Township had comparatively few Highlanders who formed two distinct settlements, one near Ilderton and the other at Hyde Park to the west of the town of London.[67] Kilmartin in Metcalfe Township, to the north of Ekfrid, had also acquired a small Argyll community by 1826, although most of its Argyll inhabitants probably arrived during the large-scale clearances of the 1840s when people were given assisted passages to Upper Canada.[68] Meanwhile, the appropriately named Scottsville in Westminster Township became established in the early 1830s.[69]

Highlanders flooded into the area during the early 1830s, a time when much of Scotland was gripped by an economic depression.[70] The Talbot settlement had many benefits. There was "the excellence of the soil, the condensed population, and the superiority of climate,"[71] but there was an additional attraction for Scots. Here they could settle among fellow-Highlanders who were upholding the customs and traditions which were so dear to them. Thus, they could aspire to the material self-betterment of the New World while continuing to cling on to their Highland values and way of living. It was an unbeatable combination.

Yarmouth and Southwold townships (Elgin County) experienced an influx of Highland settlers at this stage as did East Williams Township (Middlesex County).[72] By 1837 Reverend Daniel Allan, from Hamilton, was preaching regularly to Presbyterians at Yarmouth, "about 7 or 8 miles east of St. Thomas."[73] Having arrived in Southwold from a small hamlet near Inverness, Marjory McNicol, a widow, wasted no time in establishing her 100-acre farm. She had acquired "fine land" and

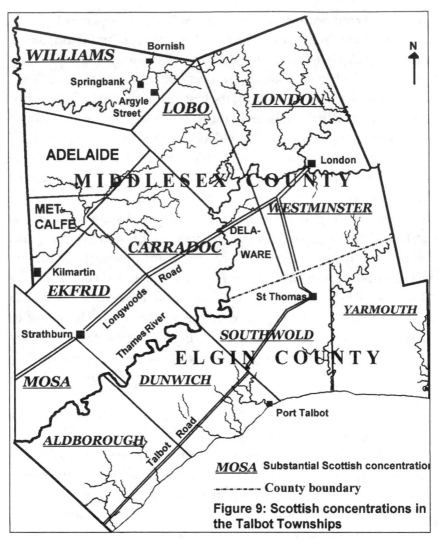

Figure 9: Scottish concentrations in the Talbot Townships

expected to buy more soon:

> One thing I know that when people get themselves properly settled
> they are much better off here than at home...When we settled here
> there was not a single tree cut down but now I have eight acres clear"
> and it is the very best of land. I got built a fine large house to live in
> – I have about four acres under Indian corn, pumpkins, potatoes, kale
> and a variety of other things...Soon I intend to sow my wheat from
> eight to nine acres. It cost me from forty five to forty six pounds before
> I got ourselves settled...The land costs about eleven shillings and three

pence an acre and a few other little expenses.[74]

John Mackintosh, her nephew, believed the chief selling point of the area was that people can "be their own Master…and if they are willing to work…they can have a better living than the best of your gentlemen [back in Inverness].[75] They had already been joined by people from home – William Mackintosh and Alexander and Hugh Clark "are about thirty miles from me," and doubtless, many more would follow.[76]

By the 1830s the Scottish influx had spread beyond the territory over which Talbot claimed jurisdiction and into the Huron Tract lands, the large region owned by the Canada Company. East Williams, on its southern extremity acquired one hundred Highland families at this time.[77] Naming the 2nd and 3rd concessions, along which they settled, "Argyle Street," and those along the 4th and 5th concessions "Petty Street," after Petty Parish in Inverness-shire, they imprinted their geographical origins onto place names which still survive (Figure 9).[78] The 8th concession was settled from 1839, by a group of Glasgow weavers, after whom "Glasgow Street" takes its name. The area later became known as Springbank and, in 1950, pipe bands added panache to its Centennial celebrations.[79] Meanwhile the London district acquired "a good many people" from Nova Scotia in 1833, all of whom were Highlanders.[80] Once arrived, "they speak in raptures of the soil and climate of this country compared with those of the land they left."[81]

East William's Highland population mushroomed from the late 1840s when it received people cleared from Colonel John Gordon of Cluny's estates in South Uist, Barra and Benbecula and Lord Macdonald's estate in North Uist.[82] The forced emigrations had followed in the wake of the Potato Famine which engulfed the Highlands from 1846 to 1855. Around 3,000 of Colonel Gordon's former tenants sailed to Quebec in a total of ten ships between 1848 and 1851.[83] On a much smaller scale, 300 people left from Lord Macdonald's North Uist estate in 1849 and required two ships to take them to Quebec.[84] All of the emigrants were financially assisted by their landlords.

Lord Macdonald's evictions at Sollas, at the northern end of North Uist, attracted great controversy while Colonel Gordon's brutal clearance methods caused a national outcry.[85] Colonel Gordon's "people go away quietly and are most anxious to leave, offering to sell their clothes and do anything

Log house interior in Williams Township drawn by William Elliott in 1845. Elliott lodged here when he was acting as school superintendent. The spartan conditions are evident. For example, there is no table, and because of the lack of chairs the children have to sit on the floor. *Courtesy of Tune Family Fonds, The University of Western Ontario Archives.*

to get away."[86] Their appalling condition when they landed in Quebec caused the Colonel's notoriety to spread quickly to the other side of the Atlantic. No other landlord at the time provoked as much contempt as this man.[87] However, a better future beckoned for his former tenants.

Describing the arrival of the South Uist emigrants in 1849, Adam Hope, a St. Thomas wheat merchant, provides a different perspective of events. Gone is the gloom and distress which accompanied the emigrants' departure and in their place is the better life which the New World had to offer:

> About the middle of last month [September], nearly 300 Highland emigrants from the Island of Uist arrived in the town [London]. They were reported to be rather destitute in their circumstances and were forwarded at the expense of the various towns between this and Quebec. They spoke very little English, were nearly all Roman Catholics and were said to be from the estates of Colonel Gordon of Cluny and some from Lord MacDonald's property. The authorities of the town sent them out to the townships of Williams where some families from Uist had settled last year... These poor emigrants will no doubt endure a good many privations during the coming winter but I predict they

will get more to eat in the township of Williams than they would have got in Uist had they remained there. Provisions are abundant and of course cheap and labour dear. The land is of the very finest quality and much of it is in the hands of the Canada Company."[88]

Hope was in no doubt that they would succeed. "These Highlanders will make good settlers in a few years. The girls of the families will make good servants for the inhabitants of the towns here who can afford to hire and keep servants...The men and boys will clear the land and convert the wilderness into cultivated fields. This is the way some of our best settlements of Highland Scotch have sprung up around London."[89] However, he was sceptical about the extent of their poverty:

One trait in the character of the Highlander struck me as caused in great measure by poverty, and that is that they are not <u>ashamed</u> to let you know that they are <u>paupers</u> and to make themselves out poorer than they are. In changing some one pound Scotch Bank Notes in our stores they let us understand they durst not allow their notes to be seen in Scotland or they would not have got their passage paid!!! In less than five years you will find that their Highland pride won't allow them to acknowledge that they got their passage paid. By that time they will own a cow and oxen, etc., etc.[90]

Perhaps some of them did get the better of the dreadful Colonel Gordon by exaggerating their poverty and feigning reluctance to emigrate. It certainly was in their interests to extract as much as they could from the man.

As many of these Hebridean emigrants streamed into Middlesex County, they quickly filled East Williams. Their settlements then spread into West Williams Township and the adjacent townships of McGillivray and Stephen at the southern end of Huron County, all of it land owned by the Canada Company.[91] Many of the new arrivals were Roman Catholics from South Uist who eventually colonized all three townships.[92] Some one hundred and twenty-two South Uist families are known to have emigrated to the two Williams townships at this time, but there were probably many more than this.[93] The South Uist emigrants founded a settlement at the intersection of the East and West

Williams township line, now Centre Road, and quickly prospered. Naming their settlement Bornish, after Lower and Upper Bornish in South Uist, they had constructed St. Columba's, their first Catholic Church, by 1853 (Figure 9).[94] Substantial numbers from Lord Macdonald's North Uist estate also settled in these townships.[95]

Having extended their colonizing endeavours across the northern boundary over which Thomas Talbot presided, emigrant Scots had also moved into areas lying to the west of the Talbot settlement. Orford, Howard, Harwich and Chatham townships (Kent County) had each attracted large numbers of Scots.[96] By 1846 the town of Chatham was "getting well settled. about a mile back from the river," having acquired "a considerable Scotch Settlement,"[97] which was said to be in need of Gaelic preachers.[98] Although fewer in number, Scots had also been taking up land in Tilbury Township even further to the west. James Aitchison, from Edinburgh, acquired his 100-acre lot on easy terms from the government in the 1830s, at a time when it had embarked on a major road building programme. "The reason that they are giving the grants free is that the government wishes to cut a new road through that part of the country and to get that done they are giving grants on each side of the road of 100 acres and we have to clear about 10 acres, which being done, we get our titles to the property."[99]

Moore and Plympton townships, in Lambton County, also had Scottish communities.[100] Having settled near Warwick in Plympton during the 1840s, George and Henry Forbes, from Aberdeenshire, tried to persuade their father and other family and friends to join them, "I have wrought very hard and very steady and been very saving but I should never have been as well off at home as what I shall be here in a very short time if God spares my health."[101] And Essex County had a "Scotch Settlement" which was founded in Maidstone Township in 1830.[102] Extending from the 6th concession (Wallace Line) to the 7th concession (Martindale Line), it was located in the northwest extremity of Maidstone.[103]

Thus, by the middle of the nineteenth century, Scots had not only established a string of settlements across Elgin and Middlesex counties, but they had also made an impression on Kent, Lambton and Essex counties.[104] Becoming concentrated in Elgin and Middlesex counties, they created a large Scottish enclave which stretched along the north shore of Lake Erie and northward into the Thames Valley (Figure 8).

While the influx had been fed primarily from Scotland, the United States, Nova Scotia and eastern Upper Canada had also contributed many of their Scottish inhabitants to this region. Without doubt, Argyll settlers dominated the early Scottish influx to the Talbot settlement. They had first been recruited by Lord Selkirk for his Baldoon settlement in 1804 and, fifteen years later, they led the influx of settlers to Aldborough and Dunwich townships. Others followed, creating an emigrant stream which lasted well into the 1830s. "So many came from Argyllshire, that when the Marquis of Lorne, as Governor General, visited St. Thomas in 1881, the descendants of these early settlers gathered in thousands and presented him with an address...The Marquis informed his audience that he had never seen, even in Argyllshire itself, so many Argyllshire people present at one time."[105] And modern-day place names such as Crinan, Campbellton, Iona, Appin and Kintyre are on-going reminders of the region's former links with Argyll.

The pull of fellow-Scots who had made the adjustment as settlers in a North American community was extremely strong. Highlanders living in the Talbot settlement were known for their "clannishness so peculiar to them; they keep together as much as possible; and, at one time, they actually proposed among themselves to petition the governor to set apart a township into which none but Scotch were to be admitted."[106] They lived in a world apart from everyone else – much to the annoyance of people like Reverend William Proudfoot, the Presbyterian minister of the Secession Church at London, who found them to be "a stiff-necked race. They will not understand anything that is not spoken in the Gaelic.... I felt very little interest in them today, chiefly because of their obstinate refusal to hear the Gospel because it is not in Gaelic."[107] They sought only what was best for their close-knit communities and were tough negotiators. And as Thomas Talbot discovered, such people are not easily manipulated.

Most of Talbot's lands had been settled by 1835. However, his reign ended in 1838 when the British and Upper Canada governments forced him to wind down his land agency and put it under the control of the provincial authorities. He derived little pecuniary reward for his colonization efforts and was driven most of all by a desire to see his settlers succeed. A great deal of his own money was spent on road building and he had presided over one of the most prosperous agricultural regions in North America. He gave a great many Scots their first taste of independence and prosperity and should be remembered more for his good deeds than for his abusive personality.

As the spread of settlement pushed westward from Lake Ontario and northward from Lake Erie, Scots streamed into the land-locked areas of the western peninsula. By the 1830s western Upper Canada had become the most popular destination of most Scots. They often came in groups, with a proprietor to lead and guide them. But some were attracted to Upper Canada by the prospect of settling on the Canada Company's lands. Through its capital investment in roads, bridges and buildings, it attracted emigrants who would otherwise have balked at the prospect of locating themselves in such a remote part of Upper Canada. Scots would now come in their thousands to transform vast wildernesses into thriving agricultural communities.

Eight

THE ATTRACTIONS OF THE WESTERN PENINSULA

From pretty close observation over the past eight years,
I have come to the conclusion that the Scots are the
best and most successful of all emigrants.[1]

THIS WAS PRAISE OF THE highest order and it came from an Englishman, Dr. Robert Alling, the Guelph Emigration Agent. His glowing account of Scottish pioneering success was snapped up by the Canada Company and inserted in its promotional literature. Dr. Thomas Rolph, a former Upper Canada Emigration Agent, also read out extracts to members of the 1841 Emigration Select Committee:

Come they with or without money, come they with great working sons or with only useless girls, it is all the same, The Scotchman is sure to better his condition and this very silently and almost without complaint.... The industry, frugality, and sobriety of the Scotch mainly contribute to their success...I have carefully watched the progress and result of the Scotch, Irish and English emigrants in the race of the goal desired by all, viz. to obtain a deed for their land and find that...the Scotchman is generally first in the winning post.[2]

Such good reports, when communicated back home to friends and family, fed the growing Scottish influx to the western peninsula. However,

John Galt, 1824. Galt was the first Secretary and Superintendent of the Canada Company. Born in Ayrshire, he was son of a sea captain. Educated in a Greenock grammar school, in later life he became an internationally renowned novelist. He was removed from his Canada Company post in 1829 when he lost the confidence of company directors, much to the regret of the settlers and many of his colleagues. His misdeed was in caring more for people than for profits. Painting by Edward Hastings, engraved by T.A. Woolnoth. *Courtesy of Library and Archives Canada C-007940.*

in spite of the region's fertile land and good climate, the influx had been late in happening. Two key developments were necessary. The first was the opening up of inland routes from the St. Lawrence ports, which only began during the 1820s, while the second was the establishment of the Canada Company which came into being during this decade.[3] Once both developments were underway, Upper Canada quickly overtook the Maritimes as the preferred destination for most Scots.

The Canada Company provided an overall framework within which colonization could proceed and it also promoted Upper Canada with a new effectiveness. Through its efforts large numbers of immigrants were attracted to the region who would otherwise have been lost to the United States. Lord Dalhousie wrote of the company's "powerful machinery" which worked "for the public good as well as their own."[4] And yet, the company got little credit for its colonizing achievements. Regularly criticized over its methods and overall performance, it never fully satisfied the needs of its shareholders nor its struggling farmers.[5]

John Galt, a well-known Scottish novelist, was the driving force behind the establishment of the company, and was its first commissioner and superintendent.[6] William "Tiger" Dunlop, another well-known Scot and literary friend, accompanied him in his work. And advising Galt had been Father Alexander Macdonell, the illustrious Highlander who became Upper Canada's first Roman Catholic bishop. Having played a prominent part in encouraging Highland emigration to Glengarry County, he could speak with some experience about the problems faced by pioneer Scots.[7] These three men gave the company undoubted appeal to emigrant Scots who responded in great numbers, especially during the first colonization phase which was well underway by 1830.

Acquiring two-and-one-half million acres of land in Upper Canada, the company's stated aim was "not to encourage or deal with speculators, but to open access to the settlement of lands by a steady, agricultural population."[8] Nearly half of its holdings fell within the Huron Tract, a vast triangular-shaped 1.1 million acreage, fronting on Lake Huron.[9] The company's remaining holdings, consisting of 1.4 million acres of Crown Reserves, were scattered widely across the province. Settlers could purchase land, either in the reserves or in the Huron Tract, on fairly easy terms, although in later years there were complaints about the company's inflated land prices.[10]

The company offered settlers land and employment opportunities, together with credit facilities which were greatly valued by those emigrants who arrived with little or no capital. It also contributed to the support of schools and churches.[11] John Galt's influence led to an annual grant of £750 being made to Presbyterian ministers. However, since the grant had to be shared among thirteen settlements, this was little more than a well-meaning gesture and compared badly with the generous funding which the Church of England clergy enjoyed from the Clergy Reserves.[12] The company also offered free inland transport to the head of Lake Ontario, but this did not always materialize.[13] Daniel Lizars, a prominent immigrant to the Huron Tract, complained bitterly about his many disappointments which included the denial of free transport and he was certainly not alone in making this complaint.[14]

In his *Caen-Iuil an Fhir-Imrich do dh'America Mu-Thuath* (*The Emigrant's Guide to North America*), written in Gaelic and published in 1841, Robert MacDougall warned fellow-Highlanders of the voluminous quantities of literature being produced by the Canada Company. "When the Company began selling their own land in the Huron Tract, they filled not only America, but nearly the whole world with papers concerning it."[15] And he cautioned great care in interpreting these papers.[16] Its sales literature quoted the countless success stories of families who come to the area with little or no capital. Settlers going to Ellice Township might be told that they "would be given land beside a road and everything would be wonderful," but the reality was very different.[17] New arrivals had to contend with extremely difficult conditions and might work for years for very little return. However, MacDougall greatly approved of the Canada Company's work in Goderich where they are "making every effort that they can in every way. They are cutting out roads, constructing bridges, building mills, and everything else they can, which they think will improve the area."[18]

Reverend Patrick Bell, a Presbyterian minister from Forfar in Angus, could see nothing praiseworthy at all in the company. He wrote of the "cruel seducers" who led unsuspecting Scots to a state of penury. "After taking possession of their lots they found that the promised well made roads were nothing better then ill formed tracks through the woods – the promised mills and bridges were in many cases never finished...The settlers on the large Huron Tract were last winter literally starving and in a state of open rebellion...."[19] However, this doom-laden account is difficult to reconcile with the positive feedback reported to the 1841 Select Committee. It heard of the many letters sent home by Highlanders "strongly recommending their friends to follow them."[20] The growing influx of Scots demonstrates their faith in the company despite its seemingly poor reputation. Their undoubted success led to the emigrant stream noted by the Quebec Immigration Agent throughout the 1840s and early 1850s. Time and again he would describe the Scots who were on they way to join "friends and relatives" in the London and Western districts.[21]

Most of the Scottish influx to Perth County was concentrated in the townships of North and South Easthope, Downie and Fullarton in the

Canada Company Coat of Arms. *Courtesy of the Ontario Archives Ref: S1362.*

eastern part of the Huron Tract (Figure 10).[22] North and South Easthope had some of the earliest arrivals who originated from the Breadalbane estate in Perthshire. Continuing clearances to make way for sheep farms had caused large-scale evictions, which in turn fuelled an outpouring of Scots to Upper Canada.[23] Their departures almost certainly explain the sudden rise in ship passenger numbers from Dundee to Quebec between 1831 and 1834.[24] The *Molson* of Dundee, the *Industry* and the *Victoria* of Dundee carried over 100 emigrants on each of their crossings while many more ships carried smaller numbers.[25] Taking up land along the recently-built Huron Road in North Easthope Township, the Breadalbane emigrants found conditions very much to their liking.[26] Within two years of their arrival, they wrote to their former Presbyterian minister at Kenmore, informing him of their good circumstances:

> The land here is good and well-watered, the terms of the Upper Canada Land Company are liberal, requiring the settler only to pay a fifth of the purchase money when the land is applied for, and the remainder in five yearly instalments with interest at six per cent. The Company at present sell their land at 12s. 6d. currency per acre being equal to about 10s. 8d. British, and the only stipulation is to clear off each year about three and a half acres for every 100 acres owned by a settler...There are grist mills and saw mills within a few miles of us east and west, also a store where goods of all kinds are sold. This settlement is mostly Scotch, almost wholly so where we are settled, and the utmost goodwill and unanimity prevails. We enjoy, though obtained at present by hard labour and perseverance, all the necessary worldly comforts and with the prospect, if we and our families are spared, of seeing them and us all independent and comfortable farmers, farming our own land.[27]

Such encouragement brought many more Breadalbane settlers to this one district. Most came unaided but some poor tenants, who emigrated from Dull and Killin in the early 1840s, received funds from the second Marquis of Breadalbane, although the giving of aid by landlords was by no means universal at this time.[28]

When Reverend William Rintoul visited the village of Stratford on the Avon River in 1835, he found a population in North and South Easthope which, "professedly belonging to the Church of Scotland, is...greater than that which belongs to any other denomination."[29] Three years later, when Reverend Daniel Allen became their first resident minister, they would be "the first.... Presbyterian [congregation] in connection with the Church of Scotland formed in the Huron Tract."[30] Having secured their minister, the Breadalbane settlers then appealed to the Lord Breadalbane for help in constructing their first church. "We form a neighbourhood, consisting of about 30 Highland families from your Grace's estates, and have in connection with 20 families of Lowland Scotch and 14 families of Irish Presbyterians...united together for the purpose of supporting a clergyman of the Kirk of Scotland and building a place of worship."[31] A "pretty frame church with a glittering spire," named St. Andrew's Church, was duly built on land which had been donated by the Canada Company.[32]

Meanwhile Downie and Fullarton townships mainly attracted Lowlanders.[33] Depressed conditions in the handloom weaving industry continued to fuel the steady exodus of people from districts in and near Glasgow during the early 1840s. Some nine hundred and ninety desperately poor people from eighteen Glasgow Emigration Societies, went to Upper Canada in 1843. Similar numbers had gone in the previous two years.[34] More lenient terms, introduced in 1842, meant that settlers could obtain land in the Huron Tract without having to make a down payment. This was one of the factors which drew many of them to the region. They went west despite having long-settled Lowland communities in the Rideau Valley which they could have joined.

Fullarton began to acquire its Lanarkshire settlers at this time, but it also attracted many more from eastern Upper Canada. Between 1842 and 1846, thirty to forty families, who had originated from weaving districts in Lanarkshire and in nearby Dunbartonshire and Stirlingshire, moved across to Fullarton from their previous homes in Dalhousie Township, Lanark County.[35] Having established themselves in the Rideau Valley, they probably arrived with some capital to invest. Also their farming experience would have been of great help to the new arrivals from their homeland who were adjusting to pioneer life for the very first time. Together, they founded a large community in the southeast corner of Fullarton, on the 17th and 18th concessions.

Emigrant Scots extended their territory eastward from Fullarton into the adjacent township of Downie (Figure 10). Arriving from the late 1830s, they originated from Lanarkshire, in the western Lowlands,

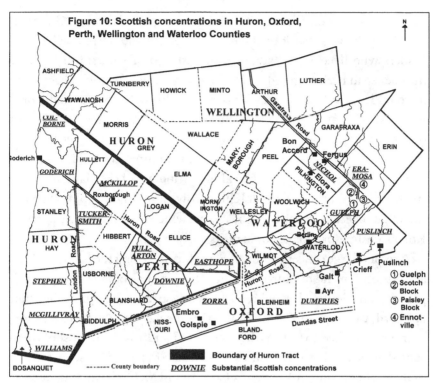

Figure 10: Scottish concentrations in Huron, Oxford, Perth, Wellington and Waterloo Counties

Dumfriesshire, Wigtownshire and Peeblesshire in the Borders, and from Fife in the eastern Lowlands.[36] When Reverend Allen, Easthope's Presbyterian minister, visited Downie in the 1840s, he had to fight his way through "solid bush." Fortunately, he could use Adam Ollier's house as "a stopping place" and, as was the custom, he was always presented "with a spiced venison ham" to help him on his way.[37] Scottish missionaries like Reverend Allen helped to reinforce Scottish values and traditions in these scattered communities. He would have been one of their few visitors and gave them an important link with the outside world. By 1844 Downie had the largest population of the townships occupied by Scots, having 1,370 inhabitants compared with Easthope, which had 1,151 people and Fullarton which had only 419 people.[38]

While Scots were well-represented in Perth County, they were the dominant group throughout much of Huron County.[39] When he visited Goderich Township in the late 1830s, Robert MacDougall found it to be a place where "Gaels abound".... They are doing very well there and it would not be a bad place for many more of them."[40] Goderich, the Huron Tract's principal town, was still "in its infancy," having only acquired its first houses from 1829.[41] And as he passed through Goderich Township, he was struck by the many "cheerful and hospitable" Highlanders who lived in the adjacent township of Tuckersmith.[42] Their numbers had been augmented by the many Scots who moved across to it from Pictou in Nova Scotia. This large influx of Scots eventually produced two separate settlement clusters, which were located a short distance apart, close to the Huron Road.[43] "The Scotch Settlement" developed along the Maitland River in Colborne Township, while a "Scotchtown" became established along a tributary of the Maitland River further to the south west, in McKillop Township (Figure 10).[44] "Scotchtown" later became Roxborough, a name which may denote the possible Roxburghshire origins of some of its early settlers.[45]

A second large concentration of Scots formed along the London Road at the southern end of Huron County. They were Roman Catholic emigrants from South Uist, who had been assisted to emigrate by their landlord, Colonel Gordon of Cluny.[46] Some 3,000 of the Colonel's former tenants sailed to Quebec between 1848 and 1851 and most of them settled in a block of townships which encompassed East and West Williams townships in Middlesex County and McGillivray and Stephen townships in Huron County.[47] Despite having had this large influx of Roman Catholics, Huron County was predominately Presbyterian, although most people belonged to Canadian Presbyterian sects, not the established Kirk.[48] A forlorn missionary from the Glasgow Colonial Society found little support for the Church of Scotland when he travelled to Goderich. Not only had "a missionary of the Secession Church...taken up residence" in Goderich,[49] but the Presbyterian congregation at Tuckersmith also felt "bound to the Secession Church."[50] This pattern would be repeated throughout the entire county.

While the Canada Company had a supervisory role within the Huron Tract, it had far less influence outside it. However, its scattered land blocks, the former Crown Reserves, attracted a good many Scots, who generally came to the area in large groups. Zorra, a township lying just to the south of the Huron Tract in Oxford County, was one of many townships in which the Canada Company had extensive land holdings. This may have been a factor in its choice by the many Highlanders who settled here during the 1830s. As was the case at Tuckersmith, Zorra's Scottish population was augmented by an influx of Highlanders transferring from Pictou, at this time.

Zorra was a Sutherland colony. Having established several Scottish communities in Nova Scotia and Cape Breton during the first two decades of the nineteenth century, Sutherland emigrants went on to colonize Zorra.[51] Angus and William Mackay, two brothers who had emigrated to Nova Scotia, used their entrepreneurial skills to good effect by obtaining large quantities of land in Zorra Township. They did so in the 1820s, just as the area was being opened up to colonizers. They then moved west and spent the next few years chopping down trees and planting crops.[52] Returning to Scotland in 1830, they reappeared later that year in Zorra with their aged mother and 360 Sutherland people who sailed to Quebec on two ships, the *Canada* and the *John*.[53] The growing economic depression in Sutherland had, no doubt, helped the brothers to attract this large response. It seems that many in the group "possessed property" and were "young and eager for adventure," having been influenced by "favourable reports from friends already settled" in Upper Canada.[54] They were the first of many Sutherland groups to settle in Zorra.

The exodus from Sutherland and nearby Inverness-shire and Ross-shire continued "at a most unprecedented rate" during the following year.[55] Five ships sailed from Cromarty to Pictou and Quebec in the summer of 1831 and two more were expected within days "taking with them, in all, a population of 1,500 souls, and not a little of the metallic currency of the country."[56] And such was the demand for gold coins that emigrants had to pay an extra shilling to purchase them.[57]

By 1833 Zorra had one hundred and ten Sutherland families, although some of them were migrants from Pictou.[58] According to Thomas Rolph, Zorra's inhabitants were "eminently successful; they are frugal, loyal, faithful and a correct body of people."[59] And although they were "not skilled in agriculture," they possessed "strength, good-will and perseverance."[60] These qualities made them outstanding pioneers:

These good Zorra pioneers were a fine and superior stock. They were, as has been said of the Pilgrim Fathers of New England, the sifted wheat – chosen men. They had a good education. Wherever they settled there rose the walls of a schoolhouse; and the few books brought into the wilderness were of a high standard and deeply valued.[61]

Zorra had its first Presbyterian church by 1833 and two years later had its first resident minister. The church,[62] built on the 5th concession, was located in the village of Embro:

> To say that our forefathers were a church-going people would be greatly to understate the truth…to attend its services they gladly travelled on foot over a winding path in the dense forest, three, six or even in some cases ten miles, returning the same day after the service was over.[63]

Having built their church they then constructed their school:

> The pioneer school-house was a very humble affair. A log shanty, thirty feet by twenty two, cornered but not hewed, with chinks between the logs, then moss, all plastered with clay. The roof consisted of rafters with poles laid across, and for shingles, pieces of elm bark three feet by four. The chimney was made of lath, covered with plaster, and served for heating, ventilating and lighting the little house. Of course it frequently caught fire; but the boys by the free use of snow were equal to the occasion.[64]

Reverend Donald McKenzie was paid £90 per annum by the congregation and served as Zorra's minister for nearly 40 years.[65] His son was "deeply impressed" by "the devotion to his father's memory which still remained among the people" in the latter part of the century.[66] McKenzie's tombstone was made of "polished granite, emblematic of a character as steadfast as it was genial, gentle and loving."[67]

By 1842 Zorra had 2,722, people, "principally Highland Scotch," who were located on the west side of Zorra.[68] Its Highlander population grew

Picture taken from *Pioneer Life in Zorra* by W.A. MacKay. It shows the Presbyterian log Church at Zorra. Its dimensions were 48 feet by 28 feet and it was 18 logs high. There was no spire, no carpet and for the first winter or two there was not even a stove. *Courtesy of Library and Archives Canada.*

throughout the 1840s as economic conditions in Sutherland deteriorated even further. Some came from the parishes of Farr and Rogart during the early 1840s, this being the time when tenants from these areas received financial aid from the Duke of Sutherland.[69] And with the deepening crisis which accompanied the Highland Famine years from 1846 to 1856, many more hundreds were assisted to emigrate. However, the mood had changed by this time. While a decade earlier people had responded with great enthusiasm to the Mackay brothers' colonization venture, now they needed to be persuaded. Agents acting for the Duke of Sutherland, circulated letters with glowing reports of life in Zorra, while more generous removal terms, which included the cancellation of rent arrears and free fares for aged relatives, were offered. This concerted effort produced the desired exodus from Assynt and Eddrachilles parishes to Upper Canada which began in 1847:

> I observe from an account in one of the Montreal papers that the Duke of Sutherland has chartered the *Panama* of Liverpool, and given a free passage to 287 persons, tenants and their wives and children residing on his estates in Sutherlandshire to Quebec, besides furnishing the whole with 10 weeks wholesome provisions for the voyage. The consequence was that they all reached Canada in good health, without a case of sickness or death occurring on board and last week the whole party I am informed have safely reached the township of Zorra in good health.[70]

The *Greenock* of Glasgow and *Scotia* came with 600 Sutherland emigrants in the following year and a further 100 were taken on the *Argo* and *Vesper* in 1850 and 1851, all receiving financial help from the Duke of Sutherland.[71] While this later influx to Zorra was from the northwest of Sutherland, modern-day place names such as Golspie and Embro (probably from Embo, near Golspie) suggest that many of the earlier arrivals had originated from southeast Sutherland.

Although the Canada Company had a major impact on settlement in western Upper Canada, it was certainly not the sole driving force. One of the most successful Scottish colonizers at the time was William Dickson, a prominent lawyer, prosperous merchant and cousin of John Galt. Having purchased an entire township of 94,000 acres, just to the east of Zorra, he named it Dumfries after his native shire in Scotland

Settler's home on the Thames River, 1842. The artist was Henry
Francis Ainslie (1803–1879). *Courtesy of Library and Archives
Canada C-000544.*

(Figure 10).[72] Initially, Dickson sought to attract settlers from other parts
of Upper Canada and from the United States, but this approach met
with little success.[73] However, when improved inland transport routes
became available from the mid-1820s, Dickson changed his policy and
recruited settlers from his native Dumfriesshire.

Dickson directed his efforts to those border areas of Scotland which
he knew best. Publishing articles in local newspapers and writing to influential people, he stimulated substantial interest in his colonizing venture.[74]
James Hogg, the well-known Scottish writer, helped Dickson to secure
some of his best settlers[75] John Telfer, a former Hudson's Bay Company
worker, acted as his recruiting agent in Scotland and was particularly successful in locating emigrants.[76] Dumfriesshire, Roxburghshire and
Selkirkshire emigrants began arriving in Dumfries in increasing numbers from 1825. This positive response owed much to Dickson's financial
terms which included credit facilities to purchase stock, implements and
provisions, as well as exemptions from down-payments.[77]

From 1830 Dumfries and Galloway newspapers were suddenly full of
advertisements of ship crossings to Quebec.[78] Among the selling features
of the *Donegal,* due to leave Maryport for Quebec in the spring of 1831,
were her captain who would show "humanity and attention to passengers," "a medical gentleman and a minister of the Church of Scotland

and his family who would be on board" and the fact that "every attention [would be] paid to them [passengers from Scottish Borders] while in Maryport."[79] Four further ships, in addition to the *Donegal,* sailed from Maryport to Quebec in 1831, carrying a total of 456 passengers, many of whom would have been on their way to Dumfries, Upper Canada.[80] Double this number sailed in the following year.[81]

By 1840 Dumfries Township had a population of 6,000 people who were almost all Scots.[82] It was well supplied with churches and schools and its settlers were said to be highly prosperous.[83] Its first settlers were also said to be "generally of a superior class."[84] Many of them brought "a thirst for knowledge which even the necessities of bush life could not eradicate."[85] Having high intellectual ideals, they formed a debating society and founded "a circulating library."[86] Galt, its principal town, had a population of 1,000 people "who are principally Scotch" while the village of Ayr, 12 miles from Galt, had two churches, both Presbyterian, which served a population of 230 people.[87]

The Scottish communities at Bon Accord and Fergus, in Nichol Township (Wellington County) were also established by prominent Scots who, having purchased their sites, led families from their homeland to them. Fergus was founded by the Perthshire-born landowner, Adam Fergusson and James Webster, a lawyer from Angus. Following a visit to the area in 1831, Fergusson, a prominent agriculturalist, had produced his *Practical Notes made during a tour in Canada...in 1831* which

The Hon. William Dickson, lawyer, merchant and settlement promoter. Born in 1769 in Dumfries, Scotland, Dickson came to Canada in 1792, settling in the Niagara District, where he practised law. After purchasing Dumfries Township, he encouraged Scots from the Border areas to establish farms on his land. By 1812 he had built his second brick house and had purchased a magnificent library of over 1,000 volumes, which were imported from Britain. The artist was Hoppner Meyer. *Courtesy of the Toronto Reference Library, J. Ross Robertson Collection JRR 1248.*

View of Galt, including the "Scotch Church" and Mr. Dickson's House. Known originally as Shade's Mills, the village was renamed Galt in honour of John Galt. Drawn by Alice E. Brown in 1857. *Courtesy of the Archives of Ontario, C 281-0-0-0-11.*

struck a chord with many Scottish farmers who were impressed by the opportunities to be realized in western Upper Canada. Fergusson's guidebook came out at a time of declining economic and agricultural prospects in Scotland, and thus had a major impact. Most of the influx

The village of Ayr , Upper Canada, was incorporated in 1824. By June 1843 the village's Presbyterian congregation had with-drawn from the General Assembly of the Church of Scotland and their first church, Knox Presbyterian, a white clapboard building was already in use. Forty-five years later, a new more imposing church was built, shown here in an undated photo-graph, and the first service to be held there took place on October 9, 1888. *Courtesy of Knox United Church, Ayr, Ontario.*

to the Fergus settlement came from Perthshire, Fergusson's home county and from Aberdeenshire, where his wife's had family connections.[88]

Having made this exploratory visit, Fergusson emigrated to the area with his family in 1833 and together with Webster purchased a 7,367 acre site in the northern part of Nichol Township.[89] However, Fergusson and his small group were certainly not the earliest arrivals. A group of Black Loyalists, led by Richard Pierpoint, had settled a decade earlier just to the east of Fergus.[90] When the Scots arrived the two communities remained apart although Pierpoint and James Webster became close friends. When Pierpoint died in 1838, it is believed that Webster sought to have him buried in the Presbyterian cemetery, but he failed to win support for this proposal from his fellow Scots. After a heated debate the church congregation decided that he could have a pauper's burial with no tombstone, but Webster disagreed with this decision. The place where Pierpoint actually was buried remains a mystery.[91]

Meanwhile, groups of Aberdeenshire people were responding to Fergusson's book and other encouraging reports which were circulating at the time. Taking the decision to emigrate, they chose George Elmslie, an Aberdeen merchant, to locate and purchase a suitable site on their behalf. Travelling to Fergus in the autumn of 1834, with his friend Alexander Watt, also from Aberdeen, Elmslie hoped to buy land from Adam Fergusson, but most of it had already been sold. So he opted instead for a 1,200 acre site a short distance to the west of Fergus on the Irvine River.[92] In less than a year the "Bon Accord" settlement was

Hon. Adam Fergusson, not dated. Ferguson, born in Woodhill, Perthshire, founded Fergus in 1834. Favourably known throughout Scotland, his recommendation of the farming opportunities to be had in western Upper Canada attracted many followers. He became a member of the Upper Canada Legislative Council in 1839. His son, the Hon. Adam Johnston Fergusson-Blair, founded the Veterinary College at Guelph, which was later taken over by the Ontario Department of Agriculture. Painting by John W.L. Forster. *Presented by the Grandsons, G. Toweer Ferguson and Robert G.B. Fergusson to the University of Guelph Collection at the MacDonald Stewart Art Centre – UG900.153.*

founded.[93] Very much an Aberdeenshire colony, it took its name from the motto on its native city's Coat of Arms.[94]

The Bon Accord settlers "were already as one family" as they contemplated their first winter:

> The winter was now approaching and the heavy rains and cold night gave indications of a severe one. With all our means and appliances and with abundance of warm clothing we were but indifferently prepared for it. The best that could be said of our houses and shanties was that they would shelter us from the violence of the storms, and that they were uncomfortable; our crops had perished and we had to weather another year on the interest of our little capital. Yet we were not discouraged: we had agreeable and intelligent society; and our new and isolated situation had increased friendship to attachment and attachment to love. There were no jealousies, no backbiting and no quarrels.[95]

Bon Accord thrived on its ability to attract "parties, relatives and friends, following each other at intervals, and all from Aberdeenshire."[96] Many hundreds of emigrants sailed from Aberdeen to Quebec during the 1830s, with the peak year being 1836 when nearly 700 sailed.[97] Writing home that year, an "intelligent and respectable Aberdonian, who emigrated to Upper Canada last Spring," described how his part of Upper Canada "was filling up, almost entirely with Scotsmen":

> This part of the country is fast filling up, almost entirely with Scotchmen, many of whom are from Aberdeenshire. Within these two weeks, nearly a dozen families have settled beside us, all 'frae the North'.... You would be astonished as I was, if you saw the very respectable class of settlers between this and Fergus. There are of them who at home, would be moving into the first class of provincial society. I dined at Fergus lately with the St. Andrew Society and became a member. There were forty of us all Scotchmen, except one Englishman.[98]

And even though Bon Accord and Fergus were only three miles apart:

> there was a distinction broader than a concession road between the people of the Bon Accord settlement and those of the Fergus settlement.

The former were very respectable, highly educated and intelligent but they could not boast of the Old Country connections that a number of the latter had. Each community kept pretty much to itself socially though they fraternised in business and religion.[99]

Fergus certainly did have settlers with "Old Country connections." Using their contacts with wealthy people back in Scotland, James Webster, Alexander Dingwall-Fordyce, Alexander Ferrier and John Valentine were able to raise extra funds for the building of a church and school at Fergus. Both were completed by December 1835, only two years after Adam Fergusson had first purchased the site.[100]

Meanwhile, George Elmslie, who had established himself as a farmer, was teaching Bon Accord children at a log schoolhouse built on his land.[101] And by 1839 the school had a Debating Society:

The settlement was not without some excellent amusement which was enjoyed by young and old. There was a Library, a Temperance Society...a Singing School and the...Bon Accord Mutual Instruction and Debating Society.[102]

Fergus was also developing a "reputation for intelligence," which was "far above most similar settlements," having attracted many exceptionally

St. Andrews Church, Fergus. The "Auld Kirk," completed in 1835, was the first church built between Guelph and Georgian Bay. It was replaced by the present Gothic stone building in 1862. Photograph, c. 1893–95 by A.J. Miller, Fergus. *Courtesy of the Wellington County Museum and Archives, ph 2829.*

View of Fergus in 1837, by Janet Dingwall-Fordyce (1819–1873).
Courtesy of the Wellington County Museums and Archives Art 176.

well educated men, many "being college graduates."[103] Alexander Ding-wall-Fordyce, who settled at Fergus in 1835, is just one example. Coming from a wealthy Aberdeen business family, he had been educated at Marischal College (Aberdeen University). Taking up residence on a 600-acre farm in the townships, he and his sister, Elizabeth, founded a lending library which was housed in their own home. Other graduates of Marischal College who settled at Fergus, include Arthur and James Ross, from a wealthy land-owning Aberdeen family and the three sons of Alexander Cadenhead, an Aberdeen lawyer.[104] However, while Fergus and Bon Accord attracted many well-educated and affluent people, the majority of settlers were farmers, tradesmen, and labourers of very modest means.

The worsening economic conditions of the late 1840s brought even more Aberdeenshire emigrants to the region and, by 1848, Bon Accord had nearly doubled in size to 3,000 acres.[105] However, by this time the Bon Accord name had gone and it was now the "Irvine Settlement."[106] Throughout the 1840s the Immigration Agent at Quebec often noted the people "in easy circumstances" or the "respectable body of passengers," who had arrived from Aberdeen. They were "amply provided" with the means to get to their destinations and always they were heading west.[107] However, he also noticed the two large contingents from Tiree, who arrived at Quebec in 1849 in a desperately poor state.[108] Having been victims of the famine in Tiree during 1846–47, many of them "had not the shirts on their backs"[109] Heading for Fergus, they would take up residence in the log houses which had been built by Richard Pierpoint and the other Black Loyalists, who had by then vacated their site.[110]

The Scots who opted for Guelph Township (Wellington County), just to the south of Nichol, were in an area which came fully under the control of the Canada Company. This was the so-called Halton Block, a tract of land consisting of 42,000 acres, which had been allocated to the company in compensation for the lack of Clergy and Crown Reserves in the Niagara region. It later became Guelph Township. The company's enormous capital investment in the township was a major factor in its rapid expansion. Founded by John Galt in 1827, the town of Guelph had "upwards of 200 houses"[111] by the 1830s.

The first group of Scots to arrive in the township founded the area's "Scotch Block" on the Elora Road, about four miles north of the town of Guelph. Having left Cromarty in 1825 on the *Planet*, forty families (198 people) from the north of Scotland had intended to settle on land in Venezuela, which was owned by the Columbian Agricultural Society of London.[112] However, the glowing picture presented by the company of its land holdings in the Topo Valley, between La Guaria and Caracas proved to be a mirage. The intention was that they would grow cotton, coffee and indigo, but when they actually got there they found an inhospitable and barren wilderness. When, a year later the company fell into bankruptcy, it abandoned all responsibility for the settlers who faced starvation. One member of the group appealed to fellow Scots for help by writing to the *Glasgow Herald*:

> I hope all Scotchmen will take pity on us. We are to petition the British Parliament by next packet [ship]. Our number is about 150 souls, without means or friends to help us in our great distress. I hope all our countrymen will have the feelings of Christians by sending us speedy relief as we are in a country where no kind of employment is to be had. My family are all well and so are all the Glengarry people.[113]

Following numerous petitions they were helped by British officials and by 1827 had arrived in New York. From there they went on to Guelph Township with the expectation of settling on Canada Company land. John Galt played a key role in assisting them, although his intervention put him at odds with the Canada Company directors who disapproved of his high-handed methods. However, the immigrants must have been relieved to find that a warm-hearted and generous Scot was in charge of their re-location.[114] Assigning £1000 of the Canada Company's money towards relief measures to help the destitute families, Galt's swift actions kept them alive and enabled them to resettle successfully in Guelph.[115]

Emigrants from Paisley in Renfrewshire came to Guelph Township in the following year and founded the "Paisley Block," which was named after their native parish.[116] Situated about six miles northeast of the town of Guelph, it attracted many followers, including substantial numbers from Roxburghshire in the Scottish Borders.[117] This part of Scotland had lost substantial numbers to Upper Canada in the early 1840s and it is highly likely that a good many of them settled in Guelph Township.[118] By 1846 the Paisley Block extended some four miles in length and was said to contain "good farms which are generally well cultivated."[119]

The large Scottish influx to Guelph Township overflowed into Puslinch Township, lying just to the south. It began attracting Gaelic-speaking Highlanders from the early 1830s, who became concentrated in the southern part of the township. Perthshire and Inverness-shire emigrants were particularly well represented. Later, in 1850, the township also attracted a large group of destitute emigrants from South Uist in the Outer Hebrides who, having reached Hamilton, "walked to Puslinch to the music of the bagpipes."[120] They initially became squatters on the 1st concession and founded a community which was located near Crieff.[121] A large Presbyterian congregation became established in the southern part of the township, requiring two churches (one at Crieff, the other at Duff) which were initially under the charge of one minister. However, the two churches had their own ministers by 1853 and they continued to hold services primarily in Gaelic until 1880.[122]

Meanwhile, as Puslinch Township was increasing its population of Highland Scots, Eramosa Township, to the north of Guelph Township, was attracting Lowlanders, especially emigrants from Roxburghshire.[123] During his 1831 tour, Adam Fergusson had met people from the Scottish Borders who were doing well in Eramosa and a decade, later when Thomas Rolph visited the township, he observed flourishing Scottish settlements.[124] John McLaren's tavern in Eramosa Township, on the east side of the main road to Guelph, attracted other buildings and soon became a hamlet, which McLaren named Ennotville, after his birthplace, Enoch (in Dumfriesshire). A library was founded in 1847 on land donated by McLaren and, by 1920, it was the second largest rural library in the province.[125] Minto Township on the western side of Wellington County also attracted substantial numbers of Scots from the 1850s; they came principally from Argyll.[126]

The remote areas between Lake Huron and Georgian Bay were some of the last areas in the western peninsula to attract settlers. Even by the 1850s they were still only sparsely populated. To encourage settlers, the government offered fifty-acre lots as free grants on either side of the new colonization roads which extended through Bruce and Grey counties. Both the Garafraxa Road, which linked Guelph with Owen Sound (formerly Sydenham) and the Durham Road, which linked Durham with Kincardine, helped to facilitate a growing influx of settlers.[127] Once again, Scots came in large numbers and in groups. Some were very poor. A good many originated from the Lowland counties of Dumfriesshire, Roxburghshire, Berwickshire and Lanarkshire as well as from the Hebridean Islands, especially Arran, Islay, Coll, Tiree, Colonsay and Lewis.[128]

Some of the first arrivals in Bruce County were the Lewis families who founded "the Lewis Settlement." Emigrating in 1851, during the clearances which followed the widespread destitution on the Island, they received financial help from their landlord, Sir James Matheson. Although most of them went to the Eastern Townships in Lower Canada, around 500 hundred people (109 families) settled in western Upper Canada.[129] Their travel arrangements had been made with great care by John Munro MacKenzie, the estate Chamberlain manager who explained Matheson's removal terms to the various tenants.[130] They faced eviction if they remained and so had little choice but to emigrate. Some people like Reverend McLean, the Presbyterian minister, raised objections and preached "against emigration," but MacKenzie's "long argument with him on that subject" would ensure that he would "be more careful of what he says in future."[131]

The Lewis emigrants spent their first winter in Hamilton, where the men worked on the Great Western Railway which was then being constructed. Having scattered to Guelph, Stratford, Galt and Goderich by December, they re-assembled in Goderich in the summer of 1852 and were joined by eighteen more families from Lewis that same year.[132] Together they settled in consecutive lots between the 4th and 10th concessions of Huron Township (Figure 11).[133] It was a tough beginning for them. During their first year they had to obtain their supplies in Goderich, "from which place they brought them on their backs, along the lake shore to the foot of the 8th concession, and thence home through the bush."[134]

In 1855, the *Melissa* brought 44 Lewis emigrants to the region; these newcomers extended the Lewis territory even further into the adjoining township of Kincardine.[135] Tiree, Mull and Iona settlers also came to Kincardine during the late 1840s, founding a settlement near Tiverton which stretched into the southern part of Bruce township.[136] Scots made further advances further north in Saugeen Township, near Southampton, founding yet another "Scotch Settlement" and they also colonized parts of Arran, Saugeen, Brant, Elderslie, Culross and Kinloss townships.[137] Huron, Kinloss and Elderslie townships mainly attracted Highlanders while Arran, Saugeen, Bruce, Kincardine and Culross townships had sizeable Lowland populations.

Bruce County's Highland links were greatly strengthened in the early 1850s when "Scotch Highlanders" began arriving from Cape Breton.[138] Since most of Cape Breton's early Scottish inhabitants originated from the Western Isles, these migrants would have had Hebridean roots. Some 554 of them arrived in Quebec in 1851. Finding Cape Breton's "climate too severe and unfavourable to agricultural production, they had disposed of their farms...with the intention of settling in the western part of the province."[139] Four years later came 417 more Highlanders from Cape Breton who, having sold their farms, "were proceeding to the borders of Lake Huron, where they may combine their former occupation of fishing with agriculture."[140] Scots would constitute some 20 per cent of the population of Bruce County by 1861 and were the second largest group after Canadian-born settlers.[141]

Grey County also proved attractive to Scots once the new colonization roads opened up the region to settlers. By as early as 1843 the government had to announce that "lots on the Garafraxa and Owen Sound road" were "no longer open for settlement on the principle of free grants" because most had been occupied. However, the government would make grants available "on the same conditions in the immediate vicinity of the roads, which will afford the means of advantageous settlement."[142]

Many of the early arrivals from Scotland settled near Owen Sound, in Sydenham Township, and near Dornoch, in the adjacent Holland Township.[143] Lowlanders settled just north of Owen Sound along the

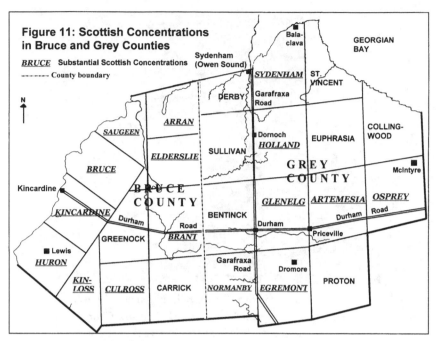

Figure 11: Scottish Concentrations in Bruce and Grey Counties

shore, while a Highland settlement was founded beyond this, also along the shore, at Balaclava.[144] A few families from Harris came to Sydenham Township in the 1860s, while others became scattered in St. Vincent, Holland, Collingwood, Sullivan and Derby townships.[145] Meanwhile, the large clearances which occurred from Colonel Gordon's estate in South Uist, during the late 1840s, brought substantial numbers of South Uist people to Glenelg Township.[146]

The great distress experienced in Tiree, Mull and Iona following the failure of the potato crops in 1846–47, was to bring many more Hebridean settlers to Grey County.[147] Most of them obtained some financial help from their landlord, the 8th Duke of Argyll, but they also had to rely on the charitable "Emigrant Fund," administered by the Upper Canada authorities, to get to their final destinations.[148] As previously noted, many of the Tiree settlers who emigrated in 1849 went to Fergus (Wellington County), but most of those who left during the famine years went to the new areas being opened up in Grey County. Forming a large consolidated settlement just south of the Durham Road near the village of Priceville, they eventually occupied the three adjacent townships of Glenelg, Egremont and Artemisia (Figure 11). This caused the displacement of a number of earlier Black settlers who had cleared the land along

Amos Presbyterian Church at Dromore in Egremont Township. Replacing a former log church, it is named after Mrs. George Amos, a Dumfriesshire lady, whose family gave the land on which the church is built. *Courtesy of The Grey Roots Archival Collection Catalogue # 980.384.1.*

the Durham Road eastward from Priceville.[149] Glenelg Presbyterians built a log church at Rocky Saugeen, just to the north of Durham in 1856, "The pulpit being supplied by missionaries."[150] A church followed three years later. Scots also established a further community in Osprey Township, whose focal point was McIntyres' Corners, named after some McIntyre brothers from Tiree.[151] However, Glenelg also attracted Lowlanders, as did Egremont, whose settlement was based at Dromore. And yet another Lowland community was formed in Normanby Township.

Meanwhile, the many Tiree emigrants who had earlier taken up residence in Brock Township (Ontario County), to the east of Lake Simcoe, began arriving in Bruce and Grey counties in the early 1850s, thus augmenting the Tiree communities even further.[152] There are indications that some of the Iona emigrants had previously settled in Peel County, possibly at Caledon, before taking up their land in Glenelg. As the Tiree settlers had done, they joined an already-established community in central Upper Canada in order to acclimatize to their new conditions before seeking permanent homesteads further west.[153]

Chief among the factors which drew Scots to the western peninsula

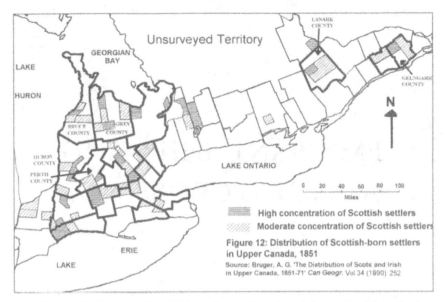

Figure 12: Distribution of Scottish-born settlers in Upper Canada, 1851
Source: Bruger, A. G. 'The Distribution of Scots and Irish in Upper Canada, 1851-71' *Can Geogr.* Vol 34 (1990) 252

was its good climate, plentiful and good land and the pull of family ties which were engendered by the first pioneer communities. And although emigrant Scots had initially been drawn to eastern Upper Canada in large numbers, by the mid-nineteenth century western Upper Canada had become their preferred choice (Figure 12). By then, there were particularly large concentrations of Scottish-born settlers at the townships of Aldborough, Dunwich, Ekfrid and Williams (Middlesex County), Zorra (Oxford County), Nichol, Puslinch and Guelph (Wellington County), Tuckersmith and McKillop (Huron County), Easthope (Perth County), Kincardine (Bruce County), Sydenham and Glenelg (Grey County) and Nottawasaga (Simcoe County).[154] A decade later, Scots would predominate in very large swathes of Huron, Perth, Bruce and Grey counties.[155]

However, irrespective of the factors which influenced Scots to choose a particular location, the crucial prerequisite for emigration was the availability of affordable transport. The choice of shipping routes and the frequency of service varied widely from one end of the country to the other. Transport opportunities influenced the regional direction of emigration and of particular importance was the growth of the North American timber trade, which revolutionized the scale and costs of transatlantic shipping.

Nine

EMIGRANT SHIPS AND ATLANTIC CROSSINGS

*I merely write a few lines, as they intend sailing tomorrow and
I may not have another opportunity. The passengers appear to be
very agreeable, but especially the two brothers which you saw
are unusually frank. There are three fiddlers aboard and I have
already got the offer of a fiddle which is very agreeable. The Captain
has got plenty of books but no kind of game…I stood long
waiting for the Earl Grey but never saw her go past…You must
excuse the rigmarole letter as they are singing all about.[1]*

A PARTY ATMOSPHERE SWEPT THROUGH THIS ship as she prepared
to leave Greenock for Quebec in 1841. Judging from the known
perils of sea voyages, her passengers ought to have been huddled
together in fear and trepidation. John McDonald's lurid description of the
agonies of his crossing on the *David* of London with 364 other passengers,
twenty years earlier, was certainly a terrible warning of what to expect. Keeping a diary, which he later published, he ended his account with these words:

I have been a sufferer, I witnessed the sufferings of my fellow travellers and am convinced that it was my duty to publish what I saw
and felt in myself and others. I leave it to every man to judge for himself, wishing that what is here stated may prove the means of saving
many lives and much property.[2]

However, the emigrants, who followed John McDonald, probably disregarded this and his other gloomy pronouncements, knowing full well that there was nothing new or alarming in what he had described. This was a time when most people lived in overcrowded and insanitary conditions. Finding these sorts of hardships on a ship was nothing new. Nor were they necessarily a sign of an inferior service. Because the transatlantic passenger trade had evolved from the shipping opportunities which had been created by the timber trade, it was in a primitive state of development. At this stage, shipping services were geared primarily to the needs of the timber trade rather than the comfort of passengers. Thus, even though emigrants provided much-valued extra revenue, the ships which they sailed on were chosen primarily for their timber-carrying capabilities. It was not that shipowners were being deliberately cruel or irresponsible. This was how shipping services operated at this time.

The North American trade developed rapidly from 1811 when already high duties on European timber were nearly doubled, thus pricing it out of the market. By this action Britain's timber purchases were effectively transferred from Europe to North America. The higher tariffs on European timber removed the disadvantage of greater distance thus making North American timber the cheaper alternative.[3] This created the explosive growth in Atlantic shipping which completely revolutionized emigrant travel. As the trade grew, more ships crossed the Atlantic and shipowners sought to minimize their costs by taking emigrants on their ships' westward journeys. Competition brought down fares and transatlantic crossings became regular occurrences. The timber trade was the sole reason why ships left in such numbers from Scottish ports, and without those ships the early Scottish influx to British North America could not have happened.

When Reverend William Bell came to the Perth settlement in 1817, he and his wife and six children, sailed on the *Rothiemurchus* of Leith, a ship which had been built five years earlier, specifically for the timber trade. While Bell had many complaints to make to Captain Watson about the food and lack of privacy in the steerage, he was satisfied with the ship's accommodation:

> She was fitted for the timber trade and had no cabin except a small one on the quarterdeck...but as there was a good deal of room

between decks and as we were not overcrowded with passengers we expected at this season of the year to make a tolerable shift.[4]

The *Rothiemurchus* sailed from Leith to Quebec in April with a cargo of gunpowder and 105 emigrants, including the Bell family, and returned to Leith a few months later with a cargo of timber.[5] Timber, loaded into the ship's hold one-way, replaced the emigrants who had been accommodated in the same hold, going the other way. Temporary wooden planking would have been placed over cross beams, after which carpenters would have been called in to build temporary berths along the sides. This was how most emigrants crossed the Atlantic. They travelled as steerage passengers, below deck, in what were often cramped and uncomfortable conditions. The only means of ventilation was through the hatches, and in stormy seas these could be kept battened down for days.

Bell complained bitterly about the poor food and foul-tasting water on board ship, while most of the other passengers had the opposite problem of not being able to face any food at all.[6] They suffered dreadfully from bouts of sea sickness, made worse by the many gales and stormy seas. Bell had wanted to pay extra for a temporary partition to be placed between his family "and the other passengers at the stern end of the between-decks room where there were two port-holes," but Captain Watson refused.[7] The niceties of social class had little place in the hold of a ship. In any case, however much Reverend Bell objected to the rough and ready conditions in the steerage, the ship in which he sailed could not have been better. Having an "A1" rating from Lloyd's of London, the *Rothiemurchus* was one of the many new ships being built at the time to meet the needs of the North American timber trade.[8] The passengers may have endured awful food, but the shipowner had not skimped in his choice of vessel. He had provided one of his best ships.

As major insurers, Lloyd's of London needed reliable shipping intelligence, which it procured through the use of paid agents in the main ports in Britain and abroad. Fortunately, such details were recorded in the *Lloyd's Shipping Register,* a documentary source, still in use today, which dates back to the late eighteenth century.[9] Ships were inspected by Lloyd's surveyors and assigned a code according to the quality of their construction and maintenance.[10] Shipowners actually complained that the codes were too stringent, particularly in the way a ship's age

> SALE ON SATURDAY, 13TH FEBRUARY.
>
> CANADA OAK, ASH, ELM,
> AND
> RED AND YELLOW PINE TIMBER,
> *Just now landed, from the Ship*
> BRILLIANT,
> ALEXANDER DUTHIE, from QUEBEC.
> THIS CARGO consists of—
> 6,500 Feet YELLOW PINE.
> 4,000 Feet RED PINE.
> 2,250 Feet OAK.
> 3,000 Feet ELM.
> 500 Feet ASH.
> 4 Large MAST-PIECES, from 70 to
> 80 feet in length, by 20 to 22 inches.
> All of the best quality; and will be exposed to Sale, by Public Roup,
> on the Ground where it lies, adjoining the Works of the ABERDEEN
> ROPE and SAIL COMPANY, Footdee, on SATURDAY the 13th February.
> The Sale will commence at 11 o'clock forenoon, and Credit will be
> given.   Apply to
>   William Duthie,
>   FOOTDEE.
> Aberdeen, 29th January, 1836.

The timber cargo of the *Brilliant* of Aberdeen, collected in Quebec and offered for sale in 1836, followed by an announcement of the ships return crossing to Quebec. She carried a total of 1,709 emigrants from Aberdeen to Quebec between 1830 and 1845. *Taken from the Aberdeen Journal Jan. 29, Feb. 16, 1836.*

and place of construction could affect its classification.[11] These codes were then used by insurers and shipowners to determine levels of risk and freight rates. Today these codes provide hard data on the quality of construction of the ships which carried emigrant Scots to Quebec during the late eighteenth and nineteenth centuries.

Because of gaps and inconsistencies in shipping sources, the identification of shipping codes can never be an exact science.[12] Shipping codes have been located for nearly 60 per cent of the 550 ships known to have carried emigrants from Scotland to Quebec during the 70-year period covered in this study (Appendix III). Seventy-eight per cent of the 307 ships with known codes were first class ships ("A1" code), or were ranked just below the top rating ("AE" code).[13] The remainder had an "E," or second class ranking, signifying that although they were seaworthy, they had minor defects. No examples at all were found of unsuitable ships. However, when the most frequently-used ships are analyzed, the high quality of emigrant shipping becomes even more apparent. A staggering eighty per cent of the one hundred ships which carried 300 or more passengers, either in a single crossing or in several, had an "A" ranking. The popular image of leaky, sub-standard shipping is not born out by the evidence.

The *Lloyd's Shipping Register* provides unequivocal evidence that emigrants actually sailed in the best ships. They were not offered the worst ships as is generally believed. Shipowners could have cut their costs by offering inferior vessels, but, if they had done so, they would have had no repeat business. Because emigrants were in such demand, competition between shippers worked in the emigrants' favour. Nevertheless, ships were chosen primarily for their stowage capabilities and manoeuvrability in heavy seas. The needs of passengers were quite secondary. Initially they were merely regarded as just another cargo to be taken across the Atlantic.

The 1802 sailings of the *Neptune* of Greenock, *Helen* of Irvine, *Jean* of Irvine and *Friends of John Saltcoats,* were some of the earliest timber ship crossings from Scotland to Quebec with emigrants.[14] Mostly A1 ships, between them, they carried the 1,152 Highlanders who were on their way to the Glengarry settlements. All of them would have endured extremely cramped conditions during their crossings. Conditions on the *Neptune* were worst of all. Some six hundred people had been packed into her hold, this being four times the number she should have carried when judged against the 1803 Passenger Act, which stipulated two tons per person.[15]

While the 1803 legislation did reduce overcrowding for a period, its space requirements were relaxed in 1817, to one-and-one-half tons per person, as a result of pressure from shipowners and agents. Ten years later, the passenger to tonnage ratio was set at three passengers for every four tons in 1828, and it was made slightly more generous in 1835, when it was increased to three passengers for every five tons.[16] Meanwhile, the emigrant's desire for cheap fares and the shipper's desire for high volume kept prices down but at the expense of occasional overcrowding. Steerage fares for passengers, supplying their own food, averaged £3.10s. in the 1820s but fell in the following decade to around £2.10s.[17] And evidence from the emigrants themselves suggests that they put a far higher premium on low fares than on their creature comforts. Thus, the avarice of shippers was not totally to blame for the excess numbers which were occasionally carried on vessels.

The onset of a severe economic depression in Scotland from 1830, together with improvements in inland travel, stimulated a mushrooming exodus of Scots to Upper Canada. By this time emigrants could take advantage of the more regular shipping services which had become available at the main Scottish timber ports. "Regular traders," as they were called, were now crossing the Atlantic at least twice a year, sometimes three times, usually under the helm of the same captain. These vessels, which always followed the same Atlantic route between their home and foreign ports, brought continuity to the service. Designed to meet specific cargo needs, they were a particular boon to passengers.[18] They had large-sized cabins which could accommodate up to thirty or forty passengers. Although cabins only benefited the minority of emigrants who could afford to pay more for greater comfort and privacy, regular traders also had the capability of providing improved conditions for steerage passengers.[19] The needs of the timber trade were still paramount but some shipowners were, at long last, being more selective in their choice of vessel.

The *Quebec Packet* of Aberdeen and the *Rebecca, Cherub, Corsair,* and *Gleniffer*, all of Greenock, regularly took cabin passengers during the 1820s. However, by the 1830s certain regular traders were proving to be popular with steerage passengers. Large numbers were sailing on vessels like the *Brilliant* of Aberdeen, the *Albion* of Greenock, the *Favourite* of Montreal and the *Jamaica* of Glasgow on a regular basis. Each had a higher than average between decks height and each had a highly experienced captain.[20] They also might have had better than average ventilation and hygiene. By concentrating on a few simple matters like clean water casks, shipowners could alleviate much suffering and ensure a good take-up of places on their ships.

Captain Alexander Allan of Saltcoats had been quick to spot the enormous economic potential of Britain's growing timber trade with Quebec. Together with his five sons, he established the Allan Line, a Clyde-based shipping fleet, which eventually dominated shipping in the Saint Lawrence. He captured a sizeable slice of Greenock's and Glasgow's passenger trade by offering the unbeatable combination of good ships under the helm of long-serving captains.[21] It was a modest beginning. After acquiring eight shares in the *Jean* in 1819, Allan bought out the other shareholders and moved his family to Greenock.[22] Six years later he acquired the *Favourite,* a Montreal-built ship, having "six feet between decks.. ample room for steerage passengers and...good accommodation in the cabin."[23] His third ship, the *Canada* of Greenock, purchased in 1831, was also built to a high standard. Establishing his son, Hugh, at a branch office in

Montreal, Alexander Allan continued to expand his fleet and was soon able to offer several crossings a year between the Clyde and Montreal.[24]

By the 1840s the firm had six additional ships – the *Arabian* of Greenock, *Brilliant* of Glasgow, *Favourite* of Greenock, *Blonde* of Montreal, *Caledonia* of Greenock and *Albion* of Greenock, each attracting large numbers of steerage passengers. Later, when shipping services became more specialized, ships like the *Glencairn, Marion, Ottawa* and *Harlequin,* built in the 1850s and registered in Glasgow, would carry as many emigrants in one crossing as these earlier Allan Line ships had taken in several (Appendix III).[25] To ensure that the Allan Line could always offer its newest ships, each ship in the fleet only saw service for an average of five years before being withdrawn. During the twenty-five year period from 1830 to 1855, the Allan Line carried around 10,000 emigrants from the Clyde to Quebec, primarily as steerage passengers. Large though this figure is, it represents only one-quarter of the total passenger trade from the Clyde (Table 8).[26] The remaining 36,000 people, who left from Greenock and Glasgow, travelled on the many regular traders, not owned by the Allan firm, which operated from the Clyde.[27]

Table 8

Emigrant Departures to Quebec from Scottish Ports, 1831–55

Scottish Port	Emigrant Totals
Glasgow	28238
Greenock	18008
Aberdeen	10409
Highlands & Islands*	8275
Misc. Small Ports#	5459
Leith	4411
Stornoway	3362
Dundee	2294
Cabin Passengers	1152
Dumfries	394
Children under 1 year	292

*Excludes Stornoway
#For example, Alloa, Annan, Ayr, Irvine, Montrose, Peterhead and Stranraer

Source: PP, Annual Reports of the Immigration Agent at Quebec.

Dinner Plate from the Allan Line Royal Mail
Steamers. The British government awarded the
Atlantic mail contract to the Allan firm in 1855.
By the late nineteenth century the Allan Line
had over 20 steamships, which provided a regular service from Glasgow to Quebec as well as
to Boston, Halifax and Philadelphia. *Courtesy
of Maritime Museum of the Atlantic, Halifax,
Canada M72.67.1.*

Regular traders like the *Tamerlane* of Greenock, *Ann Rankin* of Glasgow, *Sesostris* of Glasgow, *Conrad* of Greenock, *Tay* of Glasgow, *Erromanga*
of Greenock and *Jamaica* of Glasgow were typical of the Clyde-registered
ships which proved most popular with emigrants. Features which they all
shared were deep holds and sleek lines, perquisites for spacious passenger
accommodation and fast crossings.[28] Ships such as these were much in
demand since, in addition to having a robust local market, they attracted
emigrants from regions far removed from the Clyde. The chance survival
of the list of passengers who sailed on the *Portaferry* from Greenock in
1832 reveals the extent of the Clyde's drawing power. In addition to the
expected Lanarkshire and Renfrewshire passengers, there were also sizeable numbers from Stirlingshire, East Lothian, Berwickshire, and
Perthshire, on the east side of the country.[29] Although Leith ships regularly went to Quebec, this latter group chose to depart from Greenock.[30]
This was because they could get a much better choice of passenger ships
on the Clyde than at Leith. Once the interlinking Forth and Clyde and
Union canals had been opened in 1822, people from Edinburgh and other
places on the east, had cheap and ready access to Glasgow.[31] In these circumstances Leith lost out to the Clyde.

Aberdeen also had its regular traders but unlike the Clyde, no one
firm dominated the Atlantic passenger trade.[32] With his astute purchase of former whaling ships in the early 1830s, William Duthie was
well ahead of his time in recognizing the gains to be made from size.
His 332 ton *Brilliant* and 250 ton *Hercules* could offer six feet between
decks for passengers[33] – an almost unheard of luxury for the time.[34]
It was not until the passing of the 1842 Act that six feet would become
the minimum legal requirement.[35] By this time Donaldson Rose's *St.*

Lawrence and Alexander Duthie's *Berbice* were being put into service.[36] Having slimmer hulls, they offered faster journey times as well as a height between decks of up to seven feet. Becoming Aberdeen's most popular emigrant carrier, the *St. Lawrence* carried nearly 2,000 people to Quebec while the *Berbice* took around 1,200 people (Appendix III).[37]

In spite of its important linen trade with North America, Dundee never ranked as a major transatlantic port.[38] However, it did have the occasional entrepreneur like James Soot, a Leith shipper, who sought to build up an Atlantic passenger trade. Having had interests in both the Dundee New Whale Fishing Company and the Union Whale Fishing Company, he was William Duthie's equivalent in Dundee. During the 1830s he offered the *Fairy* and *Ebor,* both having "great height between decks," having been "doubled and fortified for the whale fishing" but he attracted few passengers. As was the case with Leith, Dundee could simply not compete with the Clyde ports.[39] While Dumfries ships regularly collected timber, first from Maritime ports and later from St. Lawrence ports, they carried relatively few emigrants (Table 8). With the coming of larger ships by the 1830s, Dumfries lost what little passenger trade it had to the large Cumbrian ports like Maryport and Whitehaven.[40]

Shipping services developed one stage further when Cromarty came to be used as a central collecting point for the northeast Highlands.

The emigration stone at Cromarty, designed and carved by Richard Kindersley, 2002. The names of 39 ships, which carried emigrants to Upper Canada and Nova Scotia, are carved around the edges. The inscription is from Hugh Miller's report, in the *Inverness Courier,* of the departure of the *Cleopatra* from Cromarty in June 1831, and reads: "The *Cleopatra* as she swept past the town of Cromarty was greeted with three cheers by the crowd of the inhabitants and the emigrants returned the salute, but mingled with the dash of the waves and the murmurs of the breeze, their faint huzzas seemed rather sounds of wailing and lamentation than of a congratulatory farewell." *Photograph by Geoff Campey.*

Situated as it was midway between the Dornoch and Moray firths and having an excellent harbour, its huge catchment area extended from Sutherland down to Inverness-shire and eastward to Morayshire and Banffshire (Figure 1). Atlantic-bound ships from Aberdeen, Leith, Dundee and other eastern ports called for emigrants at Cromarty from as early as 1815 and, as the service developed, Thurso and Loch Laxford became further collecting points.[41] By making use of spare capacity on westward-bound shipping, shipowners were able to provide regular and affordable ship crossings from Cromarty to North America. Timber ships operating from east coast ports simply made a short diversion to Cromarty to collect emigrants, before heading west across the Atlantic. Because Cromarty had no appreciable foreign timber trade there was no question of ships making round trips with passengers one way and timber the other way. These were merely opportunistic one-off collections by passing timber ships.

Many of the ships, like the *Pacific* of Aberdeen and the *Chieftain* of Kirkaldy, which collected emigrants at Cromarty, regularly crossed the Atlantic from their home ports, but there were some like the *Margaret Bogle* of Leith which followed no fixed route or pattern. Having sailed from Leith to Quebec in 1826, the *Margaret Bogle* sailed to Waterford in Ireland, and then in the following year sailed to Halifax and proceeded on to New York. She then sailed to Liverpool and, before the year had ended, had returned to New York and gone on to Baltimore.[42] Her passenger collections at Cromarty in 1837 and at Thurso and Loch Laxford in 1841, and four other collections at Leith and Glasgow, all bound for Quebec, were part of this ship's unpredictable and varied schedule.[43] Her 1833 crossings from Leith to Quebec and back again, earned a profit of £370, of which about 20 per cent came from the sale of 68 passenger fares. The timber trade was thus the main business but emigrants were an important additional source of revenue.[44] She was owned by John Smith, a Leith merchant, and his two brothers, Walter and Thomas, who were both ship captains. Her relatively large proportions and the fact that she was usually captained by the highly experienced Walter Smith probably explain why she was chartered so frequently for the Atlantic passenger trade.[45]

But, although the ships made fleeting appearances, the emigration agents who procured them were more permanent fixtures. Acting as middlemen, the emigration agents provided a succession of ships, which had the appearance of a purpose-built shipping fleet, but, of course, they had no common owner and rarely did the same journey more than once. But they sought a consistent standard of shipping since their repeat business depended on a good recommendation from passengers. William Allan, a Leith ship broker, firmly established Cromarty's role as an emigrant embarkation port by 1819. Having a network of sub-agents in Sutherland, and along the Dornoch, Cromarty and Beauly firths, as well as in Speyside, Allan managed passenger services over an extensive area. His sub-agents, who were the local merchants, shoremasters, postmasters and innkeepers, sold places on ships and organized the steamers which took emigrants to meet a particular ship at Cromarty. On the whole, crossings under his control ran smoothly although there were occasional mishaps. During the *Canada*'s crossing from Cromarty to Quebec in May, 1830, "a severe fever owing to bad water" broke out among the 244 emigrants, claiming six lives. The ship's wooden casks, having previously contained palm oil, had been used to store water. Being badly contaminated, the water "could not be used for tea or coffee or anything else."[46]

The port of Quebec had rudimentary medical facilities which were being managed by the Quebec Emigrant Society. It had been formed in 1819, a year when, in a single season, the city had to cope with 12,000 emigrants, representing some two-thirds of its entire population. Having sent back some of the "deluded and helpless beings," the Society wanted British people to realize that they "should not abandon their homes in a vague expectation of relief" when they reached Quebec.[47] However, little notice was taken of their warning and Quebec continued to be inundated with penniless emigrants. Conditions improved greatly in 1832 with the passing of the Quarantine Act, which introduced an immigrant tax of 5 shillings, payable by each overseas passenger. The funds raised enabled the authorities to build quarantine and other medical facilities at Grosse Isle.[48] Predictably, the new tax was bitterly opposed by shipowners and agents, who claimed that it would deter people from emigrating.[49] As anticipated, emigration numbers fell sharply in the following year and only began to rise again in the early 1840s. (Table 9).

Table 9

British immigrant and other arrivals at the port of Quebec, 1829–55.

Year	England	Ireland	Scotland	Europe	Maritime Provinces	Total
1829	3565	9614	2634	—	123	15945
1830	6799	18300	2450	—	451	28000
1831	10343	34133	5354	—	424	50254
1832	17481	28204	5500	15	546	51746
1833	5198	12013	4196	—	345	21752
1834	6799	19206	4591	—	339	30935
1835	3067	7108	2127	—	225	12527
1836	12188	12590	2224	485	235	27722
1837	5580	14538	1509	—	274	21901
1838	990	1456	547	—	273	3266
1839	1586	5113	485	—	255	7439
1840	4567	16291	1144	—	232	22234
1841	5970	18317	3559	—	240	28086
1842	12191	25532	6095	—	556	44374
1843	6499	9728	5006	—	494	21727
1844	7698	9993	2234	—	217	20142
1845	8883	14208	2174	—	160	23375
1846	9163	21049	1645	896	—	32753
1847	31505	54310	3747	—	—	89562
1848	6034	16582	3086	1395	842	27939
1849	8980	23126	4984	436	968	38494
1850	9887	17979	2879	849	701	32292
1851	9677	22381	7042	870	1106	41076
1852	9276	15983	5477	7256	1184	39176
1853	9585	14417	4745	7456	496	36699
1854	18175	16156	6446	11537	857	53183
1855	6754	4106	4859	4864	691	21274

Source: Annual Reports of the Immigration Agent at Quebec, 1831–55 (note: PP 1837–38 (175)XLVII contains figures for 1829–36).

By 1836 William Allan's business had been taken over by two High-landers – Duncan MacLennan and John Sutherland. MacLennan was an Inverness lawyer while Sutherland worked as the Wick agent for the British Fisheries Society, a body which promoted employment opportunities in fishing. Having lived for twenty years in Nova Scotia, Sutherland made great play of his personal knowledge of North America's farming and business opportunities.[50] And as agents for the Canada Company, the partners made full use of the company's promotional literature to

View of the busy port of Quebec in 1840, a lithograph by Thomas Picken based on a drawing by Captain Benjamin Beaufoy. *Courtesy of Toronto Reference Library, J. Ross Robertson Collection, JRR 2014.*

highlight emigrant success stories in its townships.[51] With John Sutherland managing Sutherland and Caithness, the partners extended their coverage northward and as emigration from Caithness and northwest Sutherland began its dramatic rise, Thurso came into its own as a major emigrant embarkation port. MacLennan and Sutherland did particularly brisk trade between 1840 and 1845 when they arranged transport from both Cromarty and Thurso for nearly 3,000 emigrants in 19 ships.[52] What feedback we have about the partners is mainly favourable.

The 1842 sailing of the *Lady Emily* of Sunderland to Pictou and Quebec with 150 passengers clearly went smoothly. The 86 emigrants who disembarked at Pictou were full of praise for Captain Stove. "Particularly do we appreciate the kindness of Captain Stove…and if he should continue in future to bring out passengers for Mr. Sutherland, we shall have great pleasure in recommending such of our friends as may be disposed to follow us to this, the land of our adoption, to take passage with Captain Stove."[53] Having heard consistently good reports from emigrants who had travelled in their ships, the *John O'Groat Journal* had offered its eulogies as well:

The northern counties of Scotland are peculiarly indebted to Mr. Sutherland for laying on his vessels in this part of the country – for before he established himself, those desirous of emigrating had to bear the expense of removal to Greenock, which equalled if not exceeded the whole sum now charged for the passage to America. Nearly 2,000 emigrants have been sent out by him within two years in vessels of the first class. So far as we know Mr. Sutherland has left behind him a character for uprightness and integrity. His conduct to the poorer classes of emigrants has been very praiseworthy – he very frequently granted free passages to many members of a family where the head of it could not command sufficient means to carry them all out.[54]

When the *Prince Albert* of Arbroath left Thurso for Quebec with 125 passengers, seven years later, the same newspaper lavished yet more praise on Mr. Sutherland. Having gone on deck to see the passenger accommodation for themselves, the reporters concluded that "the arrangements were such as to give entire satisfaction" and the emigrants, "ere the *Prince Albert* sailed, gave expression to this feeling and to the sense of the honourable and gentlemanly conduct of Mr. Sutherland."[55] The accommodation was light and airy and the "height between decks…was such that we could safely promenade amongst this veritable colony."[56] Sutherland insisted on some last minute improvements "to secure the greater comfort to the passengers" and "the owner, thereupon,…complained that Mr Sutherland was much more particular as to the fitting out of vessels than was customary with others in his line."[57] However, not all of Sutherland's ships were this well-received.

When the partners had arranged for the *Lady Grey* of North Shields to take 240 emigrants from Cromarty to Pictou and Quebec in 1841, they soon had a crisis on their hands. By the time that she arrived at Pictou and disembarked 135 of her passengers, there was a raging typhus epidemic on board the ship. Six people had already lost their lives and, by the time that the *Lady Grey* reached Quebec, there were eleven further deaths, two of them occurring at the Quarantine Station in Grosse Isle.[58] The emigrants, who left at Pictou, blamed Captain Grey for the deaths. "The cause of sickness on board arose from the passengers having caught cold on deck in consequence of the decks being always wet and in a filthy state."[59] Captain Grey insisted that his job was simply to get the vessel safely to Pictou and that he was not responsible for its cleanliness. But he should have been. Fortunately his appalling behaviour had been fully documented by the emigrants. In their report, they advised emigrants to "enquire into the character and disposition of the masters of vessels they intend sailing in, upon whom in a great measure, depends the lives of themselves and families, whilst under their charge."[60]

Captains were indeed very important. At sea everything depended on their navigational skills. The *Fairy* of Dundee's grateful passengers praised Captain Ritchie's "humane, caring and attentive manner" on their 1833 crossing.[61] Kind-hearted and competent captains were like magnets and attracted the bulk of the Atlantic passenger trade. Aberdeen had men like Alexander Leslie, who captained the *Albion* of Aberdeen for an amazing 25 years, and Alexander Barclay and Duncan Walker who regularly captained the *Brilliant* and *Hercules*. Thomas Fowler, who sailed from Aberdeen to Quebec on the *Brilliant* in 1831 under Captain Barclay, had come to appreciate the importance of a good captain, "I advise passengers in crossing the Atlantic to pay some attention to the selection of a sober, staid commander; as their comfort will in a great measure depend upon him whatever kind the weather may happen to be."[62] However, it was not just their comfort which was at stake. A captain's skill and cool head were important to their very survival.

The ordeal suffered by the *Albion* of Greenock's passengers in 1847 serves as a reminder of the risks which people took when they crossed the Atlantic early in the year. Having left Greenock on the 25th of March with 19 cabin passengers, who were mostly women, Captain Bryce Allan would have expected to reach Quebec by early May, but on this occasion his ship became ensnared in a large icefield. As conditions worsened, he put pen to paper and wrote home, thus leaving behind a vivid account of this miserable crossing.[63]

The *Albion* first "entered the ice" on April 10, 1847, having become stuck just off Port-aux-Basques on the tip of Newfoundland. Joining her in the ice were two other ships with emigrant Scots on board – the *Erromanga* of Greenock and the *Belleisle* of Glasgow. Captain Allan soon became "heartily sick of it" and hoped that the incident "will be a warning to the shipowners at home not to dispatch the ships so early in Spring."[64]

Allan had to manage his ship's dwindling food supplies over the following weeks without alarming his passengers. Meanwhile his crew worked all hours of the day to cut the *Albion* free from the ice with axes, "their feet being wet all of the time," but to no avail. The passengers got their exercise by walking over the ice to speak to fellow-Scots on board the *Belleisle* and on one occasion Captain Ramsay and a Presbyterian minister walked across the much greater distance from the *Erromanga* to the *Albion,* to help lift spirits, but needed to be rescued. Captain Allan thought them "very rash in attempting to come as the ice was so bad...and when they were returning the ice gave way and I was obliged to launch my lifeboat and get them safe on board for which we were very grateful."

As the 1st of May approached Captain Allan wondered whether he and the others would ever see Quebec:

> I am getting more dispirited every day, but am confident that it is very sinful, as I ought to put my trust in God, who has hitherto preserved me, but I must confess that I am at times almost despairing of getting to my journey's end...God afflicteth not willingly and I have no doubt my trials and detention are sent to try my faith.[65]

However, his faith would be tested even further. Three days later the captains of the *Bellisle* and *Erromanga* would plead with him for food. Given that they had 33 and 56 passengers respectively, he judged their needs to be the greater and released 100 lb. of beef from the *Albion's* stores.[66] He, his crew and his passengers faced starvation, although Allan was careful to disguise their predicament as much as he could.

Mercifully the *Bellisle* and *Erromanga* broke free on the 21st of May, and so did the *Albion* three days later:

> Today [24th May] I am happy to say that we have at last got into clear water. We were 46 days from the time we entered the ice until we got out again and 28 of those we never had a man at the helm; the ship was frozen so hard that it would not move.[67]

Captain Allan brought the *Albion* into the port of Quebec on the June 4, some 72 days after she had left Greenock. He could take comfort from the fact that they had arrived "thank God in perfect health." They were the lucky ones. Many thousands of mostly Irish emigrants died during the dreadful typhus and dysentery epidemic which gripped Grosse Isle and Quebec that summer. The port had been exceptionally busy that year, with arrivals being three times greater than normal (Table 9). Around 17,500 Irish emigrants died either on board ship, or shortly after landing. Never before or since had such misery and suffering been witnessed.[68]

Two years later, the 209 emigrants who sailed from Glasgow on the *Circassian* of Aberdeen also experienced a long voyage, but they were not as fortunate as the *Albion*'s passengers. Although she left in June, when the threat of ice had gone, she took 77 days to reach Quebec. Having been denied sufficient food, the passenger succumbed to disease. A total of seventy people died, 53 from cholera and 17 from typhus, with most of the deaths occurring at the Quarantine Station and hospital at Grosse Isle. "Provisions had been put on board only sufficient for six weeks and at the expiration of that time the passengers were placed on short allowance and had to purchase from the master all the articles they required beyond the pound of bread-stuffs required by law."[69] The emigrants had agreed to a despicable contract, which enabled the shipowner to charge extra for food after a fixed period. Captain Dixon's shameful conduct in enforcing the contract led to "the deficiency of food" and created "the largest proportionate mortality" experienced on any ship that season.[70]

Of all the sad incidents involving emigrant ship crossings, none sticks in the mind more than the plight of the 1,700 South Uist emigrants who came to Quebec in 1851. There was no loss of life, nor even any disease, but their suffering defies belief. They were the former tenants of Colonel Gordon of Cluny, who sailed in five ships from ports in the Outer Hebrides. Speaking only Gaelic, they arrived in a destitute state. Archibald Buchanan, the Immigration Agent, had seen nothing like it before:

> I never during my long experience at the station saw a body of emigrants so destitute of clothing and bedding; many children of 8 and 9 years old had not a rag to cover them. Mrs. Crisp, the wife of the master of the *Admiral,* (which vessel brought 413 of their number), was busily employed all the voyage in converting empty bread-bags, old canvas and blankets into coverings for them. One fully grown man passed my inspection with no other garment than a woman's petticoat.[71]

The *Circassion* of Aberdeen, a brig of 180 tons, built by William Duthie and Sons in 1835. She is shown entering the harbour at Malta. The artist is unknown. *Courtesy of the City of Aberdeen Art Gallery and Museums Collection.*

In addition to the distress of having been cleared out of their homes, they were packed off to Quebec "without the means of leaving the ship or of procuring a day's subsistence for their helpless families." With Mr. Buchanan's help and government funding the South Uist emigrants reached their final destinations in the western peninsula.[72] The colonial authorities later wrote to Colonel Gordon asking him to reimburse them for their costs, but he refused. As many people on both sides of the Atlantic would come to realize, Gordon was a tight-fisted, contemptible brute.[73]

Episodes like this reinforce the highly negative depictions of emigration which are to be found in popular literature. The forced evictions, during the Highland Famine years from 1846 to 1856, and the high death toll of Irish emigrants on sea crossings, during this same period, have understandably captured much public attention. However, these were exceptional incidents and should not be allowed to distort the overall picture. The evidence from this study shows that most emigrant Scots arrived safely and in good health. The notable exceptions were the 70 passengers who lost their life on the *Circassian* of Aberdeen in 1849. In addition, there were some near misses. The *Earl of Dalhousie* was shipwrecked near Anticosti Island, but, fortunately, her crew and 140 passengers were rescued and put on the *John Howard* of London and

Rob Roy of Aberdeen, which were in the immediate vicinity.[74] And the *Glencairn* of Glasgow was able to rescue the crew and 65 passengers from the *Shandos* of Glasgow when a fire engulfed it.[75]

Commentators like Edward Guillet and Arthur Lower have much to answer for. Their assertions that emigrants always had gruesome crossings on ill-managed ships have contributed to the gloom and foreboding which has long permeated this subject. Guillet has quoted one Grosse Isle physician who claimed that, "while there were plenty of seaworthy vessels, the worst only were generally used in the emigrant trade," to substantiate his "continuous nightmare of suffering" portrayal of emigrant shipping.[76] Arthur Lower alleged that until about 1835 conditions for emigrants "were probably worse than in the slave trade. Every slave thrown overboard meant so much money lost; every emigrant less decreased the ship's liability to feed him and gave more room for those that were left."[77] It is easy to titillate with this sort of nonsense, and to provide grisly anecdotal snippets, but these are poor substitutes for the facts.

This study has followed the progress of 963 ship crossings from Scotland to Quebec involving some 99,434 emigrants during the period from 1785 to 1855. Irrefutable and extensive evidence has been presented to show that the ships which they sailed on were generally of the highest quality. There were many exemplary captains and reliable emigration agents who managed shipping services over many years. It was no picnic travelling in the hold of a ship, but until the days of the specialist steamship, designed with passengers' needs in mind, this was all that the current technology allowed. However basic the conditions were, Scots were generally offered the best available shipping of their time.

Ten

BORDER GUARDS
AND TRAIL BLAZERS

Ontario is to a large extent a Scotch colony.[1]

S IR RICHARD CARTWRIGHT, THE KINGSTON-BORN Liberal politi-
cian, wrote these words in his *Reminiscences* of 1912. Of course, he
was not referring to the Scottish domination of Ontario in numeric
terms. At the time, people of Scottish ancestry accounted for no more than
14 per cent of the total population of Ontario.[2] He was commenting on
their impressive influence and achievements. Although they were no more
than a substantial minority group, Scots had long been dominating much
of the province's business and political life. Scottish influences were to be
found everywhere in universities and in the professions, especially in law
and medicine. In fact, Ontario had a Scottish elite who enjoyed a visibil-
ity which was totally disproportionate to their numbers in the overall
population. Part of the explanation for their high profile lies in their early
arrival to the province. Scots had spearheaded much of the early immigration to the province. Arriving as they did from the late eighteenth
century, they had grasped the many farming and economic opportunities
which were open to the first wave of colonizers. They had obvious entrepreneurial talents, but there was more to their success than this. Scots had
a strong sense of identity and self-belief and they were remarkably good
at coping with the privations of pioneer life. They were a founding people whose influence and impact set them apart from other ethnic groups.

Most of Ontario's high-profile Scots had risen "from the ranks of the common people."[3] William Rattray wrote in the 1880s of the many sons of poor crofters and tradesmen who later achieved "prosperity and fame."[4] Large numbers of them "rose from the humblest positions in life to honour and distinction."[5] Reverend William Sutherland, minister of the Presbyterian Church at Strathburn in Middlesex County, actually counted "600 of the descendants of the early pioneers" in his region who had gone on to "become teachers or entered the ministry or learned professions."[6] And yet, when one looks back one hundred years to the time when the Glengarry settlements were just beginning to take shape, Scottish pioneering success must have looked highly improbable. The initial settlers lacked any kind of axe skills. Originating from a near treeless region of the Highlands, few "had ever cut down so much as a sapling."[7] However, these people came equipped with other more important attributes. They were well used to coping with extremes of climate and hardships. This and their predilection for self-sufficiency gave them the necessary staying power needed to endure the toughness and isolation of pioneer life.

Highlander pioneering successes became widely known and eventually attracted the attention of the 1841 Select Committee on emigration. In his evidence to the committee, Reverend Norman MacLeod, a Glaswegian Presbyterian minister who was an enthusiastic proponent of Highland emigration, spoke of the great "industry and energy" shown by Highlanders in their new settlements overseas.[8] Referring to their apparent reputation for "indolence" back home, he explained that "it arises from the peculiar circumstances in their own country."[9] Set free from the constraints of a feudal society, Highlanders grasped the opportunities to be had in Upper Canada and prospered. Having been in correspondence with clergymen in Upper Canada, MacLeod described "the peculiar adaptation of the Highland population for Canada." It was "greater than any other people that can be sent out. They can turn their hands (to use a common expression) to anything; they can make carts…boats…their women can weave cloth."[10] The Hon. Christopher Hagerman commented on "the excellent farms" and "considerable wealth" which had been acquired by the Glengarry settlers – benefits which were "within reach of all of them."[11] John Bowie, who was involved in the management of several Highland estates, spoke of the many pioneers who "have sent home letters strongly recommending their friends to follow them."[12] It was a virtuous circle of success reinforcing success.

When Thomas Rolph, the Upper Canada Emigration Agent, gave evidence to this same committee, he made no distinction between Lowlanders and Highlanders. He relayed the report of a colleague which concluded quite simply that "Scots are the best and most successful of all emigrants."[13] Heads would have nodded but even, at this time, there was little appreciation of the factors behind this success. Scots tended to settle in compact groups. Each of their settlements in Upper Canada could trace its roots back to a particular region of Scotland, thus giving it a distinctive identity. By banding together, Scots gave themselves a mutual support structure. As John Howison discovered when he visited the various Highland communities in the Talbot settlement, "these people with the clannishness so peculiar to them, keep together as much as possible."[14] Although he was highly disapproving of their ways, describing them as "a lawless and unprincipled rabble," even he had to admit that they had created a harmonious environment which was highly supportive to newcomers.[15] Close-knit communities may not have been forward looking when it came to economic advancement, but they allowed shared values and traditions to flourish. This gave Scots their clear sense of identity and strong feelings of self-worth, which were such important factors in their success.

Upper Canada's Perth settlement in the Rideau Valley first came to the attention of the *Glasgow Herald* in 1820, just five years after it had been founded. It described how former weavers from Glasgow were "strutting between the stumps" of their felled trees in Lanark County "as pompous as an Edinburgh magistrate."[16] Not exactly rags to riches yet, but these former weavers clearly felt very pleased with their progress. It is hard to imagine less likely colonizers than Glasgow weavers. However they relinquished their former trades with great relish and became highly successful farmers. They too adopted a collective approach to settlement. They settled as "one neighbourhood" in separate communities.[17] And their self-help friendly societies, which had proved invaluable in the fundraising needed to finance their relocation costs, continued to function in their new environment. Many of these societies were later transformed into St. Andrew's societies whose primary role was to offer support to newly arrived immigrants. A particularly noteworthy feature of these early weaving communities was their association with books and libraries.

The Pipes and Drums of the 42nd Lanark & Renfrew Heritage Band, Perth and District, 1996. The band is proud of its associations with the Royal Highland Regiment (42nd). Lanark County's initial pioneers mainly originated from various parts of the Lowlands, and from Perthshire in the Highlands. *Courtesy of the Perth Museum, Perth, Ontario.*

Scotland has traditionally placed a high value on education. William Rattray commented on the poor Scots who came with "a sound education," thus giving them an "an obvious advantage over their neighbours."[18] And since, by 1750, virtually every town in Scotland of any size had the benefit of a lending library, a good many of them also came with a healthy appetite for reading books. Weavers, who were especially well known for their intellectual pursuits and personal libraries, brought their books with them to the Rideau Valley. Great care had been taken to entrust their book collections to commendable people like Robert Mason. "A plain weaver, he has kept himself at evening schools well near twenty years of age and he has read [Joseph] Butler's *Analogy of Religion* with intelligence. He carried with him a library for the use of the emigrants and he has often been entrusted with bibles and catechisms for them."[19] Robert Mason was indeed a credit to the Scottish education system and was also a reminder of the importance placed by Scots on their religion.[20]

Scots in Dalhousie Township had built their first lending library by 1828. "Though we have expatriated ourselves, and are now obscured in interminable forests in [Upper] Canada, we are still anxious to keep the intellectual machinery in motion."[21] One man tramped through the woods to get to the Dalhousie Library in the hope of borrowing "the whole twenty volumes of the *Encyclopaedia Britannica*," but finding this was against the rules, "turned away sorrowful."[22] This commendable thirst for knowledge is a characteristic shared by many Scots, although not necessarily with this intensity. Scots in Dumfries, Fergus and Ennotville had their libraries as did Zorra and there were probably a good many more examples. Writing in 1890, Reverend Donald McKenzie's son could recall "from my earliest childhood...that almost every home in that large parish [Zorra] had its library – small it may be, but well-chosen."[23] The Zorra example is surprising given that this was initially a Gaelic-speaking community. However, a tradition of English book collections had clearly taken over by this stage.

Initially, Church missionaries, who visited Highland communities, attracted few listeners unless they could communicate in Gaelic. In townships like Lochiel in Glengarry County, Ekfrid in Middlesex County and Puslinch in Wellington County, Presbyterian services spoken in Gaelic attracted far greater numbers than those in English, and this was the case well into the late nineteenth century.[24] Gaelic was sufficiently widespread in 1841 to warrant a monthly Gaelic newspaper, which was produced in Kingston and distributed throughout Upper Canada.[25] However, Gaelic had already begun its decline in some areas by this time. In addition to Zorra, mentioned previously, Breadalbane's Baptist community in Glengarry County had also adopted English. Their services were being conducted solely in English by 1850.[26] With Gaelic being primarily a spoken language, there had been little documentation of the centuries-old poems, songs and stories, which the Gaelic-speaking pioneers had brought with them. As memories faded, many of these traditions disappeared into the mists of time. However, this problem has at least now been recognized and institutions like the University of Guelph's Scottish Studies department are ensuring that greater attention is being paid to conserving the province's Scottish heritage.

The Highland Society of Glengarry, founded by Bishop Alexander Macdonell in 1820, was another important mechanism for promoting Highland culture, although it had ceased to function by 1870.[27] In more recent times Highland Games have given Scottish culture new life throughout Ontario. It must be said, however, that such displays bear little relation to the province's early Scottish traditions.[28] But the same can be said of the cultural symbolism which now abounds in Scotland. The Highland symbols which have come into vogue are modern inventions.

They began appearing in the nineteenth century when Scotland was seeking a more distinctive national identity. Adopting the cultural emblems of its poorest region, the Highlands and Islands, Scotland redefined its heritage and gave itself the trappings of pipe bands and tartans. This same process has also happened in the New World locations inhabited by Scots and Ontario is a shining example of these later developments.

Highland Games commemorate the feats of strength which were once practised in the Highlands and, with their pageantry and tartans, they attract great crowds. After winning a tug-of-war championship at the Chicago World Fair in 1893, six farmers from Embro in Zorra Township went on to found the Embro Highland Games. A proliferation of similar events have followed throughout the province, with most, like the North Lanark Highland Games, being quite recent developments. The Fergus Highland Games, first established in 1945, regularly attract large numbers of visitors from across the continent, making it one of the most successful festivals of its kind in Canada. In 2002, when Fergus hosted the coming together of the Clan Maxwell Societies of Canada

The Men of Zorra, the West Zorra Tug-of-war Championship Team from Oxford County. *Back row (l–r):* Alex Clark (206 lbs., 6' 3"), Robert McLeod (197 lbs., 6' 1/4"), Ira Hummason (199 lbs., 6' 2"); *front row (l–r):* Wm. R. Munro (188 lbs., 6' 1"), E.L. Sutherland (Captain), Robert McIntosh (anchor), (215 lbs., 6' 1"), dated 1893. *Courtesy of Woodstock Museum National Historic Site.*

and the United States, its Highland Games brought one hundred Maxwells together in a combined celebration of Scottish heritage. The Glengarry Highland Games and Tatoo, held in Maxville, Ontario, since 1948 attracts thousands of visitors annually.

Given that they have sprouted mainly in those districts which experienced large influxes of Scots, Highland Games clearly reflect vestiges of a genuine Scottish past. North Bay, which only attracted its immigrants Scots in the late nineteenth century after the railways had been constructed, now stages Highland Gatherings. When the Morrison family, who originated from Callander in Perthshire, moved from the Muskoka Lakes area to the shores of Lake Nipissing in 1880 they helped to found a town which commemorates their Perthshire roots in its name. Now, the town of Callander has its annual "Celtfest," which holds Highland dance, fiddling and athletic competitions.[29]

Curling was also exported from Scotland to Upper Canada, as was shinty, which subsequently developed into ice hockey.[30] The first curling club appeared in Kingston in 1820. Fergus had a curling club by 1834 – only a year after it was founded, while Galt and Guelph formed their clubs in 1838, soon after they were established.[31] Curling in Ottawa dates back to 1851 when it was first played on the Rideau Canal. In more recent times, the sport has spread to Northern Ontario. Chapleau, situated north of Sault Ste. Marie, attracted many Scottish migrants from the Rideau Valley in the early 1880s, when the railways made the district accessible to settlers. They were no doubt the driving force behind the formation of Chapleau's first curling club, which was formed two years after the town was founded.[32]

Scottish culture continues to have tremendous appeal in Ontario and inspires interest in growing numbers of St. Andrew's societies, Burns suppers and other Scottish groups. Highland music remains a living tradition in many parts of the province. Glengarry and the Ottawa Valley have developed their own distinctive styles of fiddling while pipe bands continue to multiply.[33] The Sons of Scotland Band formed in Ottawa in 1896, the Kincardine Scottish Pipe Band formed in 1908 and the Guelph Pipe Band formed in 1922 are just some of many examples.

It is hardly surprising that Scottish culture remains so vibrant. A well-informed anonymous commentator who visited Ontario in the early 1900s wrote: "If there is one thing that the true-born Scot can never do

The Fergus Curling Club, 1889. *Back row (l–r):* David Mennie, John Graham, Robert Kerr, John Bayne; *front row:* W.A. Richardson, T.J. Hamilton, H.S. Michie, John Mennie. *Courtesy of the Wellington County Museum and Archives, ph 2829.*

successfully it is to lose his nationality."[34] Having spent his childhood in Elgin County and being of Highland ancestry, John Kenneth Galbraith, the internationally-renowned Harvard economist, could observe the indomitable forces at work:

> The Scotch were proud of being the descendents of pioneers. At political meetings, on St. Andrew's Day, in sermons, in homilies for the children at the Christmas concert and even in conversation the intellectual and moral leaders reminded themselves and others of the fortitude of men and women who had left the Highlands to make their way in this strange land and of the legacy of strength and courage which they had left to their children and grandchildren. A community of livestock breeders has an almost instinctive understanding of genetics so it was easy to speak of the natural selection which has characterized this movement. The rugged and enterprising had come; the rest had remained behind.[35]

The gene bank thus formed was truly remarkable. The descendents of the first Scottish settlers excelled in business, the arts, the professions and public service. Scots ran Ontario's banking and finance systems and were the dominant force in establishing the province's early schools and universities. John Simpson, from Rothes in Morayshire, moved to the Scotch Line in Perth in 1816 when only a child and by 1857 he had become the Ontario Bank's first president. Emigrating in 1833, the Renfrewshire-born John McMurrich soon became a successful merchant and founded businesses in Toronto, Kingston and Hamilton. Adam Hope, from East Lothian, emigrated a year later, and established himself as a London merchant. By 1865 he had moved to Hamilton, where he founded another successful firm and became the director of a bank. There are countless other examples of Scottish business acumen at work in the province.

Dr. Robert Tait McKenzie, who was born in Almonte (Ramsay Township) in Lanark County, gained a high reputation as a sculptor.[36] Being descended from the McKenzies of Eilean Donan Castle in Wester Ross, he returned to his birthplace in later life and purchased a summer house which he named "Mill of Kintail" after his ancestral roots.[37] Reverend

The Owen Sound Pipe Band, 1910. *Back row (l–r):* Stew Cruickshank, John McKeen, Jock Thompson, Robert Cameron, Robert Watt; *front row:* Dougal McCaffery, Donald Kelso, Jim Cruickshank. *Courtesy of The Grey Roots Archival Collection Catalogue # 988.7.51.*

Charles William Gordon, a Presbyterian minister turned novelist, based some of his books on his reminiscences of life at Indian Lands in Glengarry County. He wrote around thirty popular novels in all under the *nom-de-plume* of Ralph Connor.[38] The Ayrshire-born Thomas Macqueen founded the *Huron Signal,* a reform newspaper, while the song-writer Alexander Muir, who was born in Lesmahagow, Lanarkshire, wrote the words and music of "The Maple Leaf Forever." William Cruikshank, a Scots who taught art in Toronto for many years, had among his students some of the Group of Seven, of which J.E. MacDonald is a member.

When Alexander Graham Bell, the son of an Edinburgh elocutionist, moved to Brantford Township (Brant County) in 1870, he invented the telephone, a device which changed the world.[39] The Kircaldy-born Sir Sandford Fleming, who settled in Peterborough from 1844, became one of Canada's greatest railway pioneers and devised the world-wide system of time zones which came to be known as standard time.[40] Agnes Campbell Macphail, who was raised in a Scottish community in Grey County, became the first woman to be elected to the Canadian parliament in 1921, the first year in which women were allowed to vote. An active supporter of disarmament, she also championed prison reform and Women's Rights.

Being people of strong convictions Scots also became noted for their stubbornness and endless squabbling. Sir John A. Macdonald, the member of parliament for Kingston and Canada's first Prime Minister, had little time for the populist and reforming views of his archenemy, George Brown, the newspaper proprietor who founded the Toronto *Globe*.[41] Since Macdonald originated from Glasgow and Brown from Edinburgh, it is hardly surprising that sparks flew between them. However, in an astonishing turn-around both men joined forces in 1864 to work for the Confederation which eventually created the Dominion of Canada.

William Lyon Mackenzie and Reverend Dr. John Strachan, both Scots, also became sworn enemies. Arriving from Dundee in 1820, Mackenzie became a supporter of radical reform and by 1824 had launched the *Colonial Advocate,* a newspaper which advocated, amongst other things, the sale of Upper Canada's Clergy Reserves and the disestablishment of the Church of England in Canada.[42] Such aims immediately put Mackenzie at loggerheads with the Aberdeen-born Strachan who sought to preserve the link between church and state and the Church of England's claims to the Clergy Reserves. To Mackenzie,

Strachan was "a diminutive, paltry, insignificant Scotch turn-coat parish schoolmaster."[43] However, Strachan shrugged off such criticisms. Becoming Toronto's first Anglican Bishop, he provided the initial stimulus to Upper Canada's education system. He was the first president of the church-controlled University of King's College, founded in 1827, and when, in 1850, King's College changed into the "godless" University of Toronto, Strachan founded the University of Trinity College.[44] Meanwhile, Mackenzie became Toronto's first mayor in 1834 and led the failed Upper Canada uprising of 1837.

Although he was an eccentric and controversial figure, William Lyon Mackenzie attracted considerable popular support. He was not afraid to speak his mind or challenge the established order, a trait which he shared with many of his fellow Scots. Right from the beginning the first arrivals had shown a healthy disregard for authority. Highlanders in particular were determined to shed all aspects of their feudal past and readily grasped the egalitarian ways of their new country. When John Howison visited Highlanders in the Talbot settlement, he met people who were completely impervious to his overbearing ways:

> The Scotch...do not fail to acquire some of those ideas and principles that are indigenous to this side of the Atlantic. They soon begin to attain some conception of the advantages of equality, to consider themselves as gentlemen, and become independent; which in North America means to sit at meals with one's hat on; never to submit to be treated as an inferior; and to use the same kind of manners toward all men.[45]

Thomas Fowler, an Aberdeen man, observed that "the very lowest here stand up briskly for equality and in general insist on being admitted to table with every master they serve."[46] Presbyterian missionaries from the established Church of Scotland faced stiff competition from the independent Presbyterian sects which were prospering. After the disruption of 1843, when the Free Church was formed, it too won considerable backing in western Upper Canada from Scots who were keen to break free from the control exercised by the established church.

Highlanders had to be subservient in Scotland but not in Upper Canada. Set free from their feudal shackles, they blossomed. Their early settlement strongholds at Glengarry gave Upper Canada its civilian border guards at a time when the country was especially vulnerable to invasion. Lanarkshire and Renfrewshire emigrants followed soon after and created a second line of defence in the Rideau Valley. Most of the early overseas influx to eastern Upper Canada came from Scotland. And Scots were always at the cutting edge of each new frontier as settlement spread westward and northward. Being the trail-blazers, their settlements were often among the earliest to be founded.

As Nancy Jean Cameron prepared to leave New York State in 1784 with the other Inverness-shire Scots, she could not have imagined the impact that they would have on the future development of Upper Canada. "We must follow the old flag wherever it takes us." They followed it to the old province of Quebec and founded the hugely important Glengarry settlement. Soon Highland immigrants were "pouring down every day in most astonishing numbers" to join them, thus helping to secure the future of what would become the Province of Ontario.[47]

Appendix I

EXTANT PASSENGER LISTS

1. The *British Queen*, of Greenock, Deniston (Master). Sailed from Arasaig to Quebec Aug. 16, 1790.
[NAC RG4A1, Vol. 48, 15874-5]

				(◄——————Age——————►)						
Names	Trade	Farms	Country From	over 12	8 to 11	6 to 8	4 to 6	2 to 4	below 2	Amount Paid
Donald McAulay	Smith	Frobost	S. Uist	3	1	2		1	1	10 5 2½
Ewing McMillan	Tenant	Laidnafiroy	Ardgour	2	2	1	1	1	1	8 8 5
Donald McDonald	Tenant	Lagana-chorum	Glengary	3		2			1	10 18 6
Dougald McMillan	Tenant	Druiulu	Moidart	2			1	1		4 2 4½
Duncan Gillies	Tenant	Roniasick	N. Morar	7						13 9 6
Angus McLellan	Taylor	Lagana-chorum	GlenGary	2			1	1	1	4 2 4½
Peggy McDougal		Cleadale	Eigg	1		1				2 1 0
Allan McDonald	Tenant	Cleadale	Eigg	4		2				7 5 1
Donald McDonald	Tenant	Cleadale	Eigg	2					1	3 7 0
John McKinnon	Tenant	Cleadale	Eigg	1						2 1 0
Lachlan McKinnon	Tenant	Cleadale	Eigg	4	1	2		2	2	15 9 0
Lachlan Campbell	Tenant	Cleadale	Eigg	3				1	1	4 8 1½
Donald McDonald for Isabella		Cleadale	Eigg	1						3 7 0
Donald McCormick	Tenant	Cleadale		1	1					3 1 6
Do	Tenant	Cleadale	Eigg	1						3 1 6
Donald Fraser	Smith	Ardnafouras	Arasaig	4						11 11 0
John McKay	Tenant	Ardnafouras	Arasaig	1						1 18 6
John Gillies	Tenant	Bierard	N Morar	2					2	4 0 6
John McDonnell	Tenant	Inverosir	Knoydart	3				1		5 18 1½
Duncan McCraw	Servant	n/k	n/k	1						3 17 0
Donald Henderson	Servant	n/k	n.k	1						3 17 0
John McAulay	Servant	Frobost	S. Uist	1						1 18 6
Janet McDonald	Servant	n/k	n/k	1						1 18 6
			Totals	51	4	8	6	8	10	

[Total of 87 people]

2. The *Helen* of Irvine, *Jean* of Irvine and *Friends of John Saltc*oats. Sailed from Fort William to Quebec in June 1802.
[LAC MG24 I183 File 2, 7-9, 11; Fleming, *The Lochaber Emigrants to Glengarry*, 5-11; MacMillan, *Bygone Lochaber*, 239.]

Passengers who Boarded at Fort William

	Alex. McPhee,	Aberchalder	40	Don'd McDonell	Laddy
	Alex. McPhee	Do.		John McDonell	
	Catherine McPhee	"		Dun: McDonell	
	Mary McPhee	"		Catherine McDonell	
5	Margt McPhee	"		~~McDonell~~	
	Anny McPhee & 1 Child	"		Mary Kennedy	
	Don'd McPhee	Do.	45	Allan McDonell	Munergy
	Anne Kennedy }	"		Mrs. McDonell	
	Janet Marshall }	"		Margaret McDonell taken in No. 298	
10	McPhee's wife & ~~1 Child~~	"		Catherine McDonell	
				Donald McDonell & 2 Children	
	Ewen Kennedy	Aberchalder			
	His wife			Don'd McDougald	Ft Augustus
	Don'd Kennedy	Kinlochlochy	50	Mrs. McDougald	
	4 Children			Marjery McDougald	
				Alex'r McDougald	
	Don. Cameron	Drimnasallie		John McDougald	
15	His Wife				
				Alex'r Stewart	
	John Corbet	Ardachy		& 1 Child	Ft Augustus
	Mrs Corbet		55	Don'd Fraser	Leck
	~~Mary Corbet~~			Mrs. Fraser & 1 Child	
	Wm. Corbet				
20	Christy Corbet & 1 Child			Mary McAlpin	Greenfield
				Mary Cameron	Letterfinlay
	John McDonald	Inchlagan		Catherin McAlpine	Do.
	His Wife		60	Eliz. Grant	Drumnadrochit
	Don'd McDonald & 2 Children				
				Alex. Grant	Achnaconeran
	Don'd Scot	Aberchalder		Mrs. Grant	
25	his Wife			John Grant & 4 Children	
	Alex'r Scot				
	Dun. Scot			Don'd Grant	Dalcattaig
	Janet Scot		65	Mrs. Grant	
	Mary Scot & 2 Children				
				Mary Grant	Duldreggan
30	Dun: Kennedy	Aberchalder		Flory Grant	
	His Wife & 3 Children			Isabella Grant	
				Anne Grant	Livisie
	Don'd Kennedy	Achluachrach	70	John Grant & 1 Child	
	Mrs. Kennedy				
	~~Mary McDonald~~ & 5 Children			James Mcdonell	Balmean
				Mrs. McDonell	
35	Alex'r McDonell	Laggan		Kath: McDonell	
	Mrs. McDonell & 2 Children			Allan McDonell & 4 Ch.	
	John McDonell	Leck	75	Don'd McDonell	Inchlagen
				His Wife	
	Don'd Kennedy	Laddy		Mary McDonell	
	Mrs. Kennedy & 2 Children				

Passengers who Boarded at Fort William

Janet McDonell
Catherine McDonell
80 Peggy McDonell
Allan McDonell & 4 Ch.

Alex'r McDonell   Boline
his Wife
Dun: McDonell
85 Don'd McDonell
Cath. McDonell & 4 Ch.

John McDonell   Invervigar
Dugald McDonell
Catherine McDonell
90 Flora McDonell
Peggy McDonell
Don'd McDonell & 1 Ch.

Arch'd McLean   Laddy
Angus McLean

---

95 John Kennedy   Invervigar
His Wife
Dun: Kennedy
Alex'r Kennedy

Don'd Kennedy   Inchlagen
100 Angus Kennedy
Alex'r Kennedy
Allan Kennedy
Mrs. Kennedy & 2 Children

John Kennedy   Inchlagen
105 his Wife
Ewen Kennedy
Mary Kennedy
Alex'r Kennedy
Janet Kennedy
110 Angus Kennedy & 3 Children

John McDonell   Ardnabie
His Wife & 1 Child
Alex'r Cameron
His Wife

---

115 John Stewart   Boline
Mary Stewart
Catherine Stewart

Ran'd McDonell   Achteraw
Alex'r McKinzie   Urquhart
120 John McDonell   Divach
Alex'r Scot   Urquhart

Chas. McArthur   Inverskilroy
John McArthur
Sarrah McArthur

---

125 Lizie McArthur
Donald McArthur

Dun: McKinnon   Donie
His Wife & 6 Children

Effy Kennedy   Caum
130 Archy McMillan
Mary McMillan
Kath: McMillan
Miles McMillan
Dun: McLean & Wife
135 Alex'r McKinnon
His Wife & 3 Childrem
Dun: McKinnon

Jas. McIntosh   Kerrowdoun
Catherin McIntosh
140 Mary McDonell
Mary McDonell

Don Kennedy   Lewiston
Marg't Kennedy & 3 Children

---

145 John Cameron   Glenturret
Angus Cameron his Bro.
Catherine Cameron   Leck
Mary Gillis
Mary Cameron
150 Marjory Cameron 2 Ch.

Don Cameron   Kenlocharkaig
His Wife & 2 Children

John Cameron   Kenmore
His Wife
155 John Cameron
Donald Cameron
Ewen Cameron

Dun: McMillan   Shanvail
His Wife
160 Catherine McMillan
Effy McMillan
4 Children

John McMillan   Shanvail
His Wife
Alex'r McKay & 3 Children

---

165 Kath: McMillan   Shanvail
Mary McMillan
Peggy McMillan & 1 Child

Angus McPhee   Crieff
170 His Wife & 3 Children

Passengers who Boarded at Fort William

John McDon'd   Kenlochnasale
His Wife
Alex'r McDonald
Don'd McDonald

175 Peggy McDonald
Mary McGilvray

Don: McMillan   Tomdoun
His Wife & 4 Children

E. McMillan   Corrybuy
180 his Wife & 4 Children
Arch'd McMillan

Ewen McMillan   Craigalachie
His Wife & 1 Child

John McMillan   Corsuck
His Wife
185 Ewen McMilland
5 Children

John McMillan   Muick
His Wife
Mary McMillan
190 Marg: McMillan
Catherin McMillab

Ewewn McMillan   Coinich
his Wife & 3 Children

John McMillan   Glenpean
195 his Wife
Dun: McMillan
Dug'd McMillan
Bell McMillan
Alex'r McMillan
1 Child

---

200 John McMillan   Camusine
3 Children

John McMillan   Coinich
His Wife
Dun: McMillan
Betty McKinnon
205 Alex'r McDonell
Mary McMillan   Munerigy
3 Children

Alex'r McMillan   Callich
His Wife & 1 Child

Ewen McMillan   Quarter
210 Cath: McMillan

Angus McMillan   Arkaig
His Wife & 2 Children

Angus McDonald   Invervigar
His Wife
215 Duncan McDonell
Katherine McDonell
Mary McDonell
Alex'r McDonell

John McDonell

---

220 Don' McMilland   Achintore
& his Wife

John McDon'd   Doers

John McDon'd for
his Broyr   Inchlagen

Donald McDonell   Leck
225 & his Wife

Dun Gillis   Aberchalder
Moread McMillan
Mary Kennedy
Mrs. Gillis
4 Children

---

230 Don'd McDonell   Aberchalder
His Wife
Anne McDonell
Dun McDonell
Ewen McDonell
2 Children

---

235 W'm Fraser   F. Augustus
His Wife & 2 Children

Alex'r Fraser   F Augustus
His Wife

Alex'r Rankin   Carnach
240 his Wife
[Blank Line]
& 2 Children

Arch'd Henderson   Glencoe
His Wife
245 [Blank Line]
& 1 Child

Ewen McLean   Aberchalder
His Wife
Don. McLean
250 Cathr. McLean
Mary McLean
4 Children

Don: McMillan   Aberchalder
His Wife
John McMillan

Passengers who Boarded at Fort William

255 Marg't McMillan
Marg't McDonell & 3 Children
_____

Don: McDonell   Thornhill
His Wife & 3 Children
_____

Alex'r Cameron   Thornhill
260 his Wife & 2 Children
_____

Arch. McDonell   Paisley
His wife
_____

Mary McLean   Laddy
Katherin Mclean
_____

265 Dun: McLean   Munergy
His Wife
Angus McLean
Duncan McLean
Janet McLean & 1 Child
_____

270 Mary McMaster   Glenpean
Anne Cameron   Muick
_____

Ewen McMillan   Lubriach
His Wife
Mary McMillan
275 Peggy McMillan
Donald McMillan
Ewen McMillan
_____

Cath McLean   Caum
_____

John Cameron   Achnacarry
280 his Wife
Don: Cameron
_____

Mary Chisholm   Strathglass
Anne Chisholm   Do
_____

Don: McDonald   Inchlagan
285 His Wife & 2 Children
_____

Dugald McMillan   Inchlagan
His Wife & 1 Child
_____

Ewen Kennedy   Invergarry
His Wife
290 ~~Christy McLean~~
Peggy Kennedy
_____

Don: McMillan   Paisley
His Wife & 2 Children
_____

Annie McMillan   Paisley
_____

295 Alex'r Kennedy   Laddy
His Wife & 2 Children
_____

Alex'r Cameron   Lochielhead
_____

Marg't McDonald   Munergy
See no 45: Omitted in that family
_____

Dun: McLean's Wife Nr 134 Omitted

Passengers who boarded at Saltcoats near Irvine

Archibald McMillan	Murlaggen	Angus McKay	Shanvall
His Wife & 5 Children		Kenneth McLean	Mull
Thamsina Gray	Maryburgh	Donald McLellan	Glenelg
		Mary McMaster	Oban
Allan McMillan	Glenpean	Alex McMillan	Late Soldier,
His wife Margaret &			Lochaber
Children – Ewen, John,			Regiment
Alexander, James, Donald,		Angus McMillan	Callich
Archibald, Helen, Janet		Don: McMillan	Callop, Glen-finnan
Alexander Cameron	Gortenorn	Donald McMillan	Rellen
Alexander Cameron	Sallachen	Dugald McMillan	Oban
Alexander Cameron	Arkaigside	James McMillan	Knoydart
Donald Cameron	Kirkton	John McMillan	Callich
Duncan Cameron	Drimnasallie	Murdoch McPherson	Noid, Badenoch
John Cameron	Kinlochiel	Dun: McRae	Glenshiel, Kintail
John Cameron	Muick	Gilchrist McRae	Lianish, Kintail
Margaret Cameron	Glengarry	Norman Morrison	Glenelg
John Campbell	Glenelg	John Wright	Millwright, from Ayrshire
Alex: McDonald	Moy, Glen Spean		
Duncan McDonell	Aviemore		

3. The *Oughton*, John Baird (Master). Sailed from Kirkcudbright to Lachine, near Montreal, in May 1804.
[LAC MG24 I8 Vol. 4, 105-8. The names have been resequenced where necessary to keep members of the same family together in separate groups.]

Name	Age	Sex	Remarks
Peter MacDonald	42	Male	
Mary MacDonald	45	Female	
John MacDonald	13	Male	
David MacDonald	12	Male	
Peter MacDonald	5 ½	Male	
Angus MacDonald	31	Male	
Jean MacDonald	40	Female	
Angus MacDonald	3	Male	
Andrew MacDonald	6	Male	
Kath MacDonald	8	Female	
Nancy MacDonald	3 months	Female	
Donald MacCallum	50	Male	
Mary MacCallum	40	Female	
Hugh MacCallum	18	Male	
Isa MacCallum	16	Female	
Flora MacCallum	14	Female	
Amelia MacCallum	9	Female	
Peggy MacCallum	7	Female	
Ann MacCallum	4	Female	
Charles Morrison	49	Male	
Peggy Morrison	34	Female	
Flora Morrison	14	Female	
Christian Morrison	2 ½	Female	
Fa: MacKay	14	Female	
James Morrison	13	Male	
John MacDougald	50	Male	Remained with a sick boy
Sarah MacDougald	47	Female	Remained with a sick boy
Angus MacDougald	17	Male	
John MacDougald	14	Male	
Hector MacDougald	10 ½	Male	Sick
Lauchlan MacDougald	8 ½	Male	Remained with his father
Archibald MacDougald	6	Male	
James MacDougald	2 ½	Male	
Munly MacDougald	18	Female	
Flora MacDougald	4	Female	Remained with father
Allan MacDougald	21	Male	
Ann MacDougald	19	Female	
Mary MacDougald	5 months	Female	
Angus MacPherson	49	Male	
Kirsty MacPherson	43	Female	
Alexander MacPherson	19	Male	
Donald MacPherson	17	Male	
Mary MacPherson	8	Female	
Dugald MacPherson	4	Male	

Name	Age	Sex	Remarks
Alexander MacDonald	35	Male	A piper
Mary MacDonald	30	Female	
John MacDonald	13	Male	
Angus MacDonald	8	Male	
Neil MacDonald	3	Male	
Anne MacDonald	9	Female	
Ann MacDonald	5	Female	
Kath MacDonald	1 ½	Female	
John McKenzie	36	Male	
Ann McKenzie	36	Female	
Keneth McKenzie	10	Male	
Donald McKenzie	8	Male	
Flora McKenzie	6	Female	
John Buchannan	42	Male	
Kath Buchannan	31	Female	
Alexander Buchannan	17	Male	
Robert Buchannan	10	Male	Died on passage from Scotland
John Buchannan	1 ½	Male	
Marion Buchannan	19	Female	
Kath Buchannan	8	Female	
Nelly Buchannan	3 ½	Female	
Donald Buchannan	5 ½	Male	
Donald MacDonald	45	Male	From Laggan
Kath MacDonald	37	Female	
Chrisy MacDonald	15	Female	
Sarah MacDonald	13	Female	
Mary MacDonald	9	Female	
Kath MacDonald	7	Female	
Flora MacDonald	5	Female	
Peggy MacDonald	3	Female	
Angus MacDonald	11	Male	
Donald MacDonald	32	Male	Tiree, Taylor
Flora MacDonald	26	Female	
John MacDonald	6	Male	
Duncan MacDonald	3	Male	
Hugh MacDonald	1 ½	Male	
Donald Brown	38	Male	
Marion Brown	35	Female	
Hector Brown	7	Male	
Alexander Brown	5	Male	
Flora Brown	7	Female	
Neil Brown[1]	n/k		
Allan MacLean	32	Male	
Mary MacLean	30	Female	
Mary McDonald	48	Female	
Kirsty MacLean	10	Female	
Mary MacLean	2 ½	Female	
Hector MacLean	8	Male	
Effie McLean	8 months	Male	

[1] His name was added, at the end, in the original list.

Name	Age	Sex	Remarks
Angus MacDonald	n/k	Male	From Oronsay
Nancy McLaughlin	n/k	Female	
Ann MacLean[2]	n/k	Female	
Allan MacDonald	18	Male	
John MacDonald	16	Male	
Archibald MacDonald	n/k	Male	
Donald MacDonald	n/k	Male	
Hector MacDonald	n/k	Male	
Neil MacDonald	n/k	Male	

[2]Ann MacLean is recorded, in the original list, with the MacDonalds who originated from the Island of Oronsay. She may have been a member of Allan MacLean's family, (listed just above) or had some connection with it.

4. General List of Settlers enrolled for Canada under the Government Regulations at Edinburgh, 1815.

[PRO CO 385/2 ff 3-26]

A total of 757 people enrolled but only 699 actually sailed from Greenock. They sailed to Quebec in one of four ships: *Atlas*, Turnbull (Master) 242 passengers; *Dorothy*, Spence (Master) 194 passengers; *Baltic Merchant*, Jeffreys (Master) 140 passengers; *Eliza*, Telfer (Master) 123 passengers. The *Atlas* sailed on July 11, the *Dorothy* on July 12, the *Baltic Merchant* on July 14 and the *Eliza* on August 3.

The list below provides a summary of data contained in the "General List of Settlers." The full settler list names all members of each family, in each case giving the person's age. Wives are recorded by their maiden names. The deposits which had to be paid by each family head are also recorded together with their former trades or occupation (if changed).

Most of the settlers resided in Scotland but some were English. Where known county or city locations have been indicated within square brackets.

Settlers	Trade or occupation of head of household	Residence in Britain
Duncan McMillan	Farmer and Weaver	Glasgow
Jn Flood	Farmer and Weaver	Anderston [Glasgow]
Wife Janet & 2 ch.		
Jas Bryce	Farmer	West Calder [Midlothian]
Wife Jane & 6 ch.		
Samuel Purdie	Wright	West Calder [Midlothian]
Isobel Purdie		
Hugh McKay	Farmer and Weaver	Gorbals [Glasgow]
Wife Betty & 5 ch.		
Alexr. McFarlane	Labourer	Kilbirnie [Ayrshire]
Wife Ann & 7 ch.		
Moses Shirra	Farmer	Old Kilpatrick [Near Glasgow]
John McNab	Labourer	Gorbals [Glasgow]
Wife Isobel & 4 ch.		
Jn Brash	Plowman	Port Dundas [Glasgow]
Wife Catherine & 3 ch.		
Alex'r McNab	Farmer	Glasgow
Wife Catherine & 2 ch.		
Arch'd Morrison	Farmer	Glasgow
Wm Anderson	Gardener	Edinburgh
Wife Ann & 3 ch.		
John Christie	Gardener	Primrose [Kincardine]
Wife Isobel		
Wm. Old	Labourer	Edinburgh
Wife Agnes & 5 ch.		
Jn. Miller	Labourer	Restonbill
Geo. Wilson	Farmer	Glencapelquay
Wife Isobel & 7 ch.		
Geo. Johnston	Labourer	Wigtown
Wife Nanny		
Thos. Barber	Tailor	Torthorwold [Dumfriesshire]
Wife Janet & 4ch.		
Rob't Newall	Farmer	Hawick [Roxburgh]
Wife Sarah & 2 ch.		
Malcolm McLean	Shepherd	Callander [Perthshire]
Wife Elizabeth & 6 ch.		
Peter McPherson	Labourer	Callander [Perthshire]

Settlers	Trade or occupation of head of household	Residence in Britain
Wife Helen & 6 ch.		
Jas. Maclaren	Weaver	Callander [Perthshire]
Wife Euphemia & 6 ch.		
Jas. MacDonald	Blacksmith	Edinburgh
Wife Margaret & 4 ch.		
Jn. Allan	Labourer	Cockburnspath [Berwickshire]
Francis Allan	Labourer	Edinburgh
Wife Janet & 1 ch.		
Thos. Cuddie	Gardener	Corstophine [Edinburgh]
Wife Marion		
Thos. Duncan	Labourer	Bedlay Inn
Wife Isobel & 4 ch.		
Jn. Ferguson	Farmer	Callander [Perthshire]
Wife Catherine & 7 ch.		
Jn. McDonald	Labourer	Callander [Perthshire]
Wife Ann & 6 ch.		
Jas. Taylor	Labourer & Dyer	Carnwath [Lanarkshire]
Wife Marg. & 5 ch.		
Thos. Borrie	Shoemaker	Dundee [Angus]
Wife Agnes & 9 ch.		
Jn. McNab	Farmer	Inverkeithing [Fife]
Wife Hannah & 2 ch.		
Jn. Cockburn	Shepherd	Mellerstain [Roxburgh]
Wife Jane & 7 ch.		
Jn. Broad	Farmer	Redfordgreen [Peebleshire]
Wife Isobel & 6 ch.		
Jn. Campbell Kerr	Saddler	Edinburgh
Jn. McLaren	Mason	Craignure [Island of Mull]
Wife Janet & 5 ch.		
Jn. Simpson	Shoemaker	Rothes [Morayshire]
Wife Marg. & 5 ch.		
Jn. Halliday	Schoolmaster	Hutton [Dumfriesshire]
Wife Marg't & 7 ch.		
Andrew Beattie	Teacher	Corrie Mill
Wm. Byers	Ploughright	Lochmaben
Wife Rosina & 7 ch.		[Dumfriesshire]
Jas. Gibson	Farmer	Broadladdyke
Wife Helen & 5ch.		
Rob't Wood	Farmer	Inverkeithing [Fife]
Wife Helen & 3 ch.		
David Oliphant	Printer & Labourer	Leith
Wife Clementina & 3 ch.		
Rob't Gardner	Farmer	Paisley
Jn. Ritchie	Blacksmith	Fintry [Stirlingshire]
Wife Janet & 9ch.		
Wm. Wallace	Farmer	Cowden [Perthshire]
Wife Martha & 1 ch.		
Jn. McConachie	Farmer	Moorhouse [England]
Wife Janet & 5 ch.		
John Hay	Labourer	St. Vigeans [Angus]
John Hay	Labourer	St. Vigeans [Angus]
Jas. Fraser	Joiner	Newcastle-upon-Tyne [England]
Wife Ann & 2 ch.		
Peter McDougall	Shoemaker	Fearnan [Perthshire]
Wife Catherine & 3 ch.		
Peter Stewart	Farmer	Balmore [Lanarkshire]
Wife Christian & 5 ch.		

Settlers	Trade or occupation of head of household	Residence in Britain
Duncan Campbell	Weaver	Lawers
Wife Catherine		
Jn. McDougall	Farmer	Carie [Perthshire]
Wife Katherine & 2 ch.		
Arch'd McLaren	Labourer/Weaver	Killin [Perthshire]
John McLeod	Labourer	Glasgow
Wife Janet		
Jas. Crawford	Farmer	Meadowhead
Wife Janet & 2 ch.		
Jn. Ferrier	Labourer/Weaver	Waterside [England]
Wife Charlotte & 4 ch.		
Abraham Ferrier	Labourer/Weaver	Waterside [England]
Wife Christian & 4 ch.		
Jas. Miller	Farmer	West Kilbride [Ayrshire]
Wife Mary & 3 Ch.		
Thos. McLean	Mason	Dunscore [Dumfriesshire]
Jn. McLaren	Farmer	Ledcharie [Perthshire]
Wife Susan & 7 ch.		
David McLaren	Farmer	Killin [Perthshire]
Wife Catherine & 6 ch.		
Jn. McDonald	Mason	Killin [Perthshire]
Wife Christian & 2 ch.		
Alex'r McDonald	Mason	Killin [Perthshire]
Wife Marjory		
Allan McDiarmid	Weaver	Killin [Perthshire]
Wife Janet & 3 ch.		
Jn. Oliver	Farmer	Kilmarnock [Ayrshire]
Wife Mary & 6 ch.		
Peter Gibson	Labourer	Muirkirk [Ayrshire]
Jas. Gibson	Labourer	Muirkirk [Ayrshire]
Jn. McDonald	Surgeon	Edinburgh
Wife Margaret		
Alex'r Laing	Farmer	Old Deer [Aberdeenshire]
Wife Ann & 4 ch.		
Wm. Hay	Farmer	Lonmay [Aberdeenshire]
Wife Ann & 9 ch.		
Alex'r McLaren	Carpenter	Killin [Perthshire]
Wife Marg't		
Wm. Holderness	Farmer	Spaldington [England]
Wife Ann & 6 ch.		
Hugh Fraser	Carpenter	Killin [Perthshire]
Wife Elizabeth & 5 ch.		
Wm. Rutherford	Wright	Liff [Angus]
Wm. Spalding	Mason	Liff [Angus]
Alex'r Spalding (brother)	Mason	Liff [Angus]
Duncan McGregor	Labourer	Killin [Perthshire]
Wife Christian & 3 ch.		
Joseph Holdsworth	Schoolmaster	Wakefield [England]
James Drysdale	Farmer	Drumtuthel
Wife Christian & 5 ch.		
Alex'r Simpson	Labourer	Longbride
Jn. Spalding	Weaver	Paisley
Wife Joan & 6 ch.		
Alex'r Kydd	House Carpenter	St. Andrews [Fife]
Duncan McArthur	Labourer	Killin [Perthshire]
Wife Christian & 2 ch.		
Allan McDonell	Labourer	Fort Augustus

Settlers	Trade or occupation of head of household	Residence in Britain
Wife Ann & 3 ch.		[Inverness-shire]
Wm. McGillivray	Labourer	Barrowfield [Glasgow]
Wife Isobel & 6 ch.		
Farquhar Smith	Labourer	Barrowfield [Glasgow]
Wife Margaret & 2 ch.		
Thos. Smith	Labourer	Barrowfield [Glasgow]
Don'd McGillivray	Labourer	Barrowfield [Glasgow]
Wife Janet & 3 ch.		
Don'd McDonald	House Carpenter	Killin [Perthshire]
Wife Ann & 2 ch.		
Roderick McRae	Farmer	Glenelg [Inverness-shire]
Wife Marion & 4 ch.		
Jon McRae	Farmer	Glenelg [Inverness-shire]
Wife Janet & 1 ch.		
Jn. Fraser	Farmer	Glenelg [Inverness-shire]
Wife Marg't & 5 ch.		
Alex'r McRae	Farmer	Glenelg [Inverness-shire]
Wife Cath'ne & 3 ch.		
Malcolm McRae	Farmer	Glenelg [Inverness-shire]
Wife Rebecca & 4 ch.		
John McRae	Farmer	Glenelg [Inverness-shire]
Wife Marion & 5ch.		
Jn. McCrimmon	Farmer	Glenelg [Inverness-shire]
Wife Cath'ne & 5 ch.		
Farquhar McCrimmon	Farmer	Glenelg [Inverness-shire]
Wife Cath'ne		
Rob't Davison	Labourer	Liverpool [England]
Wife Mary Ann		
Chas Baker	Farmer	Penkridge [Staffordshire]
Henry Baker	Farmer	Penkridge [Staffordshire]
Wife Elenor & 2 ch.		
Jn. McDonald	Labourer & Pensioner	Edinburgh
Wm. Jamieson	Labourer	Muirkirk [Ayrshire]
Janet Jamison (sister)		
Duncan McLaren	Weaver	Killin [Perthshire]
Wife Annabella & 5 ch.		
Don'd McPhee	Wright	Ardgour [Argyll]
Wife Cath'ne & 6 ch.		
Andrew Donaldson	Farmer	Kinglassie [Fife]
Wife Marg't & 1 ch.		
David Donaldson (his son)		
Margaret Donaldson (sister)		
Thos. Donaldson	Farmer	Kinglassie [Fife]
Isobella Donaldson (sister)		
Andrew Donaldson (his brother)	Farmer	Kinglassie [Fife]
John Donaldson (his bro.)	Farmer	Kinglassie [Fife]
Jas. Donaldson (his bro.)	Farmer	Kinglassie [Fife]
David Donaldson (brother in law)	Farmer	Kinglassie [Fife]
Jean Donaldson		
Thos. Jeffryes	Farmer	Edinburgh
Wife Isobella & 1 ch.		
Jos. Jeffryes	Farmer	Edinburgh
Duncan McDonell	Labourer	Fort Augustus
Wife Isobella & 3 ch.		[Inverness-shire]
Ewen Bethune	Labourer	Glenelg [Inverness-shire]

Settlers	Trade or occupation of head of household	Residence in Britain
Don'd McDonald	Labourer	Glasgow
Wife Mary & 5 ch.		
Wm. Johnston	Farmer	Stobotule [Peeblesshire]
Wife Janet & 1 ch.		
Thos. Scott	Labourer/Tailor	Tundergarth
Wife Janet & 2 ch.		[Dumfriesshire]
Alex. McDonell	Farmer	Knoydart
Wife Janet & 10 ch.		[Inverness-shire]
Ronald McDonell	Farmer	Knoydart
Wife Florence & 6 ch.		[Inverness-shire]
Jn. McDonell	Farmer	Knoydart
Wife Cath'ne & 4 ch.		[Inverness-shire]
Ron'd McDonell	Farmer	Knoydart
Wife Mary & 3 ch.		[Inverness-shire]
Duncan McDonell	Farmer	Knoydart
Wife Mary & 5 ch.		[Inverness-shire]
Angus McDonald	Farmer	Knoydart
Wife Jean & 2 ch.		[Inverness-shire]
Donald McDougale	Farmer	Knoydart
Wife Christian		[Inverness-shire]
Jas. McDougale	Farmer	Knoydart
Wife Mary		[Inverness-shire]
Alex'r McDougale	Farmer	Knoydart
Arch'd McDougale	Farmer	Knoydart
Wife Jean & 4 ch.		[Inverness-shire]
Jn. McDonell	Farmer	Knoydart
Wife Florence & 4 ch.		[Inverness-shire]
Duncan McLeoir	Farmer	Knoydart
Wife Janet & 4 ch.		[Inverness-shire]
Jn. McIntosh	Farmer	Glenelg [Inverness-shire]
Wife Mary & 2 ch.		
Alex'r McRae	Farmer	Glenelg [Inverness-shire]
Wife Marg't & 8 ch.		
Malcolm McLeod	Farmer	Glenelg [Inverness-shire]
Wife Ann & 3 ch.		
Don'd McCummon	Labourer	Glenelg [Inverness-shire]
Duncan McCummon	Labourer	Glenelg [Inverness-shire]
Don'd Campbell	Farmer	Glenelg [Inverness-shire]
Wife Cath'ne & 6 ch.		
Jn. McGillivray	Farmer	Glenelg [Inverness-shire]
Wife Marg't		
Malcolm McCraig	Farmer	Glenelg [Inverness-shire]
Wife Cath'ne & 3 ch.		
John McCraig	Farmer	Glenelg [Inverness-shire]
Wife Cath'ne & 2 ch.		
Kenneth McRae	Farmer	Glenelg [Inverness-shire]
Wife Marion & 3 ch.		
Roderick McLennon	Farmer	Glenelg [Inverness-shire]
John McRae	Farmer	Glenelg [Inverness-shire]
Wife Cath'ne & 5 ch.		
Finlay McRae	Farmer	Glenelg [Inverness-shire]
Wife Cath'ne & 1 ch.		
Christopher McRae	Farmer	Glenshiel [Ross-shire]
Wife Marg't & 4 ch.		
Donald McPherson	Labourer	Anderston [Glasgow]
Wife Marg't & 3 ch.		
Duncan McDonell	Farmer	Knoydart

Settlers	Trade or occupation of head of household	Residence in Britain
Wife Janet & 3 ch.		[Inverness-shire]
Jn. McDonald	Labourer	Fort Augustus
Wife Eliz'th & 2 ch.		[Inverness-shire]
George Gray	Farmer	Banff [Banffshire]
Wife Isobel & 8 ch.		
Alex'r Kidd	Cartwright	Blackburn
Wife Christian & 7 ch.		
Jn. Jameson	Shoemaker	Muirkirk [Ayrshire]
Rob't Gibson	Stocking	Edinburgh
Wife Jean & 5 ch.	(manufacturer?)	
Duncan McCraig	Labourer	Glenelg [Inverness-shire]
Wife Marion & 2 ch.		
Jn. Johnston	Farmer	Craighouse [Isle of Jura]
David Wilson	Farmer	Beith [Ayrshire]
Wife Janet & 6 ch.		
Jas. Stevenson	Farmer	Beith [Ayrshire]
Duncan McLellan	Farmer	Glenelg [Inverness-shire]
Wife Ann & 3 ch.		
Wm. Campbell	Farmer	Glenelg [Inverness-shire]
Wife Cristian & 4 ch.		
Peter McIntosh	Shoemaker	Killin [Perthshire]
Wife Eliza & 3 ch.		
Peter Morison	Mason	Finlarig [Perthshire]
Wife Mary & 4 ch.		
Duncan McDougall	Farmer	Knoydart
Wife Ann & 4 ch.		[Inverness-shire]
Jn. Gray	Farmer	Banff [Banffshire]

5. The *Curlew*, John Young (Master). Sailed from Greenock to Quebec with settlers from Perthshire, July 21, 1818.
(The original list records the names of all children together with their ages.)
[PRO CO 384/3 ff. 123-7]

Blair Atholl parish
John Stewart
Ellen Stewart & 1 ch.
John Robertson
Alex'r Stewart
Marg't Stewart

Dull parish
Rob't Scott
Marg't Scott & 1 ch.
John Scott
Marg't Scott
Alex'r Douglas
Eliz'th Douglas
Rob't Scott
Nelly Scott
Alex'r McNaughton
Eliz'th McNaughton
John Stewart
Eliz'th Stewart
Duncan Cameron
Mary Cameron & 2 ch.
Hugh McDiarmid
Jannet McDiarmid & 2 ch.
Findlay Cameron
Jannet Cameron
John Kennedy
Marg't Kennedy & 2 ch.
Alex'r McTavish
Cath'ne McTavish & 2 ch.
Don. Robertson
Cath'ne Robertson
Don. Robertson
Jannet Robertson
John Robertson
Cath'ne Robertson
Peter Robertson
Duncan Robertson
Marg't Robertson & 2 ch.
John McTavish
Marg't McTavish & 2 ch.
John McTavish
Cath'ne McTavish
Donald Levingston
Jannet Levingston & 3 ch.
John McTavish

Killin parish
John Robertson
Jannet Robertson & 2 ch.
Duncan McNab
Cath'ne McNab & 3 ch.
James McLean

Killin parish
Jannet McLean & 1 ch.
Jannet Stewart (wife)
Duncan Campbell
Cath'ne Campbell & 3 ch.
Duncan McKay
Jannet McKay & 1 ch.
John McLaren
Cath'ne McLaren & 2 ch.
Mary McVean (wife)
Arch'd McDiarmid
Mary McDiarmid & 2 ch.

Comrie parish
James McArthur
Ann McArthur & 3 ch.
John McArthur
Cath'ne McArthur & 2 ch.
Rob't McGregor
Mary McGregor & 2 ch.
Donald Ferguson
Mary Ferguson
Rob't Ferguson
Christine Ferguson
John Ferguson
Mary Ferguson
Duncen Ferguson
Ann Ferguson
James Ferguson
Christine Ferguson & 2 ch.
John Carmichael
Ann Carmichael
John McLaren
Jannet McLaren & 1 ch.
John McLaren
Jannet McLaren & 2 ch.
Colin McLaren
Christine McLaren & 2 ch.
James McCowan
Jannet McCowan
Wm. McEwan & 1 ch.
John McEwan & 1 ch.
Duncan Anderson & 2 ch.
Peter McGregor
Christin McGregor
John McGregor
Duncan McCowan & 2 ch.
Donald Clark
Marg't Clark
Alex'r Clark
Jannet Clark & 1 ch.
John McVie
Jannet McVie & 2 ch.

Comrie parish
Arch'd Dewar
Marg't Dewar & 2 ch.
Malcolm Dewar
Ann Dewar & 2 ch.
John Dewar
Peter Dewar
Duncan McCallum
Christine McCallum & 1 ch.
Duncan McCallim & 2ch.
Duncan McDiarmid
Mary McDiarmid & 2 ch.
Malcolm Drummond
Christine Drummond & 2 ch.
John Gow
Jannet Gow
John Cram
Isabella Cram & 1 ch.
Peter Comrie
Jane Comrie & 2 ch.

Muthill parish
David Stewart
Cath'ne Stewart & 2 ch.

Callander parish
Alex'r McGregor
Jannet McGregor & 3 ch.
James McInnes
Marion McInnes & 1 ch.

Little Dunkeld parish
John McEwan
Cath'ne McEwan & 2 ch.

Balquhidder parish
Malcolm Fisher
Christine Fisher & 5 ch.
Mary Fisher (wife)

Totals
Settlers	66
Wives	59
Children 12–17 years	13
Under 12 years	67

6. The *Sophia* of Ayr, Moore (Master). Sailed from Greenock to Quebec with settlers from Perthshire on July 26, 1818.

(The original list records the names of all children together with their ages.)

[PRO CO 384/3 ff.133-4]

Balquhidder parish
Alex'r McGregor
Mary McGregor & 1 ch.
Arch'd McGregor
Jannet McGregor & 2 ch.
Peter McGregor
Catherine McGregor & 2 ch.
Donald McLaren
Marjori McLaren & 6 ch.
Donald Munroe
Mary Munroe & 3 ch.
Finlay McEwen
Mary McEwen & 7 ch.
Duncan Ferguson
Isabella Ferguson & 2 ch.
John McVie
Jannet McVie & 5 ch.
John McGregor
Cath'ne McGregor & 1 ch.
Peter McGregor
Mary McGregor & 2 ch.

Kincardine parish
Don'd Ferguson
Cath'ne Ferguson & 4 ch.
Robert Ferguson
Jane Ferguson
Peter Ferguson
Jannet Ferguson

Kincardine parish
Daniel Ferguson
Mary Ferguson, settler
John Folford
Jannet Folford & 2 ch.
John King
Jannet King & 4 ch.
John King
Duncan King
Christine King, settler
Cath'ne King, settler

Killin parish
John Campbell
Mary Campbell & 6 ch.
Donald McIntyre
Isabella McIntyre & 2 ch.

Kenmore parish
John Anderson
Isabella Anderson & 6 ch.
Peter Anderson
Christine Anderson & 6 ch.

Totals

Settlers	22
Wives	23
Children 12-17 years	11
Children under 12 years	50

7. *Commerce* of Greenock, Coverdale (Master). Sailed from Greenock to Quebec in June 1820.

[LAC RG8 Vol. 625 ff. 219-23][1]

No.	Name	Age	Sex	Head of Household's Occupation	Place	Former residence Parish	County
1	John Cumming	39	m	Labourer	Bridgeton	Barony	Lanark-
2	Mary Cumming	39	f			[Glasgow]	shire
3	Catherine Cumming	12 ½	f				
4	John Cumming	3 ½	m				
5	Mary Cumming	6	f				
6	Agnes & Ann twins)	2	f				
7	Daniel Cumming	37	m	Labourer	Johnstone	Abbey	Renfrew-
8	Agnes Cumming	37	f			[Paisley]	shire
9	Daniel Cumming	14	m				
10	Agnes Cumming	11	f				
11	Archibald Cumming	8	m				
12	John Cumming	6	m				
13	Mair Cumming	3	f				
14	Archibald Cumming	4	m				
15	Archibald Cumming	35	m	Labourer	"	"	"
16	Eleanor Cumming	38	f				
17	David Cumming	2	m				
18	Paul Cumming	21	m	Cotton Spinner	Bridgeton	Barony	Lanark-
						[Glasgow]	shire
19	Geo. Muir Cumming	60	m				
20	Anne Cumming	26	f	Cotton Spinner	"	"	"
21	Jannet Cumming	22	f	Cotton Spinner	"	"	"
22	Charles Isdell	31	m	Wright	Cowcaddens	"	Lanark-
23	Mary Isdell	32	f				shire
24	Mary Isdell	10	f				
25	Jean Isdell	8	f				
26	James Isdell	5	m				
27	Jannet Isdell	3	f				
28	William McIntyre	24	m	Cotton Spinner	Bridgeton	"	Lanark-
29	Rebecca McIntyre	26	f				shire
30	Robert Ferguson	31	m	Weaver	Bridgeton	"	Lanark-
31	Agnes Ferguson	32	f				shire
32	James Ferguson	3	m				
33	John Robertson	38	m	Weaver	Bridgeton	Barony	Lanark-
34	Jannet Robertson	37	f			[Glasgow]	shire
35	Robert Robertson	42	m	Weaver	"	"	"
36	Spencer Robertson	7	m				
37	Anne Robertson	5	f				
38	John Robertson	2	m				
39	Thomas Robertson	1 mo	m				

[1] The passenger list also gives the height, hair colour and complexion of each person. Their stated purpose in emigrating was "to earn subsistence by industry in America for which they engage to pay £3. 5s. for every adult and so in proportion for those under age." The passenger list only records 177 of the 402 people who actually sailed on this crossing.

No.	Name	Age	Sex	Household's Occupation	Former residence Place	Former residence Parish	Former residence County
40	William Browne	22	m	Shoemaker	Calton	"	Lanark-
41	Jannet Browne	19	f				shire
42	Alexander Mercer	23	m	Taylor	Rutherglen	Rutherglen	
43	John Mair	21	m	Shoemaker	"	"	"
44	Jean Mair	21	f				
45	James Lindsay	28	m	Shoemaker	Calton	Barony	"
46	Jean Lindsay	21	f			[Glasgow]	
47	Catherine Lindsay	10	f				
48	John Lindsay	7	m				
49	James Lindsay	5 ½	m				
50	Matthew Kirkwood	40	m	Sawer	Gorbals	Gorbals	"
51	Margaret Kirkwood	35	f			[Glasgow]	
52	Agnes Kirkwood	12 ½	f				
53	Matthew Kirkwood	8	m				
54	Jannet Kirkwood	5 ½	f				
55	David Hamilton	30	m	Joiner	Rutherglen	Rutherglen	"
56	Thomas Bullock	36	m	Labourer	Glasgow	Barony	"
57	Jannet Bullock	30				[Glasgow]	
58	James Bullock	13	m				
59	William Bullock	11	m				
60	Catherine Bullock	9	f				
61	Robert Bullock	7	m				
62	Thomas Bullock	5	m				
63	Isabell Bullock	4	f				
64	John Bullock	2	m				
65	John Galbraith	33	m	Weaver	Glasgow	Barony	Lanark-
66	Isabell Galbraith	25	f			[Glasgow]	shire
67	William Galbraith	3	m				
68	Isabell Galbraith	2 mos.	F				
69	James Rae	29	m	Weaver	Bridgeton	"	"
70	Mary Rae	20	f				
71	James Colquohoun	43	m	Sawyer	Glasgow	"	"
72	Mary Colquohoun	35	f				
73	Alex'r Colquohoun	13	m				
74	Arthur Colquohoun	12	m				
75	Elizabeth Colquohoun	9	f				
76	Marrion Colquohoun	7	f				
77	Mary Colquohoun	5	f				
78	Agnes Colquohoun	2	f				
79	Uphemia Mercer[2]	20	f				
80	William Wilson	34	m	Weaver	Anderston	"	"
81	Anne Wilson	28	f				
82	Jean Wilson	8	f				
83	Thomas Wilson	6	m				
84	Catherine Wilson	1	f				

[2] This is the wife of Alex. Mercer at No 42 of this list.

No.	Name	Age	Sex	Household's Occupation	Former residence Place	Parish	County
85	Robert Cannan	47	m	Weaver	Bridgeton	"	"
86	Mary Cannan	50	f				
87	James Bell	30	m	Weaver	"	"	"
88	Robert Cannan	24	m	Weaver	"	"	"
89	Robert Cannan	2	m				
90	David Ballatine	29	m	Weaver	"	"	"
91	Mary Ballatine	30	f				
92	Mary Ballatine	2	f				
93	Matthew Ballatine	3 mos	m				
94	Alex Wylie	22	m	Weaver	"	"	"
95	Margaret Wylie	22	f				
96	Mary Wylie	3 mos	f				
97	John Blair	34	m	Dyer	Leigh Kirk	"	"
98	Archibald Bullock	36	m	Weaver	Leigh Kirk	Barony [Glasgow]	Lanark-shire
99	Jannet Bullock	30	f				
100	John Bullock	11	m				
101	Elizabeth Bullock	10	f				
102	James Bullock	8	m				
103	Archibald Bullock	5	m				
104	William Bullock	3	m				
105	Walter Bullock	1	m				
106	James Bullock	26	m				
107	David Bower	32	m	Wright	Bridgeton	"	"
108	Anne Bower	34	f				
109	Anne Bower	8	f				
110	Christian Bower	5	f				
111	John Bower	3	m				
112	James Bower	½	m				
113	John Henderson	41	m	Weaver	Cambuslang	Cambuslang	"
114	Anne Henderson	36	f				
115	John Henderson	1	m				
116	Peter Reid	39	m	Weaver	Bridgeton	Barony [Glasgow]	"
117	Jean Reid	36	f				
118	William Reid	11	m				
119	Ellinor Reid	9	f				
120	Jean Reid	7	f				
121	Peter Reid	4	m				
122	Elizabeth Reid	1	f				
123	Gilbert Forgie	46	m	Weaver	Govan	Govan	"
124	Margaret Forgie	35	f				
125	Jean Forgie	58	f				
126	Ellinor Forgie	20	f				
127	Graham Forgie	16	m				
128	Thomas Forgie	14	m				
129	Margaret Lockard	14	f				
130	Martha Forgie	12	f				
131	Elizabeth Forgie	10	f				
132	Mary Forgie	8	f				

No.	Name	Age	Sex	Household's Occupation	Former residence Place	Parish	County
133	Isabell Forgie	6	f				
134	Ann Forgie	8	f				
135	Jannet Forgie	3	f				
136	Alexander Forgie	1 ½	m				
137	Robert James	34	m	Taylor	Cambuslang	Cambuslang	Lanark-shire
138	Margaret James	35	f				
139	Elizabeth James	10	f				
140	Margaret James	7	f				
141	Catherine James	5	f				
142	William James	3	m				
143	John James	½	m				
144	Peter Barr	28	m	Smith	Bridge of Weir	n/k	Renfrew-shire
145	Peter Munro	47	m	Weaver	Paisley	High Church [Paisley]	Renfrew-shire
146	Mary Munro	43	f				
147	Catherine Munro	17	f				
148	John Munro	15	m				
149	Mary Munro	13	f				
150	Christian Munro	11	f				
151	Peter Munro	7	m				
152	Margaret Munro	3	f				
153	Jannet Munro	1	f				
154	Robert Fleming	32	m	Labourer	Calton	Barony [Glasgow]	Lanark-shire
155	Ellinor Fleming	32	f				
156	Ellinor Fleming	6	f				
157	Agnes Fleming	4	f				
158	James Fleming	1	m				
159	Mary Ballantine	13	f				
160	William Ballantine	8	m				
161	David Ballantine	4	m				
162	Hugh Ballantine	1 ½	m				
163	Alex McInnes	50	m	Weaver	Parkhead	Barony [Glasgow]	"
164	Jean McInnes	48	f				
165	John McInnes	25	m	Weaver	"	"	"
166	James McInnes	23	m	Weaver	"	"	"
167	Alex McInnes	19	m	Shoemaker	"	"	"
168	Edward McInnes	13	m				
169	Thomas McInnes	9	m				
170	Donald McKinnon	60	m	Printer	Anderston	Barony [Glasgow]	Lanark-shire
171	Sarah McKinnon	47	f				
172	John McKinnon	20	m	Printer	Anderston	"	"
173	Hugh McKinnon	18	m				
174	Elizabeth McKinnon	15	f				
175	Alex McKinnon	15	m				
176	Henry McKinnon	8	m				
177	Catherine Lindsay	38	f		Glasgow	"	"

8. George Canning, Potter (Master). Sailed from Greenock to Quebec on April 14, 1821, with 490 passengers from eleven emigration societies.

(The original list gives the names of all family members together with their ages and details of payments made for their fares.)

[PRO CO 42/189 ff.512-69]

Note: # Denotes president of emigration society. Number in parentheses after family head denotes number in family.

Family Head	Emigration Society	Family Head	Emigration Society
#Jas. Yuill Sen'r (8)	Abercrombie (1)	Walter Bain (4)	Bridgeton Transatlantic
#Jas. Yuill Jn'r (2)	"	Thos. Paterson (1)	"
John Dunlop (4)	"	Jas. Black (1)	"
John Stewart (8)	"	Andrew Brown (6)	"
Arch'd Stewart (3)	"		
Alex'r Stewart (1)	"	#John McPhearson (6)	Cambuslang
		Thos. Dobbie (7)	"
#Jas. Borrowman (9)	Barrowfield Rd	Wm. McMillan (7)	"
Hugh Anderson (1)	"	Hugh Park (6)	"
Andrew McKean (4)	"	Jas. Park (5)	"
Hugh Hunter (4)	"	Rob't Scott (7)	"
Duncan McIntosh (3)	"	Jas. McIlquham (7)	"
John McWhinnie (6)	"	Peter McIlquham (1)	"
Wm. Creighton (6)	"	Rob't Carswell (1)	"
John Moore (6)	"	Rob't Mason (7)	"
Hugh Sinclair (6)	"	John Miller (4)	"
Alex'r Matthie (5)	"	Wm. Gourlay (5)	"
Frederic McLea (7)	"	John Reid (2)	"
Wm. Croom (6)	"	Jas. Wilkie (4)	"
Alex'r Morrison (3)	"		
Peter Dunlop (1)	"	#Walter Black (7)	Glasgow Canadian
		Robert Purdon (6)	"
#John Kilpatrick (7)	Bridgeton Canadian	Andrew Smith (8)	"
John Bruce (4)	"	Crawford Gunn (2)	"
Ephraim Kilpatrick (7)	"	Jas. Miller (5)	"
George Steel (7)	"	Duncan Bain (4)	"
Hugh McMillan (4)	"		
Thomas Falconer (6)	"	Wm. Miller (7)	Glasgow Canadian
William Stirling (7)	"	David Stewart (2)	"
George Cummings (2)	"	Andrew Miller (1)	"
Arch'd Cummings (1)	"	Alex'r Galbraith (4)	"
Jas. Hendrick (8)	"	George Sutherland (9)	"
Thomas Leslie (1)	"	David Sutherland (1)	"
Jas. Calder (4)	"		
Donald McKinnon (5)	"	#Duncan McInnes (6)	Glasgow Jnr Wrights
John McKinnon (Jnr) (1)	"	George Charters (3)	"
John McKinnon (Snr) (5)	"	George Stevenson (2)	"
		Wm. Lockhead (7)	"
#Jas. Braidwood (7)	Bridgeton Transatlantic	Rob't Cameron (9)	"
Wm. McQueen (7)	"	Jas. Beveridge (3)	"
John Graham (7)	"		
Jas. Colquhoun (6)	"	#Wm. McEwan (3)	Glasgow Loyal Agr'l
Angus Colquhoun (5)	"	Daniel MacPherson (2)	"
Wm. Pollock (6)	"	John More (6)	"
Alex'r Goodwin (8)	"	Jas. McMurtie (2)	"
Walter Stirling (4)	"	John Barr (5)	"
Alex'r White (5)	"	John McPherson (1)	"
Jas. Stewart (1)	"	#Rob't McLaren (6)	Glasgow Sr. Wrights
Mrs. McLennan (3)	"	Ninian Frame (4)	"

Family Head	Emigration Society	Family Head	Emigration Society
Neil McQuarrie (1)	Glasgow Sr. Wrights	#Jas. Aitkenhead	Strathhaven & Kilbride
Wm. White (2)	"	Jas. Leitch (6)	"
Andrew Blair (4)	"	Robert Baird (8)	"
Jas. Paterson (2)	"	Wm. Baird (1)	"
Jas. Allan (1)	"	Jas. Paterson (8)	"
Alex'r Murray (1)	"	John Riddell (1)	"
#Jas. Paul (1)	Glasgow Union	Jas. Smith (1)	"
David McLay (1)	"	Rob't Struthers (1)	"
Jas. Heatherington (5)	"	Wm. Law (1)	"
Montgomery Paul (4)	"	Wm. Flemming (3)	"
Arch'd Provan (3)	"	John Munro (1)	"
Hugh McLay (2)	"		

9. *Earl of Buckinghamshire*, Johnston (Master). Sailed from Greenock to Quebec on April 29, 1821, with 607 passengers from seven emigration societies.

(The original list gives the names of all family members together with their ages and details of payments made for their fares.)

[PRO CO 42/189 ff 512-69]

Note: # Denotes president of emigration society. Number in parentheses after family head denotes number in family.

Family Head	Emigration Society	Family Head	Emigration Society
#Thomas Craig (3)	Brownfield & Anderston	John Nairn (6)	Paisley Townhead
John McPherson (1)	"	John Porter (6)	"
William Blair (2)	"	James Hart (4)	"
James Craig (1)	"	James Gemmell (4)	"
John Downie (1)	"	Arthur Stoaks Snr. (6)	"
Andrew McAlpin (6)	"	Arthur Stoaka Jnr. (1)	"
David Adam (1)	"	Robert Craig (4)	"
John Closs (1)	"	James Bryson (7)	"
Lauchlan McLean (9)	"	William Christielaw (6)	"
Robert Menzies (1)	"	Archibald Nairn (8)	"
James Johnston (4)	"	Matthew McFarlane (5)	"
		James McFarlane (1)	"
#William McLellan (10)	Cathcart	Robert McFarlane (2)	"
James Machan (5)	"	John Smith (6)	"
James Bankhead (6)	"	John Rorison (7)	"
John Morrison (1)	"	Robert Duncan (9)	"
John McDougall (1)	"	William Wilson (5)	"
James McLellan (5)	"	Hugh McPhail (3)	"
		James King (3)	"
#James Gilmour (6)	Lanarkshire	Robert Muir (1)	"
William Gilmour (1)	"	Peter McGregor (4)	"
William Miller (1)	"	Thomas Ferguson (8)	"
William Moir (6)	"	John Hart (7)	"
Thomas Buchanan (1)	"	Josiah Davies (11)	"
Alexander McVicar (7)	"	Peter Hutchison (6)	"
John McVicar (1)	"	James Mitchell (5)	"
John Virtue (6)	"		
Matthew Virtue (1)	"	Alexander Young (8)	Townhead ctd.
Gilbert Fleck (2)	"	John Armour (4)	"
		John Shaw (6)	"
#James Brown (4)	Lesmahagow	Anthony McBryde (2)	"
James Brooks (8)	"	Daniel Currie (4)	Paisley
John Lockhart (5)	"	James Crawford (8)	"
John Winning (1)	"	James McIlreath (5)	"
Alex'r Cunningham (5)	"	James Nisbet (5)	"
		William Caldwell (7)	"
#John Hutchison (3)	Mile End	John McLachlan (6)	"
		Thomas Bridget (5)	"
William Paul (4)	Mile End Ctd.	Daniel Hay (4)	"
John Buchanan (5)	"	Peter Davidson (6)	"
William McGee (7)	"	John Stewart (3)	"
Hugh Cherry (5)	"	Matthew McFarlane Jnr (6)	"
John Hutchison (3)	"	Alexander Duncan (8)	"
		Robert Adams (2)	"
#Daniel Ritchie	Paisley Townhead	William Taylor (1)	"
David Wylie (5)	"	Alexander Bain (11)	"
William Hamilton (4)	"	David Smith (8)	"
John Fumerton (4)	"	Owen Crilly (3)	"
Hugh Millar (4)	"	James eason (1)	"

Family Head	Emigration Society	Family Head	Emigration Society
George Eason (1)	Paisley	James Kattan (3)	Parkhead (Paisley)
Ebenezer Wilson (6)	"	George Herron (6)	"
Alexander Hill (9)	"	George Henderson (2)	"
John Neilson (6)	"		
John McLaren (6)	"	Robert Twaddle (10)	Parkhead (Paisley)
George Watson (6)	"		
John Anderson (6)	"	William Wilson (7)	"
Mrs. Parkin (4)	"	John Mitchell (9)	"
William Lambie (8)	"	Stewart Houston (6)	"
James Thomson (5)	"	John Burns (3)	"
Mrs. Campbell (1)	"	Thomas Hall (1)	"
Mrs. Thomson wife of		Thomas Turnbull (1)	"
James Thomson (1)	"	Gavin Smilie (1)	"
		George Gray (1)	"
#William Wallace (7)	Parkhead (Paisley)	William Houston (1)	"
William Davie (8)	"	Thomas Twaddle (1)	"
John Dunlop (8)	"	Robert Smith (1)	"
Robert Finlay (7)	"	John Mitchell (1)	"
Wm. Hammond (5)	"	Margaret McEwan (1)	"
George Aikenson (6)	"	John Smith (2)	"
Robert Smith (5)	"	Duncan McDougall (7)	"
John Leckie (11)	"	Archibald McDougall (1)	"
Thomas McLellan (1)	"		

10. *Commerce* of Greenock, Coverdale (Master). Sailed from Greenock to Quebec on May 11, 1821, from Greenock to Quebec with 422 passengers from eight emigration societies. (The original list gives the names of all family members together with their ages and details of payments made for their fares.)

[PRO CO 42/189 ff 512-69]

Note: # Denotes president of emigration society. Number in parentheses after family head denotes number in family.

Family Head	Emigration Society	Family Head	Emigration Society
#William Bryce Snr. (4)	Camlachie	#John Miller (8)	North Albion
William Rutherford (4)	"	William Graham (1)	"
And^w Buchanan Somerville (3)	"	John Parkin (2)	"
William McCallum (7)	"	Peter Baxter (1)	"
Robert Young (1)	"		
Andrew Liddle (6)	"	#Alexander Wark (5)	Rutherglen Union
Robert Love (5)	"	William Atlan (5)	"
William Robertson (3)	"	James Cochran (7)	"
John Henderson (2)	"	Duncan Campbell (2)	"
William Bryce (1)	"	Archibald Campbell (1)	"
Jonathan Tomlinson (9)	"	William Henderson (7)	"
James McConnell (4)	"	James King (1)	"
Richard McConnell (2)	"	Alx'r Graham's Wife (3)	"
Henry Thomson (8)	"	James Sneddon (4)	"
John McCall (3)	"	John Toshack Snr. (9)	"
Robert Pinkerton (1)	"	William Toshack (1)	"
Alexander Steel (6)	"	James McEndrick (2)	"
Robert Craig (6)	"	Angus Hood (1)	"
Thomas Strachan (7)	"	Mrs. Bainie (1)	"
Robert Hay (4)	"	William Anderson (8)	"
Archibald Browning (5)	"	John Paul (8)	"
William Preastly (1)	"	Samuel Gemmill (1)	"
		Andrew Angus (1)	"
#Andrew Hill (8)	Govan	Adam Paterson (4)	"
Andrew Climie (9)	"	Robert Sym (1)	"
William Robertson (7)	"	John Warnock (3)	"
James Young (4)	"		
		James Miller (6)	Rutherglen Union ctd.
#Robert Chalmers (8)	Hamilton	Archibald Buchanan (6)	"
James Scott (1)	"	Alexander Bodin (5)	"
Dugald Ferguson (4)	"	James Smith (6)	"
Archibald Thomson (4)	"	James Buchanan (2)	"
John Lowrie (8)	"	Betty Brown wife of	
John Crawford (6)	"	Robert Nisbet (4)	"
George McNeish (7)	"	John Angus (5)	"
William Barr (1)	"	John Toshack Jnr. (1)	"
Juhn Tully (10)	"		
Thomas Reid (3)	"	#Hugh Campbell (5)	Spring Bank (1)
		Joseph Campbell (2)	"
William Brownlie (1)	Hamilton	John Dunn (2)	"
David Brownlie (1)	"	Simon Alcorn (3)	"
Robert Gardner (3)	"	Robert Campbell (6)	"
John Stark (1)	"	James Barr (4)	"
John Muir (8)	"	John Campbell (10)	"
Thomas Muir (1)	"	Neil Barr (1)	"
John Brownlie (1)	"		
#James Donaldson (6)	Kirkman Finlay		
John Hamilton (3)	"		
David McIntyre (5)	"		

Family Head	Emigration Society	Family Head	Emigration Society
#Robert Grant (5)	St. John's Parish	Alexander Nicholson (3)	St. John's Parish
John Cobb (6)	"	John McIntosh (4)	"
Andrew McBeath (5)	"	Alexander Grahame (6)	"

11. *David* of London, David Gemmil (Master). Sailed from Greenock to Quebec on May 19, 1821, with 364 passengers from nine emigration societies.

(The original list gives the names of all family members together with their ages and details of payments made for their fares.)

[PRO CO 42/189 ff 512-69]

Note: # Denotes president of emigration society. Number in parentheses after family head denotes number in family.

Family Head	Emigration Society	Family Head	Emigration Society
#John Young (2)	Abercrombie (2)	James Robertson (3)	Glasgow Trongate ctd.
Arch'd McKenchie (7)	"	John Watt (2)	"
William Smith (1)	"	James Watt (3)	"
Walter Beatie (5)	"	Thomas Watt (1)	"
James McCallum (6)	"	Malcolm McDonald (4)	"
John Robertson (5)	"	John Gemmill (4)	"
		John Gilmour (2)	"
#Samuel Stevenson (3)	Alloa	Allan Gilmour (5)	"
James Matthie (8)	"	Hugh Gilmour (4)	"
Geo. Watt (8)	"	James Gilmour (2)	"
James Dow (9)	"	Thomas Deachman (5)	"
James London (1)	"	James McAlpin (1)	"
William Thomson (1)	"	Robert Barclay (1)	"
James Thomson (1)	"	William Kyle (8)	"
Thomas Dodds (10)	"	John Findley (7)	"
		John Baird (1)	"
#John Blair (8)	Balfron	Arch'd Rankin (2)	"
Andrew Scott (1)	"	James Bowes (8)	"
David Kemp (1)	"	Thomas Bowes (1)	"
Duncan Ferguson (4)	"	Alex'r Bowes (1)	"
John Nichol (6)	"	John Bowes (1)	"
John McPhee (7)	"	Mrs. Wilson (5)	"
Mary Johnston (1)	"	John Gemmill (1)	"
John Marshall (2)	"	Peter Taylor (1)	"
#George Bremner (7)	Deanston (by Doune)	#David Young (4)	Hopetown Bathgate
George Bremner Jr. (4)	"	Mrs. Young (2)	"
Charles Bremner (2)	"	Edward Young (1)	"
Alexander McNicholl (2)	"	James Dick (13)	"
Wm. Livingstone (3)	"	Henry Mungale (1)	"
#William Purdie (2)	Glasgow Trongate	#Arch'd Paterson (5)	Milton Dumbartonshire
Thomas Duncan (3)	"	David Campbell (3)	"
James Ferguson (3)	"	John Gillan (1)	"
Janet Drummond (1)	"	William Drydon (1)	"
William Purdie (1)	"		
John Gemmill (7)	"	#Walter Gardner (4)	Wishawton
John Kent (4)	"	William Lindsay (9)	"
James Rollo (4)	Glasgow Trongate ctd.	#Robert Ruthven (6)	Spring Bank
William Hamilton (1)	"	James Pollock (6)	"
James Wilson (5)	"	Thomas Pollock (6)	"
Hugh Wallace (4)	"	Peter McCulloch (5)	"
David Leckie (1)	"	John McCulloch (1)	"

12. *Portaferry*, Pollock (Master). Sailed from Greenock to Quebec in May, 1832.*
[*QM* June 13, 1832]

Donald Martin	Skye	Hector Hunter Wife	
Jno McKinlay & Wife	Glasgow	& Four	Berwick on Tweed
Robert Rankin	Glasgow	William Clark Wife	
Robert Miller	Glasgow	& Three	Berwick on Tweed
Robert Jaffray	Glasgow	William Rankin	Berwick
Joeph Gilchrist Dow	Glasgow	John Carnegie Wife	
Thomas Kennedy	Hawick	& Three	East Kilbride
John Ross & Wife	Glasgow	Donald Forbes & Wife	Inverness
John Carse & Family	Glasgow	John Anderson & Wife	Old Buttrey
Alex McAllister & Ten	Campbeltown	John Scoular	Glasgow
Thomas Gemmell		William Struthers & Six	Bothwell
& Wife	Glasgow	Peter Cameron	East Kilbride
J Edmeston & Three	Glasgow	Barnell Storie & Son	Blantyre Works
Thomas Dunn	—eland	Robert Morrison Wife	
Peter Thomson & Wife	Paisley	& Son	Crieff
John Hepburn	Edinburgh	Hugh White	Baladne Deep
John Forbes	Alyth	George Thomson & Wife	Blantyre
Alex Connal	Glasgow	Samuel Thomson	Blantyre
James Easton & Nine	Blantyre Works	James McKenzie	Blantyre
Hugh Cautter & Three	Dalry	Alex Hepburn	Athelstoneford
James Robertson	Glasgow	William Stewart & Three	Edinburgh
Peter Clark & Wife	Campbeltown	James McEwan & Six	Dumblane
Thomas McCready	New Dalry	Henry Hood & Son	Lanark
Walter Buchan	Glasgow	Matthew Lochhead	Westhord
John Graham & One	Monzie	George Reid Wife	
Alex Grant Wife		& Three	Glasgow
& Three	Calder	Duncan Stewart Wife	
John Burns Wife & Two	Rattray	& Three	Paisley
Malcolm McGregor	Inverness-shire	John Spiers	Bridge of Weir
William Stewart 6 Mother	Inverness-shire	James Hunter & Three	Glasgow
Alex Cuthbertson	Hamilton	Robert Campbell	
Robert Templeton		& Three	Bridge of Weir
& Five	Rothesay	James Black Wife	
Dun Niven	Alyth	& Child	Paisley
Robert Bennet	Wigton	William Fell	Hamilton
James Gentles	Paisley	William Smith	
Walter Jarvie Wife		& Two Nephews	Haddington
& Child	Kirkintilloch		
Thomas Cannon			
& daughter	Glasgow		
George Duncan	Glasgow		
William Farley	Airdrie		

* The passenger list is believed to be associated with the *Portaferry*'s crossing in May 1832. *Glasgow and West of Scotland Family History Society Journal* (Autumn 1990) 8-9.

13. Partial List of passengers who sailed to Quebec from Greenock on the *Portaferry*, Pollock (master) in 1833.
[*Montreal Gazette* May 30, 1833]

"Understanding that Mr. WILLIAM CANNON, surgeon, half pay Royal Navy, intends settling as a Medical Practitioner in KINGSTON, UPPER CANADA, we, the undersigned passengers by the brig *Portaferry*, from GREENOCK to MONTREAL, cannot allow him to depart from us without giving him the following testimonial...."

J. Pollock, Master of the
  William M'donald, Portaferry
William Mair, Minister
R. M'Lemont, Merchant
John Williamson, do.
James R. Orr, do.
James Greenshields
Samuel Pate
Thomas Mickle
John Birrell
John Summerville
James Cuthbertson
James Smith
James Watson
Francis Watson
James Calland
George Cuthbertson
Robert Brown
William Clelland
Thomas Baxter

John Murdy
James Dickson
George Weir
Robert Tacket
James Clelland
James Thomson
William Cuthbertson
James Carmichael
John Weir
John Tacket
Alexander M'Donald
Alexander Fraser
James Thomson
Mrs. Weir
William Weir
John Mickle
Mr. Lindsay

May 30, 1833

14. List of North Uist passengers from Lord MacDonald's estate who sailed from Greenock to Quebec in the *Waterhen* of London in 1849.

[Private communication, Clan Donald Centre, Skye]

No. of Ticket	Passenger Name	Age	No. of Ticket	Passenger Name	Age
1	Donald McLuish	64	16	Alex'r McDonald	70
	Mary McLuish	42		Flora McDonald	60
	Ann McLuish	19		Donald McDonald	28
	Neil McLuish	17		Margaret McDonald	26
	Flora McLuish	15		Flora McDonald	24
2	Catherine Neilson	50		John McDonald	23
	Allan McKenzie "	23		Marion McDonald	22
3	John McDonald	26		Ann McDonald	20
4	Roderick McDonald	20	18	William McDonald	22
5	Christian McDonald	28	19	Alex'r McDiarmid	24
6	Archie McAuley	35	21	Ronald McInnes	40
	Catherin McAuley	28		Marion McInnes	35
	Margaret McAuley	2		Finlay McInnes	6
7	Alex'r McDonald	19		Angus McInnes	3
8	Andrew McKenzie	54	22	Christy Ferguson	50
	Mary McKenzie	50		Donald Mathieson	21
	Euphemia McKenzie	22		John Mathieson	18
	Elspet McKenzie	20	24	Rod McDonald	32
	John McKenzie	19		Euphemia McDonald	26
	James McKenzie	16		John McDonald	1
	Archie McKenzie	13		Janet McDonald	26
9	John Mondl	52	25	Donald McDonald	50
	Kate Mondl	40		Catherine McDonald	50
	Hector Mondl	20		Roderick McDonald	24
	Mary Mondl	18		Donald McDonald	20
	John Mondl	12	26	Archie McAskill	17
10	Norman McIntyre	40	27	John McKeary	60
	Mary McIntyre	40		Christy McKeary	50
	Innes McIntyre	15		Christy McKeary	21
	Marion McIntyre	12		Ann McKeary	19
	Peggy McIntyre	10		Alexander McKeary	17
11	Alex'r McDonald	45		Archie McKeary	15
	Isobel McDonald	46		Catherine McKeary	7
	James McDonald	20		Ncil MacMay	23
	Ian McDonald	18		Kate MacMay	19
	Angus McDonald	16	29	Angus McDonald	34
	Alex'r McDonald	11	30	Alex McKeagan	59
12	Archie McPhail	26		Mary McKeagan	58
	Christian McPhail	25		Angus McKeagan	25
	Christian	1		John McKeagan	20
13	Donald McDonald	28	31	Archie McKinnison	50
14	Alex'r McGlashan	54		Elizabeth McKinnison	36
	Janet McGlashan	53		Neil McKinnison	7
	John McGlashan	24	32	John McDonald	46
	Angus McGlashan	22		Mary McDonald	44
	Alex'r McGlashan	20		Catherine McDonald	21
	Donald McGlashan	18		Christy McDonald	19
	Lachland McGlashan	16		Duncan McDonald	16
	Donald McGlashan	13		Mary McDonald	15
	Mary McGlashan	13		Jonathan McDonald	13
	Catherine McGlashan	11		John McDonald	11
15	Alex'r Stewart	30		Ann McDonald	9
	Rachel Stewart	25		Ann McDonald	7
	Elspet Stewart	1			

No. of Ticket	Passenger Name	Age
34	John McLean	57
	Catherine McLean	48
	Mary McLean	25
	Margaret McLean	23
	Neil McLean	20
	Elizabeth McLean	17
	Catherine McLean	13
35	Donald McPherson	53
	Catherine McPherson	21
	Flora McPherson	18
	Donald McPherson	13
	Lauchlan McPherson	11
	Angus McPherson	9
36	Malcolm McLeod	45
	Marion McLeod	35
	Margaret McLeod	16
	John McLeod	14
	Marion McLeod	12
	Ann McLeod	8
	Donald McLeod	6
	Angus McLeod	1

No. of Ticket	Passenger Name	Age
37	Neil McDougal	62
	Ann McDougal	54
	William McDougal	30
	Mary McDougal	18
	John McDougal	16
	Archie McDougal	10
	Margaret McDougal	8
	Mary McDougal	5
38	Alex. McDonald	50
	Catherine McDonald	37
	Allan McDonald	26
	Donald McDonald	23
	Roderick McDonald	19
	Archie McDonald	17
	John McDonald	14
	Margaret McDonald	12
	Christy McDonald	5
	Marion McDonald	1
53	John McGregor	41
54	Donald McDonald	22
55	William McDouall	22
56	Allan McDouall	20
57	Ronald McDonald	28

15. List of North Uist Passengers from Lord MacDonald's estate who sailed to Quebec from Greenock on the *Cashmere* of Glasgow in 1849.
[NAS GD 221/4011/53]

No. of Ticket	Passenger Name	Age	No. of Ticket	Passenger Name	Age
39	Duncan Stewart	40		Euphemia McLeod	35
	Janet Stewart	34		Katherine McLeod	12
	Catherine Stewart	8		Allan McLeod	10
	John Stewart	6		Margaret McLeod	6
40	Donald Cameron	58		Janet McLeod	3
	Catherine Cameron	30		Alexander McLeod	1
	Christy Cameron	27	47	Donald Morrison	60
	John Cameron	22		Flora Morrison	45
	Ann Cameron	20		Mary Morrison	21
	Ewen Cameron	13		Donald Morrison	17
	Ann McLellan	5		Jane Morrison	13
	James McLellan	3		Kenneth Morrison	10
41	Donald McGlachan	62		Catherine Morrison	8
	Catherine McGlachan	42		Christy Morrison	5
	Angus McGlachan	16	48	Donald McLean	50
	Alexander McGlachan	14		Flora McLean	42
	Ann McGlachan	12		Donald McLean	20
	Flora McGlachan	10		John McLean	17
	Donald McGlachan	8		Archie McLean	15
	Neil McGlachan	1		Lachlan McLean	13
42	John McLuish	51		Mary McLean	8
	Kate McLuish	37		Alexander McLean	4
	Donald McLuish	13		Ewen McLean	1
	Ewan McLuish	11	49	Donald McLean	29
	Murdo McLuish	9		Marion McLean	25
	Mary McLuish	7		Mary McLean	6
	Donald Jr McLuish	5		Euphemia McLean	2
	Christy McLuish	2	50	Alexander McLean	46
43	Norman McLuish	47		Catherine McLean	28
	Catherine McLuish	32		Euphemia McLean	20
	Marion McLuish	15		Neil McLean	13
	Donald McLuish	6	50	John McLean	11
	Angus McLuish	4		Lachlan McLean	6
	Margaret McLuish	2		Rachel McLean	4
	Archie McLuish	1		Donald McLean	2
44	Neil McPherson	50		Hector McLean	1
	Kate McPherson	35	51	Lachlan McInnes	44
	Archie McPherson	16		Marion McInnes	36
	John McPherson	14		Donald McInnes	12
	Margaret McPherson	10		Flora McInnes	10
	James McPherson	7		Finlay McInnes	8
	Flora McPherson	5		John McInnes	6
43	Alex'r McPherson	3		Donald McInnes	4
45	Neil McGlashan	59		Christy McInnes	3
	Euphemia McGlashan	58	58	Mary Ferguson	20
	Ewen McGlashan	23	59	Ronald McDonald	40
	Ann McGlashan	21		Marion McDonald	38
	Christy McGlashan	18		Ann McDonald	14
	Alexr McGlashan	13		Kitty McDonald	13
	Allan McGlashan	11		Duncan McDonald	10
	Donald McGlashan	9		Mary McDonald	7
	Mary McGlashan	7		Neil McDonald	3
46	Malcolm McLeod	35		Peggy McDonald	3

Appendix II

SHIP CROSSINGS FROM
SCOTLAND TO QUEBEC, 1785–1855

Most of the passengers shown in this list were destined for Upper Canada. Those who did not go to Upper Canada would have settled either in the United Sates or Lower Canada. The list is restricted to ship crossings with a minimum of 15 passengers. Unless otherwise stated, the passenger numbers refer only to Quebec arrivals. In those crossings where passengers also disembarked at Pictou and other Maritime ports, the figures for these are given in the comments field. Passenger figures have been obtained from a wide variety of documentary sources. Some passenger figures are approximations and some are ambiguous. Uncertainties arise as to whether passenger numbers include all adults (not just heads of households) and children and infants. For details of the ships which carried the emigrants see Appendix III.

Year	Mth	Vessel	Master	Psgr. Nos.	Departure Port
1785	06	*Philadelphia*	n/k	300	n/k

McLean, *Glengarry*, 101-8. Arrived Quebec in 1786.

1786	07	*Macdonald*	Stevenson, R.	539	Knoydart

McLean, *Glengarry*, 108-16 Glengarry settlers.

1788		*Neptune* (1)	n/k	60	n/k

Adams & Somerville, *Cargoes of Despair and Hope*, 185. Glengarry settlers.

1790	08	*British Queen* of Greenock	Deniston	87	Arisaig

Psgr list: LAC RG 4A1, Vol. 48, 15874-5; *QG* Oct. 21; McLean, *Glengarry*, 16-21. Glengarry settlers.

1792	07	*Unity*	Service	200	Grnk

QG Sept. 27; McLean, *Glengarry*, 123. Glengarry settlers; 40 Highland families.

1793	06	*Argyle*		150	Glenelg

McLean, *Glengarry*, 123-5. Wintered in PEI, went to Quebec in two schooners.

1801		*Fame* (1)	Forrest	79	Grnk

Bumsted, *People's Clearance*, 225

Year	Mth	Vessel	Master	Psgr. Nos.	Departure Port
1802	06	*Eagle* (1)	Conolly, N.	21	Grnk

QG Sept. 11.

| 1802 | 06 | *Helen* of Irvine | Service, G. | 166 | Fort William |

Psgr list: LAC MG 24 I183 file 2 pp. 7, 9-11; McLean, *Glengarry*, 142-4. Glengarry settlers.

| 1802 | 06 | *Jean* of Irvine | MacDonald, J. | 250 | Fort William |

Psgr list: LAC MG 24 I183, File 2, 7,9-11; *QG* Sept. 9; McLean, *Glengarry*, 142-4. Glengarry settlers.

| 1802 | 06 | *Neptune* of Greenock | Boyd | 600 | Loch Nevis |

QG Sept. 11; McLean, *Glengarry*, 136-9. Glengarry settlers.

| 1802 | 07 | *Albion* (1) | Service, G. | 167 | Fort William |

QG Sept. 9.

| 1802 | 07 | *Friends of John Saltcoats* | Hen, John | 136 | Fort William |

Psgr list: LAC MG 24 I183, File 2, 7, 9-11; *QG* Sept. 15; McLean, *Glengarry*, 142-4. Glengarry settlers.

| 1804 | 05 | *Oughton* | Baird, John | 102 | Kirkcudbright |

Psgr list: LAC MG 24 I8, Vol. 4, 105-8; Campey, *The Silver Chief*, 51-76. Lord Selkirk's Baldoon settlers.

| 1804 | 08 | *Commerce* | London | 42 | Oban |

NAS GD202/70/12.

| 1805 | 04 | *Jean* of Irvine | Wilson | 24 | Grnk |

QM May 18; *GA* April 5.

| 1806 | 08 | *Hope* (2) | Henry, M. | 47 | Port Glasgow |

QM Oct. 30; *GA* Aug. 20. Called at Halifax.

| 1809 | 05 | *Albion* (2) | Kidd, R. | 60 | Dundee |

QG July 6.

| 1810 | 04 | *Dunlop* | Stevenson, Allan | 54 | Glasgow |

QG June 14.

| 1811 | 04 | *Betsey* | Gordon, J. | 15 | Grnk |

QG July 11.

| 1812 | 05 | *Cambria* of Aberdeen | Perie, James | 33 | Aberdeen |

E.504/1/24; some of the 33 passengers left at Halifax.

| 1812 | 06 | *Betsey* | Gordon, J. | 15 | Grnk |

QG July 11.

| 1814 | 05 | *Montreal* | Allen | 18 | Grnk |

QG July 14.

| 1815 | 04 | *Carolina* of Aberdeen | Dunoon, A. | 24 | Aberdeen |

E 504/1/25.

| 1815 | 07 | *Atlas* (1) | Turnbull | 242 | Grnk |

Psgr list for all four vessels: PRO CO385/2; McLean, *Glengarry*, 155–57. One of four ships taking settlers who received government assistance.

Year	Mth	Vessel	Master	Psgr. Nos.	Departure Port
1815	07	*Baltic Merchant*	Jeffreys	140	Grnk

See *Atlas* (1).

1815	07	*Dorothy*	Spence	194	Grnk

See *Atlas* (1).

1815	07	*Eliza*	Telfer	123	Grnk

See *Atlas* (1).

1815	07	*Margaret* of Peterhead	Shand, J.	16	Leith

E.504/22/70.

1815	08	*Union*	Henry	15	Grnk

QG Sept. 2.

1816	03	*Carolina* of Aberdeen	Duncan, A.	25	Aberdeen

E.504/1/26.

1816	03	*Mary* of Greenock (1)	Moore, A.	15	Grnk

QM May 24; E.504/15/111.

1816	04	*Mary* of Aberdeen	Clayton, J.	21	Aberdeen

QM July 23; E.504/1/26.

1816	04	*Prescott* of Leith	Young	26	Leith

QM June 21; E.504/22/72.

1816	04	*Rothiemurchus* of Leith	Watson, G.	28	Leith

QM May 31; E.504/22/72.

1816	05	*Caledonia* of Irvine	Reid, J.	30	Grnk

E504/15/112.

1816	05	*Fancy* of Aberdeen	Struthers, J.	15	Grnk

QM Aug. 20; E.504/15/112.

1816	05	*Greenfield*	Holmes, J.	28	Grnk

QM Aug. 27; E.504/15/112.

1816	07	*Lady of the Lake*	Primrose, D.	27	Grnk

QM Sept. 10; E.504/15/112.

1816	08	*Britannia*	Spence, C.	36	Grnk

QM Sept. 27; E.504/15/113.

1816	08	*Fame* (2)	Abrams	17	Grnk

QM Sept. 17; E.504/15/113.

1816	08	*Hibernia* of Aberdeen	Lamb, R.	42	Stornoway

E504/33/3.

1816	08	*Isabella and Euphemia*	Middleton, J.	32	Stornoway

QM Nov. 5; E.504/33/3.

1816	08	*Jane* of Sunderland	Rogers, J.	16	Grnk

E.504/15/113.

Year	Mth	Vessel	Master	Psgr. Nos.	Departure Port
1816	08	*John and Samuel* of Liverpool	Cook, F.	82	Stornoway

E.504/33/3; PRO CO 42/358 ff..113-5.

| 1816 | 08 | *Morningfield* of Aberdeen | Perie, J. | 63 | Stornoway |

QM Sept. 20; E.504/33/3.

| 1816 | 08 | *Perseverence* of Aberdeen | Philip, J. | 52 | Stornoway |

E.504/33/3.

| 1817 | 03 | *Renown* of Kirkaldy | Watts, J. | 20 | Leith |

QM June 10; E.504/22/76.

| 1817 | 04 | *Rothiemurchus* of Leith | Watson, G. | 105 | Leith |

QM June 3; E.504/22/76.

| 1817 | 04 | *Juno* of Aberdeen | Henderson, J. | 20 | Dundee |

QM June 17.

| 1817 | 04 | *Mary* of Greenock (1) | Moore | 26 | Grnk |

QM June 3; *GA* Mar. 7.

| 1817 | 04 | *Nancy* of South Shields | Allan, R. | 34 | Leith |

QM Aug. 1; Martell, *Emigration from Nova Scotia*, 43. 130 passengers left at Halifax.

| 1817 | 04 | *Neptune* of Ayr | Neil | 22 | Grnk |

QM June 10.

| 1817 | 04 | *Prompt* of Bo'ness | Coverdale | 133 | Leith |

QM July 8; E.504/22/77; Martell, *Emigration from Nova Scotia*, 43; *GA* Mar. 21; *KM* June 26. 60 passengers left at Halifax.

| 1817 | 04 | *Rebecca* of Greenock | Harvey | 29 | Grnk |

QM June 3.

| 1817 | 05 | *Agincourt* of Leith | Matheson | 73 | Leith |

QM Aug. 11; *SM* LXXIX, 477. 127 passengers left at Halifax.

| 1817 | 05 | *Alexander* of Bo'ness | Henry, J. | 44 | Leith |

QM July 22; E.504/22/77; *SM* LXXIX, 477.

| 1817 | 05 | *Harmony* (1) | Abrams | 136 | Grnk |

QM July 18.

| 1817 | 05 | *James* | Jack, W. | 24 | Grnk |

QM Aug. 11.

| 1817 | 05 | *Jessie* of Aberdeen | Thomson, J. | 21 | Aberdeen |

QM Aug. 1; E. 504/1/27.

| 1817 | 05 | *John* of Bo'ness | Mitchell, J. | 118 | Leith |

QM Aug. 19; E.504/22/7.

| 1817 | 05 | *Lord Middleton* of North Shields | Kerr, G. | 163 | Leith |

QM July 22; E.504/22/77; *SM* LXXIX, 477; *DC* May 23; *KM* May 12.

| 1817 | 05 | *Tods* of Perth | McPherson, W. | 42 | Dundee |

QM July 22; E.504/27/14; *DC* Apr. 25; *PC* Apr. 24.

Year	Mth	Vessel	Master	Psgr. nos.	Departure Port
1817	05	*Trafalgar* of London	Mitchell, J.	100	Leith

QM Aug. 1; E.504/22/77; *PC* May 29; *KM* May 12.

1817	06	*Ardgour* of Fort William	Lillie, W.	108	Fort William

QM Sept. 9; E.504/12/6.

1817	06	*Minerva* of Aberdeen	Strachan, W.	26	Fort William

E504/12/6.

1817	06	*Peace*	Seator	85	Grnk

QM July 18; *GA* Apr. 22.

1817	07	*Cambria* of Aberdeen	Wilson, J.	15	Aberdeen

QM Sept. 9; E.504/1/27.

1817	07	*General Goldie* of Dumfries	Smith	18	Dumfries

QM Sept. 16; *DGC* June 24. Called at Pictou and Miramichi.

1817	07	*Pitt*	Hamilton	37	Grnk

QM Sept. 26; *GA* June 27.

1818	05	*Agincourt* of Leith	Mathwin	298	Leith

QM Aug. 7.

1818	06	*Camilla*	McCarthy, D.	109	Grnk

QM July 17.

1818	06	*Favourite* (1)	Greg	23	Grnk

QM July 17.

1818	06	*General Goldie* of Dumfries	Smith, W.	30	Dumfries

E 504/9/9.

1818	07	*Agamemnon*	Rogers	192	Leith

QM Aug. 15.

1818	07	*Curlew*	Young, J.	205	Grnk

Psgr list: PRO CO 384/3; ff. 123-7; *QM* Sept. 10. Breadalbane settlers; some went to Prince Edward Island.

1818	07	*Jane* of Sunderland	Rogers J.	131	Grnk

QM Aug. 23; PRO CO 226 Vol. 36, f.19. See comments for *Curlew*.

1818	07	*Mars*	Blin	253	Mull

QM Sept. 8.

1818	07	*Sophia* of Ayr	Moore	106	Grnk

Psgr list: PRO CO 384/3 ff.133-4; *QM* Sept. 8. See comments for *Curlew*.

1818	07	*Waterloo* of Fort William	Kendal, J.	108	Fort William

QM Sept. 10; E504/12/6.

1819	03	*Skeen* of Leith(1)	Mason	37	Leith

Martell, *Emigration from Nova Scotia*, 47; *SM* IV 1819, 465. 113 passengers left at Halifax.

1819	04	*Earl of Dalhousie* of Aberdeen	Levie, J.	19	Aberdeen

QM May 14.

Year	Mth	Vessel	Master	Psgr. nos.	Departure Port
1819	04	*Mary* (2)	Munro	32	Leith

SM 1819 IV, 465.

| 1819 | 04 | *Percival* of Leith | Scott | 85 | Leith |

SM IV 1819, 465; *PC* Feb. 25.

| 1819 | 04 | *Renown* of Kirkaldy | Watts, J. | 37 | Leith |

QM May 18; E.504/22/84

| 1819 | 05 | *Agincourt* of Leith | Matthews | 40 | Leith |

QM July 27; E.504/22/85; Martell, *Emigration from Nova* Scotia, 47; *SM* IV 1819, 465.
133 passengers left at Halifax. According to Scottish customs records, 200 people left Leith.

| 1819 | 06 | *Jean* | Allan | 28 | Grnk |

QM Aug. 2.

| 1819 | 06 | *Speculation* | Allen | 87 | Oban |

QM Sept. 14; Martell, Ibid, 49; *IJ* June 4. 63 passengers left at Pictou.

| 1819 | 07 | *Harmony* (1) | Messop, H. | 233 | Oban |

QM Aug. 24.

| 1819 | 07 | *Hope* of Greenock | Marden | 184 | Oban |

QM Aug. 24; E.504/25/3.

| 1819 | 07 | *Paragon* | Mitchell | 66 | Leith |

QM Aug. 31.

| 1819 | 07 | *Traveller* of Aberdeen | Goldie, J. | 143 | Tobermory |

E504/35/2.

| 1819 | 08 | *Nelson* | Barrick | 19 | Leith |

QM Sept. 17.

| 1820 | 04 | *Alexander* | Young | 96 | Grnk |

QM June 5.

| 1820 | 04 | *Enterprise* | Pattin | 39 | Ayr |

QM May 25.

| 1820 | 04 | *Jane* (2) | Allen, W. | 34 | Grnk |

QM May 19.

| 1820 | 04 | *Psyche* of Dundee | Erskine, T. | 38 | Dundee |

QM May 27; *DCA* CE 70 11/2; *DCA* CE 70/11/16.

| 1820 | 04 | *Rebecca* of Greenock | McKenzie | 42 | Grnk |

QM May 25.

| 1820 | 04 | *Robert* | Neil | 44 | Grnk |

QM May 21.

| 1820 | 04 | *Sally* | Cumming | 33 | Grnk |

QM June 8.

| 1820 | 04 | *Skeen* of Leith (1) | Bishop | 22 | Leith |

QM May 18.

Year	Mth	Vessel	Master	Psgr. nos.	Departure Port
1820	04	*Sovereign* (1)	Pearson	49	Leith

QM June 3.

| 1820 | 04 | *Traveller* of Aberdeen | Goldie, J. | 20 | Aberdeen |

QM May 12.

| 1820 | 04 | *True Briton* | Reid, J. | 54 | Grnk |

QM June 5.

| 1820 | 04 | *Young Norval* | Luck | 37 | Grnk |

QM May 26.

| 1820 | 05 | *Earl of Buckinghamshire* | Johnson, J. | 200 | Grnk |

QM June 24.

| 1820 | 05 | *Minerva* (1) | Williamson | 60 | Grnk |

QM June 30.

| 1820 | 05 | *Sir J H Craig* | Dease, J. | 100 | Leith |

QM July 15; E.504/22/90.

| 1820 | 05 | *Speculation* | Douglass | 120 | Grnk |

QM June 30.

| 1820 | 06 | *Benlomond* | Rattray, H. | 218 | Grnk |

QM July 21.

| 1820 | 06 | *Betsey* of Greenock | Wither | 78 | Oban |

QM Aug. 15; E504/25/3.

| 1820 | 06 | *Commerce* of Greenock | Coverdale, N. | 402 | Grnk |

Psgr list: LAC RG8 vol. 625 ff. 219-23; *QM* Aug. 5.
Passengers included emigration society members.

| 1820 | 06 | *Martha* | Denwood | 43 | Dumfries |

DWJ June 20.

| 1820 | 07 | *Alexander* | Ferguson | 112 | Grnk |

QM Sept. 5.

| 1820 | 07 | *Argus* (1) | Wilkinson | 88 | Dumfries |

QM Aug. 14; *DWJ* June 13.

| 1820 | 07 | *Broke* | n/k | 176 | Grnk |

Lamond, *Emigration from Lanark and Renfrew*, 10; McGill, *Lanark County*, 238.
Members of Abercrombie Transatlantic & Bridgeton emigration societies.

| 1820 | 07 | *Duchess of Richmond* | Cook | 266 | Oban |

QM Aug. 17.

| 1820 | 07 | *Glentanner* of Aberdeen | Murray | 18 | Tobermory |

QM Aug. 25; E.504/35/2. 123 passengers left at Cape Breton.

| 1820 | 07 | *Hope* (1) | Duncan | 44 | Grnk |

QM Aug. 14.

| 1820 | 07 | *Prompt* of Bo'ness | Nairn | 370 | Grnk |

QM Aug. 31; PRO CO 384/6 f. 261; Lesmahagow Emigration Society members.

Year	Mth	Vessel	Master	Psgr. nos.	Departure Port
1820	08	*Rebecca* of Greenock	Harvey	50	Grnk

QM Oct. 11.

| 1821 | 04 | *Earl of Buckinghamshire* | Johnston, J. | 607 | Grnk |

psgr list: PRO CO 42/189 ff. 512-69; Lamond, *Emigration from Lanark and Refrew*, 42. Members of seven emigration societies.

| 1821 | 04 | *Earl of Dalhousie* of Aberdeen | Levie, J. | 15 | Aberdeen |

QM May 15.

| 1821 | 04 | *George Canning* | Potter | 490 | Grnk |

psgr list: PRO CO 42/189 ff. 512-69; *QM* June 2; McGill, *Lanark* County, 239. Members of 11 emigration societies .

| 1821 | 04 | *Helen* of Dundee | Erskine, T. | 55 | Dundee |

QM June 12; *DC* Jan. 12.

| 1821 | 04 | *Margaret* | Oliphant | 180 | Grnk |

QM June 18; PRO CO 384/6 f. 254. Members of Anderston and Rutherglen Emigration Society.

| 1821 | 04 | *Neptune* (2) | Bell | 63 | Leith |

QM June 8.

| 1821 | 05 | *Commerce* of Greenock | Coverdale, N. | 422 | Grnk |

psgr list: PRO CO 42/189 ff. 512-69; *QM* June 22; Members of 9 emigration societies.

| 1821 | 05 | *David* of London | Gemmil, D. | 364 | Grnk |

psgr list: PRO CO 42/189 ff. 512-69; *QM* June 25; Members of 10 emigration societies.

| 1821 | 05 | *Kent* | Stirling | 50 | Grnk |

QM June 26.

| 1821 | 06 | *Benson* | Rowe, W. | 287 | Grnk |

QM July 27.

| 1821 | 06 | *Catherine* (1) | Daysdale | 63 | Leith |

QM Aug. 11.

| 1821 | 08 | *Ann* (1) | Henry | 37 | Grnk |

QM Sept. 14.

| 1821 | 08 | *John Howard* | Smith | 100 | London |

QM Sept. 24. 100 settlers from Anticosti who were saved from the Brig *Earl of Dalhousie* of Greenock which sailed from Fort William. The remainder were picked up by the *Dolphin*.

| 1821 | 09 | *Thistle* of Aberdeen | Allen, R. | 43 | Tobermory |

QM Oct. 19; *IJ* June 22.

| 1821 | 10 | *Dolphin* | n/k | 20 | Anticosti |

QM Oct. 16. People who had sailed in the *Earl of Dalhousie* (see above).

| 1822 | 04 | *True Briton* | n/k | 28 | Grnk |

QM June 7.

| 1822 | 05 | *Rose* | Johnson | 45 | Leith |

QM June 11.

Year	Mth	Vessel	Master	Psgr. nos.	Departure Port
1822	05	*Thompsons Packet* of Dumfries	Lookup	40	Dumfries

QM July 9; Martell, *Emigration from Nova Scotia...*, 53. Ninety-three passengers left at Pictou.

1822	07	*George* (1)	McAlpin, J.	42	Grnk

QM Aug. 13.

1822	07	*Ossian* of Leith	Block	127	Fort William

QM Aug. 23; *IJ* 29 June 1821.

1822	07	*Pilgrim*	Smith	62	Tobermory

QM Aug. 23.

1823	04	*Ann* (1)	Maclean	38	Glasgow

QM May 23.

1823	04	*Helen* of Dundee	Erskine, T.	20	Dundee

QM May 23.

1823	05	*Roscius*	McClaren	47	Grnk

QM June 15.

1823	06	*Eleanor*	Wallace	96	Workington

QM June 19.

1823	06	*Jane* (2)	Snowden	63	Grnk

QM June 19.

1823	06	*Pilgrim*	Smith	77	Grnk

QM Aug. 12.

1823	07	*Emperor Alexander* of Aberdeen	Watts, A.	49	Tobermory

QM Oct. 7; *IJ* Jan 30, 1824. One hundred and eleven passengers left at Sydney, Cape Breton. Campey, *After the Hector*, 217-9.

1823	07	*Monarch*	Crawford	259	Tobermory

QM Aug. 19.

1823	07	*Quebec Packet* of Aberdeen	Anderson	16	Aberdeen

QM Sept. 23.

1823	08	*Rebecca* of Greenock	Harvey	25	Grnk

QM Sept. 26.

1824	04	*Culloden*	Leyden	19	Leith

QM June 5.

1824	04	*Jean* of Ayr	Allan	16	Grnk

QM June 5.

1824	04	*Rebecca* of Greenock	Harvey	22	Grnk

QM June 1.

1824	05	*Margaret Bogle* of Leith	Boyd	17	Glasgow

QM June 16.

1824	06	*Active* (1)	Johnson	84	Whitehaven

QM July 10.

Year	Mth	Vessel	Master	Psgr. nos.	Departure Port
1824	06	*Aurora*	Hodson	61	Whitehaven

QM Aug. 10.

| 1824 | 06 | *Jane Wright* | n/k | 50 | Grnk |

QM Aug. 3.

| 1824 | 07 | *Dunlop* | Mandell | 131 | Grnk |

QM Aug. 31; Martell, *Ibid*, 54. Called at Sydney, Cape Breton, 96 passengers left.

| 1824 | 07 | *Gratitude* of Dundee | Gellatly, J. | 55 | Fort William |

QM Sept. 14; DCA CE 70/11/1. Includes 20 settlers who boarded ship at Baie des Chaleurs.

| 1824 | 08 | *Commerce* of Greenock | Wittleton | 15 | Grnk |

QM Sept. 11.

| 1824 | 08 | *Duchess of Richmond* | McClashen | 20 | Grnk |

QM Sept. 28.

| 1825 | 04 | *Niagara* | Hamilton | 115 | Grnk |

QM May 14. Settlers for McNab Township.

| 1825 | 05 | *George Stewart* | Stewart | 57 | Grnk |

QM July 16.

| 1825 | 07 | *Margaret* (1) | Boyd | 20 | Grnk |

QM Sept. 6.

| 1825 | 07 | *Tamerlane* of Greenock | McKillop | 30 | Grnk |

QM Aug. 24.

| 1825 | 08 | *Corsair* of Greenock | McAlpine | 30 | Grnk |

QM Sept. 20.

| 1826 | 04 | *Favourite* of Montreal | Allan | 22 | Grnk |

QM May 20; E.504/15/155.

| 1826 | 04 | *General Wolfe* | Johnston | 32 | Grnk |

QM May 20; E.504/15/155.

| 1826 | 04 | *Quebec Packet* of Aberdeen | Anderson | 19 | Aberdeen |

QM May 13.

| 1826 | 06 | *Gleniffer* | Stevenson | 42 | Grnk |

QM July 29; E.504/15/156.

| 1826 | 06 | *Margaret* (1) | Boyd | 22 | Grnk |

QM Aug. 5; E.504/15/156.

| 1826 | 06 | *Tamerlane* of Greenock | McKillop | 55 | Grnk |

QM Aug. 5; E.504/15/156. Called at Sydney, Cape Breton.

| 1826 | 07 | *Highland Lad* | Vickerman | 16 | Tobermory |

QM Sept. 23; Martell, *Emigration from Nova Scotia*, 57. Called at Nova Scotia.

| 1826 | 07 | *Ythan* | Cairns | 20 | Grnk |

QM Sept. 12.

Year	Mth	Vessel	Master	Psgr. nos.	Departure Port Grnk
1826	08	*Rebecca* of Greenock	Laurie	20	Grnk

QM Oct. 7; E.504/15/156.

| 1826 | 08 | *Sophia* of Greenock | Neil | 43 | Grnk |

QM Oct. 7; E.504/15/157.

| 1826 | 08 | *Welcome* | McColl | 15 | Grnk |

QM Oct. 10; E.504/15/157.

| 1826 | 09 | *Favourite* of Montreal | Allan | 17 | Grnk |

QM Oct. 14; E.504/15/157.

| 1827 | 04 | *Caledonia* | Miller | 79 | Grnk |

QM June 2; *GA* March 16.

| 1827 | 04 | *Percival* of Leith | Johnson | 47 | Leith |

QM May 19.

| 1827 | 04 | *Rebecca* of Greenock | n/k | 20 | Grnk |

QM May 5.

| 1827 | 05 | *George Canning* | Callender | 164 | Grnk |

QM June 23; *GA* April 6.

| 1827 | 05 | *Harmony* of Whitehaven | Young | 36 | Stornoway |

QM Sept. 1; Martell, Ibid, 59. 200 passengers left at Halifax.

| 1827 | 05 | *Lord Byron* | Robinson | 26 | Grnk |

QM July 21.

| 1827 | 06 | *Forth* | Robinson | 150 | Grnk |

QM July 17.

| 1827 | 06 | *Warner* | Crawford | 43 | Grnk |

QM July 24; *GA* May 8.

| 1827 | 07 | *Indian* | Matthias | 69 | Grnk |

QM Sept. 7; *GA* June 8.

| 1827 | 08 | *Active* (2) | Walker, A. | 40 | Tobermory |

QM Sept. 21; E.504/35/2. Vessel called at Cape Breton.

| 1827 | 08 | *Earl of Dalhousie* | Boyd | 20 | Grnk |

QM Oct. 9.

| 1828 | 03 | *Brilliant* of Aberdeen | Barclay, A. | 20 | Aberdeen |

QM May 17.

| 1828 | 03 | *Harmony* (2) | Young | 79 | Leith |

QM May 20.

| 1828 | 04 | *Ariadne* | McCall | 20 | Grnk |

QM May 17.

| 1828 | 04 | *Caledonia* | Miller | 90 | Grnk |

QM May 31.

Year	Mth	Vessel	Master	Psgr. nos.	Departure Port
1828	04	*Favourite* of Montreal	Allan	40	Grnk
QM May 17.					
1828	04	*Mary* (1)	Dunlop	206	Grnk
QM May 31.					
1828	05	*George Canning*	Callender	180	Grnk
QM June 24.					
1828	06	*Majestic*	Black	60	Leith
QM Aug. 9.					
1828	07	*Duchess of Richmond*	McClashan	106	Grnk
QM Aug. 19.					
1828	08	*Favourite* of Montreal	Allan	60	Grnk
QM Sept. 30.					
1829	04	*Cherub*	Miller	15	Grnk
QM May 12.					
1829	04	*George Canning*	Callender	103	Grnk
QM May 23.					
1829	04	*Mary* (1)	Duck	161	Grnk
QM May 30.					
1829	05	*Caledonia*	Miller	130	Grnk
QM June 23.					
1829	06	*Corsair* of Greenock	Hamilton	38	Grnk
QM Sept. 8.					
1829	06	*Foundling*	McLeod	170	Grnk
QM Aug. 1.					
1829	06	*Scotia*	Simpson	33	Grnk
QM Aug. 4.					
1829	07	*Amity* of Glasgow	Ray	17	Glasgow
QM Aug. 29.					
1829	07	*Huntley*	Wilson	176	Grnk
QM Aug. 15.					
1829	07	*Regent*	Steel	16	Leith
QM Aug. 15.					
1829	08	*Favourite* of Montreal	Allan	40	Grnk
QM Sept. 29.					
1830	03	*Sprightly*	n/k	60	Dundee
PC Mar. 3.					
1830	04	*Brilliant* of Aberdeen	Barclay, A.	20	Aberdeen
QM May 24.					

Year	Mth	Vessel	Master	Psgr. nos.	Departure Port
1830	04	*Margaret Balfour* of Dundee	n/k	63	Dundee

QM June 8; *PC* Mar. 1831.

1830	04	*Nailer*	n/k	120	Grnk

QM June 8.

1830	04	*Neptune* (2)	n/k	144	Leith

QM June 8.

1830	05	*Brittannia*	n/k	19	Leith

QM June 19.

1830	06	*Canada*	Potts	244	Cromarty from Leith

QM Aug. 19; *IC* June23 & Oct. 6; *IJ* Nov. 6.

1830	06	*Cartha*	Smith	144	Grnk

QM July 24.

1830	06	*Duchess of Richmond*	Alexander	129	Grnk

QM Aug. 7.

1830	06	*George Canning*	Callender	140	Grnk

QM July 27.

1830	06	*Hope* (3)	McFarlane	25	Leith

QM July 16.

1830	06	*John*	Mann	120	Cromarty

QM Aug. 10.

1830	06	*Stirling Castle* of Greenock	Fraser	224	Grnk

QM Aug. 10.

1830	07	*Deveron* of Glasgow	McGill	117	Grnk

QM Aug. 14.

1830	07	*Mary* of Newcastle	Jacobson	64	Loch Snizort, Skye

QM Sept. 4; *IJ* Dec. 10. Left Scotland with 330 passengers.

1830	07	*Triton*	McClean	64	Leith

QM Aug. 14.

1831	04	*Brilliant* of Aberdeen	Barclay, A.	75	Aberdeen

Fowler, *Journal of a tour through British North America*, 5-42.

1831	04	*Dalmarnock*	McFarlane	28	Grangemouth

QM May 17.

1831	04	*Donegal*	Matches	164	Maryport

QM May 26.

1831	04	*George* (2)	Thompson	23	Maryport

QM May 28.

Year Mth	Vessel	Master	Psgr. nos.	Departure Port
1831 04 QM May 24.	*Molson* of Dundee	Law	143	Dundee
1831 04 QM May 31.	*Nailer*	McColl	65	Grnk
1831 04 QM May 28.	*Neried*	Whitehead	49	Dumfries
1831 04 QM May 17.	*Rebecca* of Greenock	Laurie	50	Grnk
1831 04 QM May 28.	*Sarah Mariana*	Archibald	164	Maryport
1831 04 QM May 19.	*Triton*	McClean	33	Leith
1831 04 QM May 21.	*True Briton*	Balderston	43	Glasgow
1831 05 QM June 23.	*Amity* of Glasgow	Ray	30	Glasgow
1831 05 QM June 14.	*Elizabeth and Anne*	Wright, J.	296	Grnk
1831 05 QM June 2.	*Experiment*	Collins	32	Maryport
1831 05 QM June 23.	*George Canning*	Callender	300	Grnk
1831 05 QM June 21.	*Hope* (4)	Middleton	73	Maryport
1831 05 QM June 7.	*Sally*	Cumming	40	Ayr
1831 05 QM July 9.	*Salmes*	Royal, H.	250	Inverness
1831 05 QM June 4.	*Skeen* of Leith (2)	Bennett	118	Leith
1831 05 QM July 5.	*William Shand*	Hunter	299	Berwick
1831 06 QM July 19.	*Atlas* (2)	Scott	52	Dundee
1831 06 QM Sept. 8.	*Baronet*	Rankin	187	Cromarty
1831 06 QM July 19.	*Foundling*	McKenzie	161	Grnk

Year	Mth	Vessel	Master	Psgr. nos.	Departure Port
1831	06	*Sophia*	Neil	36	Grnk

QM Aug. 7.

1831	07	*Brilliant* of Aberdeen	Barclay, A.	68	Aberdeen

QM Sept. 8.

1831	07	*Corsair* of Greenock	Scott, J.	57	Cromarty

QM Aug. 30; Martell, *Emigration from Nova Scotia...*, 70; *IJ* May 27. 161 passengers left at Pictou.

1831	07	*Deveron* of Glasgow	McGill	302	Grnk

QM Aug. 27.

1831	07	*Industry*	Carr	57	Cromarty

QM Sept. 29; *IJ* June 24.

1831	07	*Iris*	Frank	240	Grnk

QM Aug. 30.

1831	07	*Margaret*	Wallace	160	Leith

QM Aug. 27.

1831	07	*Rival*	Wallace	333	Grnk

QM Aug. 18.

1831	07	*Tamerlane* of Greenock	Black	377	Grnk

QM Aug. 20.

1831	07	*Zealous*	Reed	182	Leith

QM Aug. 27.

1831	08	*Annandale* of Aberdeen	Anderson	23	Aberdeen

QM Sept. 8.

1831	08	*Canada* of Greenock	Allan	25	Grnk

QM Sept. 22.

1831	08	*Cleopatra*	Morris, J.	246	Cromarty

QM Sept. 8.

1831	08	*Dalmarnock*	McFarlane	27	Grnk

QM Sept. 8.

1831	08	*Earl of Dalhousie*	Boyd	20	Grnk

QM Sept. 22.

1831	08	*Rebecca* of Greenock	Laurie	39	Grnk

QM Sept. 22.

1832	03	*Brilliant* of Aberdeen	Barclay, A.	175	Aberdeen

QM May 17.

1832	03	*Isabella* of Dundee	Donaldson, J.	43	Dundee

QM May 16; *DC* Dec. 22 1831.

1832	03	*Margaret Balfour* of Dundee	Gellatly, J.	25	Dundee

QM May 17; *DC* Mar. 8.

Year	Mth	Vessel	Master	Psgr. nos.	Departure Port
1832	03	*Molson* of Dundee	Elliot, J.	49	Dundee
QM May 16; *DC* Dec. 29, 1831 & Feb. 9, 1832.					
1832	03	*Prince George* of Alloa	Morison	16	Alloa
QM May 14.					
1832	03	*Rebecca* of Greenock	Laurie	43	Grnk
QM May 16.					
1832	04	*Agnes Primrose*	Johnson	40	Glasgow
QM June 6.					
1832	04	*Aimwell* of Aberdeen	Morrison	24	Aberdeen
QM May 19.					
1832	04	*Annandale* of Aberdeen	Anderson, A.	61	Aberdeen
QM May 19.					
1832	04	*Betsey Howe*	n/k	42	Leith
QM May 28.					
1832	04	*Donegal*	Matches	138	Maryport
QM June 1.					
1832	04	*Dykes* of Maryport	Cockton	156	Maryport
QM May 23.					
1832	04	*Fisher*	Kay, T.	69	Stranraer
QM June 4.					
1832	04	*Hedleys* of Newcastle	n/k	209	Cromarty
QM June 3.					
1832	04	*Helen* of Aberdeen	Anderson	18	Aberdeen
QM May 23.					
1832	04	*Jane* (1)	Wilson	65	Leith
QM May 27.					
1832	04	*Maria* (1)	Hewitt	136	Maryport
QM June 3.					
1832	04	*Nailer*	McColl	172	Grnk
QM May 19; *PC* Mar. 1.					
1832	04	*Nicholson*	Craig	183	Maryport
QM June 6.					
1832	05	*Portaferry*	Pollock, J.	216	Grnk
psgr list: *QM* June 13.					
1832	04	*Sarah* (1)	Marianne	165	Maryport
QM June 2.					
1832	04	*Traveller* of Dundee	Wighton	42	Dundee
QM May 27; *DC* Mar. 20.					

Year	Mth	Vessel	Master	Psgr. nos.	Departure Port
1832	05	*Amity* of Glasgow	Mercer, J.	39	Grnk

QM July 26.

| 1832 | 05 | *Ann* (2) | Moore | 136 | Maryport |

QM June 24.

| 1832 | 05 | *Catherine* (2) | Davidson | 37 | Irvine |

QM June 2.

| 1832 | 05 | *Dalmarnock* | McFarlane | 227 | Berwick |

QM July 2; *KM* Feb. 7, 1833.

| 1832 | 05 | *Lawther* | Pewley | 121 | Workington |

QM July 9.

| 1832 | 05 | *Margaret* | Mathewson | 110 | Campbeltown |

QM July 2.

| 1832 | 05 | *Margaret Thompson* | Ogilvy, J. | 125 | Leith |

QM June 21.

| 1832 | 05 | *Sylvanus* of North Shields | Lawson | 41 | Cromarty |

QM July 26; Martell, *Emigration from Nova Scotia*...73; *IJ* Apr. 20. 196 passengers left at Pictou.

| 1832 | 05 | *Tamerlane* of Greenock | Black | 210 | Grnk |

QM July 10.

| 1832 | 06 | *Albion* of Glasgow | Boyd, J. | 84 | Glasgow |

QM July 10, Aug. 30.

| 1832 | 06 | *Blagdon* | Thomson | 132 | Cromarty |

QM Aug. 20; Martell, Ibid, 73; *IJ* May 18. Some passengers left at Pictou.

| 1832 | 06 | *Canada* | Hunter | 111 | Cromarty |

QM Aug. 22; Martell, Ibid, 73. 130 passengers left at Pictou.

| 1832 | 06 | *Chieftain* of Kirkaldy | Scott, A. | 210 | Leith |

QM July 26.

| 1832 | 06 | *Duchess* of Richmond | McGlashen | 240 | Grnk |

QM July 18.

| 1832 | 06 | *Gleniffer* | Dunlop | 152 | Grnk |

QM Aug. 5.

| 1832 | 06 | *Industry* | Chapman, J. | 130 | Dundee |

QM July 8; *DC* Apr. 12.

| 1832 | 06 | *Iris* | Welsh | 164 | Grnk |

QM July 16.

| 1832 | 06 | *Magnet* | Goulder | 146 | Whitehaven |

QM Aug. 6.

| 1832 | 06 | *Oxford* | Davidson | 300 | Leith |

QM July 25.

Year Mth	Vessel	Master	Psgr. nos.	Departure Port
1832 06	*Sharp*	Almond	206	Cromarty
QM Aug. 13.				
1832 06	*Victoria* of Dundee	Berrie, J.	126	Dundee
QM Aug. 5; *DC* May 10; DCA CE 70/11/3.				
1832 07	*Albion* of Glasgow	McMaster	181	Loch Eriboll
QM Sept. 16; Martell, Ibid, 72. 59 passengers left at Pictou.				
1832 07	*Crown*	Howie	75	Grnk
QM Aug. 27.				
1832 07	*Elizabeth*	McAlpine	74	Clyde
QM Aug. 10.				
1832 07	*Roger Stewart*	Kerr	123	Grnk
QM Aug. 20.				
1832 08	*Favourite* of Montreal	Allan	22	Grnk
QM Oct. 4.				
1832 08	*Robertson*	Neil	19	Grnk
QM Sept. 29.				
1832 09	*Sophia*	Easton	19	Grnk
QM Oct. 19.				
1833 03	*Favourite* of Montreal	Allan	73	Grnk
QM May 9.				
1833 03	*Robertson*	Neil	36	Grnk
QM May 9.				
1833 04	*Bethea*	n/k	20	Glasgow
QM June 16.				
1833 04	*Brilliant* of Aberdeen	Duthie	64	Aberdeen
QM May 17.				
1833 04	*Charles Forbes*	Beveridge	47	Kirkaldy
QM May 21.				
1833 04	*Dykes* of Maryport	n/k	33	Maryport
QM June 12.				
1833 04	*Elizabeth* of Leith	n/k	15	Leith
QM June 15.				
1833 04	*European* (1)	n/k	155	Leith
QM June 20.				
1833 04	*Fairy* of Dundee	Ritchie, D.	50	Dundee
DC Feb. 7, 1834; DCA CE 70/11/2.				
1833 04	*Gleniffer*	n/k	31	Grnk
QM May 19.				

Year	Mth	Vessel	Master	Psgr. nos.	Departure Port
1833	04	*Hedleys* of Newcastle	Morris, J.	138	Cromarty
QM June 4.					
1833	04	*Isabella* of Dundee	Donaldson, J.	22	Dundee
QM May 27; *DPC* Feb. 1.					
1833	04	*Isabella* of Irvine	Miller	102	Grnk
QM June 2.					
1833	04	*Lancaster*	Creighton	137	Dumfries
QM June 6; *KM* Feb. 28.					
1833	04	*Margaret Bogle* of Leith	n/k	68	Leith
QM May 24; *KM* Feb. 7.					
1833	04	*Nailer*	McColl	22	Grnk
QM May 29; *PC* Feb. 28.					
1833	04	*Panmore*	n/k	24	Ayr
QM May 29.					
1833	04	*Portaferry*	Pollock, J.	103	Grnk
QM May 25; *MG* May 30.					
1833	04	*Sir William Wallace* of Aberdeen (1)	Anderson, D.	28	Aberdeen
QM May 18.					
1833	04	*St. George*	Thomson	26	Maryport
QM June 5.					
1833	04	*Triton*	McClean	71	Cromarty
QM June 1; *PC* Feb. 21.					
1833	05	*Agnes*	Outerbridge	24	Grnk
QM July 25.					
1833	05	*Betsey* of Dundee	n/k	131	Leith
QM July 11.					
1833	05	*Grace*	n/k	132	Whitehaven
QM July 16.					
1833	05	*Sovereign* (2)	n/k	44	Grnk
QM June 13.					
1833	05	*Stranraer*	n/k	75	Stranraer
QM July 10.					
1833	05	*William & Ann*	n/k	24	Glasgow
QM July 2.					
1833	06	*Amity* of Glasgow	n/k	91	Glasgow
QM Aug. 10.					
1833	06	*Argus* (2)	n/k	115	Maryport
QM Aug. 3.					

Year	Mth	Vessel	Master	Psgr. nos.	Departure Port
1833	06	*Balfour* of Whitehaven	Bee	272	Whitehaven

QM July 28.

| 1833 | 06 | *Economist* of Newport | Stokeham | 47 | Cromarty |

QM Aug. 25; Martell, *Emigration from Nova Scotia...*76; *IJ* May 17. 42 passengers left at Pictou.

| 1833 | 06 | *Jane Kay* | Toft, D. | 66 | Cromarty |

QM Aug. 12; Martell, *Ibid*, p. 75; *IJ* May 17. 106 passengers left at Pictou.

| 1833 | 06 | *Marjory* | Stocks, J. | 24 | Thurso |

QM Aug. 29; *IJ* June 7, 14 & 21.

| 1833 | 06 | *Minerva* (2) | Adamson | 59 | Leith |

QM Aug. 5.

| 1833 | 06 | *Molson* of Dundee | Elliot, J. | 108 | Dundee |

QM Aug. 1; *DC* May 3.

| 1833 | 06 | *Tamerlane* of Greenock | Martin | 278 | Grnk |

QM July 28; *PC* Apr. 18.

| 1833 | 06 | *Zephyr* | Tucker | 99 | Cromarty |

QM Aug. 21; Martell, *Emigration from Nova Scotia...*76; *IJ* May 31. 51 passengers left at Pictou.

| 1833 | 07 | *Cartha* | Morrison | 51 | Grnk |

QM Aug. 22; *PC* June 13.

| 1833 | 07 | *Favourite* of Montreal | Burns | 47 | Grnk |

QM Aug. 20.

| 1833 | 07 | *Retrench* of Greenock | Cooper | 299 | Grnk |

QM Aug. 22.

| 1833 | 07 | *Robert & Margaret* | n/k | 66 | Cromarty |

IJ May 14, June 21.

| 1833 | 08 | *Adrian* | Forster | 106 | Tobermory |

QM Oct. 5.

| 1833 | 08 | *Brilliant* of Aberdeen | Duthie | 84 | Dundee |

QM Oct. 1.

| 1833 | 08 | *Gleniffer* | Dunlop | 21 | Grnk |

QM Sept. 29.

| 1833 | 08 | *Prince George* of Alloa | Morrison | 48 | Leith |

QM Oct. 1.

| 1833 | 08 | *Robertson* | Neil | 31 | Grnk |

QM Sept. 14.

| 1834 | 04 | *Brilliant* of Aberdeen | Duthie | 137 | Aberdeen |

QM May 15.

| 1834 | 04 | *Canada* of Greenock | Allan | 51 | Grnk |

QM May 8; *PC* Apr. 17.

Year Mth	Vessel	Master	Psgr. nos.	Departure Port
1834 04 QM May 17.	*Cherokee* of Glasgow	Miller	52	Glasgow
1834 04 PC Apr. 17.	*Cherub*	n/k	24	Grnk
1834 04 QM May 15.	*Cyrus*	Scott	33	Dundee
1834 04 QM May 13.	*Fairy Queen*	Ritchie, D.	28	Dundee
1834 04 QM May 8; PC Apr. 17.	*Favourite* of Montreal	Burns	31	Grnk
1834 04 QM May 17.	*General Graham* of Alloa	Craigie	66	Alloa
1834 04 QM May 13.	*Hercules* of Aberdeen	Walker, D.	75	Aberdeen
1834 04 QM May 17.	*Margaret Bogle* of Leith	Smith	41	Leith
1834 04 QM May 13.	*Springhill* of Irvine	Auld	16	Grnk
1834 04 QM May 24.	*Stranraer*	Irvine	72	Stranraer
1834 04 QM May 15.	*Victoria* of Dundee	Berrie	34	Dundee
1834 05 QM June 10.	*Rosebud*	Roy	80	Glasgow
1834 06 QM July 15.	*Alfred*	n/k	243	Leith
1834 06 QM July 8.	*Amity* of Glasgow	Mercer, J.	33	Grnk
1834 06 QM July 20.	*Cartha*	Morrison	184	Grnk
1834 06 QM July 29.	*Conference* of Newcastle	Buchan	112	Leith
1834 06 QM July 12.	*Favourite* (2)	Girvan	33	Ayr
1834 06 QM July 17.	*Henry*	Anderson	154	Glasgow
1834 07 QM Aug. 14.	*Bowes*	Faulkner	172	Cromarty

Year Mth	Vessel	Master	Psgr. nos.	Departure Port
1834 07 *QM* Aug. 14.	*Fame* (3)	Wright	35	Grnk
1834 07 *QM* Aug. 26.	*Favourite* of Montreal	Burns	87	Grnk
1834 07 *QM* Aug. 7.	*Gleniffer*	Watson	181	Grnk
1834 07 *QM* Aug. 14.	*John & Mary*	Nicholson	79	Leith
1834 07 *QM* Aug. 14.	*Portia*	Hirst	171	Grnk
1834 07 *QM* Aug. 19.	*Stirling Castle* of Greenock	Fraser	358	Islay
1834 08 *QM* Sept. 30.	*Canada* of Greenock	Allan	46	Grnk
1834 08 *QM* Sept. 20.	*Hercules* of Aberdeen	Walker, D.	133	Aberdeen
1834 08 *QM* Sept. 13.	*Janet Izat* of Alloa	n/k	100	Tobermory
1834 09 *QM* Oct. 7.	*Brilliant* of Aberdeen	Duthie	169	Aberdeen
1834 09 *QM* Oct. 7.	*Cherokee* of Glasgow	Miller	26	Grnk
1835 04 *QM* June 6. "Respectable farmers with considerable capital." PP w/e June 6.	*Amity* of Aberdeen	Rae, W.	39	Aberdeen
1835 04 *QM* May 30.	*Berwick on Tweed*	Muers	20	Berwick
1835 04 *QM* May 29.	*Cyrus*	Scott	33	Leith
1835 04 *QM* June 18, *AH* April 18.	*Hercules* of Aberdeen	Walker, D.	70	Aberdeen
1835 04 *QM* May 23.	*Lother*	Murphy	29	Annan
1835 04 *QM* May 19.	*Victoria* of Dundee	n/k	19	Dundee
1835 05 *QM* June 6.	*Carleton* of Aberdeen	Anderson	64	Aberdeen
1835 05 *QM* June 4.	*Caroline*	Lowergran	50	Berwick

Year	Mth	Vessel	Master	Psgr. nos.	Departure Port
1835	05	*Favourite* of Montreal	Burns	39	Grnk
QM June 18.					
1835	05	*Pacific* of Aberdeen	Morrison, J.	24	Aberdeen
QM June 27.					
1835	06	*Cartha*	n/k	48	Grnk
QM July 11.					
1835	06	*Maria* (2)	Davieson	111	Cromarty
QM Aug. 1; PP w/e Aug. 22. Smallpox aboard.					
1835	07	*Chieftain* of Kirkaldy	Spark	85	Cromarty
QM Aug. 4.					
1835	07	*Gleniffer*	Wilson	31	Grnk
QM Aug. 22.					
1835	07	*Hector*	Davison	49	Islay
QM Aug. 22.					
1835	07	*Pilgrim* of Aberdeen	Allan, G.	49	Aberdeen
QM Aug. 4.					
1835	07	*Retreat*	Hamilton	92	Grnk
QM Aug. 4.					
1835	08	*Canada* of Greenock	Allan	70	Grnk
QM Sept. 24.					
1835	08	*Robert McWilliam* of Aberdeen	Williamson	25	Aberdeen
QM Sept. 19.					
1835	09	*Brilliant* of Aberdeen	Duthie	70	Aberdeen
QM Oct. 13.					
1835	09	*Paragon*	Goodchild	46	Cromarty
QM Oct. 27. 54 passengers left at Pictou.					
1836	03	*Favourite* of Montreal	Allan, B.	43	Grnk
QM May 17; *IJ* March 5.					
1836	04	*Brilliant* of Aberdeen	Duthie	80	Aberdeen
QM June 4; *AH* April 16.					
1836	04	*Cyrus*	Nicoll	33	Leith
QM June 18.					
1836	04	*Globe*	Lindsay	15	Montrose
QM May 31.					
1836	04	*Monarch* of Glasgow	Welsh	15	Grnk
QM May 28.					
1836	04	*Pacific* of Aberdeen	Morrison, J.	122	Aberdeen
AH April 23.					

Year	Mth	Vessel	Master	Psgr. nos.	Departure Port
1836	04	*Robertson*	Neil	25	Grnk

QM May 17.

| 1836 | 04 | *Sir William Wallace* of Aberdeen (2) | Anderson, D. | 17 | Aberdeen |

QM May 28; *AH* April 23.

| 1836 | 05 | *Augusta* of Aberdeen | Rae, W. | 46 | Aberdeen |

QM June 22.

| 1836 | 05 | *Corsair* of Greenock | Ritchie | 95 | Grnk |

QM July 16.

| 1836 | 05 | *Shakespeare* of Aberdeen | Rosie | 84 | Aberdeen |

QM July 19.

| 1836 | 06 | *Albion* of Scarborough | Hicks, M. | 28 | Cromarty |

QM Sept. 16; Martell, *Emigration from Nova Scotia...* p. 84; *IJ* 10 June, 1 July. 75 passengers left at Sydney, Cape Breton.

| 1836 | 06 | *Favourite* of Montreal | Allan, B. | 29 | Grnk |

QM Sept. 10.

| 1836 | 06 | *Hercules* of Aberdeen | Walker, D. | 158 | Aberdeen |

QM Aug. 27; *AH* June 18.

| 1836 | 06 | *Tweed* | Slocombe | 245 | Cromarty |

QM July 19; *EC* May 20.

| 1836 | 06 | *Viewforth* of Kirkaldy | Elden | 150 | Cromarty |

QM July 19; *EC* May 20.

| 1836 | 07 | *Belmont* of Greenock | Ford | 77 | Grnk |

QM Aug. 25.

| 1836 | 07 | *Canada* of Greenock | n/k | 52 | Grnk |

QM Sept. 22.

| 1836 | 07 | *Circassian* of Aberdeen | Ritchie, T. | 117 | Aberdeen |

QM Sept. 3.

| 1836 | 07 | *Henry* | Gibson | 60 | Grnk |

QM Sept. 6.

| 1836 | 07 | *Highlander* of Aberdeen | Fluckhart | 150 | Cromarty |

QM Aug. 19.

| 1836 | 07 | *Mariner* of Sunderland | Collins | 145 | Loch Eriboll |

QM Sept. 6; *IJ* July 1; *JJ* July 1; *PP* w/e Sept. 10. 67 of the 145 passengers had intended to disembark at Pictou.

| 1836 | 08 | *Brilliant* of Aberdeen | Elliot, J. | 28 | Aberdeen |

QM Oct. 6.

| 1836 | 08 | *Cherokee* of Glasgow | Miller | 16 | Grnk |

QM Sept. 27.

Year	Mth	Vessel	Master	Psgr. nos.	Departure Port
1836	08	*Deveron* of Glasgow	Anderson	174	Loch Indaal
QM Oct. 13.					
1836	08	*Monarch* of Glasgow	Welsh	23	Glasgow
QM Oct. 11.					
1836	08	*Palmona*	Morison	15	Grnk
QM Oct. 6.					
1836	08	*Rebecca* of Greenock	Galetly	24	Grnk
QM Oct. 6.					
1836	08	*Sir William Wallace* of Aberdeen (2)	Anderson	18	Aberdeen
QM Sept. 27.					
1837	04	*Brilliant* of Aberdeen	Elliot, J.	40	Aberdeen
QM May 23.					
1837	04	*Canada* of Greenock	Allan, B.	28	Grnk
QM May 6.					
1837	04	*Cherokee* of Glasgow	Miller	44	Glasgow
QM June 7.					
1837	04	*Jane Christie*	Scott	34	Leith
QM May 30.					
1837	04	*Richibucto* of Aberdeen	Ganson, H.	45	Grnk
QM May 30.					
1837	05	*Arabian* of Greenock	Allan	81	Grnk
QM June 7.					
1837	05	*Blackness* of Dundee	Paton	49	Leith
QM June 18.					
1837	05	*Margaret Bogle* of Leith	Smith	179	Cromarty
QM July 1; *JJ* Mar. 31, Apr. 14 & May 26; *EC* Apr. 21.					
1837	05	*Pacific* of Aberdeen	Thompson	50	Aberdeen
QM May 30.					
1837	06	*Corsair* of Greenock	Ritchie	29	Grnk
QM Aug. 11.					
1837	06	*Hercules* of Aberdeen	Walker, D.	42	Stornoway
QM July 27; Martell, *Emigration from Nova Scotia*, 86. Seventy passengers left at Pictou.					
1837	06	*Norfolk*	Harrison	41	Berwick
QM July 27.					
1837	06	*Quebec Packet* of Aberdeen	Stephen	35	Aberdeen
QM July 22.					
1837	06	*Royal Adelaide* of Greenock	Dewar	152	Grnk
QM July 27.					

Year	Mth	Vessel	Master	Psgr. nos.	Departure Port
1837	06	*Swift* of Sunderland	Beveridge	215	Cromarty

QM July 27; *EC* Apr. 28. Steerage fare for adults was 52 shillings.

| 1837 | 07 | *Thomas Worthington* | Morrison | 96 | Grnk |

QM Aug. 31.

| 1837 | 08 | *Arabian* of Greenock | Allan | 28 | Grnk |

QM Oct. 5.

| 1838 | 04 | *Ann* (3) | Wallace | 20 | Leith |

QM May 26.

| 1838 | 04 | *Brilliant* of Aberdeen | Elliot, J. | 24 | Aberdeen |

QM May 12.

| 1838 | 04 | *Carleton* of Aberdeen | Anderson, A. | 32 | Aberdeen |

QM May 22.

| 1838 | 06 | *Pilgrim* of Aberdeen | Allan | 81 | Aberdeen |

QM Aug. 19.

| 1838 | 06 | *Superb* of Greenock | Shannon | 17 | Grnk |

QM Aug. 19.

| 1838 | 07 | *Canada* of Greenock | Allan, B. | 41 | Grnk |

QM Sept. 8.

| 1838 | 07 | *Corsair* of Greenock | Ritchie | 250 | Tobermory |

QM Sept. 18; Martell, *Emigration from Nova* Scotia, 90. 155 passengers left at Sydney, Cape Breton.

| 1838 | 07 | *Eliza* | McEwen | 42 | Grnk |

QM Aug. 21; PP w/e 25 Aug. Emigrants had "considerable capital."

| 1838 | 08 | *Arabian* of Greenock | Allan | 16 | Grnk |

QM Sept. 21.

| 1839 | 04 | *Cruickston Castle* of Greenock | McKinlay | 47 | Grnk |

QM May 14.

| 1839 | 06 | *Kilmuir* | Blair | 18 | Grnk |

QM Aug. 24.

| 1839 | 06 | *Kincardineshire* of Aberdeen | Goven | 55 | Aberdeen |

QG Aug. 31; *MT* Sept. 3.

| 1839 | 06 | *Sir William Wallace* of Aberdeen (2) | Tulloch, J. | 19 | Aberdeen |

QM Aug. 24.

| 1839 | 08 | *Canada* of Greenock | Allan | 35 | Grnk |

QM Sept. 10.

| 1840 | 04 | *Caroline* of Aberdeen | Marsh, J. | 16 | Aberdeen |

PP w/e May 23.

| 1840 | 04 | *Cruickston Castle* of Greenock | McInlay | 18 | Grnk |

PP w/e May 23.

Year	Mth	Vessel	Master	Psgr. nos.	Departure Port
1840	04	*Henry* of Montrose	Ross	30	Dundee

PP 1841 (369) xv.

| 1840 | 04 | *Osprey* of Leith | Kirk | 90 | Cromarty |

IC Aug. 5; JJ Apr. 10; EC Apr. 3. 60 passengers left at Pictou.

| 1840 | 04 | *Sarah* of Aberdeen | Allan | 29 | Aberdeen |

PP 1841 (369) xv.

| 1840 | 04 | *Victoria* of Dundee | Peters, G. | 21 | Leith |

PP w/e May 23.

| 1840 | 05 | *Ann Grant* of Sligo | Murdoch | 72 | Glasgow |

PP w/e July 18.

| 1840 | 05 | *Hercules* of Aberdeen | Davidson | 42 | Aberdeen |

PP w/e July 11.

| 1840 | 05 | *Leven Lass* of Glasgow | Wright | 59 | Glasgow |

PP w/e July 18.

| 1840 | 05 | *Sisters* of Aberdeen | Hull | 41 | Aberdeen |

PP w/e July 18.

| 1840 | 06 | *Westmorland* | Duncan | 76 | Leith |

PP w/e Aug. 22.

| 1840 | 07 | *Brilliant* of Aberdeen | Elliot, J. | 23 | Aberdeen |

PP w/e Sept. 12.

| 1840 | 07 | *British King* of Dundee | Brown, A. | 20 | Cromarty |

IC Aug. 5; PP w/e Aug. 22; JJ May 29. Brought capital of £7,000 to £8,000. 137 passengers left at Pictou.

| 1840 | 07 | *Jamaica* of Glasgow | Martin | 58 | Grnk |

PP w/e Aug. 29.

| 1840 | 07 | *Lord Panmure* of Dundee | McNeill, J. | 22 | Dundee |

PP w/e Sept. 19.

| 1840 | 07 | *Quebec Packet* of Aberdeen | Stephen | 60 | Cromarty |

IC Aug. 5; JJ June 26; PP w/e Sept. 12. Passengers had £800 to £1,000 in gold.

| 1840 | 07 | *Sarah* of Aberdeen | Allan, G. | 22 | Aberdeen |

PP w/e Sept. 19.

| 1840 | 08 | *Canada* of Greenock | Allan, B. | 31 | Grnk |

PP w/e Sept. 19.

| 1841 | 04 | *Alarm* of Cork | Brown, J. | 133 | Glasgow |

PP 1842 (301) xxxi.

| 1841 | 04 | *Brilliant* of Aberdeen | n/k | 82 | Aberdeen |

PP 1842 (301) xxxi.

| 1841 | 04 | *Cornelia* of Greenock | Croall, D. | 98 | Glasgow |

PP w/e June 19; PP 1842 (301) xxxi. Members of Glasgow emigration society.

Year	Mth	Vessel	Master	Psgr. nos.	Departure Port
1841	04	*Duke of Buccleugh*	Blair, J.	41	Dumfries

PP 1842 (301) xxxi; *DT* Mar. 22.

| 1841 | 04 | *Fairy* of Dundee | Peters, G. | 123 | Cromarty |

PP 1842 (301) xxxi; *JJ* March 12.

| 1841 | 04 | *Favourite* of Greenock | Bannerman | 42 | Glasgow |

PP 1842 (301) xxxi.

| 1841 | 04 | *Mary Ann* of London | Moody, J. | 220 | Grnk |

PP w/e June 19; PP 1842 (301) xxxi. Members of Glasgow emigration society.

| 1841 | 04 | *Mohawk* of Greenock | n/k | 37 | Glasgow |

PP 1842 (301) xxxi.

| 1841 | 04 | *Pacific* of Aberdeen | Morrison, J. | 171 | Thurso |

PP 1842 (301) xxxi; *JJ* Feb 5. 22 passengers left at Pictou.

| 1841 | 04 | *Sarah Botsford* of Glasgow | Wallace, M. | 219 | Glasgow |

PP 1842 (301) xxxi.

| 1841 | 05 | *Ann and Mary* | n/k | 87 | Banff |

PP w/e July 17; PP 1842 (301) xxxi.

| 1841 | 05 | *Isabella* of Irvine | Miller, D. | 33 | Grnk |

PP 1842 (301) xxxi.

| 1841 | 05 | *Stirling* | Jessie, A. | 154 | Glasgow |

PP w/e Aug. 7; PP 1842 (301) xxxi. Members of Glasgow emigration society.

| 1841 | 06 | *Andrew White* of Sunderland | Clark, B. | 138 | Glasgow |

PP w/e Aug. 28.

| 1841 | 06 | *Bon Accord* of Aberdeen | Sim, J. | 70 | Aberdeen |

PP w/e Sept. 4; *EC* June 11.

| 1841 | 06 | *Hants* of Greenock | Neill, W. | 71 | Glasgow |

PP w/e Sept 4; PP 1842 (301) xxxi.

| 1841 | 06 | *Independence* of Belfast | n/k | 245 | Liverpool |

PP w/e Aug. 14; PP 1842 (301) xxxi.

| 1841 | 06 | *Lady Grey* of North Shields | Grey, W. | 105 | Cromarty |

IJ June 25; PP w/e Aug. 28; PP 1842 (301) xxxi; NAS RH 1/2/908. 135 passengers left at Pictou.

| 1841 | 06 | *Margaret Bogle* of Leith | Smith, W. | 117 | Thurso and Loch Laxford |

PP w/e July 24; PP 1842 (301) xxxi; *IJ* June 4; *JJ* April 30.

| 1841 | 06 | *Patriot* | n/k | 19 | Leith |

PP w/e Aug. 28.

| 1841 | 06 | *Saphiras* of Whitby | Brown, R. | 202 | Loch Laxford |

PP 1842 (301) xxxi; *IJ* June 4.

| 1841 | 06 | *Taurus* of Aberdeen | n/k | 134 | Aberdeen |

PP w/e July 17; PP 1842 (301) xxxi.

Year	Mth	Vessel	Master	Psgr. nos.	Departure Port
1841	06	*Wanderer*	Cowan, F.	141	Glasgow

PP w/e Aug 21; PP 1842 (301) xxxi. 58 (8 families) assisted by their landlord – Neill Malcolm.

| 1841 | 07 | *Canada* of Greenock | Allan. B. | 115 | Glasgow |

PP w/e Sept. 4.

| 1841 | 07 | *Charles* | n/k | 145 | Stornoway |

PP 1842 (301) xxxi.

| 1841 | 07 | *Jessy Logan* | n/k | 27 | Grnk |

PP w/e Sept. 4.

| 1841 | 07 | *John Walker* of Liverpool | n/k | 49 | Skye |

PP w/e Aug. 28.

| 1841 | 07 | *Lady Hood* of Stornoway | n/k | 78 | Stornoway |

PP w/e Sept. 4.

| 1841 | 07 | *Stillman* | Williamson, C. | 60 | Glasgow |

PP 1842 (301) xxxi.

| 1841 | 08 | *Caledonia* of Greenock | n/k | 54 | Grnk |

PP w/e Sept. 11.

| 1841 | 08 | *Favourite* of Greenock | Bannerman | 34 | Glasgow |

PP w/e Sept. 25; PP 1842 (301) xxxi.

| 1841 | 09 | *Universe* of Aberdeen | n/k | 19 | Thurso |

PP w/e Oct. 9. 105 passengers left at Pictou.

| 1842 | 03 | *Bowling* of Glasgow | Gentle, R. | 157 | Glasgow |

PP w/e June 11; SRA TCN-21(2). Members of Glasgow emigration societies.

| 1842 | 03 | *Harper* | Murphy | 235 | Glasgow |

PP w/e June 11; SRA TCN-21(2). 29 passengers were members of Glasgow emigration societies.

| 1842 | 03 | *James Dean* of Greenock | Wilson | 29 | Glasgow |

PP w/e May 28; SRA TCN-21(2).

| 1842 | 03 | *Kent* | Gardner, J. | 54 | Glasgow |

PP w/e May 28; SRA TCN-21(2).

| 1842 | 03 | *Mohawk* of Greenock | Miller | 45 | Glasgow |

PP w/e May 21; SRA TCN-21(2); *GH* Mar. 4.

| 1842 | 03 | *Monarch* of Glasgow | Allan | 36 | Glasgow |

PP w/e May 21; SRA TCN-21(2); *GH* Mar. 4.

| 1842 | 03 | *Queen of the Isles* of Stromness | Leask | 105 | Glasgow |

PP w/e June 18; SRA TCN-21(2); *GH* Mar. 4.

| 1842 | 04 | *Apollo* of Dundee | Walker, H. | 48 | Dundee |

PP w/e May 28; DCA CE 70/11/6.

| 1842 | 04 | *Blonde* of Montreal | Crawford | 396 | Glasgow |

PP w/e July 2; SRA TCN-21(2); *GH* Mar. 18. Passengers had considerable capital.

Year	Mth	Vessel	Master	Psgr. nos.	Departure Port
1842	04	*Brilliant* of Aberdeen	Elliot, J.	32	Aberdeen

PP w/e May 28; *AH* Mar. 19, Apr. 23.

| 1842 | 04 | *Carleton* | | 70 | Glasgow |

PP w/e June 4. Members of North Quarter Glasgow Emigration Society.

| 1842 | 04 | *Emma* of Dundee | Innis | 18 | Dundee |

PP w/e June 4.

| 1842 | 04 | *Feronia* | Grant, R. | 87 | Glasgow |

PP w/e July 2; SRA TCN-21(2); *GH* Apr. 22. Passengers had considerable capital.

| 1842 | 04 | *General Graham* of Alloa | n/k | 27 | Alloa |

PP w/e May 28.

| 1842 | 04 | *Leven Lass* of Glasgow | Wright | 39 | Glasgow |

PP w/e June 11; SRA TCN-21(2).

| 1842 | 04 | *Pacific* of Aberdeen | Morrison, J. | 89 | Cromarty |

PP w/e June 4; *IJ* Mar. 11; *AH* Mar. 19; *JJ* Feb. 11. Called at Orkney Islands.

| 1842 | 04 | *Sarah* of Aberdeen | Allan, G. | 28 | Aberdeen |

PP w/e May 28; *AH* Apr. 23.

| 1842 | 04 | *St Lawrence* of Aberdeen | Tulloch, J. | 25 | Aberdeen |

PP w/e May 28; *AH* Mar. 5.

| 1842 | 04 | *Wingrove* of Newcastle | Hughes | 160 | Glasgow |

PP w/e June 25; SRA TCN-21(2).Members of Glasgow emigration societies.

| 1842 | 05 | *Elizabeth* of Leith | Stocks | 15 | Leith |

PP w/e June 11.

| 1842 | 05 | *Mahaica* of Greenock | Jump, W. | 145 | Glasgow |

PP w/e July 9; SRA TCN-21(2); *GH* May 20.

| 1842 | 05 | *Pactolus* | Lloyd, T. | 182 | Glasgow |

PP w/e Aug. 6; SRA TCN-21(2); *GH* May16. 51 passengers aided by public & private contributions.

| 1842 | 05 | *Renfrewshire* | Barnes | 568 | Glasgow |

PP w/e June 11. Members of Glasgow emigration societies.

| 1842 | 05 | *Robert Morrow* of Kirkaldy | n/k | 60 | Leith |

PP w/e June 25.

| 1842 | 05 | *Superior* of Peterhead | Manson | 191 | Cromarty |

PP w/e July 9; *IJ* Mar. 18, 25, July 29. 52 passengers left at Pictou.

| 1842 | 05 | *Troubadour* of Irvine | McDowell, J. | 224 | Glasgow |

PP w/e Aug. 6; SRA TCN-21(2); *GH* Apr. 22.

| 1842 | 05 | *Wexford* of Wexford | Slatterly, J. | 200 | Grnk |

PP w/e July 9; SRA TCN-21(2). 130 passengers were members of emigration societies.

| 1842 | 06 | *Alice* of Milford | Rees, S. | 107 | Glasgow |

PP w/e Aug. 20; SRA TCN-21(2); GH May 20.

Year	Mth	Vessel	Master	Psgr. nos.	Departure Port
1842	06	*Joseph Green* of Peterhead	Volum, J.	239	Cromarty

PP w/e July 23; *IJ* March 25. 38 passengers received financial help.

1842	06	*Margaret Wilkie* of Greenock	Miller, J.	111	Grnk

PP w/e Sept. 17; SRA TCN-21(2); *GH* June 17.

1842	06	*Royal Bride* of Dundee	Welsh, G.	78	Dundee

PP w/e Aug. 13; DCA CE 70/11/6; *DC* May 13.

1842	06	*St Andrew* of New Brunswick	Leith, J.	133	Lochmaddy

PP w/e Aug. 6; *IJ* Aug. 19.

1842	06	*William Glen Anderson* of Glasgow	Gillespie	152	Aberdeen

PP w/e Aug. 13; *AH* June 18.

1842	07	*Bellona* of Glasgow	Mitchell, R.	18	Grnk

PP w/e Oct. 1; SRA TCN-21(2); *GH* July 22.

1842	07	*Caledonia* of Greenock	Allan, B.	86	Glasgow

PP w/e Aug. 27; SRA TCN-21(2); *GH* June 20.

1842	07	*Elephanta* of Glasgow	Ross, D.	130	Grnk

GH June 13; PP w/e Aug. 27.

1842	07	*Gem* of Aberdeen	Ross, P.	30	Leith

PP w/e Aug. 27; *AH* June 4.

1842	07	*Hercules* of Liverpool	Postill, F.	59	Lochmaddy

PP w/e Sept. 17; *IJ* Aug. 19.

1842	07	*James Campbell* of Glasgow	Miller, J.	27	Glasgow

PP w/e Sept. 17; SRA TCN-21(2); *GH* June 13.

1842	07	*Jane Brown* of Glasgow	Wylie, J.	30	Glasgow

PP w/e Oct. 1; SRA TCN-21(2); *GH* June 13.

1842	07	*Lady Falkland*	Parker	361	Port Glasgow

PP w/e Sept. 3; *GH* June 24.

1842	07	*Merlin*	Thompson, D.	185	Grnk

PP w/e Sept. 3; *GH* June 10.

1842	07	*Mohawk* of Greenock	Bannerman	62	Glasgow

PP w/e Sept. 17; SRA TCN-21(2).

1842	07	*Sir William Wallace* of Aberdeen (2)	Anderson, R.	78	Thurso

PP w/e Aug. 20; *IJ* June 3; *AH* June 4; *JJ* June 10.

1842	08	*Apollo* of Dundee	Walker, H.	20	Dundee

PP w/e Oct. 15.

1842	08	*Brilliant* of Aberdeen	Elliot, J.	32	Aberdeen

PP w/e Oct. 15.

Year	Mth	Vessel	Master	Psgr. nos.	Departure Port
1842	08	*Favourite* of Greenock	Greenhorn, A.	62	Glasgow

PP w/e Oct. 15; SRA TCN-21(2).

Year	Mth	Vessel	Master	Psgr. nos.	Departure Port
1842	08	*Lady Emily* of Sunderland	Smith, J.	64	Loch Laxford

PP w/e Oct .1; *IJ* June 10, Sept. 30. 86 passengers left at Pictou.

Year	Mth	Vessel	Master	Psgr. nos.	Departure Port
1842	08	*Sarah* of Aberdeen	Allan	25	Aberdeen

PP w/e Oct. 15.

Year	Mth	Vessel	Master	Psgr. nos.	Departure Port
1843	03	*Eleutheria* of South Shields	McDonaugh, W.	160	Glasgow

PP 1844 (181) xxxv; PP w/e May 27. 1 of 5 vessels taking a total of 900 members of 18 Glasgow emigration societies.

Year	Mth	Vessel	Master	Psgr. nos.	Departure Port
1843	04	*Ann and Mary*	n/k	29	Banff

PP 1844 (181) xxxv

Year	Mth	Vessel	Master	Psgr. nos.	Departure Port
1843	04	*Apollo* of Dundee	n/k	42	Dundee

PP 1844 (181) xxxv; *DC* Feb. 24.

Year	Mth	Vessel	Master	Psgr. nos.	Departure Port
1843	04	*Bona Dea*	Brown, H.	446	Grnk

PP 1844 (181) xxxv; PP w/e June 24; PRO CO 384/74. 1 of 5 vessels taking a total of 900 members of 18 Glasgow emigration societies.

Year	Mth	Vessel	Master	Psgr. nos.	Departure Port
1843	04	*Brilliant* of Aberdeen	Barr, R.	23	Aberdeen

PP 1844 (181) xxxv.

Year	Mth	Vessel	Master	Psgr. nos.	Departure Port
1843	04	*Caledonia* of Greenock	n/k	171	Glasgow

PP 1844 (181) xxxv.

Year	Mth	Vessel	Master	Psgr. nos.	Departure Port
1843	04	*Commodore*	Miller, J.	27	Glasgow

PP 1844 (181) xxxv.

Year	Mth	Vessel	Master	Psgr. nos.	Departure Port
1843	04	*Eagle* (2)	Morton, R.	94	Glasgow

PP 1844 (181) xxxv; *IC* Mar. 15.

Year	Mth	Vessel	Master	Psgr. nos.	Departure Port
1843	04	*Emma* of Dundee	n/k	34	Dundee

PP 1844 (181) xxxv; *DC* March 3.

Year	Mth	Vessel	Master	Psgr. nos.	Departure Port
1843	04	*Essex*	n/k	29	Glasgow

PP 1844 (181) xxxv.

Year	Mth	Vessel	Master	Psgr. nos.	Departure Port
1843	04	*Favourite* of Greenock	n/k	78	Glasgow

PP 1844 (181) xxxv.

Year	Mth	Vessel	Master	Psgr. nos.	Departure Port
1843	04	*Flora* of Dundee	n/k	57	Dundee

PP 1844 (181) xxxv.

Year	Mth	Vessel	Master	Psgr. nos.	Departure Port
1843	04	*Hector*	n/k	16	Glasgow

PP 1844 (181) xxxv.

Year	Mth	Vessel	Master	Psgr. nos.	Departure Port
1843	04	*Heroine* of Aberdeen	n/k	48	Aberdeen

PP 1844 (181) xxxv.

Year	Mth	Vessel	Master	Psgr. nos.	Departure Port
1843	04	*James Redden* of Dumfries	n/k	31	Dumfries

PP 1844 (181) xxxv.

Year	Mth	Vessel	Master	Psgr. nos.	Departure Port
1843	04	*Jane Brown* of Glasgow	Wylie, J.	23	Glasgow

PP 1844 (181) xxxv.

1843	04	*Jane Duffus* of Irvine	Donald, H.	257	Glasgow

PP 1844 (181) xxxv; PP w/e June 17; PRO CO 384/74. 1 of 5 vessels taking a total of 900 members of 18 Glasgow emigration societies. Members of Parkhead, Camlachie, Hamilton & Govan societies.

1843	04	*Jeanie Deans*	Miller, D.	75	Glasgow

PP 1844 (181) xxxv; PP w/e June 17.

1843	04	*Mahaica* of Greenock	Jump, W.	39	Glasgow

PP 1844 (181) xxxv; PP w/e June 17.

1843	04	*Mohawk* of Greenock	Bannerman, G.	17	Glasgow

PP 1844 (181) xxxv.

1843	04	*New York Packet*	n/k	80	Grnk

PP 1844 (181) xxxv.

1843	04	*Pacific* of Aberdeen	n/k	39	Thurso

PP 1844 (181) xxxv.

1843	04	*Robert Murrow*	n/k	41	Leith

PP 1844 (181) xxxv.

1843	04	*Sarah* (2)	McLean, W.	58	Glasgow

PP 1844 (181) xxxv; *GSP* Apr. 23.

1843	04	*Sarah* of Aberdeen	n/k	33	Aberdeen

PP 1844 (181) xxxv.

1843	04	*Springfield*	n/k	42	Glasgow

PP 1844 (181) xxxv.

1843	04	*St Lawrence* of Aberdeen	n/k	32	Aberdeen

PP 1844 (181) xxxv.

1843	04	*Superb* of Greenock	n/k	194	Glasgow

PP 1844 (181) xxxv.

1843	04	*Symmetry*	n/k	110	Thurso

PP 1844 (181) xxxv; PP w/e July 1. 18 passengers left at Pictou and PEI.

1843	05	*Blonde* of Montreal	n/k	297	Glasgow

PP 1844 (181) xxxv; PP w/e June 24.

1843	05	*Brilliant* of Aberdeen	Bank, R.	191	Glasgow

PP 1844 (181) xxxv; PP w/e June 10; *IC* Apr. 19. 1 of 5 vessels taking a total of 900 members of 18 Glasgow emigration societies. 47 passengers (10 families) aided by their landlords from Johnson village near Glasgow.

1843	05	*Caspian*	n/k	35	Glasgow

PP 1844 (181) xxxv.

1843	05	*Catherine* (2)	McKechney	22	Tobermory

PP 1844 (181) xxxv; PP w/e Oct. 14. 275 steerage passengers, shipwrecked; transhipped on *John & Robert*; all but 22 landed at Cape Breton.

Year	Mth	Vessel	Master	Psgr. nos.	Departure Port
1843	05	*Hamilton* of Glasgow	Dick, J.	283	Grnk

PP 1844 (181) xxxv; PP w/e July 15; *IC* May 10.

| 1843 | 05 | *Jean Baptiste* of Glasgow | n/k | 15 | Glasgow |

PP 1844 (181) xxxv.

| 1843 | 05 | *Lady Kinnaird* of Dundee | n/k | 65 | Dundee |

PP 1844 (181) xxxv; PP w/e July 1; *DC* Apr. 7.

| 1843 | 05 | *Margaret Bogle* of Leith | n/k | 70 | Leith |

PP 1844 (181) xxxv; PP w/e July 1.

| 1843 | 05 | *Roger Stewart* | n/k | 56 | Grnk |

PP 1844 (181) xxxv; PP w/e June 24.

| 1843 | 05 | *Romulus* of Greenock | Coll, T. | 165 | Grnk |

PP 1844 (181) xxxv; PP w/e June 24. 1 of 5 vessels taking a total of 900 members of 18 Glasgow emigration societies.

| 1843 | 06 | *California* of Greenock | Auld | 328 | Glasgow |

PP 1844 (181) xxxv; PP w/e July 15; *IC* May 24.

| 1843 | 06 | *Canada* of Greenock | McArthur, J. | 43 | Glasgow |

PP 1844 (181) xxxv.

| 1843 | 06 | *George* of Dundee | Hanley, F. | 120 | Loch Laxford |

PP 1844 (181) xxxv; PP w/e Sept. 16; *DC* Apr. 28. 95 passengers left at Pictou.

| 1843 | 06 | *John Cumming* | n/k | 83 | Glasgow |

PP 1844 (181) xxxv.

| 1843 | 06 | *Margaret* of Greenock | McBride, A. | 238 | Glasgow |

PP 1844 (181) xxxv; *IC* June 14.

| 1843 | 06 | *Menapia* | Queen, J. | 183 | Glasgow |

PP 1844 (181) xxxv; PP w/e July 29.

| 1843 | 06 | *Messenger* | Mather, W. | 42 | Glasgow |

PP 1844 (181) xxxv.

| 1843 | 06 | *Monument* | n/k | 87 | Glasgow |

PP 1844 (181) xxxv.

| 1843 | 06 | *Navarino* | n/k | 27 | Glasgow |

PP 1844 (181) xxxv.

| 1843 | 06 | *Rose* of Aberdeen | n/k | 94 | Aberdeen |

PP 1844 (181) xxxv.

| 1843 | 06 | *Tay* of Glasgow | Langwell | 327 | Grnk |

PP 1844 (181) xxxv; PP w/e August 5. Included 118 emigrants who were assisted by their landlords.

| 1843 | 06 | *Wilson* | n/k | 21 | Grnk |

PP 1844 (181) xxxv.

| 1843 | 07 | *Albion* of Aberdeen | Leslie, A. | 16 | Aberdeen |

PP 1844 (181) xxxv.

Year	Mth	Vessel	Master	Psgr. nos.	Departure Port
1843	07	*Blackness* of Dundee	n/k	58	Dundee

PP 1844 (181) xxxv; *DC* May 12.

Year	Mth	Vessel	Master	Psgr. nos.	Departure Port
1843	07	*Hector* of Dundee	Anderson, W.	92	Glasgow

PP 1844 (181) xxxv; PP w/e Sept. 16.

| 1843 | 07 | *Henry Kneeland* | n/k | 19 | Glasgow |

PP 1844 (181) xxxv.

| 1843 | 07 | *Jean Hastie* of Grangemouth | Robertson, J. | 44 | Thurso |

PP 1844 (181) xxxv; *DC* June 2.

| 1843 | 07 | *Octovara* | n/k | 59 | Glasgow |

PP 1844 (181) xxxv.

| 1843 | 08 | *Acadian* of Glasgow | n/k | 26 | Grnk |

PP 1844 (181) xxxv.

| 1843 | 08 | *Apollo* of Dundee | n/k | 26 | Dundee |

PP
1844 (181) xxxv; *DC* July 7.

| 1843 | 08 | *Brilliant* of Aberdeen | n/k | 36 | Aberdeen |

PP 1844 (181) xxxv; PP w/e Sept. 23.

| 1843 | 08 | *Caledonia* of Greenock | Allan, B. | 61 | Glasgow |

PP 1844 (181) xxxv; PP w/e Sept. 16.

| 1843 | 08 | *Canmore* of St. John | n/k | 23 | Glasgow |

PP 1844 (181) xxxv.

| 1843 | 08 | *Entaw* | n/k | 54 | Glasgow |

PP 1844 (181) xxxv.

| 1843 | 08 | *Favourite* of Greenock | Greenhorn, A. | 53 | Glasgow |

PP 1844 (181) xxxv.

| 1843 | 08 | *Jane Brown* of Glasgow | Wyllie, J. | 41 | Glasgow |

PP 1844 (181) xxxv.

| 1843 | 08 | *Margaret Pointer* | Miller, J. | 51 | Glasgow |

PP 1844 (181) xxxv.

| 1843 | 08 | *Warsaw* | n/k | 31 | Glasgow |

PP 1844 (181) xxxv.

| 1843 | 09 | *Jupiter* | n/k | 18 | Glasgow |

PP 1844 (181) xxxv.

| 1843 | 09 | *Perdonnet* | n/k | 37 | Glasgow |

PP 1844 (181) xxxv.

| 1843 | 10 | *Herald* of Greenock | Coubro | 319 | Grnk |

PP 1844 (181) xxxv.

| 1844 | 04 | *Messenger* | Miller | 18 | Glasgow |

QM June 8.

Year Mth	Vessel	Master	Psgr. nos.	Departure Port
1844 04 AH Apr. 27.	*St Lawrence* of Aberdeen	Tulloch, J.	139	Aberdeen
1844 05 QM July 3.	*Ann Henzell*	Henzell	75	Glasgow
1844 05 QM June 20.	*Brilliant* of Glasgow	Barr	219	Glasgow
1844 05 QM June 27.	*Congress*	Greig	22	Leith
1844 05 QM July 3.	*Hector*	Anderson	134	Glasgow
1844 06 QM July 23.	*Abigail*	Daly	341	Glasgow
1844 06 QM Aug. 3.	*Canada* of Greenock	McArthur, J.	118	Glasgow
1844 06 QM July 23.	*St Nicholas*	Morgan	29	Inverness
1844 06 QM July 23.	*William Hutt*	Rankin	138	Glasgow
1844 07 QM Aug. 27.	*Caledonia* of Greenock	Allan	45	Glasgow
1844 07 QM Sept. 10.	*Papineau*	Morland	28	Glasgow
1844 07 QM Aug. 27.	*Tay* of Glasgow	Longwell	146	Grnk
1844 07 QM Aug. 27.	*Watermillock*	Conner	34	Glasgow
1844 08 QM Sept. 24.	*St Lawrence* of Aberdeen	Tulloch, J.	76	Aberdeen
1845 03 QM May 27.	*St Lawrence* of Aberdeen	Tulloch, J.	17	Aberdeen
1845 04 QM May 20.	*Apollo* of Dundee	Walker, H.	33	Dundee
1845 04 QM June 5.	*Brilliant* of Glasgow	Barr	39	Glasgow
1845 04 QM May 15.	*Favourite* of Greenock	Crawford	30	Glasgow
1845 04 QM May 27.	*Margaret Boyle*	Scott	20	Leith

Year	Mth	Vessel	Master	Psgr. nos.	Departure Port
1845	05	*Abercrombie*	Louttef	27	Glasgow
QM July 1.					
1845	05	*Agitator*	Henry	33	Glasgow
QM June 28.					
1845	05	*Blonde* of Montreal	Crawford	226	Glasgow
QM July 10.					
1845	05	*Brilliant* of Aberdeen	Elliot, J.	37	Aberdeen
QM June 7; *AH* May 10.					
1845	05	*Heroine* of Aberdeen	Walker, D.	70	Aberdeen
AH May 24, 31; *QM* July 15.					
1845	05	*Jeanie Deans*	Miller	36	Glasgow
QM July 1.					
1845	05	*Mary* of Greenock (2)	Harrison, J.	25	Glasgow
QM July 12.					
1845	05	*St Lawrence* of Aberdeen	Tulloch, J.	98	Aberdeen
AH May 10.					
1845	06	*Afghan*	Black	229	Grnk
QM Aug. 5.					
1845	06	*Canada* of Greenock	McArthur, J.	110	Glasgow
QM July 31.					
1845	06	*Lerwick*	Giffney	83	Dundee
QM June 28.					
1845	06	*Messenger*	Miller	48	Glasgow
QM July 19.					
1845	06	*New York Packet*	Hossack	108	Glasgow
QM July 31.					
1845	06	*Romulus*	Sangster	86	Glasgow
QM July 22.					
1845	06	*Romulus* of Greenock	Esson	58	Glasgow
QM July 15.					
1845	07	*Caledonia* of Greenock	Greenhorn, A.	50	Glasgow
QM Aug. 30.					
1845	07	*Erromanga* of Greenock	Kelso	38	Glasgow
QM Sept. 4.					
1845	07	*European* (2)	McBride, A.	91	Glasgow
QM Sept. 11.					
1845	07	*John Hutchison*	Harrison	76	Thurso
QM Aug. 26, *IC* May 28, July 16.					

Year	Mth	Vessel	Master	Psgr. nos.	Departure Port
1845	07	*Lord Seaton* of Aberdeen	Talbot, W.	64	Aberdeen
QM Sept. 9.					
1845	08	*St Lawrence* of Aberdeen	Tulloch, J.	52	Aberdeen
QM Sept. 25.					
1845	09	*Mary Sharp*	Woolf	17	Glasgow
QM Oct. 21.					
1846	04	*Cambria* of Greenock	Kelso	19	Glasgow
QM June 9.					
1846	04	*Fame* (4)	Miller	27	Glasgow
QM June 13.					
1846	04	*Favourite* of Greenock	Grant	39	Glasgow
QM May 14.					
1846	04	*Lord Seaton* of Aberdeen	Talbot, W.	18	Thurso
IC April 1; *QM* May 19.					
1846	04	*Norway*	Hughes	22	Glasgow
QM June 20.					
1846	04	*St Lawrence* of Aberdeen	Tulloch, J.	97	Aberdeen
QM May 19.					
1846	05	*Ianthe*	Hunter	37	Glasgow
QM July 17.					
1846	05	*Jamaica* of Glasgow	Martin	76	Glasgow
QM July 7.					
1846	06	*Blonde* of Montreal	Crawford	374	Glasgow
QM July 7.					
1846	06	*Brilliant* of Aberdeen	Brown	164	Grnk
QM Aug. 15.					
1846	06	*Heroine* of Aberdeen	Walker, D.	132	Aberdeen
QM Aug. 25.					
1846	06	*Mary* of Glasgow	Harrison, J.	42	Glasgow
QM July 28.					
1846	07	*Albion* of Greenock	Allan	70	Glasgow
QM Aug. 15.					
1846	07	*Caledonia* of Greenock	Greenhorn, A.	30	Glasgow
QM Aug. 31.					
1846	07	*Kate* of Newcastle	Taylor, T.	43	Cromarty
IC June 17; *QM* Sept. 8.					
1847	03	*Albion* of Greenock	Allan, B.	18	Glasgow
PP 1847-48 (964) xlvii.					

Year	Mth	Vessel	Master	Psgr. nos.	Departure Port
1847	03	*Caledonia* of Greenock	Greenhorn, A.	15	Glasgow

PP 1847-48 (964) xlvii.

| 1847 | 04 | *Belleisle* of Glasgow | Reid | 33 | Glasgow |

PP 1847-48 (964) xlvii.

| 1847 | 04 | *Cambria* of Greenock | Birnie, W. | 19 | Glasgow |

PP 1847-48 (964) xlvii.

| 1847 | 04 | *Earl Powis* of Dundee | n/k | 52 | Dundee |

PP 1847-48 (964) xlvii.

| 1847 | 04 | *Favourite* of Greenock | Crawford, M. | 79 | Glasgow |

PP 1847-48 (964) xlvii.

| 1847 | 04 | *Glenswilly* of Glasgow | Henderson, T. | 43 | Glasgow |

PP 1847-48 (964) xlvii.

| 1847 | 04 | *Mary* of Greenock (2) | Shotton, J. | 36 | Glasgow |

PP 1847-48 (964) xlvii.

| 1847 | 04 | *St Lawrence* of Aberdeen | n/k | 55 | Aberdeen |

PP 1847-48 (964) xlvii.

| 1847 | 05 | *Charlotte Harrison* of Greenock | McIntyre | 305 | Grnk |

PP 1847-48 (964) xlvii. 66 assisted from parish & private funds.

| 1847 | 05 | *Clansman* of Glasgow | Peck | 218 | Grnk |

PP 1847-48 (964) xlvii.

| 1847 | 05 | *Lord Panmure* of Dundee | Henderson, J. | 116 | Glasgow |

PP 1847-48 (964) xlvii.

| 1847 | 05 | *Peruvian* of Glasgow | Boyd, J. | 35 | Glasgow |

PP 1847-48 (964) xlvii.

| 1847 | 06 | *Ann Rankin* of Glasgow | McArthur, J. | 336 | Glasgow |

PP 1847-48 (964) xlvii.

| 1847 | 06 | *Britannia* of Newcastle | Simpson | 388 | Glasgow |

PP 1847-48 (964) xlvii.

| 1847 | 06 | *Euclid* of Liverpool | Bainbridge, G. | 330 | Glasgow |

PP 1847-48 (964) xlvii; *GH* May 31.

| 1847 | 06 | *Heroine* of Aberdeen | n/k | 81 | Aberdeen |

PP 1847-48 (964) xlvii.

| 1847 | 06 | *Jamaica* of Glasgow | Martin | 212 | Grnk |

PP 1847-48 (964) xlvii. 200 passengers assisted by Duke of Argyll.

| 1847 | 06 | *Panama* of Liverpool | n/k | 279 | Loch Laxford |

PP 1847-48 (964) xlvii; *IC* Sept. 7. All passengers assisted by Duke of Sutherland.

| 1847 | 07 | *Caledonia* of Greenock | Greenhorn, A. | 45 | Glasgow |

PP 1847-48 (964) xlvii.

Year	Mth	Vessel	Master	Psgr. nos.	Departure Port
1847	07	*Cambria* of Greenock	Birnie, W.	67	Glasgow
PP 1847-48 (964) xlvii.					
1847	07	*Canada* of Greenock	McArthur, J.	136	Glasgow
PP 1847-48 (964) xlvii.					
1847	07	*Eliza* of Cardiff	Jones, J.	269	Glasgow
PP 1847-48 (964) xlvii. 140 passengers assisted by Duke of Argyll.					
1847	07	*Erromanga* of Greenock	Ramsay, R.	56	Glasgow
PP 1847-48 (964) xlvii.					
1847	08	*Albion* of Greenock	Allan, B.	64	Glasgow
PP 1847-48 (964) xlvii.					
1847	08	*Belleisle* of Glasgow	Reid	28	Glasgow
PP 1847-48 (964) xlvii.					
1847	08	*Earl Powis* of Dundee	n/k	20	Dundee
PP 1847-48 (964) xlvii.					
1847	08	*Favourite* of Greenock	Crawford, M.	19	Grnk
PP 1847-48 (964) xlvii.					
1847	08	*Lord Metcalfe* of Aberdeen	Bain	51	Aberdeen
PP 1847-48 (964) xlvii.					
1847	08	*Mary* of Greenock (2)	Harrison, J.	20	Glasgow
PP 1847-48 (964) xlvii.					
1847	08	*St Lawrence* of Aberdeen	n/k	26	Aberdeen
PP 1847-48 (964) xlvii.					
1848	03	*Albion* of Greenock	Allan, B.	17	Glasgow
PP 1847-48 (971) xlvii.					
1848	03	*Caledonia* of Greenock	Greenhorn, A.	20	Glasgow
PP 1847-48 (971) xlvii.					
1848	03	*Royalist* of Alloa	Beveridge	15	Grnk
PP 1847-48 (971) xlvii.					
1848	04	*Berbice* of Aberdeen	Elliot, J.	33	Aberdeen
PP 1847-48 (971) xlvii.					
1848	04	*Cambria* of Greenock	Birnie, W.	31	Glasgow
PP 1847-48 (971) xlvii.					
1848	04	*Circassian* of Greenock	Dixon, G.	106	Glasgow
SRA T/CN 26/2.					
1848	04	*Earl Powis* of Dundee	Walker, H.	34	Dundee
PP 1847-48 (971) xlvii.					
1848	04	*Erromanga* of Greenock	Ramsay, R.	79	Glasgow
PP 1847-48 (971) xlvii.					

Year	Mth	Vessel	Master	Psgr. nos.	Departure Port
1848	04	*Favourite* of Greenock	Wylie, H.	91	Glasgow

PP 1847-48 (971) xlvii.

1848	04	*Lord Metcalfe* of Aberdeen	Bain	31	Aberdeen

PP 1847-48 (971) xlvii.

1848	04	*Mary* of Greenock (2)	Harrison, J.	25	Glasgow

PP 1847-48 (971) xlvii.

1848	04	*St Lawrence* of Aberdeen	Tulloch, J.	120	Aberdeen

PP 1847-48 (971) xlvii.

1848	05	*Greenock* of Glasgow	n/k	399	Loch Laxford

PP w/e June 30; Devine, *Highland Famine*, 324. Passengers assisted by the Duke of Sutherland.

1848	05	*Jessie Stephens* of Irvine	Miller, D.	131	Glasgow

PP w/e July 8; SRA T/CN 26/2.

1848	05	*Scotia* of Belfast	n/k	196	Loch Eribol

PP w/e July 8; Devine, Ibid, 324.

1848	06	*Blonde* of Montreal	n/k	272	Glasgow

SRA T/CN 26/2.

1848	06	*Jamaica* of Glasgow	Martin	108	Glasgow

SRA T/CN 26/2.

1848	06	*Rosina* of Campbeltown	n/k	247	Grnk

SRA T/CN 26/2; *IC* May 23.

1848	07	*Albion* of Greenock	n/k	87	Glasgow

SRA T/CN 26/2.

1848	07	*Caledonia* of Greenock	Greenhorn, A.	113	Glasgow

SRA T/CN 26/2.

1848	07	*Tay* of Glasgow	Adams	106	Glasgow

SRA T/CN 26/2; IC June 27.

1848	08	*Canada* of Greenock	Barclay	98	Glasgow

PP w/e 15 Sept; Devine, Ibid, 325. Passengers assisted by Col. John Gordon.

1848	08	*Erromanga* of Greenock	Ramsay, R.	99	Glasgow

PP w/e Sept. 15; Devine, Ibid, 325. Passengers assisted by Col. John Gordon.

1848	08	*Favourite* of Greenock	Wylie, H.	22	Glasgow

SRA T/CN 26/2.

1849	04	*Berbice* of Aberdeen	Elliot	28	Aberdeen

QM May 29.

1849	04	*Earl Powis* of Dundee	Walker, H.	42	Dundee

QM June 1.

1849	04	*Erromanga* of Greenock	Ramsay, R.	25	Glasgow

QM May 12.

Year	Mth	Vessel	Master	Psgr. nos.	Departure Port
1849	04	*Favourite* of Greenock	Wylie, H.	101	Glasgow

QM May 29.

| 1849 | 04 | *Helen* | Johnson | 18 | Montrose |

QM May 29.

| 1849 | 04 | *Lord Seaton* of Aberdeen (Orkney) | Talbot, W. | 23 | Longho |

IC March 8; *QM* May 22.

| 1849 | 04 | *St Lawrence* of Aberdeen | Tulloch, J. | 36 | Aberdeen |

QM May 29.

| 1849 | 05 | *Atlantic* | Ross | 366 | Ardrossan |

QM Aug. 14; PP 1850 (173) xl; Devine, *Highland Famine*, 326. Col. John Gordon's tenants.

| 1849 | 05 | *Blonde* of Montreal | Crawford | 300 | Glasgow |

QM July 3.

| 1849 | 05 | *Clansman* of Glasgow | Johnston | 40 | Glasgow |

QM June 23.

| 1849 | 05 | *Lanarkshire* of Glasgow | Turner | 80 | Glasgow |

QM June 23.

| 1849 | 05 | *Scotia* of Belfast | Carrey | 194 | Glasgow |

QM July 5.

| 1849 | 05 | *Springhill* of Irvine | Gunn | 67 | Glasgow |

QM June 7.

| 1849 | 06 | *Barlow* | Fraser, P. | 246 | Grnk |

PP 1850 (173) xl; Devine, Ibid, 325-6; *QM* Aug. 14. Passengers were tenants of the Duke of Argyll.

| 1849 | 06 | *Champion* of Greenock | Cochrane | 219 | Glasgow |

QM July 29.

| 1849 | 06 | *Charlotte* | Vasey, T. | 333 | Glasgow |

PP 1850 (173) xl; *IC* June 7; *QM* Aug. 14. Passengers were Duke of Argyll's tenants.

| 1849 | 06 | *Circassian* of Greenock | Dixon, G. | 209 | Glasgow |

PP 1850 (173) xl; *QM* July 10. Seventy died from disease.

| 1849 | 06 | *Jamaica* of Glasgow | Martin | 158 | Grnk |

QM July 26.

| 1849 | 06 | *Prince Albert* of Arbroath | Rodger, A. | 125 | Thurso |

JJ April 27, June 15; *IC* May 3; *QM* Aug. 14.

| 1849 | 07 | *Albion* of Greenock | McArthur, J. | 81 | Glasgow |

QM Aug. 14.

| 1849 | 07 | *Caledonia* of Greenock | Greenham | 48 | Glasgow |

QM Aug. 28.

| 1849 | 07 | *Cambria* of Greenock | Harrison, J. | 82 | Glasgow |

QM Aug. 14.

Year	Mth	Vessel	Master	Psgr. nos.	Departure Port
1849	07	*Erromanga* of Greenock	n/k	85	Glasgow

QM Sept. 1.

| 1849 | 07 | *Liskeard* of Liverpool | n/k | 341 | Inverness |

PP 1850 (173) xl; Devine, *Highland Famine*, 323. Passengers were tenants of James Baillie.

| 1849 | 07 | *Mount Stewart Elphinstone* of Glasgow | Stuart, J. | 129 | Loch Boisdale |

Devine, Ibid, 325; *IC* Nov. 8; *QM* Aug. 30. Passengers were tenants of Col. John Gordon.

| 1849 | 07 | *Tuskar* of Liverpool | n/k | 496 | Stornoway |

PP 1850 (173) xl; Devine, Ibid, 325-6. Passengers were Col. John Gordon's tenants.

| 1849 | 08 | *Berbice* of Aberdeen | Elliot, J. | 56 | Aberdeen |

QM Sept. 11.

| 1849 | 08 | *Cashmere* of Glasgow | Paton, R. | 115 | Glasgow |

psgr list: NAS GD 221/4011/53; PP 1850 (173) xl; Devine, Ibid, 325; *QM* Sept. 13. Passengers were tenants of Lord Macdonald.

| 1849 | 08 | *Favourite* of Greenock | Wylie, H. | 42 | Glasgow |

QM Sept. 13.

| 1849 | 08 | *Home* | Grey | 33 | Glasgow |

QM Sept. 15.

| 1849 | 08 | *Mary* of Greenock (2) | Munro | 25 | Glasgow |

QM Sept. 25.

| 1849 | 08 | *St Lawrence* of Aberdeen | Tulloch, J. | 17 | Aberdeen |

QM Sept. 11.

| 1849 | 08 | *Waterhen* of London | Dodds, W. | 167 | Grnk |

Psgr list: Clan Donald Centre Skye; *QM* Sept. 6. Assisted by Lord Macdonald.

| 1850 | 04 | *Berbice* of Aberdeen | Elliot, J. | 45 | Aberdeen |

AH Apr. 13.

| 1850 | 04 | *St Lawrence* of Aberdeen | Tulloch, J. | 95 | Aberdeen |

AH Apr. 20.

| 1850 | 06 | *Argo* | Breslace | 50 | Thurso |

PP 1851 (348) xi; Devine, Ibid, 324; *IC* Apr. 18, May 30. Passengers were Duke of Sutherland's tenants.

| 1850 | 06 | *Conrad* of Greenock | Barclay, J. | 200 | Glasgow |

PP 1851 (348) xl; Devine, Ibid, 326; *IC* May 9. Passengers were Duke of Argyll's tenants.

| 1850 | 06 | *George* of Dundee | Hanley, F. | 82 | Loch Laxford |

PP 1851 (348) xl; *IC* May 16. Assisted by Mr. MacDonald. [of Lochshiel].

| 1850 | 06 | *Three Bells* of Glasgow | n/k | 262 | Glasgow |

PP 1851 (348) xl.

| 1850 | 06 | *Wandsworth* of Glasgow | n/k | 377 | Grnk |

PP 1851 (348) xl.

Year	Mth	Vessel	Master	Psgr. nos.	Departure Port
1850	08	*Berbice* of Aberdeen	Elliot, J.	60	Aberdeen
AH Aug. 3.					
1850	08	*St Lawrence* of Aberdeen	Tulloch, J.	69	Aberdeen
AH Aug. 3.					
1851	04	*Berbice* of Aberdeen	Elliot	98	Aberdeen
QM May 26.					
1851	04	*Glencairn* of Glasgow	Allan	57	Glasgow
SRA T/CN 26/5.					
1851	04	*Mary* of Greenock (2)	Watson	22	Glasgow
SRA T/CN 26/5.					
1851	04	*Minerva* of Greenock	Stewart	41	Glasgow
SRA T/CN 26/5.					
1851	04	*Sarah* of Aberdeen	Sim, J.	85	Aberdeen
AJ Apr. 23.					
1851	04	*St Lawrence* of Aberdeen	Tulloch, J.	139	Aberdeen
QM May 26, *AJ* Apr. 23.					
1851	05	*Ann Rankin* of Glasgow	Burns	113	Glasgow
SRA T/CN 26/5.					
1851	05	*California* of Greenock	Gall, R.	103	Glasgow
SRA T/CN 26/5.					
1851	05	*Clutha* of Greenock	Muir	134	Glasgow
SRA T/CN 26/5; *QM* June 24.					
1851	05	*Harrison Chilton* of Liverpool	n/k	130	Glasgow
QM June 24.					
1851	05	*Islay*	n/k	68	Stornoway
Devine, *Highland Famine*, 219. Sir James Matheson's tenants.					
1851	05	*Marquis of Stafford*	n/k	500	Stornoway
Devine, Ibid, 219; *IC* June 12. Sir James Matheson's tenants.					
1851	05	*Pekin* of Irvine	Crawford	44	Glasgow
SRA T/CN 26/5.					
1851	05	*Prince George* of Alloa	n/k	203	Stornoway
PP 1852 (1474) xxxiii; Devine, Ibid, 325. Sir James Matheson's tenants.					
1851	05	*Sappho* of Sunderland	MacDonald	78	Glasgow
SRA T/CN 26/5.					
1851	05	*Susan* of Glasgow	Taylor	69	Glasgow
PP 1852 (1474) xxxiii; *IC* May 29; SRA T/CN 26/5; *QM* July 5.					
1851	05	*Urgent* of Belfast	n/k	370	Stornoway
PP 1852 (1474) xxxiii. Sir James Matheson's tenants.					

Year	Mth	Vessel	Master	Psgr. nos.	Departure Port
1851	05	*Woodfield*	n/k	69	Glasgow

QM June 24.

| 1851 | 06 | *Barlow* | n/k | 287 | Stornoway |

PP 1852 (1474) xxxiii; Devine, *Highland Famine*, 220. Sir James Matheson's tenants.

| 1851 | 06 | *Barlow* | n/k | 287 | Loch Reag |

QM July 19.

| 1851 | 06 | *Birman* of Greenock | Fuller | 270 | Grnk |

PP 1852 (1474) xxxiii; SRA T/CN 26/5; *QM* Aug. 5. 180 passengers assisted by the Duke of Argyll or Sir James Matheson.

| 1851 | 06 | *Brooksby* of Glasgow | McEwan | 285 | Loch Boisdale |

PP 1852 (1474) xxxiii; *QM* Aug. 28. Col. John Gordon's tenants.

| 1851 | 06 | *Ellen* of Liverpool | n/k | 100 | Liverpool |

PP 1852 (1474) xxxiii.

| 1851 | 06 | *Jamaica* of Glasgow | Martin | 179 | Grnk |

QM Aug. 5; PP 1852 (1474) xxxiii; SRA T/CN 26/5. 104 passengers were assisted by landlords.

| 1851 | 06 | *Justyn* of Leith | Thomson, R. | 313 | Grnk |

QM July 5; SRA T/CN 26/5; *JJ* May 16.

| 1851 | 06 | *Montezuma* of Liverpool | n/k | 440 | Loch Boisdale |

PP 1852 (1474) xxxiii. Col. John Gordon's tenants.

| 1851 | 06 | *Sesostris* of Glasgow | Logan | 302 | Glasgow |

QM July 12; PP 1852 (1474) xxxiii; SRA T/CN 26/5.

| 1851 | 06 | *Spartan* of Greenock | Morrison | 244 | Glasgow |

QM July 12; SRA T/CN 26/5; JJ June 6.

| 1851 | 06 | *Vesper* | Bennett | 52 | Thurso |

QM July 12; PP 1852 (1474) xxxiii; Devine, Ibid, 324; *IC* May 1, June 26. Duke of Sutherland's tenants.

| 1851 | 06 | *Wolfville* of Ardrossan | McMillan, J. | 149 | Loch Roag |

QM July 5; PP 1852 (1474) xxxiii; *IC* July 3; SRA T/CN 26/5. Sir James Matheson's tenants.

| 1851 | 07 | *Cambria* of Greenock | Harrison, J. | 49 | Glasgow |

QM Aug 16; T/CN 26/5.

| 1851 | 07 | *Canmore* of St John | Secyle | 104 | Glasgow |

QM Aug. 16; PP 1852 (1474) xxxiii; SRA T/CN 26/5. 16 passengers assisted by their landlord.

| 1851 | 07 | *Conrad* of Greenock | Kelso | 388 | Grnk |

QM Aug. 5; PP 1852 (1474) xxxiii; Devine, *Highland Famine*, 326; T/CN 26/5. Duke of Argyll's tenants.

| 1851 | 07 | *Onyx* of Grangemouth | Hogg | 120 | Glasgow |

QM Aug. 5; SRA T/CN 26/5.

| 1851 | 07 | *Ottawa* of Glasgow | McArthur, J. | 32 | Glasgow |

SRA T/CN 26/5.

Year	Mth	Vessel	Master	Psgr. nos.	Departure Port
1851	08	*Admiral* of Glasgow	Dixon	413	Stornoway

PP 1852 (1474) xxxiii; *IC* Aug. 7. Col. John Gordon's tenants.

| 1851 | 08 | *Berbice* of Aberdeen | Elliot, J. | 80 | Aberdeen |

AJ Aug. 20.

| 1851 | 08 | *Hope* of Glasgow | Kidston | 28 | Glasgow |

SRA T/CN 26/5.

| 1851 | 08 | *Liskeard* of Liverpool | n/k | 104 | Stornoway |

PP 1852 (1474) xxxiii. Col. John Gordon's tenants.

| 1851 | 08 | *Perthshire* of Glasgow | Scott | 437 | Lochboisdale |

QM Sept. 11; PP 1852 (1474) xxxiii. Col. John Gordon's tenants.

| 1852 | 04 | *Ann Rankin* of Glasgow | Burns | 193 | Glasgow |

PP 1852 (542) xlix; SRA T/CN 26/6, 26/7.

| 1852 | 04 | *Berbice* of Aberdeen | Elliot, J. | 115 | Aberdeen |

QM May 23; *AH* Feb. 21, July 31.

| 1852 | 04 | *Birman* of Greenock | Fuller | 29 | Glasgow |

QM May 5; SRA T/CN 21/7, 10.

| 1852 | 04 | *Empress* of Banff | Leslie | 136 | Stromness |

QM May 25.

| 1852 | 04 | *Mary* of Glasgow | Shearer | 16 | Glasgow |

QM May 15; TCN 21/7, 10; *DGC* June 1; SRA T/CN 26/6.

| 1852 | 04 | *Retreat* of Alloa | Hudlass | 32 | Alloa |

QM June 6.

| 1852 | 04 | *Sarah* of Aberdeen | Sim, J. | 81 | Aberdeen |

QM June 21; *AH* Apr. 24; *JJ* Mar. 12, Apr, 16.

| 1852 | 04 | *Springhill* of Irvine | Elliott | 96 | Ardrossan |

QM May 12; *DGC* July 21.

| 1852 | 04 | *St Lawrence* of Aberdeen | Tulloch, J. | 136 | Aberdeen |

QM May 25; *AH* Feb. 21, Apr. 24; *JJ* Mar. 12, Apr. 16.

| 1852 | 04 | *Susan* of Glasgow | Wylie | 105 | Glasgow |

PP 1852 (542) xlix; SRA T/CN 26/7.

| 1852 | 04 | *Wolfville* of Ardrossan | McMillan, J. | 179 | Glasgow |

PP 1852 (542) xlix; SRA T/CN 26/6, 26/7.

| 1852 | 05 | *California* of Greenock | Gall, R. | 194 | Glasgow |

PP 1852 (542) xlix; SRA T/CN 26/6.

| 1852 | 05 | *Commodore* of Sunderland | Hall | 15 | Glasgow |

SRA T/CN 26/7.

| 1852 | 05 | *Harlequin* of Glasgow | Craig, G. | 272 | Glasgow |

QM June 12; PP 1852 (542) xlix; SRA T/CN 26/6.

Year	Mth	Vessel	Master	Psgr. nos.	Departure Port
1852	05	*Tay* of Glasgow	Adams	274	Glasgow

QM June 28; SRA T/CN 21/7, 10.

1852	06	*Abeona* of Glasgow	McArthur, J.	216	Glasgow

PP 1852 (542) xlix; SRA T/CN 26/6, 26/7; QM June 28.

1852	06	*Ann Harley* of Glasgow	MacDonald	206	Glasgow

QM July 10; SRA T/CN 21/7, 10.

1852	06	*Blanche* of Liverpool	Rudolf, G.	453	Stornoway

QM July 31; PP 1852-53 (1650) lxviii. Sir James Matheson's tenants.

1852	06	*Clutha* of Greenock	Bruce, A.	352	Glasgow

QM July 3; PP 1852 (542) xlix; SRA T/CN26/6, 26/7; *IA* June 1; *DGC* June 1.

1852	06	*Glencairn* of Glasgow	Crawford R.	245	Glasgow

QM July 10; SRA T/CN 21/7, 10; *IA* June 1, 8.

1852	06	*Marion* of Glasgow	Reid	265	Glasgow

PP 1852 (542) xlix; SRA T/CN 26/6, 26/7.

1852	06	*Melissa* of Greenock	n/k	350	Glasgow

QM July 10; SRA T/CN 21/7, 10.

1852	07	*Albion* of Greenock	Barclay	55	Glasgow

QM Aug. 26; SRA T/CN 26/7; PP 1852-53 (113) xcviii; *IA* June 22; *IH* June 19.

1852	07	*Cambria* of Greenock	Harrison, J.	99	Glasgow

QM Aug. 26; PP 1852-53 (113) xcviii; SRA T/CN 26/6, 26/7; *DGC* June 1.

1852	07	*Helen* of Montrose	Johnston	64	Montrose

QM Aug. 12.

1852	07	*Janet* of Glasgow	McIntosh	190	Glasgow

PP 1852 -53 (113) xcviii; SRA T/CN 26/6, 26/7.

1852	07	*Polly* of Glasgow	Wilson	267	Glasgow

PP 1852 -53 (113) xcviii; SRA T/CN 26/6, 26/7; *IA* June 1; *AH* June 19.

1852	08	*Caledonia* of Greenock	Hood	102	Glasgow

QM Sept. 20; SRA T/CN 26/7; PP 1852-53 (113) xcviii; *IA* June 22; *AH* June 19.

1852	08	*California* of Greenock	Gall, R.	95	Glasgow

QM Sept. 28; TCN 26/6; PP 1852-53 (113) xcviii.

1852	08	*Erromanga* of Greenock	Watson	75	Glasgow

QM Sept. 20; PP 1852-53 (113) xcviii; TCN 26/7; *DGC* June 1.

1852	08	*Ottawa* of Glasgow	McArthur, J.	34	Glasgow

QM Sept. 10; SRA T/CN26/7; *IA* June 22; *AH* June 19.

1852	08	*St Lawrence* of Aberdeen	Tulloch, J.	59	Aberdeen

QM Sept. 28.

1853	03	*Caledonia* of Greenock	Wylie	26	Glasgow

QM May 17.

Year	Mth	Vessel	Master	Psgr. nos.	Departure Port
1853	03	*Empress* of Banff	Leslie	129	Stromness
QM May 28.					
1853	03	*Helen* of Aberdeen	Johnston	103	Montrose
QM May 19.					
1853	04	*Berbice* of Aberdeen	Elliot, J.	143	Aberdeen
QM June 14.					
1853	04	*Clutha* of Greenock	Bruce, A.	126	Glasgow
QM June 2.					
1853	04	*Earl Powis* of Dundee	Walker	18	Dundee
QM May 28.					
1853	04	*Harringer*	Morrison	170	Aberdeen
QM June 7.					
1853	04	*Home*	Kidston	23	Glasgow
QM May 28.					
1853	04	*Jane Boyd* of Aberdeen	Ganson, H.	134	Aberdeen
QM May 31; *IC* Mar. 24.					
1853	04	*Juliet*	Teulon, J.	101	Glasgow
QM June 4; *IC* Apr. 21.					
1853	04	*Springhill* of Irvine	Elliott	16	Ardrossan
QM May 28.					
1853	05	*California* of Greenock	Gall	230	Glasgow
QM July 28; *IC* May 19.					
1853	05	*Glencairn* of Glasgow	Crawford	274	Glasgow
QM June 16.					
1853	06	*Albion* of Greenock	Barclay	23	Glasgow
QM Aug. 16.					
1853	06	*Benlomond*	Meldrum	388	Grnk
QM Aug. 6.					
1853	06	*Harlequin* of Glasgow	Logan	284	Glasgow
QM Aug. 9.					
1853	06	*Rosina* of Campbeltown	Gale	375	Glasgow
QM Aug. 16; *IC* May 19, Aug. 16.					
1853	06	*Shandon*	Greig	33	Glasgow
QM Aug. 13.					
1853	06	*Susan* of Glasgow	Adams	124	Glasgow
QM Aug. 6.					
1853	06	*Thornhill*	Bogart	253	Glasgow
QM July 28.					

Year	Mth	Vessel	Master	Psgr. nos.	Departure Port
1853	07	*Allan Kerr*	Turbit	144	

Glasgow/Greenock
QM Sept. 3; PP 1852-53 (1650) lxviii; *IC* June 16. Duke of Argyll's tenants.

1853	07	*Caledonia* of Greenock	Wylie	28	Glasgow

QM Sept. 8.

1853	07	*Cambria* of Greenock	Russell	17	Glasgow

QM Sept. 8.

1853	07	*Ottawa* of Glasgow	McArthur, J.	29	Glasgow

QM Sept. 6.

1853	07	*Polly* of Glasgow	Allan	27	Glasgow

QM Sept. 6.

1853	07	*St Lawrence* of Aberdeen	Tulloch, J.	72	Aberdeen

QM Sept. 22.

1853	07	*Three Bells* of Glasgow	Campbell	36	Glasgow

QM Sept. 6.

1853	08	*Annie Jane*	n/k	400	Liverpool

IC Oct. 13; Ship wrecked off Vatersay, Barra. 450 lives lost including 100 Glasgow carpenters.

1853	08	*Sillery* of Liverpool	Jackson	339	Skye (Isle Oronsay)

QM Sept. 5; Devine, *Highland Famine*, 323; PP w/e Sept. 17; *IC* July 14. Tenants of Mrs. Josephine MacDonell.

1853	09	*Glencairn* of Glasgow	Crawford	52	Glasgow

QM Oct. 22.

1854	04	*Alexander Hall*	Leslie	172	Aberdeen

QM June 10; *AH* Mar. 4.

1854	04	*Aurora* of Aberdeen	Morison, A.	277	Aberdeen

QM May 23; *AH* Feb. 4, June 7.

1854	04	*Berbice* of Aberdeen	Elliot, J.	126	Aberdeen

AH Jan. 28.

1854	04	*Empress* of Banff	Leslie	152	Stromness

QM May 27.

1854	04	*Erromanga* of Greenock	Watson	16	Glasgow

QM May 23.

1854	04	*Helen Thompson*	n/k	145	Troon

PP 1854-55 (464) xxxix; *AH* June 24. Shipwrecked; 15 passengers reached Quebec in brig *Dykes*; 130 taken on board *Sarah* and landed at Richibucto.

1854	04	*Jane Boyd* of Aberdeen	Ganson, H.	119	Aberdeen

AH Jan. 14.

1854	04	*Marion* of Glasgow	Borland	32	Glasgow

QM May 27.

Year	Mth	Vessel	Master	Psgr. nos.	Departure Port
1854	04	*Mayflower*	Nichol	242	Glasgow

QM May 27.

1854	04	*Renown* of Aberdeen	Walker, W.	115	Aberdeen

QM June 1; *AH* Mar. 11.

1854	04	*Springhill* of Irvine	Anderson	57	Ardrossan

QM June 10.

1854	04	*St Lawrence* of Aberdeen	Tulloch, J.	300	Aberdeen

AH Jan. 21.

1854	04	*Susan* of Glasgow	Martin	179	Glasgow

QM July 8.

1854	04	*Three Bells* of Glasgow	McCallum	39	Glasgow

QM May 23.

1854	05	*Commodore*	Cove	344	Glasgow

QM July 1.

1854	06	*Bannockburn*	Swan	166	Glasgow

QM Aug. 8.

1854	06	*John Hamilton* of Greenock	Sillers	326	Grnk

QM Aug. 5.

1854	06	*Lord Sidmouth* of Glasgow	McIntosh	306	Glasgow

QM Aug. 10.

1854	06	*Tadmor*	Bovie	387	Glasgow

QM Aug. 1; *IC* June 1.

1854	06	*Wallace* (1)	Wilkie	111	Glasgow

QM Aug. 10.

1854	07	*Berbice* of Aberdeen	n/k	59	Aberdeen

AH June 17.

1854	07	*Champion* of Greenock	Cochrane	278	Glasgow

QM Aug. 24.

1854	07	*Dahlia*	Trobridge	31	Glasgow

QM Aug. 26.

1854	07	*Glencairn* of Glasgow	Crawford	23	Glasgow

QM Sept. 5. On Aug. 3 stopped by the ship *Shandos* of Glasgow, which was on fire. Took on board the crew and passengers, amounting to 65 souls.

1854	07	*Jane Boyd* of Aberdeen	n/k	126	Aberdeen

AH June 10.

1854	07	*John McKenzie* of Greenock	Tilley	302	Grnk

QM Sept. 5.

1854	07	*St Lawrence* of Aberdeen	n/k	118	Aberdeen

AH June 17.

Year Mth	Vessel	Master	Psgr. nos.	Departure Port
1854 07 *QM* Aug. 12.	*Wallace* (2)	Sim, J.	117	Fraserburgh
1854 08 *QM* Sept. 30.	*Harlequin* of Glasgow	Logan	23	Glasgow
1854 08 *QM* Sept. 21.	*Hyndeford*	Carmichael	148	Glasgow
1854 08 *QM* Oct. 7.	*Ottawa* of Glasgow	Wylie	30	Glasgow
1854 08 *QM* Oct. 10.	*St Lawrence* of Aberdeen	Tulloch, J.	118	Aberdeen
1854 08 *QM* Sept. 23.	*Three Bells* of Glasgow	McCallum	44	Glasgow
1855 04 *QM* May 16, 17.	*Berbice* of Aberdeen	Scott	124	Aberdeen
1855 04 *QM* May 15.	*Caledonia* of Greenock	Shearer	28	Glasgow
1855 04 *QM* May 17.	*Helen* of Montrose	Johnston	200	Montrose
1855 04 *QM* May 19.	*Home*	Poe	31	Glasgow
1855 04 *QM* June 5.	*Renown* of Aberdeen	Walker	58	Aberdeen
1855 04 *QM* June 10, 12.	*Sir William Wallace* of Aberdeen (2)	Andrews	98	Aberdeen
1855 05 *QM* 19 June.	*Aurora* of Aberdeen	Morison, A.	340	Aberdeen
1855 05 *QM* June 26.	*George Rogers*	Younger	375	Glasgow
1855 05 *QM* June 23.	*Polly* of Glasgow	Bruce	115	Clyde
1855 05 *QM* June 3.	*Renown* of Aberdeen	Walker, W.	55	Aberdeen
1855 05 *QM* June 19.	*Sunbeam*	Dow	367	Grnk
1855 06 *QM* Aug. 7.	*Charlotte Harrison* of Greenock	Welsh	264	Grnk
1855 06 *QM* July 24.	*Chieftain* of Glasgow	Scott	303	Glasgow

Year	Mth	Vessel	Master	Psgr. nos.	Departure Port
1855	06 QM Aug. 10.	*City of Quebec*	Graham	29	Glasgow
1855	06 QM Aug. 10.	*Harlequin* of Glasgow	Logan	256	Glasgow
1855	06 QM July 31.	*John McKenzie* of Glasgow	Tilley	357	Grnk
1855	06 QM Aug. 9.	*Shandon*	Greig	52	Glasgow
1855	07 QM Aug. 28.	*Albion* of Greenock	Wylie	25	Glasgow
1855	07 QM Aug. 28.	*California* of Greenock	Fowler	25	Glasgow
1855	07 QM Aug. 28.	*Helen* of Montrose	Fluckhart	85	Montrose
1855	07 QM Aug. 20.	*Melissa*	Reid	330	Lewis Loch
1855	08 QM Sept. 13.	*Acteon*	Benson	28	Port Glasgow
1855	08 QM Sept. 25.	*Berbice* of Aberdeen	Scott	134	Aberdeen
1855	08 QM Sept. 25.	*Caledonia* of Greenock	Shearer	22	Glasgow
1855	08 QM Sept. 13.	*Cambria* of Greenock	Russell	38	Glasgow
1855	08 QM Oct. 11.	*Home*	Poe	30	Glasgow
1855	09 QM Oct. 16.	*Aurora* of Aberdeen	Morison, A.	93	Aberdeen

Appendix III

THE SHIPS WHICH CARRIED THE UPPER CANADA SCOTS ACROSS THE ATLANTIC

Explanatory Notes

Vessel Names

Vessel names often include the port at which the vessel is registered – e.g. *Rebecca* of Greenock. However, the port of registration is not always given. Where several vessels bear the same name – e.g. *Fame*, they are distinguished by a number in brackets – e.g. *Fame* (1), *Fame* (2), etc.

Passenger Data

The number of crossings and cumulative passenger totals are provided for each vessel. For details of the individual crossings see Appendix II.

Vessel Details

Information on the tonnage, vessel type, year built, place built and the Lloyd's Code have been taken from the *Lloyd's Shipping Register*.

Tonnage

This was a standard measure used to determine customs dues and navigation fees. Because it was a calculated figure, tonnage did not necessarily convey actual carrying capacity. Before 1836, the formula used to calculate tonnage was based only on breadth and length, but after 1836 it incorporated the vessel's depth as well.

Vessel Type

The word "ship" can signify a particular vessel type as well as having a generic usage in denoting all types of sea-going vessels. Sailing ship rigs were many and varied. A major distinction was the alignment of the sails. There were the square-rigged vessels in which the sails were rigged across the vessel and the fore-and-aft rigs which followed the fore-and-aft-line of the vessel. The square rig was normally used on ocean-going vessels:

    Brig (bg)   a two masted vessel with square rigging on both masts.

Snow (sw)   rigged as a brig, with square sails on both masts but with a small triangular sail mast stepped immediately towards the stern of the main-mast.

Barque (bk)   three-masted vessel, square rigged on the fore and main masts and fore-and-aft rigged on the third aftermost mast.

Ship (s)   three-masted vessel, square rigged on all three masts.

Schooner (sr)   fore-and-aft sails on two or more masts. Some had small square topsails on the foremast. They were largely used in the coasting trade and for fishing, their advantage being the smaller crew than that required by square rigged vessels of a comparable size.

Lloyd's Shipping Codes

These were assigned to vessels after periodic surveys according to their quality of construction, condition and age:

A   first class condition, kept in the highest state of repair and efficiency and within a prescribed age limit at the time of sailing.

AE   "second description of the first class," fit for safe conveyance, no defects but may be over a prescribed age limit.

E   second class vessels which, although unfit for carrying dry cargoes, were suitable for long distance sea voyages.

I   third class vessels only suitable for short voyages (i.e. not out of Europe).

The letters were followed by the number 1 or 2 which signified the condition of the vessel's equipment (anchors, cables and stores). Where satisfactory, the number 1 was used, and where not, 2 was used.

Failure to locate vessels in the *Register* does not in itself signify its exclusion from the Lloyd's classification system. To select the relevant vessel from the *Register* it is usually necessary to know the tonnage and captain's name, information which is often elusive and problematic because of gaps in the available shipping and customs records.

Vessel	Type	Tons	Capt.	No. of Voyages	Depart	Psgr Nos	Year built	Place built	Lloyd's Code
Abeona of Glasgow	n/k	611	McArthur, J.	1	Glasgow	216	1847	Quebec	n/k
Abercrombie	bk	n/k	Louttef	1	Glasgow	27	n/k	n/k	n/k
Abigail	bk	n/k	Daly	1	Glasgow	341	n/k	n/k	n/k
Acadian of Glasgow	bk	385	n/k	1	Grnk	26	1832	Greenock	A1
Acteon	bk	n/k	Benson	1	Port Glasgow	28	n/k	n/k	n/k
Active (1)	bg	166	Johnson	1	Whitehaven	84	1803	Yarmouth	E1
Active (2)	s	351	Walker, A.	1	Tobermory	40	1826	Nova Scotia	A1
Admiral of Glasgow	s	707	Dixon	1	Stornoway	413	1850	Dumbarton	A1
Adrian	s	374	Forster	1	Tobermory	106	1819	Newcastle	E1
Afghan	bk	n/k	Black	1	Grnk	229	n/k	n/k	n/k
Agamemnon	n/k	n/k	Rogers	1	Leith	192	n/k	n/k	n/k
Agincourt of Leith	s	347	Matheson	3	Leith	411	1804	North Shields	E1
Agitator	bk	n/k	Henry	1	Glasgow	33	n/k	n/k	n/k
Agnes	n/k	n/k	Outerbridge	1	Grnk	24	n/k	n/k	n/k
Agnes Primrose	n/k	n/k	Johnson	1	Glasgow	40	n/k	n/k	n/k

Vessel	Type	Tons	Capt.	No. of Voyages	Depart	Psgr Nos	Year built	Place built	Lloyd's Code
Aimwell of Aberdeen	sw	232	Morrison	1	Aberdeen	24	1816	Aberdeen	A1
Alarm of Cork	sr	186	Brown, J.	1	Glasgow	133	1838	PEI	A1
Albion (1)	n/k	n/k	Service, G.	1	Fort William	167	n/k	n/k	n/k
Albion (2)	bg	152	Kidd, R.	1	Dundee	60	1805	Dysart	A1
Albion of Aberdeen	sw	266	Leslie, A.	1	Aberdeen	16	1826	Aberdeen	AE1
Albion of Glasgow	bg	190	Boyd, J.	2	Glasgow	265	1826	Campbeltown	E1
Albion of Greenock	s	414	Allan	9	Glasgow	440	1845	Greenock	A1
Albion of Scarborough	sw	287	Hicks, M.	1	Cromarty	28	1836	Sunderland	A1
Alexander	bg	333	Young	2	Grnk	208	1811	Sunderland	A1
Alexander Hall	n/k	n/k	Leslie	1	Aberdeen	172	n/k	n/k	n/k
Alexander of Bo'ness	n/k	n/k	Henry, J.	1	Leith	44	n/k	n/k	n/k
Alfred	n/k	n/k	n/k	1	Leith	243	n/k	n/k	n/k
Alice of Milford	bg	156	Rees, S.	1	Glasgow	107	1832	Milford	A1
Allan Kerr	n/k	n/k	Turbit	1	Glasgow/ Greenock	144	n/k	n/k	n/k
Amity of Aberdeen	bg	312	Rae	1	Aberdeen	39	1825	N. Brunswick	E1
Amity of Glasgow	bg	116	Mercer, J.	5	Grnk	210	1827	Bowlg	A1
Andrew White of Sunderland	sw	256	Clark, B.	1	Glasgow	138	1838	Sunderland	A1
Ann (1)	bg	n/k	Henry	2	Grnk	75	n/k	n/k	n/k
Ann (2)	sw	195	Moore	1	Maryport	136	1810	Workington	E1
Ann (3)	bk	n/k	Wallace	1	Leith	20	n/k	n/k	n/k
Ann and Mary	n/k	213	n/k	2	Banff	116	n/k	n/k	n/k
Ann Grant of Sligo	bk	378	Murdoch	1	Glasgow	72	1806	Whitby	AE1
Ann Harley of Glasgow	bk	455	MacDonald	1	Glasgow	206	1844	Miramichi, N.B.	AE1
Ann Henzell	bg	n/k	Henzell	1	Glasgow	75	n/k	n/k	n/k
Ann Rankin of Glasgow	s	466	McArthur, J.	3	Glasgow	642	1840	Quebec	n/k
Annandale of Aberdeen	bg	254	Anderson, A.	2	Aberdeen	84	1828	New Brunswick	A1
Annie Jane	n/k	n/k	n/k	1	Liverpool	400	n/k	n/k	n/k
Apollo of Dundee	bk	248	Walker, H.	5	Dundee	169	1819	Bristol	AE1
Arabian of Greenock	bk	330	Allan	3	Grnk	125	1837	Greenock	A1
Ardgour of Fort William	sw	166	Lillie, W.	1	Fort William	108	1817	Fort William	A1
Argo	n/k	500	Breslace	1	Thurso	50	n/k	n/k	n/k
Argus (1)	bg	168	Wilkinson	1	Dumfries	88	1805	Workington	E1
Argus (2)	n/k	n/k	n/k	1	Maryport	115	n/k	n/k	n/k
Argyle	bg	139	n/k	1	Glenelg	150	1790	Nova Scotia	A1
Ariadne	s	n/k	McCall	1	Grnk	20	n/k	n/k	n/k
Atlantic	s	n/k	Ross	1	Ardrossan	366	n/k	n/k	n/k
Atlas (1)	s	435	Turnbull	1	Grnk	242	1801	Shields	E1
Atlas (2)	n/k	n/k	Scott	1	Dundee	52	n/k	n/k	n/k
Augusta of Aberdeen	s	417	Rae, W.	1	Aberdeen	46	1828	N. Brunswick	E1
Aurora	n/k	n/k	Hodson	1	Whitehaven	61	n/k	n/k	n/k

Vessel	Type	Tons	Capt.	No. of Voyages	Depart	Psgr Nos	Year built	Place built	Lloyd's Code
Aurora of Aberdeen	s	709	Morison, A.	3	Aberdeen	710	1843	Miramichi, N.B.	AE1
Balfour of Whitehaven	bg	310	Bee	1	Whitehaven	272	1809	Whitehaven	E1
Baltic Merchant	n/k	n/k	Jeffreys	1	Grnk	140	n/k	n/k	n/k
Bannockburn	s	n/k	Swan	1	Glasgow	166	n/k	n/k	n/k
Barlow	bk	436	Fraser, P.	3	Grnk	246	1834	Saint John, N.B.	AE1
Baronet	n/k	n/k	Rankin	1	Cromarty	187	n/k	n/k	n/k
Belleisle of Glasgow	s	499	Reid	2	Glasgow	33	1847	Dumbarton	A1
Bellona of Glasgow	s	368	Mitchell, R.	1	Grnk	18	1838	Greenock	A1
Belmont of Greenock	bg	294	Ford	1	Grnk	77	1825	N. Brunswick	AE1
Benlomond	s	345	Rattray, H.	2	Grnk	606	1815	N. Brunswick	A1
Benson	s	265	Rowe, W.	1	Grnk	287	1798	Lancaster	E1
Berbice of Aberdeen	bk	340	Elliot	14	Aberdeen	1225	1847	Miramichi	AE1
Berwick on Tweed	n/k	n/k	Muers	1	Berwick	20	n/k	n/k	n/k
Bethea	n/k	n/k	n/k	1	Glasgow	20	n/k	n/k	n/k
Betsey	bg	148	Gordon, J.	2	Grnk	30	n/k	Prize	E1
Betsey Howe	bg	n/k	n/k	1	Leith	42	n/k	n/k	n/k
Betsey of Dundee	bk	291	n/k	1	Leith	131	1828	Montreal	A1
Betsey of Greenock	sw	205	Wither	1	Oban	78	1803	Scotland	E1
Birman of Greenock	bk	448	Fuller	2	Grnk	299	1840	Greenock	A1
Blackness of Dundee	bk	266	n/k	2	Dundee	107	1835	Dundee	A1
Blagdon	bg	289	Thomson	1	Cromarty	132	1825	Shields	A1
Blanche of Liverpool	s	966	Rudolf, G.	1	Stornoway	453	1850	Saint John, N.B.	A1
Blonde of Montreal	bk	604	Crawford	6	Glasgow	1865	1841	Montreal	A1
Bon Accord of Aberdeen	bk	365	Sim, J.	1	Aberdeen	70	1812	Blythe	AE1
Bona Dea	n/k	n/k	Brown, H.	1	Grnk	446	n/k	n/k	n/k
Bowes		n/k	Faulkner	1	Cromarty	172	n/k	n/k	n/k
Bowling of Glasgow	bk	242	Gentle,R.	1	Glasgow	157	1842	Blng	A1
Brilliant of Aberdeen	s	332	Barclay, A.	24	Aberdeen	1709	1814	Aberdeen	AE1
Brilliant of Glasgow	s	428	Barr	2	Glasgow	258	1834	n/k	A1
Britannia(1)	bg	172	Spence, C.	1	Grnk	36	1813	Montreal	A1
Britannia (2)	n/k	n/k	n/k	1	Leith	19	n/k	n/k	n/k
Britannia of Newcastle	s	542	Simpson	1	Glasgow	388	1840	N. Brunswick	AE1
British King of Dundee	bg	239	Brown, A.	1	Cromarty	20	1825	Sunderland	AE1
British Queen of Greenock	s	191	Deniston	1	Arisaig	87	1786	Greenock	A1
Broke	s	252	n/k	1	Grnk	176	1812	Salem	A1

Vessel	Type	Tons	Capt.	No. of Voyages	Depart	Psgr Nos	Year built	Place built	Lloyd's Code
Brooksby of Glasgow	s	423	McEwan	1	Loch Boisdale	285	1843	Greenock	A1
Caledonia	bg	160	Miller	3	Grnk	299	1806	Scotland	E1
Caledonia of Greenock	s	383	Greenhorn	18	Grnk	944	1841	Greenock	A1
Caledonia of Irvine	n/k	154	Reid, J.	1	Grnk	30	1806	Irvine	E1
California of Greenock	bk	563	Gall, R.	6	Glasgow	975	1841	Miramichi, N.B.	A1
Cambria of Aberdeen	bg	120	Perie, James	2	Aberdeen	48	1808	Aberdeen	A1
Cambria of Greenock	s	397	Kelso	9	Glasgow	421	1846	Greenock	A1
Camilla	s	287	McCarthy, D.	1	Grnk	109	1798	New York	E1
Canada	s	269	Hunter	2	Cromarty	355	1811	Montreal	E1
Canada of Greenock	s	330	Allan	15	Grnk	999	1831	Greenock	A1
Canmore of Saint John	bk	264	n/k	2	Glasgow	127	1843	N. Brunswick	A1 AE1, 1851
Carleton	n/k	n/k	n/k	1	Glasgow	70	n/k	n/k	n/k
Carleton of Aberdeen	bk	404	Anderson, A.	2	Aberdeen	96	1834	N.B.	AE1
Carolina of Aberdeen	n/k	170	Dunoon, A.	2	Aberdeen	49	n/k	n/k	n/k
Caroline	n/k	n/k	Lowergran	1	Berwick	50	n/k	n/k	n/k
Caroline of Aberdeen	bk	393	Marsh, J.	1	Aberdeen	16	1839	N. Brunswick	A1
Cartha	bg	358	Smith	4	Grnk	427	1827	N. Brunswick	A1
Cashmere of Glasgow	bk	347	Paton, R.	1	Glasgow	115	1841	Nova Scotia	AE1
Caspian	n/k	n/k	n/k	1	Glasgow	35	n/k	n/k	n/k
Catherine (1)	bg	n/k	Daysdale	1	Leith	63	n/k	n/k	n/k
Catherine (2)	n/k	448	Davidson	2	Irvine	59	n/k	n/k	n/k
Champion of Greenock	bk	673	Cochrane	2	Glasgow	497	1838	Canada	AE1
Charles	n/k	580	n/k	1	Stornoway	145	n/k	n/k	n/k
Charles Forbes	sw	295	Beveridge	1	Kirkaldy	47	1816	Aberdeen	E1
Charlotte	n/k	1000	Vasey, T.	1	Glasgow	333	n/k	n/k	n/k
CharlotteHarrison of Greenock	bk	557	McIntyre	2	Grnk	569	1841	Quebec	AE1
Cherokee of Glasgow	bk	278	Miller	4	Grnk	138	1834	Greenock	A1
Cherub	bg	269	Miller	2	Grnk	39	1814	Workington	A1
Chieftain of Glasgow	bk	n/k	Scott	1	Glasgow	303	1842	N. Brunswick	AE1
Chieftain of Kirkaldy	bk	333	Scott, A.	2	Leith	295	1832	Leith	A1
Circassian of Aberdeen	bg	180	Ritchie, T.	1	Aberdeen	117	1835	Aberdeen	A1
Circassian of Greenock	bk	520	Dixon, G.	2	Glasgow	315	1839	N. Brunswick	A1
City of Quebec	n/k	n/k	Graham	1	Glasgow	29	n/k	n/k	n/k
Clansman of Glasgow	bk	348	Peck	2	Grnk	258	1823	N. Brunswick	AE1
Cleopatra	bg	267	Morris, J.	1	Cromarty	246	1817	Whitby	E1
Clutha of Greenock	bk	462	Muir	3	Glasgow	612	1839	N. Brunswick	AE1

Vessel	Type	Tons	Capt.	No. of Voyages	Depart	Psgr Nos	Year built	Place built	Lloyd's Code
Commerce	n/k	n/k	London	1	Oban	42	n/k	n/k	n/k
Commerce of Greenock	s	425	Coverdale, N.	3	Grnk	839	1813	Quebec	A1
Commodore	n/k	n/k	Miller, J.	2	Glasgow	371	n/k	n/k	n/k
Commodore of Sunderland	n/k	n/k	Hall	1	Glasgow	15	n/k	n/k	n/k
Conference of Newcastle	s	298	Buchan		Leith	112	n/k	Bristol	AE1
Congress	bg	n/k	Greig	1	Leith	22	n/k	n/k	n/k
Conrad of Greenock	s	759	Barclay, J.	2	Glasgow	588	1847	Quebec	A1
Cornelia of Greenock	bg	260	Croall, D.	1	Glasgow	98	1840	N.B.	A1
Corsair of Greenock	bg	273	McAlpine	6	Grnk	499	1823	N.B.	E1
Crown	bg	338	Howie	1	Grnk	75	1824	N.B.	E1
Cruickston Castle of Greenock	bk	382	McInlay	2	Grnk	65	1822	N. Brunswick	AE1
Culloden	n/k	n/k	Leyden	1	Leith	19	n/k	n/k	n/k
Curlew	bg	260	Young J.	1	Grnk	205	1815	Newcastle	A1
Cyrus	n/k	n/k	Scott	3	Dundee	99	n/k	n/k	n/k
Dahlia	bk	n/k	Trobridge	1	Glasgow	31	n/k	n/k	n/k
Dalmarnock	s	315	McFarlane	3	Berwick	282	1828	Workington	E1
David of London	s	390	Gemmil, D.	1	Grnk	364	1812	Pictou	E1
Deveron of Glasgow	bg	333	Anderson	3	Grnk	593	1824	Nova Scotia	AE1
Dolphin	n/k	n/k	n/k	1	Anticosti	20	n/k	n/k	n/k
Donegal	sw	190	Matches	2	Maryport	302	1808	Belfast	E1
Dorothy	s	530	Spence	1	Grnk	194	Prize	Denmark	E1
Duchess of Richmond	s	324	Cook	5	Grnk	761	1807	Dublin	E1
Duke of Buccleugh	bg	205	Blair, J.	1	Dumfries	41	1829	Leith	A1
Dunlop	bg	331	Stevenson, A.	2	Glasgow	185	1805	Montreal	A1– 1810 E1– 1824
Dykes of Maryport	n/k	n/k	Cockton	2	Maryport	189	n/k	n/k	E1
Eagle (1)	s	179	Conolly, N.	1	Grnk	21	1791	Whitehaven	A1
Eagle (2)	n/k	n/k	Morton, R.	1	Glasgow	94	n/k	n/k	n/k
Earl of Buckinghamshire	n/k	n/k	Johnson, J.	2	Grnk	807	n/k	n/k	n/k
Earl of Dalhousie	bg	222	Boyd	2	Grnk	40	1826	Scotland	A1
Earl of Dalhousie of Aberdeen	bg	183	Levie, J.	2	Aberdeen	34	1817	Aberdeen	A1
Earl Powis of Dundee	bk	299	n/k	5	Dundee	166	1836	Liverpool	A1
Economist of Newport	bk	324	Stokeham	1	Cromarty	47	1829	P.E.I	A1
Eleanor	n/k	n/k	Wallace	1	Workington	96	n/k	n/k	n/k
Elephanta of Glasgow	bk	310	Ross, D.	1	Grnk	130	1836	Newport	A1
Eleutheria of South Shields	bk	340	McDonaugh, W.	1	Glasgow	160	1835	Shields	A1
Eliza	n/k	n/k	Telfer	2	Grnk	165	n/k	n/k	n/k

Vessel	Type	Tons	Capt.	No. of Voyages	Depart	Psgr Nos	Year built	Place built	Lloyd's Code
Eliza of Cardiff	bk	384	Jones, J.	1	Glasgow	269	1846	Quebec	AE1
Elizabeth	n/k	n/k	McAlpine	1	Clyde	74	n/k	n/k	n/k
Elizabeth and Anne	sw	296	Wright, J.	1	Grnk	296	1779	Shields	E1
Elizabeth of Leith	bg	165	n/k	2	Leith	30	1831	Leith	n/k
Ellen of Liverpool	bk	397	n/k	1	Liverpool	100	1834	N. Brunswick	AE1
Emma of Dundee	bg	215	Innis	2	Dundee	52	1822	Suffolk	A1
Emperor Alexander of Aberdeen	sw	236	Watts, A.	1	Tobermory	49	1814	Sunderland	A1
Empress of Banff	bk	359	Leslie	3	Stromness	417	1845	Nova Scotia	n/k
Entaw	n/k	n/k		1	Glasgow	54	n/k	n/k	n/k
Enterprise	n/k	n/k	Pattin	1	Ayr	39	n/k	n/k	n/k
Erromanga of Greenock	bk	351	Ramsay, R.	8	Glasgow	473	1845	Greenock	A1
Essex	n/k	n/k	n/k	1	Glasgow	29	n/k	n/k	n/k
Euclid of Liverpool	bk	501	Bainbridge, G.	1	Glasgow	330	1841	Pictou	AE1
European (1)	n/k	n/k	n/k	1	Leith	155	n/k	n/k	n/k
European (2)	s	n/k	McBride	1	Glasgow	91	n/k	n/k	n/k
Experiment	n/k	n/k	Collins	1	Maryport	32	n/k	n/k	n/k
Fairy of Dundee	s	248	Ritchie, D.	2	Dundee	173	1801	York	E1
Fairy Queen	bk	n/k	Ritchie, D.	1	Dundee	28	n/k	n/k	n/k
Fame (1)	bg	144	Forrest	1	Grnk	79	1790	Chester	E1
Fame (2)	bg	204	Abrams	1	Grnk	17	1815	Quebec	A1
Fame (3)	bk	n/k	Wright	1	Grnk	35	n/k	n/k	n/k
Fame (4)	n/k	n/k	Miller	1	Glasgow	27	n/k	n/k	n/k
Fancy of Aberdeen	bg	141	Struthers, J.	1	Grnk	15	1808	Aberdeen	A1
Favourite	n/k	n/k	Greg	1	Grnk	23	n/k	n/k	n/k
Favourite	n/k	n/k	Girvan	1	Ayr	33	n/k	n/k	n/k
Favourite of Greenock	bk	355	Bannerman	13	Glasgow	692	1839	Montreal	A1
Favourite of Montreal	bg	296	Allan	13	Grnk	550	1825	Montreal	A1
Feronia	n/k	n/k	Grant, R.	1	Glasgow	87	n/k	n/k	n/k
Fisher	bg	175	Kay, T.	1	Stranraer	69	1804	Hrngt	E1
Flora of Dundee	sw	174	n/k	1	Dundee	57	1824	Dundee	AE1
Forth	sw	369	Robinson	1	Grnk	150	1826	Leith	A1
Foundling	bg	205	McKenzie	2	Grnk	331	1810	America	E1
Friends of John of Saltcoats	n/k	107	Hen, John	1	Fort William	136	n/k	n/k	n/k
Gem of Aberdeen	bg	186	Ross, P.	1	Leith	30	1839	Aberdeen	A1
General Goldie of Dumfries	sp	61	Smith	2	Dumfries	48	1812	Whitehaven	A1
General Graham of Alloa	s	426	Craigie	2	Alloa	93	1811	Hull	E1
General Wolfe	n/k	n/k	Johnston	1	Grnk	32	n/k	n/k	n/k
George (1)	bg	n/k	McAlpin, J.	1	Grnk	42	n/k	n/k	n/k
George (2)	n/k	n/k	Thompson	1	Maryport	23	n/k	n/k	n/k
George Canning	s	482	Potter	6	Grnk	1377	1812	Montreal	A1

Vessel	Type	Tons	Capt.	No. of Voyages	Depart	Psgr Nos	Year built	Place built	Lloyd's Code
George of Dundee	s	676	Hanley, F.	2	Loch Laxford & Lochmaddy	202	1839	Pictou	n/k
George Rogers	s	n/k	Younger	1	Glasgow	375	n/k	n/k	n/k
George Stewart	n/k	n/k	Stewart	1	Grnk	57	n/k	n/k	n/k
Glencairn of Glasgow	s	850	Allan	5	Glasgow	651	1850	Quebec	A1
Gleniffer	bg	318	Stevenson	6	Grnk	458	1826	Saint John, N.B.	E1
Glenswilly of Glasgow	s	565	Henderson, T.	1	Glasgow	43	1838	N. Brunswick	AE1
Glentanner of Aberdeen	bg	160	Murray	1	Tobermory	18	1811	Aberdeen	A1
Globe	n/k	n/k	Lindsay	1	Montrose	15	n/k	n/k	n/k
Grace	n/k	n/k	n/k	1	Whitehaven	132	n/k	n/k	n/k
Gratitude of Dundee	bg	170	Gellatly, J.	1	Fort William	55	1823	Sunderland	A1
Greenfield	bg	114	Holmes, J.	1	Grnk	28	1815	Irvine	A1
Greenock of Glasgow	bg	159	n/k	1	Loch Laxford	399	1837	Greenock	A1
Hamilton of Glasgow	s	589	Dick, J.	1	Grnk	283	1842	Restigouche	A1
Hants of Greenock	bk	275	Neill, W.	1	Glasgow	71	1838	Nova Scotia	A1
Harlequin of Glasgow	bk	702	Craig, G.	4	Glasgow	835	1851	Quebec	A1
Harmony (1)	n/k	n/k	Abrams	2	Grnk	369	n/k	n/k	n/k
Harmony (2)	bk	n/k	Young	1	Leith	79	n/k	n/k	n/k
Harmony of Whitehaven	bg	244	Young	1	Stornoway	36	1812	Whitehaven	A1
Harper	n/k	n/k	Murphy	1	Glasgow	235	n/k	n/k	n/k
Harringer	bk	n/k	Morrison	1	Aberdeen	170	n/k	n/k	n/k
Harrison Chilton of Liverpool	bk	398	n/k	1	Glasgow	130	1839	Whitby	AE1
Hector	n/k	n/k	Davison	3	Various	199	n/k	n/k	n/k
Hector of Dundee	sw	192	Anderson, W.	1	Glasgow	92	1801	n/k	A1
Hedleys of Newcastle	bk	279	n/k	2	Cromarty	347	1823	Newcastle	E1
Helen	n/k	n/k	Johnson	1	Montrose	18	n/k	n/k	n/k
Helen of Aberdeen	bk	366	Anderson	2	Aberdeen	121	1826	n/k	E1
Helen of Dundee	bg	203	Erskine, T.	2	Dundee	75	1821	n/k	n/k
Helen of Irvine	sw	157	Service, G.	1	Fort William	166	1775	Leith	A1
Helen of Montrose	bk	346	Johnston	3	Montrose	349	1846	N. Brunswick	AE1
Helen Thompson	n/k	n/k	n/k	1	Troon	145	n/k	n/k	n/k
Henry	n/k	n/k	Anderson	2	Glasgow	214	n/k	n/k	n/k
Henry Kneeland	n/k	n/k	n/k	1	Glasgow	19	n/k	n/k	n/k
Henry of Montrose	bk	315	Ross	1	Dundee	30	1827	Newcastle	AE1
Herald of Greenock	s	801	Coubro	1	Grnk	319	1840	N. Brunswick	AE1
Hercules of Aberdeen	bk	250	Walker, D.	6	Aberdeen	520	1781	Stockton	E1
Hercules of Liverpool	s	757	Postill, F.	1	Lochmaddy	59	1836	Richibucto	AE1
Heroine of Aberdeen	s	387	Walker, D.	4	Aberdeen	331	1831	Dundee	AE1

Vessel	Type	Tons	Capt.	No. of Voyages	Depart	Psgr Nos	Year built	Place built	Lloyd's Code
Hibernia of Aberdeen	bg	113	Lamb, R.	1	Stornoway	42	1816	Aberdeen	A1
Highland Lad	s	343	Vickerman	1	Tobermory	16	1816	Quebec	E1
Highlander of Aberdeen	bg	174	Fluckhart	1	Cromarty	150	1817	Aberdeen	E1
Home	n/k	n/k	Grey	4	Glasgow	117	n/k	n/k	n/k
Hope (1)	bg	186	Duncan	1	Grnk	44	1802	Nova Scotia	E1
Hope (2)	bg	180	Henry, M.	1	Port Glasgow	47	1803	Nova Scotia	A1
Hope (3)	n/k	n/k	McFarlane	1	Leith	25	n/k	n/k	n/k
Hope (4)	n/k	n/k	Middleton	1	Maryport	73	n/k	n/k	n/k
Hope of Glasgow	bk	513	Kidston	1	Glasgow	28	1839	N. B.	AE1
Hope of Greenock	bk	231	Marden	1	Oban	184	n/k	n/k	n/k
Huntley	s	n/k	Wilson	1	Grnk	176	n/k	n/k	n/k
Hyndeford	bk	n/k	Carmichael	1	Glasgow	148	n/k	n/k	n/k
Ianthe	n/k	n/k	Hunter	1	Glasgow	37	n/k	n/k	n/k
Independence of Belfast	s	584	n/k	1	Liverpool	245	1839	Quebec	A1
Indian	n/k	n/k	Matthias	1	Grnk	69	n/k	n/k	n/k
Industry	bk	291	Carr	2	Dundee	187	n/k	Prize, 1808	n/k
Iris	bk	n/k	Frank	2	Grnk	404	n/k	n/k	n/k
Isabella and Euphemia	n/k	n/k	Middleton, J.	1	Stornoway	32	n/k	n/k	n/k
Isabella of Dundee	bg	304	Donaldson, J.	2	Dundee	65	1825	Dundee	E1
Isabella of Irvine	bg	281	Miller	2	Grnk	135	1830	Quebec	AE1
Islay	n/k	n/k	n/k	1	Stornoway	68	n/k	n/k	n/k
Jamaica of Glasgow	s	334	Martin	6	Grnk	791	1796	Greenock	AE1
James	bg	226	Jack, W.	1	Grnk	24	1812	Quebec	A1
James Campbell of Glasgow	bk	305	Miller, J.	1	Glasgow	27	1842	Dumbarton	A1
James Dean of Greenock	bk	370	Wilson	1	Glasgow	29	1840	Quebec	A1
James Redden of Dumfries	sw	244	n/k	1	Dumfries	31	1841	PEI	AE1
Jane (1)	bg	193	Wilson	1	Leith	65	1830	Quebec	AE1
Jane (2)	sw	208	Allen, W.	2	Grnk	97	1819	Sunderland	A1
Jane Boyd of Aberdeen	bk	387	Ganson, H.	3	Aberdeen	379	1843	Aberdeen	n/k
Jane Brown of Glasgow	bk	282	Wylie, J.	3	Glasgow	94	1834	Greenock	A1
Jane Christie	n/k	n/k	Scott	1	Leith	34	n/k	n/k	
Jane Duffus of Irvine'	bk	352	Donald, H.	1	Glasgow	257	1840	Pictou	A1
Jane Kay	sw	235	Toft, D.	1	Cromarty	66	1831	Sunderland	A1
Jane of Sunderland	s	340	Rogers, J.	2	Grnk	147	1805	Sunderland	E1
Jane Wright	n/k	n/k	n/k	1	Grnk	50	n/k	n/k	n/k
Janet Izat of Alloa	bk	229	n/k	1	Tobermory	100	1828	Kinnear	A1
Janet of Glasgow	bk	444	McIntosh	1	Glasgow	190	1830	Quebec	AE1
Jean	bg	n/k	Allan	1	Grnk	28	n/k	n/k	n/k
Jean Baptiste of Glasgow	bk	259	n/k	1	Glasgow	15	1836	Quebec	AE1

Vessel	Type	Tons	Capt.	No. of Voyages	Depart	Psgr Nos	Year built	Place built	Lloyd's Code
Jean Hastie of Grangemouth	s	280	Robertson, J.	1	Thurso	44	1829	N. Brunswick	E1
Jean of Ayr	n/k	n/k	Allan	1	Grnk	16	n/k	n/k	n/k
Jean of Irvine	s	167	MacDonald, J.	2	Fort William	274	1799	Saltcoats	A1
Jeanie Deans	n/k	n/k	Miller, D.	2	Glasgow	111	n/k	n/k	n/k
Jessie of Aberdeen	bg	154	Thomson, J.	1	Aberdeen	21	1814	Spey	A1
Jessie Stephens of Irvine	bk	440	Miller, D.	1	Glasgow	131	1847	Quebec	A1
Jessy Logan	n/k	855	n/k	1	Grnk	27	n/k	n/k	n/k
John	n/k	n/k	Mann	1	Cromarty	120	n/k	n/k	n/k
John and Samuel of Liverpool	bg	188	Cook, F.	1	Stornoway	82	n/k	Levant	E1
John Cumming	n/k	n/k	n/k	1	Glasgow	83	n/k	n/k	n/k
John Hamilton of Greenock	s	809	Sillers	1	Grnk	326	1849	N. Brunswick	A1
John Howard	bk	n/k	Smith	1	London	100	n/k	n/k	n/k
John Hutchison	n/k	n/k	Harrison	1	Thurso	76	n/k	n/k	n/k
John & Mary	n/k	n/k	Nicholson	1	Leith	79	n/k	n/k	n/k
John McKenzie of Greenock	s	791	Tilley	2	Grnk	659	1846	Nova Scotia	A1
John of Bo'ness	n/k	252	Mitchell, J.	1	Leith	118	n/k	n/k	n/k
John Walker of Liverpool	bk	523	n/k	1	Skye	49	1832	N. Brunswick	AE1
Joseph Green of Peterhead	s	353	Volum, J.	1	Cromarty	239	1819	Sunderland	AE1
Juliet	n/k	n/k	Teulon, J.	1	Glasgow	101	n/k	n/k	n/k
Juno of Aberdeen	bg	150	Henderson, J.	1	Dundee	20	1814	Newburgh	A1
Jupiter	n/k	n/k	n/k	1	Glasgow	18	n/k	n/k	n/k
Justyn of Leith	bk	803	Thomson, R.	1	Grnk	313	1849	Quebec	A1
Kate of Newcastle	bk	478	Taylor, T.	1	Cromarty	43	1846	Sunderland	A1
Kent	bg	n/k	Stirling	2	Grnk	104	n/k	n/k	n/k
Kilmuir	n/k	n/k	Blair	1	Grnk	18	n/k	n/k	n/k
Kincardineshire of Aberdeen	bg	193	Goven	1	Aberdeen	55	1838	Cape Breton	AE1
Lady Emily of Sunderland	sw	285	Smith, J.	1	Loch Laxford	64	1840	Sunderland	A1
Lady Falkland	n/k	n/k	Parker	1	Glasgow	361	1846	Nova Scotia	AE1
Lady Grey of North Shields	sw	285	Grey, W.	1	Cromarty	105	1841	Sunderland	A1
Lady Hood of Stornoway	bg	107	n/k	1	Stornoway	78	1816	Aberdeen	AE1
Lady Kinnaird of Dundee	bk	321		1	Dundee	65	1839	Dundee	A1
Lady of the Lake	bg	118	Primrose, D.	1	Grnk	27	1815	Quebec	A1
Lanarkshire of Glasgow	bk	629	Turner	1	Glasgow	80	1840	Quebec	AE1
Lancaster	bk	220	Creighton	1	Dumfries	137	1787	Lancaster	E1
Lawther	n/k	n/k	Pewley	1	Workington	121	n/k	n/k	n/k
Lerwick	bg	n/k	Giffney	1	Dundee	83	n/k	n/k	n/k
Leven Lass of Glasgow	bg	199	Wright	2	Glasgow	98	1839	Dumbarton	A1
Liskeard of Liverpool	bk	648	n/k	2	Inverness	445	1847	Nova Scotia	AE1

Vessel	Type	Tons	Capt.	No. of Voyages	Depart	Psgr Nos	Year built	Place built	Lloyd's Code
Lord Byron	bk	380	Robinson	1	Grnk	26	1825	Quebec	A1
Lord Metcalfe of Aberdeen	bk	510	Bain	2	Aberdeen	82	1845	Quebec	AE1
Lord Middleton of North Shields	sw	341	Kerr, G.	1	Leith	163	n/k	Carolina	E1
Lord Panmure of Dundee	bg	263	McNeill, J.	2	Dundee	138	1838	Dundee	A1
Lord Seaton of Aberdeen	s	440	Talbot, W.	3	Aberdeen	105	1840	Quebec	A1
Lord Sidmouth of Glasgow	bk	595	McIntosh	1	Glasgow	306	1835	Quebec	AE1
Lother	bk	n/k	Murphy	1	Annan	29	n/k	n/k	n/k
Macdonald	n/k	n/k	Stevenson	1	Knoydart	539	n/k	n/k	n/k
Magnet	sw	229	Goulder	1	Whitehaven	146	1812	Whitby	E1
Mahaica of Greenock	bk	256	Jump, W.	2	Glasgow	184	1837	Greenock	A1
Majestic	bg	n/k	Black	1	Leith	60	n/k	n/k	n/k
Margaret (1)	bg	125	Boyd	2	Grnk	42	1815	Irvine	A1
Margaret (2)	bg	218	Oliphant	2	Grnk	290	1820	Kirkaldy	A1
Margaret (3)	n/k	n/k	Wallace	1	Leith	160	n/k	n/k	n/k
Margaret Balfour of Dundee	bg	248	Gellatly, J.	3	Dundee	151	1828	Quebec	A1
Margaret Bogle of Leith	s	324	Boyd	6	Glasgow	492	1804	Ayr	E1
Margaret Boyle	bk	n/k	Scott	1	Leith	20	n/k	n/k	n/k
Margaret of Greenock	bk	566	McBride, A.	1	Glasgow	238	1839	Miramichi, N.B.	AE1
Margaret of Peterhead	sw	201	Shand, J.	1	Leith	16	1811	Peterhead	A1
Margaret Pointer	n/k	n/k	Miller, J.	1	Glasgow	51	n/k	n/k	n/k
Margaret Thompson	bk	272	Ogilvy, J.	1	Leith	125	1832	Kincardine	A1
Margaret Wilkie of Greenock	bk	240	Miller, J.	1	Grnk	111	1832	n/k	A1
Maria (1)	sw	200	Hewitt	1	Maryport	136	1819	Quebec	E1
Maria (2)	n/k	n/k	Davieson	1	Cromarty	111	n/k	n/k	n/k
Mariner of Sunderland	n/k	255	Collins	1	Loch Eriboll	145	n/k	n/k	n/k
Marion of Glasgow	s	670	Reid	2	Glasgow	297	1848	Quebec	A1
Marjory	bg	500	Stocks, J.	1	Thurso	24	n/k	n/k	n/k
Marquis of Stafford	n/k	n/k	n/k	1	Stornoway	500	n/k	n/k	n/k
Mars	sw	208	Blin	1	Mull	253	1806	Sunderland	A1
Martha	n/k	n/k	Denwood	1	Dumfries	43	n/k	n/k	n/k
Mary (1)	bg	n/k	Dunlop	2	Grnk	367	n/k	n/k	n/k
Mary (2)	s	308	Munro	1	Leith	32	1780	Hull	E1
Mary Ann of London	bk	275	Moody, J.	1	Grnk	220	1827	Bridlington	AE1
Mary of Aberdeen	sw	139	Clayton, J.	1	Aberdeen	21	1810	Aberdeen	n/k
Mary of Glasgow	bk	343	Shearer	2	Glasgow	58	1844	Nova Scotia	AE1
Mary of Greenock (1)	s	290	Moore	1	Grnk	26	1818	Whitby	A1
Mary of Greenock (2)	bg	218	Shotton, J.	6	Glasgow	153	1832	Greenock	A1

Vessel	Type	Tons	Capt.	No. of Voyages	Depart	Psgr Nos	Year built	Place built	Lloyd's Code
Mary of Newcastle	bg	n/k	Jacobson	1	Loch Snizort, Skye	64	n/k	n/k	n/k
Mary Sharp	n/k	n/k	Woolf	1	Glasgow	17	n/k	n/k	n/k
Mayflower	s	n/k	Nichol	1	Glasgow	242	n/k	n/k	n/k
Melissa	s	652	Reid	1	Lewis Loch	330	1843	Quebec	AE1
Melissa of Greenock	n/k	n/k	n/k	1	Glasgow	350	n/k	n/k	n/k
Menapia	n/k	n/k	Queen, J.	1	Glasgow	183	n/k	n/k	n/k
Merlin	n/k	n/k	Thompson, D.	1	Grnk	185	n/k	n/k	n/k
Messenger	n/k	n/k	Mather, W.	3	Glasgow	108	n/k	n/k	n/k
Minerva (1)	bg	166	Williamson	1	Grnk	60	1819	Anstruther	A1
Minerva (2)	bg	n/k	Adamson	1	Leith	59	n/k	n/k	n/k
Minerva of Aberdeen	sw	202	Strachan, W.	1	Fort William	26	1813	Aberdeen	A1
Minerva of Greenock	bk	349	Stewart	1	Glasgow	41	1813	Whitby	AE1
Mohawk of Greenock	s	426	n/k	4	Glasgow	161	1840	Greenock	A1
Molson of Dundee	sw	214	Elliot, J.	3	Dundee	300	1830	Dundee	AE1
Monarch	n/k	n/k	Crawford	1	Tobermory	259	n/k	n/k	n/k
Monarch of Glasgow	bk	316	Welsh	3	Grnk	74	1835	Greenock	A1
Montezuma of Liverpool	bk	462	n/k	1	Loch Boisdale	440	1846	Quebec	A1
Montreal	s	306	Allen	1	Grnk	18	1814	Irvine	A1
Monument	n/k	n/k		1	Glasgow	87	n/k	n/k	n/k
Morningfield of Aberdeen	bg	141	Perie, J.	1	Stornoway	63	1816	Aberdeen	A1
Mount Stewart Elphinstone of Glasgow	s	387	Stuart, J.	1	Loch Boisdale	129	1826	Greenock	AE1
Nailer	s	313	McColl	4	Grnk	379	1828	Quebec	A1
Nancy of South Shields	s	330	Allan, R.	1	Leith	34	1772	Scarborough	E1
Navarino	n/k	n/k	n/k	1	Glasgow	27	n/k	n/k	n/k
Nelson	bg	n/k	Barrick	1	Leith	19	n/k	n/k	n/k
Neptune (1)	n/k	n/k	n/k	1		60	n/k	n/k	n/k
Neptune (2)	bg	n/k	Bell	2	Leith	207	n/k	n/k	n/k
Neptune of Ayr	bg	167	Neil	1	Grnk	22	1799	Ayr	E1
Neptune of Greenock	s	308	Boyd	1	Loch Nevis	600	1802	N.B.	A1
Neried	n/k	n/k	Whitehead	1	Dumfries	49	n/k	n/k	n/k
New York Packet	bk	n/k	Hossack	2	Glasgow	188	n/k	n/k	n/k
Niagara	bg	276	Hamilton	1	Grnk	115	1824	Quebec	n/k
Nicholson	n/k	n/k	Craig	1	Maryport	183	n/k	n/k	n/k
Norfolk	s	n/k	Harrison	1	Berwick	41	n/k	n/k	n/k
Norway	n/k	n/k	Hughes	1	Glasgow	22	n/k	n/k	n/k
Octovara	n/k	n/k	n/k	1	Glasgow	59	n/k	n/k	n/k
Onyx of Grangemouth	bk	389	Hogg	1	Glasgow	120	1823	Stockton	AE1
Osprey of Leith	s	382	Kirk	1	Cromarty	90	1819	Greenock	AE1
Ossian of Leith	bg	194	Block	1	Fort William	127	1813	Leith	A1
Ottawa of Glasgow	s	480	McArthur, J.	4	Glasgow	125	1851	Dumbarton	A1
Oughton	bg	207	Baird, John	1	Kirkcudbright	102	1787	Leith	E2
Oxford	s	401	Davidson	1	Leith	300	1804	Whitby	E1

Vessel	Type	Tons	Capt.	No. of Voyages	Depart	Psgr Nos	Year built	Place built	Lloyd's Code
Pacific of Aberdeen	bk	386	Morrison, J.	6	Aberdeen	495	1826	Aberdeen	AE1
Pactolus	n/k	n/k	Lloyd, T.	1	Glasgow	182	n/k	n/k	n/k
Palmona	s	n/k	Morison	1	Grnk	15	n/k	n/k	n/k
Panama of Liverpool	n/k	n/k	n/k	1	Loch Laxford	279	n/k	n/k	n/k
Panmore	n/k	n/k	n/k	1	Ayr	24	n/k	n/k	n/k
Papineau	bg	n/k	Morland	1	Glasgow	28	n/k	n/k	n/k
Paragon	bg	n/k	Mitchell	2	Leith	112	n/k	n/k	n/k
Patriot	n/k	n/k	n/k	1	Leith	19	n/k	n/k	n/k
Peace	n/k	n/k	Seator	1	Grnk	85	n/k	n/k	n/k
Pekin of Irvine	n/k	n/k	Crawford	1	Glasgow	44	n/k	n/k	A1
Percival of Leith	bg	269	Scott	2	Leith	132	1811	Sunderland	A1
Perdonnet	n/k	n/k	n/k	1	Glasgow	37	n/k	n/k	n/k
Perseverence of Aberdeen	bg	116	Philip, J.	1	Stornoway	52	n/k	Foreign	n/k
Perthshire of Greenock	bk	459	Scott	1	Lochboisdale	437	1841	Nova Scotia	A1
Peruvian of Glasgow	n/k	n/k	Boyd, J.	1	Glasgow	35	n/k	n/k	n/k
Philadelphia	s	300	n/k	1	n/k	300	1773	Hull	E1
Pilgrim	n/k	n/k	Smith	2	Tobermory	139	n/k	n/k	n/k
Pilgrim of Aberdeen	bg	170	Allan, G.	2	Aberdeen	130	1828	Aberdeen	A1
Pitt	s	308	Hamilton	1	Grnk	37	1800	Ulverston, Cumbria	E1
Polly of Glasgow	bk	629	Wilson	3	Glasgow	409	1845	Quebec	AE1
Portaferry	bg	283	Pollock, J.	2	Grnk	319	1819	Workington	E1
Portia	bk	n/k	Hirst	1	Grnk	171	n/k	n/k	n/k
Prescott of Leith	bg	163	Young	1	Leith	26	1799	Leith	E1
Prince Albert of Arbroath	sw	257	Rodger, A.	1	Thurso	125	1842	Arbroath	AE1
Prince George of Alloa	bg	312	Morison	3	Alloa	267	1789	London	AE1
Prompt of Bo'ness	s	333	Nairn	3	Grnk	521	1816	Montreal	A1
Psyche of Dundee	bg	147	Erskine, T.	1	Dundee	38	1815	Montrose	A1
Quebec Packet of Aberdeen	bg	196	Anderson, A.	4	Cromarty	130	1822	Aberdeen	A1
Queen of the Isles of Stromness	bk	261	Leask	1	Glasgow	105	1842	Aberdeen	A1
Rebecca of Greenock	s	305	Laurie	11	Grnk	364	1816	Greenock	E1
Regent	bg	n/k	Steel	1	Leith	16	n/k	n/k	n/k
Renfrewshire	n/k	n/k	Barnes	1	Glasgow	568	n/k	n/k	n/k
Renown of Aberdeen	bk	289	Walker, W.	3	Aberdeen	228	1842	Aberdeen	AE1
Renown of Kirkaldy	bg	159	Watts, J.	2	Leith	57	1795	Ely	E1
Retreat	n/k	n/k	Hamilton	1	Grnk	92	n/k	n/k	n/k
Retreat of Alloa	bg	356	Hudlass	1	Alloa	32	1805	Newcastle	AE1
Retrench of Greenock	bg	314	Cooper	1	Grnk	299	1826	N. Brunswick	AE1
Richibucto of Aberdeen	bk	401	Ganson, H.	1	Grnk	45	1835	Richibucto	A2

Vessel	Type	Tons	Capt.	No. of Voyages	Depart	Psgr Nos	Year built	Place built	Lloyd's Code
Rival	bg	335	Wallace	1	Grnk	333	1825	N. Brunswick	E1
Robert	n/k	n/k	Neil	1	Grnk	44	n/k	n/k	n/k
Robert & Margaret	s	420	n/k	1	Cromarty	66	n/k	n/k	n/k
Robert McWilliam of Aberdeen	sw	298	Williamson	1	Aberdeen	25	1825	N. Brunswick	AE1
Robert Morrow of Kirkaldy	bg	273	n/k	1	Leith	60	1841	PEI	A1
Robert Murrow	n/k	n/k	n/k	1	Leith	41	n/k	n/k	n/k
Robertson	s	n/k	Neil	4	Grnk	111	n/k	n/k	n/k
Roger Stewart	s	300	Kerr	2	Grnk	179	1811	Massa	E1
Romulus	bk	n/k	Sangster	1	Glasgow	86	n/k	n/k	n/k
Romulus of Greenock	bk	467	Coll, T.	2	Grnk	223	1831	Miramichi	AE1
Roscius	n/k	n/k	McClaren	1	Grnk	47	n/k	n/k	n/k
Rose	bg	n/k	Johnson	1	Leith	45	n/k	n/k	n/k
Rose of Aberdeen	bk	253	n/k	1	Aberdeen	94	1843	Aberdeen	A1
Rosebud	n/k	n/k	Roy	1	Glasgow	80	n/k	n/k	n/k
Rosina of Campbeltown	bk	614	n/k	2	Grnk	622	1845	Quebec	A1
Rothiemurchus of Leith	n/k	322	Watson, G.	2	Leith	133	1812	Speymouth	A1
Royal Adelaide of Greenock	bk	417	Dewar	1	Grnk	152	1830	Miramichi	AE1
Royal Bride of Dundee	sw	196	Welsh, G.	1	Dundee	78	1840	Dundee	A1
Royalist of Alloa	n/k	n/k	Beveridge	1	Grnk	15	n/k	n/k	n/k
Sally	n/k	n/k	Cumming	2	Grnk	73	n/k	n/k	n/k
Salmes	bg	287	Royal, H.	1	Inverness	250	1826	Quebec	A1
Saphiras of Whitby	sw	277	Brown, R.	1	Loch Laxford	202	1838	Sunderland	A1
Sappho of Sunderland	n/k	n/k	MacDonald	1	Glasgow	78	n/k	n/k	n/k
Sarah (1)	n/k	n/k	Marianne	1	Maryport	165	n/k	n/k	n/k
Sarah (2)	n/k	n/k	McLean, W.	1	Glasgow	58	n/k	n/k	n/k
Sarah Botsford of Glasgow	bk	306	Wallace, M.	1	Glasgow	219	1840	N. Brunswick	A1
Sarah Mariana	sw	194	Archibald	1	Maryport	164	1816	Chester	E
Sarah of Aberdeen	bg	232	Allan, G	7	Aberdeen	303	1839	Aberdeen	n/k
Scotia	bk	n/k	Simpson	1	Grnk	33	n/k	n/k	n/k
Scotia of Belfast	s	624	Carrey	2	Grnk	390	1844	Richibucto	AE1
Sesostris of Glasgow	s	632	Logan	1	Glasgow	302	1840	New Glasgow, N.S.	AE1
Shakespeare of Aberdeen	sw	179	Rosie	1	Aberdeen	84	1825	Aberdeen	AE1
Shandon	s	n/k	Greig	2	Glasgow	85	n/k	n/k	n/k
Sharp	sw	240	Almond	1	Cromarty	206	1831	Sunderland	A1
Sillery of Liverpool	s	994	Jackson	1	Skye (Isle Ornsay)	339	1853	Quebec	A1
Sir J H Craig	s	250	Dease, J.	1	Leith	100	1811	Quebec	E1
Sir William Wallace of Aberdeen (1)	bg	232	Anderson, D.	1	Aberdeen	28	1821	Aberdeen	n/k
Sir William Wallace of Aberdeen (2)	bg	183	Anderson, D.	6	Aberdeen	325	1835	Aberdeen	n/k

Vessel	Type	Tons	Capt.	No. of Voyages	Depart	Psgr Nos	Year built	Place built	Lloyd's Code
Sisters of Aberdeen	bg	177	Hull	1	Aberdeen	41	1833	Aberdeen	n/k
Skeen of Leith (1)	bg	250	Mason	2	Leith	59	1815	Leith	A2
Skeen of Leith (2)	n/k	212	Bennett	1	Leith	118	1827	Perth	n/k
Sophia	n/k	n/k	Neil	2	Grnk	55	n/k	n/k	n/k
Sophia of Ayr	bg	230	Moore	1	Grnk	106	1811	Ayr	A1
Sophia of Greenock	bg	266	Neil	1	Grnk	43	1825	Greenock	A1
Sovereign (1)	n/k	n/k	Pearson	1	Leith	49	n/k	n/k	n/k
Sovereign (2)	n/k	n/k		1	Grnk	44	n/k	n/k	n/k
Spartan of Greenock	s	681	Morrison	1	Glasgow	244	1845	N. Brunswick	AE1
Speculation	s	205	Douglass	2	Grnk	207	n/k	America	E1
Sprightly	n/k	n/k	n/k	1	Dundee	60	n/k	n/k	n/k
Springfield	n/k	n/k	n/k	1	Glasgow	42	n/k	n/k	n/k
Springhill of Irvine	bk	348	Auld	5	Grnk	252	1826	N. Brunswick	E1
St Andrew of New Brunswick	s	553	Leith, J.	1	Lochmaddy	133	1835	Nova Scotia	n/k
St George	n/k	n/k	Thomson	1	Maryport	26	n/k	n/k	n/k
St Lawrence of Aberdeen	bk	352	Tulloch, J.	22	Aberdeen	1896	1841	Aberdeen	A1
St Nicholas	bg	n/k	Morgan	1	Inverness	29	n/k	n/k	n/k
Stillman	n/k	216	Williamson, C.	1	Glasgow	60	n/k	n/k	n/k
Stirling	n/k	203	Jessie, A.	1	Glasgow	154	n/k	n/k	n/k
Stirling Castle of Greenock	bg	351	Fraser	2	Grnk	582	1829	Miramichi, N.B.	AE1
Stranraer	n/k	n/k	n/k	2	Stranraer	147	n/k	n/k	n/k
Sunbeam	s	810	Dow	1	Grnk	367	1850	Quebec	A1
Superb of Greenock`	bk	599	Shannon	2	Grnk	211	1837	Miramichi N.B.	A1
Superior of Peterhead	bk	306	Manson	1	Cromarty	191	1813	Shields	AE1
Susan of Glasgow	bk	321	Taylor	4	Glasgow	477	1847	PEI	A1
Swift of Sunderland	sw	280	Beveridge	1	Cromarty	215	1837	Sunderland	A1
Sylvanus of North Shields	sw	263	Lawson	1	Cromarty	41	1826	Sunderland	A1
Symmetry	n/k	n/k	n/k	1	Thurso	110	n/k	n/k	n/k
Tadmor	bk	638	Bovie	1	Glasgow	387	1848	N. Brunswick	A1
Tamerlane of Greenock	s	390	Martin	5	Grnk	950	1824	N. Brunswick	A1
Taurus of Aberdeen	sr	184	n/k	1	Aberdeen	134	1841	Aberdeen	A1
Tay of Glasgow	bk	512	Langwell	4	Grnk	853	1832	N. Brunswick	AE1
Thistle of Aberdeen	sw	133	Allen, R.	1	Tobermory	43	1818	Aberdeen	A1
Thomas Worthington	s	n/k	Morrison	1	Grnk	96	n/k	n/k	n/k
Thompsons Packet of Dumfries	bg	201	Lookup	1	Dumfries	40	1817	n/k	A1
Thornhill	s	n/k	Bogart	1	Glasgow	253	n/k	n/k	n/k
Three Bells of Glasgow	s	730	n/k	4	Glasgow	381	1850	Dumbarton	A1

Vessel	Type	Tons	Capt.	No. of Voyages	Depart	Psgr Nos	Year built	Place built	Lloyd's Code
Tods of Perth	bg	109	McPherson, W.	1	Dundee	42	1816	Perth	A1
Trafalgar of London	bg	175	Mitchell, J.	1	Leith	100	1805	Hull	E1
Traveller of Aberdeen	bg	195	Goldie, J.	2	Tobermory	163	1819	Aberdeen	n/k
Traveller of Dundee	bg	195	Wighton	1	Dundee	42	1819	n/k	n/k
Triton	s	405	McClean	3	Cromarty	168	1815	Whitby	E1
Troubadour of Irvine	bk	298	McDowell, J.	1	Glasgow	224	1840	Nova Scotia	A1
True Briton	sw	216	Reid, J.	3	Grnk	125	1818	Blythe	A1
Tuskar of Liverpool	s	900	n/k	1	Stornoway	496	1845	Saint John, N.B.	AE1
Tweed	bk	n/k	Slocombe	1	Cromarty	245	n/k	n/k	n/k
Union	s	231	Henry	1	Grnk	15	1807	America	E1
Unity	s	219	Service	1	Grnk	200	1791	Ayr	A1
Universe of Aberdeen	n/k	n/k	n/k	1	Thurso	19	n/k	n/k	AE1
Urgent of Belfast	s	592	n/k	1	Stornoway	370	1839	Quebec	AE1
Vesper	n/k	n/k	Bennett	1	Thurso	52	n/k	n/k	n/k
Victoria of Dundee	sw	252	Berrie, J.	4	Dundee	200	1832	Dundee	AE1
Viewforth of Kirkaldy	bk	289	Elden	1	Cromarty	150	1830	Shields	A1
Wallace (1)	s	n/k	Wilkie	1	Glasgow	111	n/k	n/k	n/k
Wallace (2)	bg	n/k	Sim	1	Fraserburgh	117	n/k	n/k	n/k
Wanderer	bg	280	Cowan, F.	1	Glasgow	141	1839	N. Brunswick	A1
Wandsworth of Glasgow	s	767	n/k	1	Grnk	377	1839	Quebec	A1
Warner	bg	161	Crawford	1	Grnk	43	1817	Saltcoats	A1
Warsaw	n/k	n/k	n/k	1	Glasgow	31	n/k	n/k	n/k
Waterhen of London	bk	355	Dodds, W.	1	Grnk	167	1825	Hull	AE1
Waterloo of Fort William	n/k	n/k	Kendal, J.	1	Fort William	108	n/k	n/k	n/k
Watermillock	bg	n/k	Conner	1	Glasgow	34	n/k	n/k	n/k
Welcome	n/k	n/k	McColl	1	Grnk	15	n/k	n/k	n/k
Westmorland	n/k	n/k	Duncan	1	Leith	76	n/k	n/k	n/k
Wexford of Wexford	s	254	Slatterly, J.	1	Grnk	200	1829	Quebec	AE1
William & Ann	n/k	n/k	n/k	1	Glasgow	24	n/k	n/k	n/k
William Glen Anderson of Glasgow	bk	389	Gillespie	1	Aberdeen	152	1827	Richibucto N.B.	AE1
William Hutt	s	n/k	Rankin	1	Glasgow	138	n/k	n/k	n/k
William Shand	n/k	n/k	Hunter	1	Berwick	299	n/k	n/k	n/k
Wilson	n/k	n/k	n/k	1	Grnk	21	n/k	n/k	n/k
Wingrove of Newcastle	sw	261	Hughes	1	Glasgow	160	1839	Sunderland	A1
Wolfville of Ardrossan	bk	415	McMillan, J.	2	Loch Roag	328	1841	Nova Scotia	AE1
Woodfield	n/k	n/k	n/k	1	Glasgow	69	n/k	n/k	n/k
Young Norval	s	n/k	Luck	1	Grnk	37	n/k	n/k	n/k
Ythan	n/k	n/k	Cairns	1	Grnk	20	n/k	n/k	n/k
Zealous	n/k	n/k	Reed	1	Leith	182	n/k	n/k	n/k
Zephyr	n/k	650	Tucker	1	Cromarty	99	n/k	n/k	n/k

Notes

One – The Vulnerable Colony

1   Bumsted, J.M. (ed.), *The Collected Writings of Lord Selkirk*, Vol. I, (1799–1809): *Observations on the Present State of the Highlands of Scotland, with a view of the causes and probable consequences of emigration*, (Winnipeg: The Manitoba Record Society, 1984) 161. Hereafter this source is referred to as *Selkirk's Observations*.

2   Ibid.

3   Anon., *A Short Account of the Emigration from the Highlands of Scotland to North America; and the Establishment of the Catholic Diocese of Upper Canada* (Kingston, Ontario, 1839) 9. Addington made these comments to Father Alexander Macdonell, who would later become Upper Canada's first Bishop (Roman Catholic).

4   Between 1763 and the outbreak of the American Revolution in 1775, some 125,000 British emigrants came to North America, although most settled in what would later become the United States. Philip Buckner, *English Canada – The founding generations: British migration to British North America, 1815–1865*. Canada House, Lecture Series No. 54 (ISBN 0265–4253), Canadian High Commission, Grosvenor Square, London.

5   An example of this policy at work was the case of the Mississauga First Nation, who controlled land along the north shore of what is now Lake Ontario. Following the American Revolution, the Mississauga were removed from this area and replaced by Loyalists. See Donald B. Smith, "British Indian Policy in the wake of the American Revolution" in Bumsted, J.M., *Interpreting Canada's Past*, Vol. I, (Toronto: Oxford University Press, 1993) 290–312.

6   The Native Peoples could be removed to new ground relatively easily because there was an abundance of space. After the War of 1812–14, when their usefulness as allies diminished, government officials showed little regard for Indian land claims. Because of their relatively small numbers and lack of military power, they could offer little resistance to the continuing spread of settlement onto their lands.

7   NLS Adv MS 35.6.18, ff. 8–15, Melville Papers, State of Emigration from the Highlands of Scotland, its extent, causes and proposed remedy, London, March 21, 1803.

8   Passenger data accounts for a total Scottish influx of around 4,000 of which around 3,000 had Inverness-shire origins.

9   Joseph Bouchette, *The British Dominions in North America: a Topographical and Statistical Description of the Provinces of Lower and Upper Canada, New Brunswick, Nova Scotia, the Islands of Newfoundland, Prince Edward Island and Cape Breton,* (London, 1832) Vol. II, 235.

10   Sir John Sinclair, *First Statistical Account of Scotland,* 21 vols. (Edinburgh, 1791–99) Vol. XVII, 76.

11   In addition to Belfast, Lord Selkirk also founded Highland settlements at Baldoon (later Wallaceburg) in Upper Canada in 1804, and at Red River (later Winnipeg) in 1812.

12   The government continued to operate its "grace and favour" land policies well into the 1850s. Lillian F. Gates, *Land Policies of Upper Canada* (Toronto: University of Toronto Press, 1968) 303–7.

13   Wilderness land was regarded as the legitimate property of *bona-fide* settlers. They thus felt justified in taking unauthorized possession of land and in doing so claimed that they were assisting the process of colonization. Government officials rarely challenged them and most squatters eventually were able to legitimize their holdings.

14   The Sutherland Highlanders (93rd) took part in a bungled attack on the well-fortified American position at New Orleans in January 1815, and suffered many casualties. The battle was fought two weeks after the peace treaty ending the war had been signed.

15   This regiment was formed in 1804 from the veterans of the Glengarry Fencibles Regiment which had been raised in 1794. Marianne McLean, *People of Glengarry 1745–1820: Highlanders in Transition* (Montreal: McGill-Queen's University Press, 1991) 198–200.

16   Norman MacDonald, *Canada, Immigration and Settlement 1763–1841* (London: Longmans, 1939) 501.

17   The rebellions in Upper Canada reflected widespread popular unrest over the state of agriculture, dissatisfaction with the ruling elite and French/English animosity. See J.M. Bumsted, *The Peoples of Canada, a Pre-Confederation History,* Vol. 1 (Toronto: Oxford University Press, 1992) 248–50.

18   For background on Robert Gourlay, see *Dictionary of Canadian Biography* (hereafter *DCB*), Vol. IX, 330–6.

19   Bouchette, *The British Dominions in North America,* 235.

20   The Annual Reports of the Immigration Agent at Quebec, 1830–55. The official figures show that 94,096 Scots arrived at Quebec during this 25-year period. However, there are problems in interpreting this figure. Some Scots sailed to New York because it was usually a quicker sea voyage than was the crossing to Quebec. Thus, they would be excluded from this figure. Moreover, this figure includes Scots who did not necessarily settle in Upper Canada. The United States, with its cheaper land and better economic opportunities, attracted a good many of the British immigrants who landed at Quebec – Scots included. In addition, some of the Quebec arrivals from Britain would have been heading for Lower Canada, although they would have been a relatively small number.

21   The overall statistics for British North America show a similar pattern. N.H. Carrier, and J.R. Jeffrey, *External Migration: A Study of the Available Statistics 1815–1950* (London, HMSO, 1953) 27.

22   Scottish immigration grew once again during the first three decades of the twentieth century. With the arrival of steamships and the railways, unprecedented numbers arrived, dwarfing the earlier influx.

23   The Scottish influx to Upper Canada petered out by the late 1850s, as the United States and Australia became increasingly attractive to Scots. Carrier and Jeffrey, ibid, 95–6.

24   Emigrants could halve their journey time to Hamilton by taking road transport from Montreal to Prescott, but this cost nearly six times the amount payable when the entire journey was made by river. In 1832, emigrants would pay £6 and take about 6 days to get to York if they travelled from Montreal to Prescott by land; otherwise the cost of going the 550 miles from Montreal to York was £1. 11s. 6d. and the journey time was around 12 days. See NAS GD 46/13/184: *Information published by His Majesty's Commissioners for Emigration respecting the British Colonies in North America* (London: Feb., 1832) 7–8. For details of transatlantic fares see Chapter 9.

25   Arthur E. Wright, *Pioneer Days in Nichol* (Mount Forest, ON: self-published, 1932) 49.

26   Helen Cowan, *British Emigration to British North America; the first hundred years* (Toronto: University of Toronto Press, 1961) 57.

27   However, Western Isle Scots were the one exception. They remained fiercely loyal to their long-established communities in Cape Breton.

28   Nevertheless, as was the case in the Maritimes, Upper Canada's economy depended heavily on the timber trade with Britain. A.R.M. Lower, "Settlement and the Forest Frontier in Eastern Canada" in W.A. MacKintosh and W.L.G. Jaergs (eds.), *Canadian Frontiers of Settlement,* Vol. IX (Toronto: Macmillan, 1936) 40–7. See also Douglas McCalla, "Forest Products and Upper Canadian Development," in *Canadian Historical Review,* Vol. 68 (1987) 159–98.

29   With the opening of the Welland Canal in 1829, linking Lake Erie with Lake Ontario, the lush forests in the region around Lake Erie were opened up for the first time.

30   Donald MacKay, *The Lumberjacks* (Toronto: Natural Heritage, 1998) 13–6, 22–7, 40–5.

31   Although Irish-born immigrants were evident in the western peninsula by 1851, a much higher proportion were to be found in eastern Upper Canada than was the case with the Scots. See A.G. Brunger, "The Distribution of Scots and Irish in Upper Canada 1851–71," *Canadian Geographer,* Vol. 34 (1990) 250–7.

32   LAC M-1353: Rev. MacNaughton to Rev. Robert Burns, Aug. 27, 1833.

33   Ibid.

34   See for example PP, w/e Aug. 22, 1840. The Quebec Immigration Agent's Annual Reports have been published in the Parliamentary Papers. They often give information on the geographical origins and destinations of immigrants and sometimes give details of their former occupations.

35   Ibid.

36   LAC MG29 C29: George Sandfield Macdonald fonds, File 1, 5.

37   LAC MG30-C77: H. McColl fonds, Sketches written in 1904, 11.

Two – The Glengarry Settlements

1 John MacTaggert, *Three Years in Canada, An account of the actual state of the country in 1826–7–8 comprehending its resources, productions, improvements and capabilities and including sketches of the state of society, advice to emigrants, etc.* Two Volumes (London, H. Colburn, 1829) Vol. 1, 193. John MacTaggart, a civil engineer, was employed by the British government.

2 Sir Francis Bond Head, *The Emigrant,* (London: John Murray, 1846) 116.

3 Ibid.

4 MacTaggart, *Three Years in Canada*, 193.

5 Cowan, *British Emigration*, 3–17.

6 Only a small minority of the New York Loyalists went to Upper Canada. Some 28,000 of them had gone to Nova Scotia. Gates, *Land Policies of Upper Canada*, 11–23; Gerald, M. Craig, *Upper Canada, The Formative Years 1784–1841* (Toronto: McClelland & Stewart, 1993), 1–19 (originally published in 1963).

7 *New York Journal,* Oct. 28, 1773, quoted in McLean, *People of Glengarry*, 87.

8 *SM*, Vol. 35 (1773) 499. The *Pearl* carried 225 adults and 200 children. Twenty five children died of smallpox on the voyage. According to the *Scots Magazine*, the group comprised "three gentlemen of the name of Macdonell with their families and 400 Highlanders" who had obtained a grant of land in Albany, New York.

9 John Macdonell had a varied career which included service in a Spanish regiment. See William McLennan, *Spanish John: being a memoir, now first published in complete for, of the early life and adventures of Colonel John McDonell, known as "Spanish John," when a lieutenant in the Company of St. James of the Regiment Irlandia, in the service of the king of Spain operating in Italy* (London: Harper, 1898).

10 Tacksmen were an elite class in the Scottish feudal system who acted as factors or farm managers under a laird. They usually sublet much of their own land to sub-tenants who did most of the work on the great Highland estates. With the introduction of improved farming methods in the 1770s, the tacksmen's role became increasingly obsolete and many reacted to the sweeping changes by promoting emigration within their local population and were highly influential in encouraging large numbers to emigrate.

11 The part played by tacksmen in instigating emigration from Highland estates is discussed in Margaret I. Adam, "The Highland Emigration of 1770," in *Scottish Historical Review,* Vol. xvi (1919) 280–93.

12 Seventeen Scottish families had also arrived in the area before the *Pearl* emigrants and had settled on William Johnson's land. McLean, *People of the Glengarry,* 89.

13 Ibid, 87–9.

14 Ian Adams and Meredyth Somerville, *Cargoes of Despair and Hope, Scottish Emigration to North America 1603–1803* (Edinburgh: John Donald, 1993) 40–50.

15 Sir John Johnson was authorized to raise the King's Royal Regiment of New York shortly after his arrival in Montreal in June, 1776. Most of its members were Mohawk Valley Highlanders. McLean, 90–6.

16 LAC MG23 HII19: Mrs. Nancy Jean Cameron to Mrs. Kenneth Macpherson, May 15, 1785. They would travel to the St. Lawrence from Albany by going north along the Hudson River to Lake George then after travelling overland they would take boats along the length of Lake Champlain and continue northwards along the Richelieu River to Sorel.

17 Ibid.

18 Ibid.

19 The old province of Quebec was formally divided into the new provinces of Upper and Lower Canada in 1791. Glengarry was on Upper Canada's eastern boundary with Lower Canada.

20 They were joined by men from Major Rogers' Corps, another group led by Major Van Alstine and detachments of other soldiers who included some Germans. Craig, *Upper Canada, The Formative Years*, 1–19.

21 McLean, 170–4. Most of the Glengarry Loyalists settled in Charlottenburg Township. The first arrivals were to be found principally along the north and south shores of the Raisin River.

22 The 84th Regiment, which was raised at the beginning of the American War in 1775, acquired its recruits mainly from Highland emigrants loyal to the British side, who were living at the time in North America. In addition to getting land in Glengarry County, former members of the 84th Regiment were also allocated land grants at Chatham, in Lower Canada, on the north side of the Ottawa River. John Butler's Rangers were composed of New York and Pennsylvania Loyalists. When the regiment was disbanded, most agreed to settle at Niagara.

23 Allan Macdonell later became a Justice of the Peace in Glengarry County. McLean, 98–103. His younger brother, Alexander, later became Bishop Macdonell of Kingston.

24 LAC RG19, Vol. 4447, No. 14: "Victualling list of emigrants lately come from Scotland by way of New York and Albany who meaned to settle in this province commencing 25th and ending 31st of August, 1786." Why only half of them were recorded remains a mystery. There may have been more than one provisioning list. It is also possible that some of the emigrants remained for varying periods of time in New York before moving on to Glengarry. McLean, 104–108.

25 The *Macdonald* was "an old war or troop ship." See LAC MG29 C29: George Sandfield Macdonald fonds, File 1, 49.

26 Translated from Gaelic verse. It appears as a newspaper clipping kept in a scrapbook owned by John J. MacLeod of Glengarry County, Ontario. It was likely published in the *Glengarry News*, (no date). McLean, 114.

27 Ibid, 108–16. Angus McDonell was also known as Angus Sandaig (the name of his Knoydart farm).

28 Quoted in Miss A.M. Pope, "A Scotch Catholic Settlement in Canada," *Catholic World*, Vol. 34 (Oct., 1881) 74. According to the *Quebec Mercury,* the *Macdonald* had 19 cabin and 520 steerage passengers.

29 LAC RG4 A1 f. 9910: John Craigie to Stephen Delaney, Inspector of Loyalists at Lachine, Sept. 4, 1786.

30 LAC RG4 A1 f. 9912: Brig. General Hope to Lt. Angus McDonell, Sept. 25, 1786.

31 LAC, f. 9911, Craigie to Delaney, ff. 9912–4: Hope to McDonell. Adults had a
    weekly allowance of four-and-one-half pounds potatoes, one and a half pounds
    of salt fish, three pounds five ounces of flour and two pounds beef.

32 Many of the 300 emigrants who arrived via Philadelphia in 1786 also obtained
    land in these concessions.

33 The names of these people are to be found in LAC RG19, Vol. 4447, No. 28:
    List of Sundry Persons as Emigrants from North Britain who were located by
    Mr. James McDonell in the townships of Lancaster and Charlottenburg in the
    years 1786–87. George Sandfield Macdonald, who wrote down his interviews
    with local Glengarry people in the 1880s, produced a list which confirms that
    the majority of the 1786 arrivals originated from Knoydart. LAC MG29 C29:
    George Sandfield Macdonald fonds (Part 6).

34 In the Christian faith, St. Raphael is one of the seven archangels who stand in
    the presence of God. The name in Hebrew means "God heals."

35 Charlottenburg was sub-divided in 1798 and Lancaster's sub-division occurred
    in 1818.

36 In 1791, the population of the province of Quebec west of the Baudet River
    (which would become the colony of Upper Canada) was 10,000. Gates, *Land
    policies of Upper Canada,* 22; McLean, 180.

37 LAC RG4 A1, Vol. 48 ff. 15874–5: The passenger list for the *British Queen* cross-
    ing appears in Appendix I. The passengers originated from Glen Garry, North
    Morar and Knoydart in the Glengarry estate and from Ardgour, Arisaig,
    Moidart, Eigg and South Uist in the Clanranald estate. The *British Queen's*
    arrival was reported by the *Quebec Gazette* on Oct. 21, 1790.

38 Lucille H. Campey, *'A Very Fine Class of Immigrants': Prince Edward Island's
    Scottish Pioneers, 1770–1850* (Toronto: Natural Heritage, 2001) 24–5, 112–8.

39 McLean, 116–21, 182–3. The merchants supplied beef and bread to the emi-
    grants for their trip inland and also sent them a further 726 pounds of beef after
    their arrival in Glengarry County.

40 For the Prince Edward Island influx, see Campey, *Very Fine Class of Immi-
    grants,* 25, 138; for the Nova Scotia influx, see Lucille H. Campey, *After the Hector:
    The Scottish Pioneers of Nova Scotia and Cape Breton, 1773–1852* (Toronto: Nat-
    ural Heritage, 2004) 56–82.

41 *QG,* Sept. 27, 1792. Alexander was the son of Ewan McMillan of Glenpean.
    According to George Sandfield Macdonald, the ship, *Cochrane,* also arrived in
    1792 "with a few immigrants." See LAC MG29 C29 File 1, 49.

42 *Diary of Mrs. John Graves Simcoe,* June 24, 1792 quoted in Edwin C. Guillet,
    Pioneer Days in Upper Canada (Toronto: University of Toronto Press, 1966) 6.
    Col. John McDonell had been a captain in Butler's Rangers. He served in the
    Legislative Assembly of Upper Canada from 1792 to 1800 and was its first
    speaker.

43 While most of the 1793 emigrants originated from Glenelg, some came from
    Glen Moriston, Strathglass and Knoydart.

44 McLean, 121–25, 173–80.

45 *QG,* June 5, June 12, 1794.

46 LAC RG1 L3: Upper Canada Land Petitions MC 21 (1837–39) Petition of
    Alexander McLeod of the 6th concession of Lochiel.

47   Ibid.

48   During this period from 1790 to 1793, the Highlands and Islands lost around 900 people to Prince Edward Island, 650 people to Nova Scotia and just over 400 people to Upper Canada. See Campey, *Very Fine Class of Immigrants,* 138–9 and Campey, *After the Hector,* 57–8, 236.

49   McLean, 134–5.

50   Sinclair, *First Statistical Account of Scotland,* Vol. XVII. 135–6.

51   NLS MS 9646: "Essay On Emigration from the Scottish Highlands and Islands" (an original manuscript attributed to Edward S. Fraser of Inverness-shire) f. 27.

52   Robert Brown, *Strictures and remarks on the Earl of Selkirk's observations on the present state of the Highlands* (Edinburgh: Abernethy & Walker, 1806) 36–38, Appendix (State of Emigrations 1801, 1802 and 1803); NLS MS 9646 ff. 19, 21, 23.

53   NLS MS 35.6.18: State of emigration from the Highlands of Scotland its extent, causes and proposed remedy (March 21, 1803) f. 19.

54   NAS RH 4/188/2: "Prize essays and Transactions of the Highland Society of Scotland," (original manuscript – mainly minutes for meetings of the Society), Vol. iii, 1802–03, 531–4. Second Report of the Committee on Emigration, June 1802.

55   Pressure from the Highland Society caused the government to introduce the Passenger Act of 1803 which stipulated minimum food and space requirements for emigrants. However, the immediate effect of the Act was to cause fares to nearly double and thus greatly reduce the numbers of people who could afford to emigrate.

56   In addition to these four ships, the *Quebec Gazette* also recorded the arrival of the *Eagle* from Greenock "with 21 men, women and children" and of the *Albion* from Fort William with 167 passengers (*QG* 9, Sept. 11, 1802).

57   *QG,* Sept. 16, 1802. Thomas Telford, *A Survey and Report of the Coasts and Central Highlands of Scotland* (London: 1803) 15. As only adults paid full fares, children were computed as being a fraction of an adult. Through the use of such a formula, the *Neptune's* 600 passengers were converted to 400 "full passengers."

58   Archibald McMillan was assisted by his first cousin, Allan McMillan of Glenpean (Lochiel), whose brother had led the 1792 emigration to Upper Canada. The emigrants paid fares of £5. 5s. McLean, 139–44. The ship arrivals were reported in the *Quebec Gazette* on 5th and 15th of Sept. 1802.

59   LAC MG24 I183 ff. 7–9, 11. The passengers lists for the *Helen, Jean* and *Friends* crossings appear in Appendix 1. They are described in detail in Rae Fleming (ed.), *The Lochaber Emigrants to Glengarry* (Toronto: Natural Heritage, 1994) 5–16. Also see Somerled MacMillan, *Bygone Lochaber, historical and traditional* (Glasgow: K. & R. Davidson, 1971) 239 for a list of the additional passengers who boarded ship at Saltcoats, near Irvine, in the Firth of Clyde.

60   LAC MG24 I183 ff. 35, 73; *Lloyd's Shipping Register,* 1802.

61   McLean, 142–3. McMillan would eventually receive a total of £1,979 in fares from the emigrants, leaving him with a profit of around £118.

62   *QG,* Sept. 16, 1802. The group had three spokesmen: Norman Morrison, Duncan McDonald and Murdoch McLennan.

63   McLean, 136–39.

64   LAC MG24 I183 (File 3) f. 40: Case heard in Montreal, Sept. 23, 1802. The J.P.s were James McGill and John M. Kindlay.

65   McLean, 139–44.

66 The name, Blue Chapel, derived from the colour of its ceiling.

67 John Graham Harkness, *Stormont, Dundas and Glengarry, A History 1784–1945* (Ottawa: Mutual Press, 1972) 118–31. Williamstown's first frame church, built by the late eighteenth century, was replaced by a stone building which was constructed from 1812. A small frame church, built in 1803 at Martintown, was replaced by a more substantial building in 1825.

68 Patrick Cecil Telford White (ed.), *Lord Selkirk's Diary 1803–04; A journal of his travels through British North America and the Northeastern United States* (Toronto: The Champlain Society, 1958), 197. Hereafter referred to as *Lord Selkirk's Diary*. Father Alexander Macdonell, who had the "Blue Chapel" built, was succeeded by another Rev. Alexander Macdonell who later became Upper Canada's first Roman Catholic Bishop. Rev. John Bethune also preached at Lancaster, Cornwall and Martintown. In 1787, he was Chaplain of the First Battalion of the Royal Highland Emigrant Regiment. Guillet, *Pioneer Days*, 8.

69 *Lord Selkirk's Diary,* 198.

70 The wooden frame church was replaced by a large stone church in the 1860s.

71 An endowment system was introduced in 1792 for Protestant clergy (interpreted as the Church of England) and the Crown, thus creating reserves which could only be acquired by settlers through renting.

72 MacDonald, *Canada, Immigration and Settlement*, 480.

73 McLean, 191–2.

74 Papineau later became Ottawa County. The combined efforts of Scottish-born ex-servicemen and proprietors eventually created the conditions which gave Chatham, Grenville and Lochaber townships their substantial Scottish populations (see *Lower Canada Census, 1861*).

75 *DCB*, for more information on Archibald McMillan, see Vol. VI, 475–9.

76 LAC MG24 I 183: Letter-book, McMillan to Duncan Cameron, Sept. 30, 1803, and to Ewan Cameron, Oct. 20, 1805.

77 Ibid, Letter-book, McMillan to John Munro, July 21, 1806.

78 Ibid, Sept. 10, 1807.

79 DCA Dundee and District Shipping Local Collection, D3113. The *Quebec Gazette,* July 6, 1809, recorded the arrival of the *Albion* (Master R. Kidd) from Dundee with 60 passengers.

80 *DCB*, Vol. VI, 478–9. McMillan always had to struggle to meet the settlement regulations set by government. His failure to attract sufficient settlers by 1821 caused him to nearly lose his land grants.

81 *Lord Selkirk's Diary,* 199; McLean, 193–5.

82 MacMillan, *Bygone Lochaber*, 11–2, in *DCB*, Vol. VI, 478–9. The 1852 Census shows that 545 MacMillans lived in Glengarry County.

83 J.A. Macdonell, *Sketches illustrating the early settlement and history of Glengarry in Canada* (Belleville, ON: Mika Publishing Co. 1984, (first published 1893); *DCB*, Vol. VII, 544–51.

84 Fencible regiments were used for the internal defence of the country. The Glengarry Fencibles Regiment served in Jersey and Guernsey and in the Irish Rebellion of 1798. Michael Brander, *The Scottish Highlanders and their Regiments* (Haddington Scotland: Gleneil Press, 1996) 81, 209–12. James Browne, *History of the Highlands and the Highland Clans* (Glasgow: A. Fullarton & Co., 1840) Vol. iv, 378–81.

85   Anon., *A Short Account of the Emigration from the Highlands of Scotland to North America;* 9.
86   Ibid, 10.
87   LAC MG24 J13: "The Glengarry Highlanders," 25.
88   PRO CO 42/360 ff. 93–4: Hobart to Peter Hunter, March 1, 1803. Father Macdonell was granted 1,200 acres and each family he recruited would get 200 acres. The location in Upper Canada of his land grant is not known.
89   LAC MG24 J13: "Glengarry Highlanders," 25.
90   Although the 1803 Act was introduced ostensibly for humanitarian reasons, it was generally accepted throughout Scotland that it would provide a temporary deterrent to emigration and allow time for the Highland improvement schemes being recommended by Thomas Telford to be implemented. For further details of the space and food regulations of the Act see Lucille H. Campey, *Fast Sailing and Copper-Bottomed, Aberdeen Sailing Ships and the Emigrant Scots they carried to Canada* (Toronto, Natural Heritage, 2002) 105–7.
91   McLean, 146–8; J.M. Bumsted, *The People's Clearance: Highland Emigration to British North America 1770–1815,* (Edinburgh: Edinburgh University Press, 1982) 77, 111, 158.
92   Selkirk's Baldoon land, near present-day Wallaceburg Ontario, was granted on roughly the same terms as Father Macdonell's land.
93   Lucille H. Campey, *The Silver Chief, Lord Selkirk and the Scottish Pioneers of Belfast, Baldoon and Red River* (Toronto: Natural Heritage, 2003) 52, 78, 145.
94   LAC MG24 J13: "Glengarry Highlanders," 30.
95   Ibid.
96   PRO CO 42/342, 5–6, Alexander Macdonell to Alexander Grant, April 1806.

Three – The Perth Military Settlement

1   William Bell's "Journal," quoted in Isabel Skelton, *A Man Austere* (Toronto: Ryerson Press, 1947) 85. Bell's "Journals" have been deposited in the Douglas Library of Queen's University, Kingston. There are 17 volumes.
2   PRO CO 385/2, ff. 3–26. The combined passenger list for the *Atlas, Dorothy, Eliza* and *Baltic Merchant* crossings appears in Appendix I. See Skelton, *Man Austere,* 85–7.
3   The *Atlas, Dorothy,* and *Baltic Merchant* arrived at Quebec on September 3, while the *Eliza* arrived on October 1 (*QG*, Sept. 7, Oct. 5, 1815).
4   Skelton, *Man Austere,* 86.
5   PRO CO 42/164: John Campbell to Henry Goulburn, May 13, 1815. Because of the many hindrances of the 1803 Act, a new act was soon passed imposing less stringent terms.
6   Another Perthshire group, numbering around 80, mainly from Kenmore and Callander, emigrated to New Brunswick in 1815. They sailed on the *Favourite* from Port Glasgow to Saint John, having had their passages paid by the New Brunswick government (passenger list in *Generations,* New Brunswick Genealogical Society (65, 1995, 22–6).
7   According to Bumsted, just under seventy per cent of the Scots who emigrated to British America between 1770 and 1815 chose to settle in the Maritimes. Bumsted, *Peoples Clearance,* 228.

8   Evidence of Lt. Col. Cockburn, *Select Committee, Emigration, 1826*, A1497.

9   G.P. de T., Glazebrook, *A History of Transportation in Canada*, Vol. 1 (Toronto, McClelland & Stewart, 1964) 78–9. George K. Raudzens, "The Military Impact on Canadian Canals, 1815–25," in *Canadian Historical Review*, Vol. LIV (1973) 273–86.

10 Although the scheme was not publicized in England, some thirty English settlers accepted the government's terms and sailed to Quebec from Deptford. Cowan, *British Emigration to British North America*, 40–4.

11 Public opinion was not yet ready to accept that emigration could provide a practical escape route for the poor and destitute. The government, thus, had to stress that its assisted emigration scheme was not intended to promote emigration. Its purpose was to divert those who had already intended to emigrate to go to Upper Canada.

12 PRO CO 42/165, f. 134.

13 H.J.M Johnston, *British Emigration Policy 1815–1830: Shovelling out paupers* (Oxford: Clarendon Press, 1972) 17–27.

14 See M.E. Vance, "Emigration and Scottish Society: The background of government assisted emigration to Upper Canada 1815–21," unpublished Ph. D. thesis, University of Guelph, 1990, 15–44.

15 PRO CO 42/165 ff. 180–5: Campbell to Bathurst, Oct. 14, 1815.

16 Ibid.

17 PRO CO 42/165 ff 305–7: Memorial of Allan McDonell, from Kerrivemore near Fort Augustus, March 11, 1815.

18 Ibid. The full list of 29 families, who consisted of around 150 people, appears in Table 2. Only Duncan McDonell's family, can be found in the 1815 passenger list. (See Appendix I.)

19 PRO CO 42/165 ff 97–8, 180–5: Campbell to Bathurst March 15, Oct. 14, 1815.

20 PRO CO 42/165 ff. 180–5: Campbell to Earl Bathurst, Oct. 14, 1815.

21 Before 1815, the Maritimes attracted Scots principally from the Western Isles and the mainland counties of Inverness-shire, Argyll, Ross-shire and Sutherland. For details of the early Highland and Island influx to Prince Edward Island see Campey, *Very Fine Class of Immigrants*, 136–43, and for the Nova Scotia and Cape Breton influx see Campey, *After the Hector*, 234–42.

22 PRO CO 385/2 ff. 3–26: "General list of settlers enrolled for Canada under the government regulations at Edinburgh, 1815," (See Appendix I for full list.)

23 An added factor in Callander was the spread of sheep farming which had been stimulating emigration from as early as 1791.

24 Drummond to Gore, March, 15 1816, quoted in McLean, *People of Glengarry*, 198.

25 Thirteen Lowland families also chose to settle in Glengarry County. They were granted land in Lochiel Township. McLean, 200.

26 The 350 figure is approximate. According to McLean, a total of 362 emigrants went to Glengarry under the 1815 government scheme.

27 Ibid, 155–57, 200–01. The Knoydart emigrants got their land in the 10th, 11th and 15th concessions of what was then Lancaster Township (later Lochiel). The Glenelg settlers were given land in the 12th and 13th concessions of Lancaster Township (later Lochiel) and in the 4th, 5th, 7th and 8th concessions of West Hawkesbury Township. The Perthshire emigrants were granted their land in the 16th and 17th concessions of Lancaster Township (later Lochiel).

28　A later stone church was built in 1865. Donald E. Meek, 'Evangelicalism and Emigration: Aspects of the role of dissenting evangelicalism in Highland emigration to Canada' in Gordon MacLennan (ed.), *Proceedings of the First North American Congress of Celtic Studies* (1986) 15–37. The Breadalbane settlers had sailed on the *Dorothy* in 1815. The settlers were predominantly McDiarmids, McDougals, McLaurins and Campbells.

29　LAC H-1807 f. 326: McLaurin family fonds, Mary Beaton's transcript of the register of baptisms and marriages, 1820–1911. Harkness, *Stormont, Dundas and Glengarry*, 121–2.

30　The Colonial Office had intended to send 2,000 emigrants from Scotland, 2,000 emigrants from Ireland and a small number from England. Johnston, *British Emigration Policy*, 18–9.

31　NAS RH9/17/237: List of letters received from applicants wishing to settle in Canada (Feb. 27 to March 9, 1815). A comparison of this list with the 1815 combined passenger list for the *Atlas, Dorothy, Eliza* and *Baltic Merchant* reveals that many of the initial applicants actually enlisted in the scheme.

32　LAC RG5 A1, Vol. 25, 367–9: Petition of Scottish Settlers, Dec. 28, 1815.

33　Each soldier received 100 acres of free land, a year's provisions and farm implements. Officers normally received 200 acres. Ex-soldiers who arrived with their families were more likely to become long-term settlers than was the case with single men.

34　The ex-soldiers included men from two disbanded Swiss regiments, the de Wattevilles and the de Meurons. Larry Turner, *Perth, Tradition and Style in Eastern Ontario* (Toronto: Natural Heritage, 1998) 16–9.

35　Turner, *Perth,* 11–24; PRO MPG 484 (1): Sketch of the Rideau Settlement.

36　The townships to the south of them – Crosby, Burgess, Elmsley, Montague and Marlborough had already been surveyed.

37　Heads of family got 100 acre lots. Sons, on coming of age, obtained similar allotments, and food was issued free of charge for the first six months.

38　The Tay, formerly called the Pike River, is a major tributary of the Rideau River.

39　Gates, *Land Policies of Upper Canada,* 85–9. Virginia Howard Lindsay, "The Perth Military Settlement, Characteristics of its permanent and transitory settlers 1815–22," unpublished M.A. thesis, Carleton University, 1972, 40–7 and the Appendix. Lindsay demonstrates that land quality was an important factor in determining whether emigrants became permanent settlers.

40　Clarence Halliday, *John Holliday, a Forthright Man* (Cobourg, ON: privately published, 1962) 1–4, 27–39.

41　Andrew Haydon, *Pioneer Sketches of the District of Bathurst* (Toronto: Ryerson Press, c. 1925) 24–9.

42　Rev. William Bell was a Secessionist Presbyterian Minister who joined with William Smart, William Taylor and Robert Easton to form the Presbytery of the Canadas. By the 1820s there were ten secession Presbyterian ministers and only five Church of Scotland ministers in eastern Upper Canada.

43.　PRO CO 42/358.

44　Skelton, *Man Austere,* 118–9.

45　Jean S. McGill, *A Pioneer History of the County of Lanark* (Toronto: self-published, 1974) 41–4. Turner, *Perth,* 53–6.

46 Robert F. Gourlay, *Statistical Account of Upper Canada,* Vol. I (London: Simpkin & Marshall, 1822) 549–50.

7 Ibid, 524–6, 549–50.

48 Ibid, 549–50.

49 Rev. William Bell, *Hints to Emigrants in a series of letters from Upper Canada,* (Edinburgh: Waugh & Innes, 1824) Letter IX, 64–9.

50 PRO CO 42/165 ff. 143: Campbell to Henry Goulburn, May 6, 1815. Between 1813 and 1815 the Kildonan parish in Sutherland lost around one hundred and eighty people to Lord Selkirk's Red River Colony. Campey, *The Silver Chief,* 77–105

51 PRO CO 42/165 f.143.

52 Notices in Lord Bathurst's name appeared, for example, in the *Dumfries and Galloway Courier* (April 2, 1816) and the *Aberdeen Journal* (April 3, 1816).

53 Ibid.

54 Johnston, *British Emigration Policy,* 23.

55 PRO CO 42/358 ff. 113–5: Memorial on behalf of Norman Stewart and others from the parish of Duirinish, Skye, Aug. 27, 1817.

56 McLean, 162, 249–50. Five Duirinish families moved out of Glengarry County to Godmanchester in Huntingdon County, Lower Canada.

57 E.504/15/112, 15/113.

58 E.504/22/77, *QM,* July 8, 18, 1817; Aug. 19, 1817. Many of these people acquired their land in Bathurst, Drummond, Burgess and Beckwith townships. McGill, *History Lanark County,* 233–7.

59 For example, in May 1817, the *Dundee, Perth and Cupar Advertiser* published an advertisement for the *Pilot,* which described the grants of land and special benefits available "on the river Rideau" and another advertisement for the *Trafalgar,* in which readers were invited to write to the agent, William Allan for details of the government's "encouragement."

60 By requiring payment of a deposit, the government hoped to attract people of means who would have the required initiative and ability. In addition to this large Perthshire contingent, two English groups, led by Thomas Milburn of Aston, Cumberland, and Captain Francis Spilsbury of Newark, Nottinghamshire, and one Irish group, led by Richard Talbot, also took advantage of this scheme. See Bruce S. Elliott, *Irish Migrants in the Canadas; A New Approach* (Kingston, ON: McGill-Queen's University Press, 1988) 63–7.

61 PRO CO 384/1 ff. 71–2: Campbell to Goulburn, Feb. 11, 1817. The group also included people from Blair Atholl and Kincardine. John Campbell's father had been the third Earl's "man of business." See Vance, "Emigration and Scottish Society," 25. The Breadalbane estate extended from Aberfeldy to Tyndrum and was bounded on the north by Loch Rannoch and Loch Tummel and on the south by Loch Katrine and St. Fillans.

62 Ibid.

63 Ibid.

64 Eric Richards, *A History of the Highland Clearances: People, Landlords and Rural Turmoil,* (Edinburgh: Berlinn Ltd., 2005) 113, 116, 187. For a detailed analysis of the economic problems being experienced at the time on the Breadalbane estate, see Vance, "Emigration and Scottish Society," 45–124.

65 Moreover, the Earl "had kept up a pension list for widows and others in distressed circumstances...nothing is dearer to his heart than his tenants." PRO CO 384/1 ff. 71–2: Campbell to Goulburn, Feb. 11, 1817.

66 PRO CO 384/1 ff. 317–8: McDermid to Lord Bathurst, March 18, 1817.

67 PRO CO 384/3 ff. 115–34, 1225: Report to Navy Office, July 8, 1818. Cowan, *British Emigration,* 44–5. They were assisted in their fund raising by John Robertson of Breadalbane who probably organized charitable donations on their behalf. The passenger lists for the *Curlew* and *Sophia* appear in Appendix I.

68 Many settled in that part of Beckwith which was known as "the Derry." See Carol Bennett, *In Search of Lanark* (Renfrew, ON: Juniper Books, 1980).

69 PRO CO 384/20, 95: Petitioners from the Breadalbane estate to the Colonial Office, Jan. 5, 1828.

70 Their petition in 1820 to Lord Bathurst requesting financial aid is to be found in: PRO CO 226/36, 19. The names of the petitioners are listed in Campey, *Very Fine Class of Immigrants,* 62–64.

71 There were 239 civilian males and 708 discharged soldiers. Bell, *Hints to Emigrants*, Letter X, 69–78.

Four – The Lanark Military Settlement

1 *GC,* April 22, 1820.

2 Johnston, *British Emigration Policy,* 35–6; R.H. Campbell, *Scotland Since 1707, The Rise of an Industrial Society* (Edinburgh: John Donald, 1985) 135–42. Also see Bruce Lenman, *An Economic History of Modern Scotland 1600–1976* (London: 1977) 116–21.

3 The economic vitality of the Clyde area attracted huge numbers of Irish workers who were concentrated in the lowest paid sectors of the labour market. Handloom weavers experienced growing competition from these workers. Power looms were gradually introduced from 1813.

4 Some Scottish landowners, including the Duke of Hamilton, considered adopting a scheme which would have enabled distressed weavers to obtain small allotments of land. However the Scottish laws of entail, which ensured that estate property remained within families, proved to be an insuperable barrier and the scheme had to be dropped. Vance. "Emigration and Scottish Society," 147–8.

5 J.M. Cameron., "A Study of the factors that assisted and directed Scottish Emigration to Upper Canada 1815–55," unpublished Ph. D. thesis, University of Glasgow, 1970, 515–20. According to evidence given at the Select Committee on Emigration in 1826, the average total emigration cost was £22 per person (PP 1826 IV(404) 217). Clyde timber ships, which regularly crossed the Atlantic, charged the lowest fares. These could range from £3.10s (food not provided) to £6.6s (food provided). For example see *GH* July 19, 1822.

6 Entry fees and subscriptions were paid by each member creating a common fund which people, in hard times, could call upon. Norman Murray, *The Scottish Handloom Weavers 1790–1850* (Edinburgh: John Donald, 1978) 141–7. Vance, "Emigration and Scottish Society," 201–6.

7   PRO CO 384/4 f. 88. The petitioners also included John Couper, John Reid and
    Gabriel Wilson. Petitions were also received at this time from areas outside of
    the Clyde. For example, a group of labourers from Knapdale in Argyll asked
    to be "sent to his Majesty's Colonies of North America." PRO CO 384/5 f. 651.

8   PRO CO 384/4 ff. 482–3. James A. Colvin, "Scottish Emigration Societies
    1820–1830," (unpublished M.A. thesis, University of Guelph, 1979), 21–4. Many
    weavers took up general labouring jobs during periods of unemployment. Hence
    they sometimes appear in petitions as labourers. See for example the petition
    of the Glasgow Union Emigration Society, Oct. 16, 1820 in PRO 384/6 f. 544.

9   GC, June 10, 1819. Johnston, British Emigration Policy, 36–40.

10 PRO CO 384/5 ff. 454–5: Memorial of Bridgeton inhabitants, July 8, 1819.

11 The Inverness Courier's acid comments on the government's refusal to assist the
    weavers to go to Upper Canada were published on July 1, 1819.

12 The economic depression spawned a rising tide of political agitation. People
    believed that their misery stemmed from bad government and campaigned for
    parliamentary reform – especially universal suffrage and annual parliaments.
    The people who supported the growing radical movement disapproved of emi-
    gration, believing that their conditions could be improved by better government.
    Johnston, British Emigration Policy, 36–7.

13 The rebels, mainly unemployed artisans, included many impoverished weavers.
    T.M. Devine, The Scottish Nation, 1700–2000 (London: Penguin Books, 1999)
    196–230; Vance, "Emigration and Scottish Society," 142; Johnston, British Emi-
    gration Policy, 48–50.

14 The emigration societies had to act as guarantors for charitable donations and
    all advances of money paid by the government. Robert Lamond, A Narrative
    of the progress of Emigration from the Counties of Lanark and Renfrew to the New
    Settlements in Upper Canada on Government Grant (Ottawa, ON: Canadian Her-
    itage Publications, 1978 [first published 1821]) 5–11; Johnston, British Emigration
    Policy, 52.

15 Brown, Strictures and Remarks.

16 An additional £500 was raised in London. Vance, "Emigration Scottish Soci-
    ety," 167–70.

17 PRO CO 384/6 ff. 788–9. Note on behalf of Lanarkshire Emigration Societies,
    April 27, 1820.

18 PRO CO 384/6 ff. 249–50, 253–8, 260–1, 263, 519; NAC RG8 Vol. 625 ff. 219–23.
    Lamond, Emigration from Lanark and Renfrew to Upper Canada, 14–5. Eleven
    families from the Glasgow Emigration Society were due to travel on the Com-
    merce. The list of the 177 Emigration Society members who travelled on the
    Commerce appears in Appendix I. The Commerce arrived at Quebec with 402
    passengers (QM Aug. 5, 1820).

19 PRO CO 384/6 ff. 477, 799. Highlanders often migrated to Lowland towns and
    cities, to take up seasonal employment although relatively few migrated per-
    manently. It is difficult to quantify the actual numbers of Highlanders who
    settled in areas like Glasgow and Greenock. According to reports in the First
    Statistical Account of Scotland, there were 1,825 heads of family in Greenock, in
    1792, who had originated from the Highlands. By 1841 the numbers of High-
    landers in Glasgow was put as high as 30,000 (Select Committee, Emigration,

1841 A 522). Sinclair, *First Statistical Account of Scotland,* Vol. vii, 704–7. T.M. Devine, "Temporary Migration and the Scottish Highlands in the Nineteenth Century," in *Economic History Review,* Vol. 32, (1979) 344–59; T.M. Devine, "Highland Migration to Lowland Scotland 1760–1860," in *Scottish Historical Review,* Vol. LXII (1983) 347–51.

20 PRO CO 384/6 ff. 249–50, 254. The group was led by their president, William Granger.

21 Johnston, *British Emigration Policy...,* 52–3. See Colvin, "Scottish Emigration Societies...," 114–8, for the full list of Scottish emigration societies formed between 1820 and 1830.

22 There were only three English emigration societies. Unlike English local authorities, which were required to provide poor relief for those capable of working, Scottish parishes had no similar obligation under the Scottish Poor Law. Thus, while English parishes might have had an incentive to use their funds to assist paupers to emigrate, Scottish parishes did not. This explains why emigration societies were largely confined to Scotland. See Johnston, *British Emigration Policy,* 5–6, 40, 102–3.

23 Kirkman Finlay reported that just over 800 people had been assisted to emigrate in 1820. Passenger information is only available for 700 people. Johnston, Ibid, 53.

24 For example, the *Benlomond* arrived at Quebec with 218 emigrants, the *Earl of Buckinghamshire* with 200, the *Speculation* with 120, the *Alexander* with 112 and the *Minerva* with 60. *QM,* June 24, June 30, July 21, Sept. 5, 1820.

25 According to Robert Lamond, "the average expense for 1883 men, women and children, who sailed last Spring from Greenock [in 1821] was £2.18s.3d. for each individual." This covered the cost of provisions and their passage to Quebec "and left besides sufficient provisions to serve the Societies to their place of settlement." The government paid for their onward journey to the Rideau Valley, advanced loans for their support in the first year and provided blankets and farm implements. Lamond, *A Narrative of the progress,* 112.

26 Those who sailed on the *Earl of Buckinghamshire* belonged to the following emigration societies: Paisley Townhead, Brownfield and Anderston, Cathcart, Lanarkshire, Lesmahagow, Mile End, Parkhead (Paisley). Those who sailed on the *George Canning* belonged to the Abercrombie (1), Barrowfield Road, Bridgeton Canadian, Bridgeton Transatlantic, Cabuslang, Glasgow Canadian, Glasgow Junior Wrights, Glasgow Loyal Agricultural, Glasgow Senior Wrights, Glasgow Union, Strathaven and Kilbride societies; Those who sailed on the *Commerce* belonged to the Camlachie, Govan, Hamilton, Kirkman Finlay, North Albion, Rutherglen Union, Spring Bank (2), St. John's Parish and Bridgeton Canadian societies. Those who sailed on the *David* belonged to the Abercrombie (2), Alloa, Balfron, Deanston (by Doune), Glasgow Trongate, Hopetown Bathgate, Milton Dumbartonshire, Wishawton and Spring Bank (1) societies. Passenger lists for the four ship crossings have been reconstructed from data given in PRO CO 42/189 ff. 512–69 and these appear in Appendix I. The 104 families from Paisley Townhead, who sailed on the *Earl of Buckinghamshire,* are listed in PRO CO 384/6 ff. 540–1; also see CO 384/7 f. 1221

27 *GH* May 25, 1821.

28   The cost to the government was £31,200 and the Glasgow Committee paid £6,800. This was far less that the £111,000 spent on 3,500 emigrants who went to the Cape of Good Hope. Johnston, *British Emigration Policy*, 54.

29   John Climie to his brother & sister, Feb. 8, 1821 in Lamond, *A Narrative of the progress*, 90.

30   William Gourley, Jan. 28, 1821 in Lamond, Ibid, 102.

31   William Miller had been a member of the Anderston and Rutherglen Emigration Society. Letter quoted in Carol Bennett, *The Lanark Society Settlers, 1820–1821* (Renfrew, ON: Juniper Books, 1991) 49.

32   A. Boag to his sister, Aug. 24, 1821, in Lamond, *A Narrative of the progress*, 103.

33   They would have included many tenants who had been cleared from Lowland estates from the late eighteenth century. See Malcolm Gray's "The Social Impact of Agrarian Change in the Rural Lowlands" in T.M. Devine and Rosalind Mitchison (eds.), *People and Society in Scotland 1760–1830*, Vol. I (Edinburgh: John Donald, 1988) 53–69. Also see Peter Aitchison and Andrew Cassell, *The Lowland Clearances, Scotland's Silent Revolution* (East Linton: Tuckwell, 2003) 127–41.

34   MacTaggart, *Three Years in Canada*, Vol. 2, 243.

35   An emigrant Scot writing home, May 5, 1821 in Lamond, *A Narrative of the progress*, 104.

36   *GC*, April 18, 1820.

37   Ibid.

38   NAS GD 45/3/363; Return of men, women and children in military settlements, Dec. 24, 1821. Nearly one-third of the male population were former soldiers. Vance, "Emigration and Scottish Society," 249–50.

39   Letter quoted in Bennett, *The Lanark Society Settlers…*, 70. Peter Munro had been a member of the Bridgeton Canadian Emigration Society.

40   Ibid, 181. Andrew Angus had been a member of the Rutherglen Union Emigration Society.

41   Duncan Campbell claimed that poverty had driven him to move to New York. His letter to Peter McLaren, May 16, 1818, is quoted in Turner, *Perth*, 43.

42   John McDonald, *Narrative of a Voyage to Quebec and journey from thence to New Lanark in Upper Canada, detailing the Hardships and Difficulties which an Emigrant has to Encounter, before and after his Settlement; with an account of the Country, as regards its Climate, Soil and the Actual Conditions of its Inhabitants* (Edinburgh: 1823) 11. His account of the suffering he and other emigrants endured in crossing the Atlantic and in getting to their final destinations is discussed in Chapter 9.

43   Ibid, 16.

44   McGill, *Pioneer History of Lanark County*, 61–88.

45   LAC M-1354: Rev. William Rintoul to Rev. Robert Burns, Sept. 22, 1835.

46   LAC M-1353: Rev. William McAlister to Rev. David Welsh, May 25, 1831.

47   Bouchette, *The British Dominions in North America*, 80.

48   LAC M-1353: Rev Matthew Miller to Rev. Burns, Nov. 1832. However, the western part of Ramsay had very poor land. See McGill, *Lanark County*, 78. The Ramsay Presbyterian congregation built a stone church at Almonte in 1836. Later known as the "Auld Kirk," it attracted Presbyterians from neighbouring townships. Several woollen mills were constructed in Almonte during the 1850s and by 1870 it was one of the leading woollen cloth manufacturing centres in Ontario.

49   Bell, *Hints to Emigrants,* Letter XV, 106–19.

50   LAC M-1352: Petition from James Brown, George Easton, John McIntyre to the Glasgow Colonial Society, Sept. 5, 1825.

51   LAC M-1352: Matthew Leech to Rev. Burns, June 13, 1828.

52   LAC M-1354: Rev. George Romanes to Rev. Burns, Oct. 14, 1834. However, progress in both Beckwith and Goulbourn townships would have been hampered by the large amounts of rock and swamp. Gates, *Land Policies of Upper Canada,* 93.

53   Jessie Campbell, *Some reminiscences of the life and labours of the Rev. George Buchanan, first Presbyterian Minister of Beckwith, Lanark County, Upper Canada* (Toronto: self-published, 1900) 19. Rev. Dr. George Buchanan, a Secessionist Presbyterian minister, served the Beckwith congregation from 1821. By the 1830s when most of the congregation supported the established Church of Scotland, Rev. Buchanan was asked to join with them, but he refused and was replaced by Rev. John Smith.

54   Elliott, *Irish Migrants in the Canadas,* 61–81. Some of Richard Talbot's group went west to take up land in the settlements being developed by Thomas Talbot.

55   Cowan, *British Emigration,* 45–6, 65–84.

56   McGill, *Pioneer History of Lanark County,* 89–101.

57   Gates, *Land Policies of Upper Canada,* 85–96.

58   Ontario Genealogical Society, *1842 Census Records for Lanark County for the townships of Bathurst, Beckwith, Dalhousie, Darling, Drummond, Lanark and North and South Sherbrooke* (Kingston: 1992). Detailed data on land quality in Bathurst and Drummond townships is given in Lindsay, "The Perth Military Settlement," Appendix A.

59   McDonald, *Narrative of a Voyage to Quebec,* 13–4.

60   The Abercrombie Emigration Society, the Abercrombie Street Emigration Society, the Second Division of the Abercrombie Street Emigration Society and the Abercrombie Friendly Emigration Society. Colvin, "Scottish Emigration Societies," 3–4.

61   Letter from Alexander Watt to his friend in Quebec who remitted it to a person in Glasgow, Oct. 10, 1820 in Lamond, 85.

62   NAS GD 1/814/5/3: Arthur Stocks to his brother, John Colquhoun, in Paisley, Dec. 10, 1825.

63   Ontario Genealogical Society, *1842 Census Records for Lanark County.* North Sherbrooke had also attracted settlers from the Lesmahagow Emigration Society who settled at Elphin. See Bennett, *In Search of Lanark.*

64   Johnston, *British Emigration Policy,* 54–5.

65   PRO CO 384/8 f. 41, 226–7, 327, 394–7, 434–5.

66   They requested 100 acres per family, "the means of subsistence for a few months. £6 for every adult and £ 3 for children under 14." Alexander McCallum to the Colonial Office, Feb. 1821: PRO CO 384/7 ff. 643–45; also see Ayrshire petition in PRO CO 384/15, 623.

67   PRO CO 384/11 ff. 1575, 1603.

68   PRO CO 384/11 f. 1123: Archibald McNiven to Lord Bathurst, Dec. 13, 1825.

69   In fact, the government's costs in financing the scheme were more than was intended. While the weavers had become comfortably off, it soon became apparent that they had no hope of repaying their government loans amounting to

£30 to £40 per family. In 1836, the government finally cancelled their debts of some £22,000. NAS GD 45/3/140//10: Lord Bathurst to Earl of Dalhousie, March, 1 1826; Cowan, *British Emigration,* 62–3.

70 Lamond, 64–5.

Five – The Continuing Influx to Eastern Upper Canada

1 *Lord Selkirk's Diary,* 199.
2 Ibid.
3 John Howison, *Sketches of Upper Canada, domestic, local and characteristic, to which are added practical details for the information of emigrants of every class* (Edinburgh: Oliver & Boyd, 1822) 34–9. Howison worked for the East India Company at the time of his visit.
4 Ibid.
5 Ibid.
6 *Lord Selkirk's Diary,* 198.
7 Father MacDonell writing in 1808 to Bishop Plessis, quoted in McLean, *Glengarry,* 215.
8 Ibid.
9 *DCB,* Vol. XI, 764–5. 1841 Select Committee, A1565. Dr. Rolph was emigration agent from 1840 to 1843.
10 1841 Select Committee, A1566.
11 Ibid, A1565–1571.
12 Ibid, A1971, A2034.
13 McLean, *People of the Glengarry,* 83. See Appendix II for the list of ship crossings.
14 Glenelg and Glenshiel are in Inverness-shire, and Kintail, Lochalsh and Loch Carron are in Wester Ross. PRO CO 42/170 362–63: Letter from Donald Mac-Crummer, merchant Broadford, Skye, Nov. 20, 1816. PRO CO 384/8, 230–31: Letter from John McRa, shipowner, Fadoch by Lochalsh, Jan. 29, 1822.
15 PRO CO 384/8 f.f. 230–1.
16 PRO CO 384/5 f.7; CO 384/15 f. 485.
17 E.504/12/6; *QM,* Sept. 9, 1817; Sept. 10, 1818; Sept. 14, 1819. The *Speculation* also called at Pictou. See J.S. Martell, *Immigration to and Emigration from Nova Scotia 1815–1838* (Halifax, PANS, 1942) 49.
18 The *1861 Census* reveals that a sizeable proportion of the population in these particular townships were Presbyterians (established and free): Roxborough – 52%, Finch – 51% Caledonia – 40%, West Hawkesbury – 33%. These figures understate the preponderance of Scots since they exclude Roman Catholic Scots.
19 LAC RG5 A1 Upper Canada Sundries, Vol. 51, quoted in Clark Barrett, "The Glengarry Indian Lands," in *Ontario Genealogical Society Bulletin,* Vol. 8 (1969) 5–6.
20 Ibid. These Highlanders had holdings on the 14th to 21st Concessions. The petitioners were: Alex. McKenzie, Duncan McDonell, Alex. McKercher, James Anderson, Robert McLaren, Malcolm Campbell, Duncan Kippen, Donald McKercher, John Campbell, William McGrigor, John Kippen, John McTavish, James Anderson, John McNaughton, Peter Cameron, Duncan Cameron, John Kippen, John McRae, John McEwen, Hugh McEwen, Widow McDougal with a large family, Malcolm Fisher,

John McRae, Donald Fisher, Angus McIntyre, William Munro, John Fisher, Daniel Kennedy, Alex. Kennedy, Donald McPhee, Donald McDonald, Alex. Fisher, Murdoch Campbell, Angus McPhee and Malcolm Campbell.

21   Peter Kenneth MacLeod, "A Study of Concentrations of Scottish Settlements in Nineteenth Century Ontario," (unpublished M.A. thesis, Carleton University, 1972) 144. The "Indian Lands" were sold in 1849 by the St. Regis Iroquois to the Crown.

22   PRO CO 384/8 f. 283. Ronald McDonald to Lord Bathurst, Oct. 15, 1822.

23   Prospective emigrants had high expectations that they would be entitled to government help with transport and provisions. Their requests were always turned down, although land was usually made available to them on easy terms provided they could demonstrate that they had the necessary skills to become pioneer farmers.

24   They sailed on the *Ossian* of Leith. *QM* Aug. 23, 1822; *IJ* June 29, 1821.

25   MacDonald, *Canada, Immigration and Settlement, 1763–1841,* 499.

26   W.H. Smith, *Smith's Canadian Gazetteer: statistical and general information respecting all parts of the Upper Province or Canada West* (Toronto: H. & W. Rowsell, 1846) 30. Charlottenburg's population was 4,975 in 1846. The Eastern District was comprised of the counties of Glengarry, Stormont, Dundas, Prescott and Russell.

27   The first St. Raphaels church was built in 1789. Work commenced on a stone church in 1821 under the direction of Father Alexander Macdonell, later Bishop of Upper Canada. The Highland Society of Canada placed a memorial to him in the church.

28   Rev. John Bethune, who was the minister at Williamstown, attended to the Presbyterian congregations at Lancaster and Summerstown before they acquired their resident ministers. Martintown initially had a Free Church congregation, served by lay preachers, but from 1825 it became part of the established church. Rev. Archibald Connell was its first resident minister.

29   LAC M-1352: Rev. John Burns to Rev. Burns, May 23, 1825.

30   Ibid.

31   LAC M-1354: Alexander MacNaughton to Rev. Burns, July 12, 1834.

32   LAC M-1352: Rev. John McLaurin to Rev. John Scott, July 5, 1825. L'Orignal (Longueil Township) had formed a Presbyterian congregation by 1822, but its Presbyterian Church, St. Andrew's, was not built until 1832. Mary Ellen Perkins, *Discover Your Heritage, a Guide to Provincial Plaques in Ontario* (Toronto, Natural Heritage, 1989) 225.

33   The Presbytery of Glengarry encompassed: Glengarry County – 3 Presbyterian churches in Charlottenburg, 1 in Lochiel, 2 in Lancaster, 1 in "Indian Lands"; Stormont County – 1 in Finch, 1 in Osnabrook, 1 in Cornwall; Prescott County – 1 in Hawkesbury; Lower Canada – 1 in Côte St. George.

34   The Kenyon Presbyterian congregation was originally part of the Indian Lands parish. LAC M-1355: Alexander McNaughton to Rev. Burns, Aug. 26, 1839.

35   Ibid.

36   Lieutenant, J.C. Morgan, *The Emigrants Notebook and Guide with Recollections of Upper and Lower Canada during the Late War* (London: 1824) 205. Rev. Hugh Urquhart was the first minister of St. John's Presbyterian Church in Cornwall. Harkness, *Stormont, Dundas and Glengarry,* 111–5.

37 PRO CO 384/10 f. 206: Fergus Matheson to the Colonial Office, Feb. 7, 1824;
    CO 384/15 ff. 587–9: Petition of emigrants from the Western Highlands, Decem-
    ber 1826.

38 PP w/e Aug. 27, 1836.

39 NAS HD 21/35: List of Glenelg tenants from J. Baillie's estate who are to emi-
    grate to the Colonies.

40 PP 1850 (173) XL. Cameron, "Scottish Emigration to Upper Canada," 384–5.
    T.M. Devine, *The Great Highland Famine, Hunger, Emigration and the Scottish
    Highlands in the Nineteenth Century* (Edinburgh: John Donald, 1988) 323.

41 NAS HD 21/53: List of recipients of relief who intend emigrating to America
    from districts of Lochalsh, Plocktown, Ross-shire (n.d.); Devine, ibid, 206, 208.

42 The government had to pay their transportation costs inland from Quebec. PP
    1851 (348) XL. Devine, Ibid, 324.

43 PP 1852(1474)XXXIII.

44 Devine, *The Great Highland Famine...*, 323.

45 Donald Ross, *Glengarry evictions or scenes at Knoydart in Inverness-shire,* (Glas-
    gow: (W.G. Blackie & Co., 1853).

46 The Emigration Advances Act of 1851 made loans available to landlords, seek-
    ing to assist their tenants to emigrate, at an interest rate of 6 1/4 per cent. Devine,
    The Great Highland Famine..., 202, 204

47 PP w/e Sept. 17, 1853.

48 However, the 1815 contingent actually consisted of 700 people. Half of them,
    who were mainly Highlanders, settled in Glengarry County while the other
    half went to the Rideau Valley (see Chapter 3).

49 Letter from McNab to a near relative, Dr. Francis Hamilton Buchanan, writ-
    ten in August 1824, and quoted in Marjorie J.F. Fraser, "Feudalism in Upper
    Canada 1823–1843," *Ontario Historical Society,* Vol. 12 (1914) 145.

50 Tenants of the tenth Duke of Hamilton who lived on the island of Arran had
    intended, in 1829, to emigrate to Horton Township in Renfrew County, but
    instead they went to Lower Canada. PRO CO 384/22 ff. 2–5: M. Stewart to
    Colonial Office, March 12, 1829. Cameron "Scottish Emigration to Upper
    Canada," 380–1.

51 Rev. William A. Gillies, *In Famed Breadalbane, The story of the antiquities, lands
    and peoples of a Highland district* (Perth, Scotland: Munro Press, 1938) 108–111.

52 The *Quebec Mercury* announced the arrival of 115 passengers (May 14, 1825).
    It is not certain how many settlers McNab actually brought to Upper Canada
    in 1825. The various settler lists which survive are to be found in Garnet McDi-
    armid, "The Original Emigrants to McNab Township Upper Canada," in
    Scottish Genealogy, Vol. xxviii (1981) 109–21.

53 The emigrants had to begin their repayments to McNab after three years. For
    further details of the agreement, see A. Shortt and A.G. Doughty (eds.), *Canada
    and its Provinces. A History of the Canadian people and their institutions, by one
    hundred associates* (Toronto: Publishers Association of Canada, 1913–17) Vol.
    xvii, 94–5.

54 Cowan, *British Emigration,* 120–21.

55 Wilfred Campbell, *The Scotsman in Canada,* Vol. 1 (London: Sampson Low &
    Co., 1911) 198–200.

56 *Smith's Canadian Gazetteer*, 103. Gilbert Paterson, *Land Settlement in Upper Canada, 1783–1840* (Toronto: C.W. James, 1921) (Report of the Department of Archives for the Province of Ontario for the year 1920) 193–5; Fraser, "Feudalism in Upper Canada," 142–52. *DCB*, Vol. XI, 584–9.

57 PRO CO 384/20 ff. 195,199; CO 384/7 ff. 347, 349.

58 PRO CO 384/8 ff. 394–7, CO 384/15 f. 514.

59 PRO CO 384/8 f. 435.

60 A great many petitions for help were considered by the Select Committee in 1826–27, including one sent on behalf of 3,581 individuals from Glasgow and Paisley. PRO CO 384/15, 571–83.

61 The deliberations of the 1826–27 Emigration Select Committee are discussed in Johnston, *British Emigration Policy*, 91–108.

62 Reports from the Select Committee appointed to inquire into the expediency of encouraging emigration from the United Kingdom, 1826 Abstract of Petitions.

63 In 1832, "the super-abundance" of weavers in the area was blamed on "the influx of Irish and others into the trade," see C.R. Baird, "Observations on the poorest class of operatives in Glasgow in 1832" in *Journal of the Statistical Society of London*, Vol. 1 (1839) 172.

64 *PA*, April 19, 1828; *QM*, May 31, 1828.

65 *PA*, Aug. 23, 1828.

66 *PA*, Aug. 30, 1828.

67 *PA*, Aug. 23, 1828.

68 *PA*, Aug. 30, 1828.

69 The Paisley shawl weaving trade brought increasing prosperity to Paisley from 1825. However, the traditional weavers' role was downgraded as a result of increasing mechanisation and the division of labour. Valerie Reilly, *The Illustrated History of the Paisley Shawl*, (Glasgow: Richard Drew, 1996) 44–61.

70 Sixty per cent were civilians and forty per cent were discharged soldiers. Gates, *Land Policies of Upper Canada*, 92.

71 Bell, *Hints to Emigrants*, Letter XVII, 144–5.

72 Turner, *Perth*, 32. Bell, Ibid, 64–9.

73 Extracts from emigrant letters quoted in Cowan, *British Emigration*, 64, 250.

74 LAC M-1353: Rev. William McAlister to Rev. David Welsh, May 25, 1831.

75 Elliott, *Irish Migrants in the Canadas*, 63–77, 126–7.

76 NAS GD 45/3/140/1: Lt. Col. William Marshall to Earl Dalhousie, April 27, 1824. For details of the later Irish dominance of the area, see Elliott, Ibid, 116–29.

77 *1827 Emigration Select Committee*, A142–145: Evidence of James Foster and James Little, both members of the Glasgow Emigration Society.

78 LAC M-1352: John Robertson to Rev. David Welsh, May 14, 1828. Also see McGill, *Lanark County*, 67–8.

79 Lamond, *Emigration from the counties of Lanark and Renfrew*, 40.

80 Reilly, *History of the Paisley Shawl*, 48.

81 Inspired by the Dalhousie Library, Scots at Ramsay established their library in 1829. McGill, *Pioneer History of Lanark County*, 184–7.

82 Andrew Carnegie dispersed large quantities of his vast wealth in the late 1800s and early 1900s by founding libraries, especially in Scotland and the United States. The son of a Dunfermline handloom weaver, he acquired a love of books

from his father who used to borrow books from a local Tradesman's Subscription Library, which had been established by his brother in Dunfermline. See Joseph Frazier Wall, *Andrew Carnegie* (Pittsburgh: University of Pittsburgh Press, 1989) 37–8, 815–19.

83 The group led by Thomas Scott formed the St. Andrew's Philanthropic Society of Dalhousie Township.

84 LAC M-1352: John McIntyre to Rev. Burns, Oct. 23, 1828; NAS GD 45/3/140/8, /15: Lt. Col. William Marshall to Earl Dalhousie, May 27, Sept. 3, 1828. The managers of the Dalhousie Public Library in 1828 were: Thomas Scott, John McIntyre, Charles Baillie, William Lambie, James Muir and James Robertson. Charles Baillie of the Lesmahagow Emigration Society, who had emigrated in 1820, also sought book donations from Robert Brown, the Duke of Hamilton's factor. See Colvin, "Scottish Emigration Societies," 49–50.

85 Ibid, 186.

86 Ibid, 187.

87 Haydon, *Pioneer Sketches of the District of Bathurst*, 188. By 1847 the library had 832 books.

88 Perkins, *Provincial Plaques in Ontario,* 125.

89 LAC M-1354: Rev. George Romanes to Rev. Burns, Oct. 14, 1834. However, these townships had relatively few Scots but had high concentrations of Irish settlers.

90 LAC M-1354: Romanes to Burns, May 30, 1835.

91 Ibid, Oct. 14, 1834.

92 Ibid, May 30, 1835.

93 LAC M-1353: Rev. Matthew Miller to Rev. Burns, Nov. 1832.

94 North Easthope township in Perth County, in the Huron Tract, attracted sizeable numbers of settlers from the Breadalbane estate from the early 1830s (see Chapter 8).

95 NAS GD 112/61/16. The Breadalbane settlers who went to Reach Township near Toronto appealed to the Marquis of Breadalbane in 1848 for funds to build a church there. NAS GD 112/61/5. See Chapter 6.

96 In just two years, nearly 600 emigrants left Dundee for Quebec compared with less than 100 during the previous ten years.

97 *Perthshire Courier and General Advertiser,* March 3, 1831.

98 Scotland's iron and metallurgical industries gained rapid ground from the 1830s and were mainly centred on the Clyde. Most of the Scottish coal field development was in the vicinity of Glasgow and in Fife and Ayrshire. However, large-scale Irish immigration to the Clyde increasingly depressed wages and reduced job prospects for local people who had been made redundant. See Henry Hamilton, *The Industrial Revolution in Scotland,* (Oxford: Clarendon Press, 1932) 7–11.

99 See, for example, PP w/e July 18, 1840; Sept. 4, 1841; July 2, 1843. However, other destinations such as Home and Gore districts, further to the west, were also given. See Chapter 8.

100 For example, see the Quebec Immigration Agent's Report, PP w/e June 11, 1843.

101 PP 1841, w/e August 7; PP 1842, w/e June 11, June 25, PP 1843; w/e May 27, June 10, June 24; PP 1842(301)XXXI; PP 1844 (181) XXXV.

102 For example, see the petitions of the Glasgow Central Emigration Society (PRO CO 384/67 ff. 108– 10, 116) and the First Glasgow Protestant Emigration Society (PRO CO 384/67 ff. 124–6) which were submitted in 1841.

103 PP w/e June 11, 1843; also see PP w/e June 19 and July 12, 1842.
104 PRO CO 384/74, ff. 247–8: J.W. Campbell to Lord Stanley, May 6, 1843 and Lord Stanley to the Lord Provost of Glasgow, May 15, 1843.
105 Ibid.
106 *Emigration Select Committee,* 1841, A 232.
107 Brunger, "The Distribution of Scots and Irish in Upper Canada" 250–58.

Six – Scottish Colonization Moves West

1 LAC MG24-I67: John Millar Collection, File 1, letter to his brother James, Aug. 19, 1841. James Millar lived at Waterbeck, Dumfriesshire.
2 John Millar originated from Dalton Parish (Dumfriesshire) and emigrated shortly after his wife's death in 1834.
3 Arthur Richard Preston (ed.), *For Friends at Home, A Scottish emigrant's letters from Canada, California and the Cariboo 1844–64* (London: McGill-Queen's University Press, 1974) 13–6. The settlers also included veterans from the King's Royal Regiment of New York, Jessup's Rangers and Butler's Rangers.
4 These were North Sherbrooke, Dalhousie, Lanark, Ramsay, Bathurst, Drummond and Beckwith townships in Lanark County and Osgoode Township in Carleton County. Nearby McNab Township in Renfrew County was also founded in 1825 by Scots, but they did not receive any government aid.
5 Gordon Donaldson, *The Scots Overseas* (London: Robert Hale, 1966) 133.
6 Irish Roman Catholics had also been assisted to emigrate by the government. One group, led by Peter Robinson, went to the Rideau Valley in 1823 and a second group went to the Peterborough area in 1825.
7 This endowment system was introduced in 1792 for Protestant clergy and the Crown.
8 Montgomery R. Martin, *History, Statistics and Geography of Upper and Lower Canada* (London: Whittaker, 1838) 218.
9 Craig, *Upper Canada,* 124–44; William Norton, "The Process of Rural Land Occupation in Upper Canada," in *Scottish Geographical Magazine*, Vol. 91 (1975) 145–52;
10 William Kingdom, *America and the British Colonies* (London: Whittaker, 1820) 107.
11 Edwardsburgh later acquired a particularly large concentration of Irish Catholics. Attracted to the area in the 1840s by the prospect of finding employment in the building of local canals, many stayed and established themselves as settlers. Preston, *For Friends at Home,* 14–5.
12 LAC MG24-I67, File 1: John Millar to his brother, Nov. 23, 1843.
13 This anonymous letter first published in Dumfriesshire newspapers was reprinted in *GC,* June 15, 1817.
14 Ibid. Some of the families who emigrated under the government's assisted scheme of 1815 originated from the Border counties of Berwickshire, Dumfriesshire, Peeblesshire and Roxburghshire. See Appendix I.
15 For Dumfriesshire settlers to Prince Edward Island see Campey, *Very Fine Class of Immigrants,* 66–79. For Dumfriesshire settlers to Nova Scotia, see Campey, *After the Hector,* 244–53.

16 The *Argus* left in 1820 with 88 passengers and the *Martha* had 43, *DWJ*, June
    13, June 20, 1820. In 1831, the *Neried* sailed with 49 passengers, while in 1833
    the *Diana* of Dumfries carried 13 and the *Lancaster* carried 137: *QM* May 28,
    1833; *QM* May 25, June 6, 1833.

17 These ports were in Cumbria. Shipowners who operated from these ports, employed
    agents in the Scottish borders to help them locate passengers. See Chapter 9.

18 See Chapter 8.

19 Cowan, *British Emigration,* 123.

20 Ibid.

21 LAC MG24-I67, File 1: John Millar to James, his brother, Dec. 14, 1852.

22 1841 Emigration Select Committee, Evidence of Thomas Rolph, A1594–A1596.

23 *JJ*, Feb. 19, 1841. He probably sailed to Quebec in 1841 on the *Universe* of
    Aberdeen.

24 Ibid.

25 LAC M-1353: Rev. Matthew Miller to Rev. Burns, Sept. 29, 1832. The town-
    ship acquired its first British settlers in 1792.

26 Ibid.

27 Ibid.

28 Ibid.

29 LAC M-1352: Directors for the building of a church (Colborne) to Glasgow
    Colonial Society, May 3, 1830.

30 Perkins, *Provincial Plaques in Ontario,* 28.

31 Rev. Miller's letter, Sept. 29, 1832. Peter Robinson's group of Irish settlers set-
    tled in the Peterborough area in 1825. However, they were Roman Catholic,
    not Presbyterian. Elliott, *Irish Migrants in the Canadas,* 117.

32 LAC M-1354: Rev. Thomas Alexander to Rev. James Gibson, April 1, 1835.

33 LAC M-1354: Rev. William Rintoul to Rev. Burns, Dec. 13, 1834.

34 LAC MG25-G272: Barclay Family Fonds.

35 Malcolm Gray, "Transcript of Letter from Canada," in *Central Scotland FHS,*
    No. 29, Autumn 2004, 19–24. Published extracts of letters written by former
    Breadalbane tenants reveal that some families, having left Scotland in 1832,
    lived for a short while at Eldon Township (Victoria) before moving to Reach.

36 NAS GD 112/61/5: Petition dated April 1848, signed by 10 Christies (John, Don-
    ald, Duncan, Duncan, Donald, John, Duncan, Donald, Peter, John); 3
    Andersons (Peter, Duncan, Alexander); George Harrison; 4 McKerchers (John,
    Duncan, John, Donald); John Taylor; 3 McDermids (John, Archibald, Colin);
    Edward Walker; John Waggoner and Paul Sugden. By 1850 some of the Reach
    Township Scots would move to West Williams Township (Middlesex County).

37 Rev. R.F. Binnington, "The Glasgow Colonial Society and its work in the devel-
    opment of the Presbyterian Church in British North America 1825–1840,"
    (unpublished Th. D., University of Toronto, 1960) 238–41.

38 Large concentrations of Protestant Irish settlers were also to be found north
    and west of Toronto, especially in Simcoe County. See Elliott, *Irish Migrants in
    the Canadas,* 78–9, 116–7, 158–9.

39 Kelp, made from burnt seaweed, was exported and used in various chemical
    processes. The kelp industry declined in the 1820s due to cheap foreign imports
    of similar products.

40   For instance, a great many Skye emigrants settled in Prince Edward Island (see Campey, *Very Fine Class of Immigrants*, 32–47, 80–9, 140–3) while Barra's links were principally with Cape Breton (see Campey, *After the Hector*, 234–77.

41   E.504/35/2; *QM* Aug. 9, 1823.

42   The *Speculation, Harmony*, and *Hope* of Greenock sailed from Oban to Quebec in 1819 with 504 passengers while the *Betsey* of Greenock and the *Duchess of Richmond* carried 344 passengers in 1820 (*QM*, Aug. 24, Sept. 14, 1819; Aug. 15, Aug. 17, 1820; E.504/25/3).

43   Norton, "Rural Land Occupation in Upper Canada," 146–8. The Penetanguishene Road was constructed in 1814 to act as a military route between Kempenfeldt Bay and Penetanguishene.

44   *IJ*, Jan. 17, Feb. 28, 1823.

45   *IJ*, Feb. 28, 1823; June 18, 1824.

46   Cowan, *British Emigration*, 52.

47   PRO CO 384/10, 86. Possibly the thirty-five emigrants who sailed in 1824 on the *Gratitude* of Dundee from Fort William to Quebec were members of Cameron's group.

48   Patterson, *Land Settlement in Upper Canada*, 196.

49   Cowan, *British Emigration*, 52, 122–23.

50   PRO CO 42/202 ff. 142–45. Petition from Kilmalie families to Lord Bathurst dated April 5, 1824.

51   A petition to the Colonial Office requesting financial aid, received on February 19, 1827, lists 550 people who were mainly from west Inverness-shire. It was sent in the name of John Cameron of Fort William – possibly a relative. See PRO CO 384/15 ff. 587–9.

52   The Argyll settlers wanted to rename Eldon Township "Caledonia" but the government refused their request. W. Stanford Reid (ed.), *The Scottish Tradition in Canada* (Toronto: McClelland & Stewart, 1976) 320.

53   LAC M-1353: Rev. Peter MacNaughton to Rev. Burns, Aug. 27, 1833.

54   LAC M-1353: Rev. Matthew Miller to Rev. Burns, Sept. 29, 1832.

55   Argyll emigrants generally settled in North Carolina and did so from as early as 1738. They mainly originated from the islands of Islay, Jura and Gigha, and from the following mainland parishes: Appin, Lismore, Glenorchy and Campbeltown, North and South Knapdale and Inishail. While some went to New York, the great majority were family groups who settled in North Carolina. See Vane D. Meyer, *The Highland Scots of North Carolina*, [Chapel Hill, NC: University of Carolina Press, 1961] 84, 86; *SM* Vol. xxx (1768) 446; *SM*, Vol. xxxiI (1769) 501. Adams and Somerville, *Cargoes of Despair*, 87, 89, 90, 218; Cameron, "Scottish Emigration to Upper Canada" 88–90; Sinclair, *First Statistical Account of Scotland*, Vol. viii, 40; *Colonial Records of North Carolina*, Vol. ix (1772) 364.

56   PRO CO 384/28 ff. 24–26: Memorial of the inhabitants of Tiree, Jan. 24, 1831. The Duke of Argyll once again requested government aid on behalf of his tenants in 1840. NAS GD 133/170/ 3, 4: Duke of Argyll to Robertson of Inches, June 1840.

57   1841 Emigration Select Committee. A829.

58   *QM* Oct. 5, 1833.

59 Some also settled at Fergus (Nichol Township) in Wellington County. See Chapter 8.

60 Margaret MacKay, "Tiree Migrants in Canada," in *Oral History Journal,* Vol. 9 (1981) 49–60.

61 The Tiree emigrants, who left in the period from 1847 to 1853, had their travel costs paid by their landlord, the Duke of Argyll. Devine, *Highland Famine,* 332.

62 E. Mairi MacArthur, *Iona: Living memory of a crofting community 1750–1914* (Edinburgh: University Press, 1990) 102. E. Mairi MacArthur, "Iona, History Tradition and Settlement," in *Northern Studies,* Vol. xxvi (1989) 1–14.

63 The *Albion* of Glasgow (181) in 1832, the *Stirling Castle* of Greenock (358) in 1834, the *Hector* (49) in 1835 and the *Deveron* of Glasgow (174) in 1836. *QM* Sept. 16, Aug. 19, 1834; Aug. 22, 1835; Oct. 13, 1836.

64 MacArthur, *Iona: Living Memory,* 103; MacKay, "Tiree Migrants," 51–52; Glasgow Colonial Society, *Seventh Annual Reports of the Glasgow Colonial Society for promoting the religious interests of the Scottish settlers in British North America* (Glasgow: 1833) 15; LAC M-1354: Rev. William Rintoul to Rev. Burns, Dec. 13, 1834. Mara Township also acquired several South Uist families during the 1840s. See Bill Lawson, *A Register of Emigrants from the Western Isles of Scotland 1750–1900,* 2 vols. (Harris: self-published, 1992), Vol. 2 (South Uist and Benbecula).

65 Perkins, *Provincial Plaques in Ontario,* 192–3. Beaverton's St. Andrew's Church took 13 years to build.

66 Margaret Storrie, *Islay: Biography of an Island,* (Port Ellen, ON: self-published, 1981) 135.

67 John Ramsay's tenants sailed on the *S.S. Damascus* on June 28, 1862. The passenger list is printed in Freda Ramsay, *John Ramsay of Kildalton – being an account of his life in Islay and including the diary of his trip to Canada in 1870,* (Toronto: Peter Martin, 1970) 142–5.

68 Speech given by John Ramsay at the Annual Meeting of the Islay Association, 1878, 29 reprinted in Storrie, *Islay,* 147.

69 John Ramsay documented his visit in the form of a diary which was later published and republished in 1970. The latter includes a biographical sketch which was compiled by John Ramsay's grandson's widow. Ramsay, *John Ramsay of Kildalton,* 61. A number of Islay families petitioned the Colonial Office for assistance to emigrate to Canada in 1850. PRO CO 327/1, 102.

70 Ibid, 104.

71 LAC M-1352: John Crichton to Rev. Thomas Crichton, Oct. 24, 1826.

72 Ibid, June 27, 1826.

73 Ibid.

74 Colin Read, *The Rising in Western Upper Canada 1837–8, the Duncombe Revolt and After* (Toronto: University of Toronto Press, 1982) 183.

75 LAC M-1352: John Crichton to Rev. Thomas Crichton, Jan. 22, 1827.

76 See Chapter 8.

77 Robert McVicar, *Letters on Emigration from the British Isles and the Settlement of the Waste Lands in the Province of Canada* (Hamilton, ON: S. Hewson, 1853) 7–11. Alexander Fraser to Robert McVicar, April 30, May 9, 1842.

78 LAC M-1353: Rev. Matthew Miller to Rev. Burns, Sept. 29, 1832. John Graves Simcoe had Yonge Street built as a military road. Construction began in the late eighteenth century.

79 Ibid, Rev. Miller. A second Presbyterian church, named St. Andrew's, was built in 1862 at Maple in Vaughan Township. The congregation was said to have been formed some 30 years earlier. Perkins, *Provincial Plaques in Ontario*, 326.

80 Rev. Miller's letter, 1832.

81 LAC M-1353: Rev. Peter MacNaughton, Aug. 27, 1833.

82 The group consisted of 103 settlers and 31 Hudson's Bay Company workers. The settlers consisted of 40 Sutherland families who had sailed on the *Prince of Wales* from Stromness to Churchill in 1813. See Campey, *The Silver Chief*, 77–105, 150–52.

83 See Chapter 7.

84 Andrew F. Hunter, *A History of Simcoe County* (Barrie: Historical Committee of Simcoe County, 1948) 21–2, 311–2. Five more Red River colonists are said to have arrived at Holland River in 1816, coming by way of Parry Sound and Orillia.

85 They were joined in the following year by James and Angus Sutherland, Andrew McBeth, George Ross and "one Murray." The initial group also included Robert Sutherland, Robert and Donald MacKay, John Matthewson, Arthur Campbell and George Bannerman. *Illustrated Historical Atlas, County of Simcoe, Ontario, 1881* (Port Elgin: Cumming Atlas Reprints, 1975) 12,30.

86 LAC M-1352: John Carruthers to Rev. Burns, Feb. 27, 1830; LAC M-1353: Matthew Miller to Rev. Burns, Sept. 29, 1832. Elliott, *Irish Migrants in the Canadas*, 158–9.

87 LAC M-1353: Rev. Matthew Miller to Rev. Burns, Feb. 6, 1833. Also see LAC M-1354: Rev. William Rintoul to Rev. Burns, Dec. 13, 1834.

88 It probably lost its Scottish inhabitants to the large Scottish enclaves which were developing in the western peninsula. The 1861 Census reveals that, by this time, only 27% of its population had Scottish Presbyterian affiliations.

89 The still recognizable "Scotch Line" in west Essa probably marks the site of this former Scottish settlement.

90 Hunter, *Simcoe County*, 63–5.

91 By the 1830s Oro had acquired a substantial Black settlement. It was founded by Black veterans of the War of 1812 who came to the area under a government-sponsored scheme. However, having poor soil, the site was later abandoned. Perkins, *Provincial Plaques in Ontario*, 239.

92 Emigration Select Committee 1826, 219–21: Minutes of Evidence, Lt. Col. Cockburn. He had previously been the superintendent of the Rideau Valley military settlements. The forks of the Nottawasaga River was the location chosen in 1814 to build boats for use in conveying troops and supplies. Barry Gough, *Fighting Sail on Lake Huron and Georgian Bay, the war of 1812 and its aftermath* (St. Catherines, ON: Vanwell, 2002) 69–70.

93 *Smith's Canadian Gazetteer*, 132.

94 Hunter, *Simcoe County*, 63–5.

95 Around 40% of Mono's population was Scottish Presbyterian (see 1861 Census).

Seven – The Lake Erie and Thames Valley Settlements

1 John MacDougald to Hugh MacDougald, Mull, April 29, 1806. The original letter is in the possession of Barb Thornton of Wallaceburg, a descendant of this family. A copy appears in LAC SP (C-14) 14739–40. John MacDougald also fell victim to malaria and died soon after writing this letter.

2   Ibid.

3   By 1822 Shawnee Township had been renamed, becoming the Township of Sombra.

4   Big Bear Creek later became the Sydenham River.

5   LAC MG24 I8: Alexander McDonell Papers: Vol. 4, 105–8. This passenger list, for the *Oughton's* crossing in 1804, appears in Appendix I.

6   *Lord Selkirk's Diary,* 331. Selkirk was travelling east from Lake St. Clair to York.

7   Campey, *The Silver Chief,* 51–76.

8   Alexander McDonell was appointed Sheriff of the Home District in 1792 and in 1800 was elected to the House of Assembly for Glengarry and Prescott. He was Speaker from 1805 to 1807.

9   A.E.D. MacKenzie, *Baldoon: Lord Selkirk's settlement in Upper Canada* (London ON: Phelps Publishing Co., 1978) 33–61. *DCB,* Vol. vii, 554–6.

10   LAC MG24 I8: Vol. 1, 143–5. Also see Vol. 13. The settler lots stretched along the shores of the Chenal Ecarté River, Great Bear Creek and Little Bear Creek.

11   The house was to be 35 feet long by 18 feet wide, with a separate kitchen measuring 16 feet by 14 feet. By 1882 the one storey-and-a-half structure was in a ruinous state and nothing remains of it now. Donna Jean Cornelius, *History of Wallaceburg, Part Two* (Wallaceburg Research and Information Study, 1974) 38.

12   With the exception of Alan MacLean, the original 15 family heads were indentured servants. Because of the flooding and loss of life, Selkirk released the settlers prematurely from their indenture contracts. Campey, *The Silver Chief,* 63–4, 66, 190.

13   The settlers received 50-acre lots soon after their arrival. LAC SP (C-14) 14628–52: Plans and Undertakings for the Baldoon settlement, c. 1804.

14   When Selkirk had first visited the Baldoon site in 1804, the water levels in the rivers and lakes were at an all time low, some five or six feet lower than would be the case over the next thirty years.

15   LAC SP (C-13) 14130-36. Fred Coyne Hamil, *The Valley of the Lower Thames, 1640–1850,* (Toronto: University of Toronto Press, 1951) 46–56. The Gore of Chatham, occupied an area of about 12 miles square. It had been purchased by the British government from Chipewyan chiefs in 1797. Selkirk's Baldoon property abutted on its southern boundary.

16   MacKenzie, *Baldoon,* 62–78. *Wallaceburg Old Boys' and Girls' Reunion* (Wallaceburg, 1936) 21–3.

17   SP (C-14) 14617: Selkirk to Thomas Clark, Dec. 21, 1809.

18   Lord Selkirk, *Observations on the Present State of the Highlands,* 178.

19   SP (C-14) 14590-1: List of the Baldoon settlers in 1809 produced by Alexander McDonell. Only eighty of the original one hundred and two emigrants were alive in 1809.

20   For example, Chester Martin, in *Lord Selkirk's Work in Canada,* Oxford Historical and Literary Studies, Vol. 7 (Oxford at the Clarendon Press, 1916) claimed that Baldoon had "scarcely passed beyond the stage of a straggling pioneer village" (24). John Morgan Gray, in *Lord Selkirk of Red River* (London: MacMillan, 1963) believed that Selkirk "had all but given up, in dismay at its lack of success and ruinous cost." (49).

21   SP (C-14) 14611-20: Selkirk to Thomas Clark, Dec. 21, 1809. Because of gaps in the accounts, the total cost of the Baldoon venture cannot be given with any accuracy. But it must have been at least £10,000.

22   SP (C-13) 13919-26: Outline of a Plan for the Settlement and Security of Canada, July 29, 1805. Also see SP (C-13) 13930-31: Suggestions Respecting Canada, March 27, 1806.

23   Pierre Berton, *The Invasion of Canada, 1812–1813* (Toronto: Anchor Canada, 2001) 137.

24   For example, Marilyn Wild's, "Native's of Scotland who emigrated to Kent County" shows that 31% of the Scots who settled in Kent County originated from Argyll. They were the largest single, identifiable group. (*Central Scotland FHS Bulletin*, No. 9 (1994); No. 10, 11 (1995); No. 12, 13, (1996).

25   Edwin Guillet, *Early Life in Upper Canada* (Toronto: University of Toronto, 1963) 133; reprint – original written in 1933.

26   Fred Coyne Hamil, *Lake Erie Baron, The Story of Colonel Thomas Talbot,* (Toronto: Macmillan, 1955) 177. Quote from William Lyon MacKenzie – a Highlander, who later led the Reformers during the Upper Canada Rebellion of 1837–38.

27   Anna Jameson as quoted in Guillet, *Early Life in Upper Canada,* 135. Anna, wife of Attorney General Jameson, was one of the most celebrated female writers of her time. Having visited Col. Talbot in 1837, she wrote a graphic account of her tour in *Winter Studies and Summer Rambles in Canada,* which was published in 1838.

28   Pierre Berton, *The Invasion of Canada,* 142.

29   Anna Jameson, quoted in Guillet, 135.

30   Hamil, *Lake Erie Baron,* 100–13.

31   Talbot supervised the allocation and settlement of vacant Crown lands far removed from his holdings. He kept control over his settlers until they had completed their settlement duties and withheld their fees to government. Guillet, 129.

32   AO MU2928: Talbot Settlement Lease Book, 1825–1845. Talbot had a supervisory role within these townships: Elgin County – Aldborough, Bayham, Dunwich, Malahide, Southwold, Yarmouth; Middlesex County – Carradoc, Delaware, Ekfrid, London, Mosa, Westminster; Norfolk County: Charlotteville, Houghton, Middleton; Essex County – North and South Colchester, Gosfield, Maidstone, Mersea, Sandwich, West Tilbury; Kent County: Harwich, Howard, Orford, Raleigh, Romney, East Tilbury; Oxford County: Blandford.

33   *DCB*, Vol. xi, 857–62. Talbot's territory extended from Sandwich and Colchester (Essex County) in the west to Middleton and Haughton (Norfolk County) in the east. He never controlled land settlement in an entire township, but in some townships like Dunwich and Aldborough there were large areas under his supervision.

34   Ibid. Contrary to Upper Canada regulations which were supposed to prohibit Americans from acquiring land, Talbot accepted large numbers of settlers from the United States.

35   According to his arrangement with the government, Thomas Talbot obtained 200 acres of land for every settler whom he placed on 50 acres of his own land.

36   There were 134 former Red River colonists. The earliest arrivals, who included William Bannerman, Angus Gunn and John Matheson, settled along the Talbot Road, between the 7th and 8th concessions in Dunwich. These early settlers are listed in James H. Coyne (ed.), "The Talbot Papers, Parts I & II," in *Transactions of the Royal Society of Canada*, 3rd series, 1909–1910, Vol. iii, Section II (Ottawa: Royal Society of Canada, 1910) 75–7.

37   However, they were one of two groups of Red River colonists. The second group went to West Gwillimbury in Simcoe County. See Chapter 6.

38   Edward Ermatinger, *Life of Col. Talbot and the Talbot Settlement* (St. Thomas, ON: A. McLachin's Home Journal Office, 1859) 62–3. When he visited the Genesee River region in 1803, Selkirk learned of the "10 or 12 [Blair] Athol Highlanders" who, having arrived in 1799, founded "the Caledonia Settlement." *Lord Selkirk's Diary*, 117.

39   Donald E. Meek, "Evangelicalism and Emigration: Aspects of the role of dissenting evangelicalism in Highland emigration to Canada," in Gordon MacLennan (ed.), *Proceedings of the First North American Congress of Celtic Studies*, 1986, 15–37. Hamil, *Lake Erie Baron*, 100–1.

40   Wilfred Campbell, *The Scotsman in Canada* Vol. ii (London: Sampson Low & Co., 1911) 210.

41   Meek, "Evangelicalism and Emigration," 15–37.

42   Argyll people had also been attracted to Prince Edward Island and Cape Breton. For example, large numbers of Mull emigrants settled in Prince Edward Island between 1806 and 1810 (see Campey, *Very Fine Class of Immigrants*, 140–3) and some Mull people went to Cape Breton from 1816 (see Campey, *After the Hector*, 107, 114–6, 146–7).

43   *QM*, Aug. 24, 1819; Aug. 15, Aug. 17, 1820; E.504/25/3. In 1819, a number of emigrants were drowned "as they were loading their baggage at Port Talbot." Hamil, *Lake Erie Baron*, 100.

44   Letter written to the *Perthshire Courier* by James and Archibald McFarlane, James Campbell and John Carmichael. Originating from the parishes of Comrie, Balquhidder, Weem and Killin, they sailed to Quebec in 1818 on the *Curlew* and *Jane*. *PC*, Aug. 19, 1819.

45   The Breadalbane group had departed for London Township in 1815. A large number of Breadalbane emigrants settled in Glengarry County in 1815 and a second large group settled in the Rideau Valley in 1818.

46   *PC*, Aug. 19, 1819.

47   MacLeod, "Scottish Settlements in Nineteenth Century Ontario," 93–5. Many of the heads of family, who were living in Aldborough and Dunwich in 1820, are listed in Campbell, *Scotsman in Canada*, Vol. ii, 211–13.

48   K.J. Duncan, "Patterns of Settlement in the East" in Stanford W. Reid (ed.), *The Scottish Tradition in Canada*, (Toronto: McClelland & Stewart, 1976) 61–3.

49   Hamil, *Lake Erie Baron*, 100–9.

50   Ermatinger, *Life of Col. Talbot and the Talbot Settlement*, 63. Talbot himself had several public offices including, legislative councillor, county lieutenant and district magistrate.

51   LAC Upper Canada Sundries, March 19, 1824, quoted in Hamil, *Lake Erie Baron*, 177.

52 Coyne, "The Talbot Papers, Parts I & II," 114.

53 Ibid, 154.

54 Quotation from Archibald McKellar, *Recollections of Colonel Talbot and His Times,"* in Publications, Vol. 1, Wentworth Historical Society, 118) taken from Guillet, *Early Life in Upper Canada,* 126.

55 Hamil, *Lake Erie Baron,* 107. It is difficult to quantify the numbers of Americans in the population, but it is likely that they were a substantial segment of the population. Colin Read, *The Rising in Western Upper Canada 1837–8, the Duncombe Revolt and After.* (Toronto: University of Toronto Press, 1982) 11–23.

56 Talbot had been authorized to extend his supervision far beyond his initial holdings in Aldborough and Dunwich townships. However, the Canada Company also owned Crown reserves in the region over which Talbot presided. See Chapter 8.

57 Read, *The Rising in Western Upper Canada,* 23–46, 180, 182–3. Some of the early Scottish settlers of Ekfrid and Lobo are listed in Campbell, *Scotsman in Canada,* Vol. ii, 214–8.

58 "The Society, in connection with the Established Church of Scotland, for Promoting the Religious Interests of Scottish Settlers in British North America" was founded in 1825. Having been established by Glaswegians, it later came to be known by its condensed name – "the Glasgow Colonial Society." The Niagara congregation also acquired a Glasgow Colonial Society minister at this time. Binnington, "Glasgow Colonial Society," 148–9.

59 LAC M-1352: Rev. Ross to Rev. Burns, Dec. 30, 1829. The Aldborough Scots were concentrated in the 12th and 13th concessions. See AO MU 2928: Talbot Settlement Lease Book 1825–1845.

60 Binnington, "Glasgow Colonial Society," 148–9.

61 LAC MG30-C77: H. McColl fonds, 53.

62 Jennifer Grainger, *Vanished Villages of Middlesex* (Toronto: Natural Heritage, 2002) 88–91.

63 McColl fonds, 66. Grainger, Ibid, 171–2.

64 Ermatinger, *Life of Col. Talbot and the Talbot Settlement,* 192–3.

65 Ibid, 80.

66 Duncan Beaton, "Clan Mackellar, The Mackellars in Glassary parish – Emigration to Canada," in *Scottish Genealogist,* Vol. l (3) Sept., 2003, 114–21. They were led by Rev. Dugald Sinclair, a Baptist minister. Aldborough also had a substantial number of Baptists. See Read, *The Rising in Western Upper Canada,* 28.

67 London became a city from 1854. McColl fonds, 104. Grainger, *Vanished Villages of Middlesex,* 300–4. In the 1870s, Presbyterian services at Hyde Park were still being conducted in Gaelic in the home of the Widow Ross.

68 Neil Martin of Poltalloch assisted tenants from his Kilmartin and North Knapdale properties to emigrate during the early 1840s. For example, he assisted the 16 families (118 people) who sailed on the *Tay* to Quebec in 1843. PP 1844(181)xxxv. Cameron, *Scottish Emigration to Upper Canada,* 381–3; Richards, *Highland Clearances,* 258–9.

69 Scottsville was named after the Scottish-born Mungo Scott; see Grainger, *Vanished Villages of Middlesex,* 324–6. The Kilmartin settlement, to the north of Glencoe, developed along Dundonald Road. Kilmartin's Burns Presbyterian Church was built in 1867 but had to be demolished in 1891. The dedication

service for the new church, built the following year, was conducted partly in Gaelic. See Grainger, 171–4. Knapdale, lying a short distance to the south, was probably also founded by Argyll settlers. See Grainger, 197.

70   However, a sizeable proportion of emigrants from the Hebridean Islands chose to settle in Cape Breton at this time, even though their prospects would have been far better in Upper Canada. See Campey, *After the Hector,* 144–63.

71   Howison, *Sketches of Upper Canada*, (1822) 182.

72   The land settled by Highlanders in both Yarmouth and East Williams was owned by the Canada Company.

73   LAC M-1354: Rev. Allan to Rev. Burns, March 6, 1837.

74   NLS Acc 7020: Marjorie McNicol to James McNicol, her brother, Aug. 12, 1831.

75   NLS Acc 7020: John Mackintosh to James McNicol, May 8, 1853.

76   Ibid.

77   Some of the arrivals were Perthshire people who had previously settled in "the Caledonia Settlement," in New York. Hugh McColl, *Some Sketches of the Early Pioneers of the County of Middlesex* (Ottawa: Canadian Heritage Publications, 1979) 43.

78   Originating mainly from Argyll, Inverness-shire, Perthshire and Easter Ross, they were led by Donald McIntosh of Nairnshire, a Canada Company agent. A list of the early settlers appears in McColl, ibid, 43–4. The west end of Argyle Street and Petty Street lie close to the modern-day community of Beechwood.

79   Grainger, *Vanished Villages of Middlesex,* 75–8.

80   Read, *The Rising in Western Upper Canada,* 24.

81   LAC M-1353: Rev. Matthew Miller to Rev. Burns, Feb. 6, 1833.

82   A huge exodus followed the Highland Famine as deteriorating circumstances caused around 11,000 Highlanders and Islanders to emigrate to British North America in the decade from 1846 to 1856. While some Highlanders left unassisted, most were given financial help by landlords and various philanthropic societies.

83   Ships are listed with passengers numbers in parentheses. 1848: *Canada* of Greenock (98), *Erromanga* of Greenock (99) [see Devine, *Highland Famine,* 325]; 1849: *Atlantic* (366), *Mount Stewart Elphinstone* of Glasgow (250), *Tuskar* of Liverpool (496) [see Devine, 325–6, PP 1850(173)XL]; 1851: *Brooksby* of Glasgow (285), *Montezuma* of Liverpool (440), *Admiral* (413), *Liskeard* of Liverpool (104), *Perthshire* (437) See PP 1852 (1474) xxxiii.

84   The *Cashmere* of Glasgow took 115 passengers and the *Waterhen* of London 167. Both passenger lists appear in Appendix I.

85   The North Uist clearances produced resistance from the people, legal action and widespread newspaper publicity. Richards, *Highland Clearances,* 214–30.

86   *Scotsman,* Aug. 11, 1849 quoted in Richards, Ibid, 215. Gordon of Cluny assisted his tenants to emigrate while additional funds were provided to the most destitute by the Glasgow Destitution Board.

87   See Chapter 9.

88   NAS RH1/2/612/9: Adam Hope to George Hope, in Haddington, Scotland, Oct. 8, 1849.

89   Ibid.

90   Ibid.

91   East and West Williams only became separate townships from 1860. McGillivray and Stephen were in the Huron Tract. In addition to settling in Middlesex and Huron counties, many in the group also went to Grey County. See Chapter 8.

92   Before the arrival of the South Uist emigrants most of the Scots who had come to the region were either Presbyterians or Baptists. Read, *The Rising in Western Upper Canada,* 28, 30, 77.

93   Lawson, *A Register of Emigrants from the Western Isles,* Vol. 2, South Uist and Benbecula.

94   Emigrating in 1849, Lachlan McDonald and family, who established a farm known as Bornish, are credited with having established the place name. Grainger, *Vanished Villages of Middlesex,* 62–5. See also, Donald E. Read, "House-building in Rural Canada West, 1850" in *Families,* Vol. 43, 2004, 213–8.

95   McColl, *Some Sketches of the Early Pioneers,* 42–8.

96   Hamil, *Lower Thames,* 116–7, 214–5. In 1873, Chatham Township had a "Scotch Settlement" located at present-day Darrell. See *Lovell's Gazetteer of British North America* (Montreal: John Lovell, 1873).

97   *Smith's Canadian Gazetteer,* 32.

98   LAC M-1354: Mr. Allan to Rev. Burns, July 1, 1837.

99   NAS GD 1/92/12: James Aitchison to his father William, Nov. 23, 1834. His father hoped that pioneer life would cause James to mend his spendthrift ways and sent him off with more than £200. However, James' farming venture failed. After attempting other lines of business, he fell deeply into debt and fled to the United States to escape imprisonment.

100 Hamil, *Lake Erie Baron,* 154.

101 NAS RH 4/80: George and Henry Forbes to their father, Oct. 4, 1853.

102 Malcolm Wallace, "Pioneers of the Scotch Settlement on the Shore of Lake St. Clair," in *Ontario Historical Society,* Vol. xli, 1949, 173–206.

103 Many of its first settlers were migrants from the United States.

104 Brunger, "Distribution of Scots and Irish in Upper Canada 1851–71," 252–3.

105 Campbell, *Scotsman in Canada,* Vol. ii, 210–1. The Marquis of Lorne (1845–1910) became the 9th Duke of Argyll from 1900.

106 Howison, *Sketches of Upper Canada,* 188.

107 The Proudfoot Papers in *Papers and Records, Ontario Historical Society,* Vol. xxvi (1930) 566.

Eight – The Attractions of the Western Peninsula

1   Anon., *A Statement of the satisfactory results which have attended emigration to Upper Canada from the establishment of the Canada Company until the present period* (London, 1841) 14–5. Extracts of Dr. Alling's letter to the Commissioners of the Canada Company, dated Dec. 16, 1840, were quoted in this pamphlet which was published by the Canada Company in 1841.

2   When he gave his evidence, Dr. Rolph had been living in Upper Canada for some eight years. Emigration Select Committee, A1561.

3   The Canada Company had begun its operations eight years before its main rival, the British American Land Company, whose land holdings were concentrated in the Eastern Townships of Lower Canada. The latter land company was far less successful in attracting British settlers.

4   NAS GD 45/3/226: Earl of Dalhousie to John Galt, Aug. 13, 1833.

5   For the background to the setting up of the company, its operations and the key people who promoted and directed it, see Robert C. Lee, *The Canada Company and the Huron Tract, 1826–1853* (Toronto: Natural Heritage, 2004).

6   Lee, 45–84. Galt founded the town of Guelph in 1827. The town of Galt, later becoming part of Cambridge, was named after John Galt.

7   John Galt gave Father Macdonell a prime site in Guelph for a Roman Catholic church. See Lee, 240–1.

8   PP 1827, V (550), 461–3: "Prospectus of terms upon which the Canada Company proposes to dispose of their lands."

9   It was originally intended that the company would be offered 829,430 acres of Clergy Reserves, but after opposition raised by Church of England clergy they were withdrawn and the Huron Tract was substituted in their place. It had been purchased by the government from the Chipewyan First Nation.

10 Gates, *Land Policies of Upper Canada,* 168–70. In 1829, the average price per acre in the Huron Tract was 7s. 6d. It rose steadily, and by 1840 the average price was 13s. 3d.

11 *Emigration Select Committee, 1841,* A 2941–47.

12 Elizabeth Ann Kerr McDougall and John S. Moir (eds.), *Selected Correspondence of the Glasgow Colonial Society 1825–1840* (Toronto: Champlain Society, 1994) xlv.

13 Huron Tract settlers could claim free transport once they paid their first instalments. H.J. Johnston, "Immigration to the Five Eastern Townships of the Huron Tract," in *Ontario History,* Vol. liv (1962) 207–24.

14 Emigrants themselves contributed to the growing literature on New World destinations. More and more guidebooks and travelogues were also appearing, varying greatly in their quality and reliability. See Marjory Harper, "Image and Reality in Early Emigrant Literature," in *British Journal of Canadian Studies,* Vol. 7 (1992) 3–14.

15 Robert MacDougall, *The Emigrant's Guide to North America*, edited by Elizabeth Thompson (Toronto: Natural Heritage, 1998) 52. Originating from Perthshire, MacDougall had emigrated with his father and brother to the Huron Tract in 1836.

16 See for example the many positive reports in *A Statement of the satisfactory results which have attended emigration to Upper Canada.*

17 MacDougall, *The Emigrant's Guide to North America,* 52

18 Ibid, 56.

19 AU MS 2137–8: Rev. Patrick Bell, "Journals or Rather Observations made in Upper Canada during the years 1834–35–36 and 37," 199–200. Bell had little understanding of Upper Canada and had unrealistic expectations of pioneer life. Bell, a graduate of St. Andrews University, invented the world's first mechanized reaping machine in 1828. He lived in Fergus for three years during which time he was employed as a tutor to the Hon. Adam Fergusson's children. After this stint he returned to Scotland. In addition to Bell, the company had other critics. For example, W.H. Smith, author of *Smith's Canadian Gazetteer* (1846) disapproved of the Canada Company's leasing methods. Johnston, "Immigration to the Five Eastern Townships of the Huron Tract," 210.

20 A221–A222.

21 For example, see PP w/e August 20, 1843.

22 The Huron Tract townships were situated mainly in Perth and Huron coun-
    ties but also encompassed Bosanquet in Lambton County and East and West
    Williams in Middlesex County. Goderich on Lake Huron was the main pop-
    ulation centre. For background information on each township, see Appendix
    ix, *Huron Tract Township Names and Their Origins*, in Lee, *The Canada Com-
    pany*, 226–233.

23 Richards, *Highland Clearances,* 116, 187.

24 PP, Annual Reports of the Immigration Agent at Quebec.

25 *QM,* May 24, 1831; July 8, Aug. 5, 1832; Aug. 1, 1833.

26 Vance, "Emigration and Scottish Society," 307–9; Johnston, "Immigration to
    the Five Eastern Townships, 214, 223. Perthshire settlers who arrived 1832–1834
    are listed in the *Illustrated Atlas of the County of Perth County* (Toronto: H. Belden
    & Co., 1879) xiv–v. German and Irish emigrants also settled in North and South
    Easthope townships.

27 NAS GD 112/61/8: Peter McNaughton to Rev. D. Duff, Kenmore, Oct. 24,
    1835.

28 Statistics gathered for the Scottish Poor Law Commission which reported to
    the British Parliament in 1844 give details of the numbers of poor people who
    emigrated from individual parishes, their destinations and the extent of any
    financial help they may have received. See "Answers to Questions 30 to 32" in
    the Appendices of *Report from the Commissioners appointed for inquiring into the
    Administration and Practical Operation of the Poor Laws in Scotland* (HMSO, 1844).
    For emigration from the Perthshire parishes, see pages 210–87.

29 LAC M-1354: Rev. Rintoul to Rev. Burns, Sept. 25, 1835. Stratford was founded
    in 1832 by Thomas Mercer Jones, the Canada Company Commissioner. He
    also changed the name of the Little Thames River to the Avon River. See Lee,
    The Canada Company, 120, 123.

30 Rintoul to Burns, Sept. 25, 1835.

31 NAS GD 112/61/6: Breadalbane tenants' petition to the Marquis of Breadal-
    bane.

32 Robina Lizars and Kathleen MacFarlane, *In the Days of the Canada Company
    1825–1850. The story of a Settlement in the Huron Tract and a View of the Social
    Life of the Period* (Toronto: William Briggs, 1896) 444.

33 Fullarton also attracted settlers from Devon and Cornwall. Johnston, "Immi-
    gration to the Five Eastern Townships of the Huron Tract," 221–2.

34 PRO CO 384/74: J.W. Campbell to Lord Stanley, May 6, 1843. The 1843 group
    sailed on the *Eleutheria* of South Shields, the *Brilliant* of Aberdeen, the *Jane
    Duffus* of Irvine, the *Bona Dea* and *Romulus* of Greenock. PP 1844 (181) xxxv.

35 Johnston, "Immigration to the Five Eastern Townships," 215.

36 Ibid, 221–3. Settlers from Northern Ireland were concentrated in the southern
    part of Downie. Ibid, 214.

37 Lizars, *In the Days of the Canada Company...,* 445.

38 Johnston, "Immigration to the Five Eastern Townships," 212.

39 James Scott, *The Settlement of Huron County* (Toronto: Ryerson Press, 1966)
    98–9.

40 Ibid, 60–1.

41 MacDougall, *The Emigrant's Guide...*, 55.

42 Ibid, 55.

43 The Huron Road, which ran from Wilmot Township to Goderich, was completed in 1828.

44 *Historical Atlas of Huron County, Ontario* (Toronto: H. Belden & Co., 1879) 19. McKillop also had an "Irishtown." Scott, The Settlement of *Huron County* 60, 142.

45 Scott, Ibid, 60, 163.

46 See discussion of South Uist clearances in Chapter 7.

47 Lawson identifies 14 South Uist families who settled in Stephen Township. See Lawson, *Emigrants from the Western Isles,* Vol. 2. Stephen and McGillivray were adjacent to Biddulph Township, an Irish stronghold. Elliott, *Irish Migrants,* 132–4.

48 Scott, *The Settlement of Huron County,* 99, 145.

49 LAC M-1354: Rev. Rintoul to Rev. Burns, Sept. 25, 1835.

50 Ibid.

51 For emigration from Sutherland to Nova Scotia and Cape Breton see Campey, *After the Hector,* 110–2, 134–7.

52 Campbell, *Scotsman in Canada,* Vol. II, 222–3. Zorra had earlier Loyalist colonizers who originated from several countries. Rev. W.A. MacKay, *Pioneer Life in Zorra* (Toronto: William Briggs, 1899) 154–5.

53 *QM,* Aug. 10, Aug. 19, 1830.

54 *IC,* June 23, 1830.

55 *AJ,* July 13, 1831.

56 Ibid.

57 Sovereigns cost 21s. each at this time.

58 LAC M-1353: Rev. John Geddes to Rev. Burns, Jan. 26, 1833.

59 Emigration Select Committee, 1841, A1634.

60 Thomas Rolph, *Emigration and Colonization; Embodying the Results of a Mission to Great Britain and Ireland during the years, 1839, 1840, 1841 and 1842* (London: J. Mortimer, 1894) 290–1.

61 Campbell, *Scotsman in Canada,* 226.

62 LAC MG24-J50. The resolutions to build the church were agreed by a General Meeting of the Trustees and Delegates, held on Aug. 30, 1833: Hector Ross (President), John MacKay (Treasurer), Donald Matheson (Clerk), Alexander Ross (Constable), James Fraser, Robert Ross, Alexander Matheson, Donald Mackay, George McDonald, James Munro, James Sutherland, John Mackay, Angus McKay, Robert McDonald, Alexander McKenzie, Donald McPherson. A meeting house was built on the 7th concession.

63 MacKay, *Pioneer Life in Zorra,* 64.

64 Ibid, 236.

65 LAC MG24-J50: Donald McKenzie Fonds. Eighty family heads agreed to make this payment. Their names are listed in the "call to the Rev. Donald McKenzie dated Jan. 30, 1835.

66 LAC MG24-J50: Clipping from *Toronto Mail and Empire,* Aug. 27, 1890.

67 Ibid.

68 *Smith's Canadian Gazetteer*, 226.

69 *Report from the Scottish Poor Law Commission*, 402–4. The Duke assisted 20
    families in 1841 who sailed from Loch Laxford on the *Saphiras* of Whitby (PP
    1842(301)xxxi) and 20 families who sailed on the *George* of Dundee in 1843 (PP
    1844(181)xxxv). See Cameron, "Scottish Emigration to Upper Canada," 371–2.

70 NAS RH/1/2/612/8: Adam Hope to George Hope, Aug. 12, 1847.

71 PP 1847–48 (964)xlvii; PP 1849 (1025)xxxviii; PP 1851(348)xl; PP
    1852(1474)xxxiii; Devine, *Great Highland Famine,* 324. The Duke spent £6000
    on assisting his tenants to emigrate during the late 1840s and early 1850s. See
    Cameron, "Scottish Emigration to Upper Canada," 379.

72 It would become the two townships of North Dumfries (Waterloo County) and
    South Dumfries (Brant County) by 1850.

73 William Dickson was frustrated by the government regulations which effec-
    tively barred him from making land grants to Americans. *DCB,* Vol. vii, 25–2.

74 Dickson was a member of the Legislative Council of Upper Canada. The first
    community founded on his lands was named "Shade's Mills," after Absalom Shade,
    Dickson's first agent. He later changed the name to Galt in honour of his cousin,
    John Galt. Today Galt is an area within the city of Cambridge (Waterloo County).

75 James Hogg is also known as the "Ettrick Shepherd," having been born at
    Ettrick in the Scottish Borders. See Andrew W. Taylor, *Our Todays and Yester-
    days; A history of the township of North Dumfries and the village of Ayr, Ontario,
    Canada* (North Dumfries & Ayr Centennial Committee, 1969) 37–8.

76 Edward J. Cowan, "From the Southern Uplands to Southern Ontario: Nine-
    teenth Century Emigration from the Scottish Borders" in T.M. Devine (ed.)
    Scottish Emigration and Scottish Society (Edinburgh: John Donald, 1992) 61–83.

77 For names of the early settlers see Taylor, *History of North Dumfries,* 37–8 and
    G. Clark, "North Dumfries, Ontario," in *Borders Family History Society Bul-
    letin,* June, 1996, 17–8.

78 Before the mid 1820s, most emigration from Dumfriesshire was directed at the
    Maritimes. See Campey, *Very Fine Class of Emigrants,* 66–79.

79 *Dumfries and Galloway Courier*, Feb. 15, 1831.

80 The ships were: *Donegal* (164), *Sarah Mariana* (164), *George* (23), *Experiment*
    (32), *Hope* (73). See *QM*, May, 26, 28; June 2, 21, 1831. The passengers would
    have also included English emigrants as well as groups from the Scottish Bor-
    ders. One ship, the *Neried,* sailed to Quebec directly from Dumfries in 1831,
    carrying 49 passengers.

81 The additional ships in 1832 were: *Ann* (136), *Donegal* (138), *Dykes* (156), *Maria*
    (136), *Nicholson* (183), *Sarah* (165). See *QM,* May 23; June 1, 2, 3, 6, 24, 1832.

82 Rolph, *Emigration and Colonization*, 292.

83 James Young, *Reminiscences of the Early History of Galt and the Settlement of
    Dumfries* (Toronto: Hunter, Rose & Co., 1879) 30–45, 70–3.

84 Ibid, 70.

85 Ibid.

86 *Smith's Canadian Gazetteer*, 62.

87 Ibid, 8, 62.

88 Marjory Harper, *Emigration from North-East Scotland* Vol. 1, and *Willing Exiles*
    (Aberdeen: Aberdeen University Press, 1988) 215–24.

89 Fergus was comprised of concessions XIV, XV and XVI. In 1832, William Gilkison, from Ayrshire, purchased 14,000 acres in Nichol Township and founded Elora. A year later he established a sawmill and general store.

90 Known as Captain Dick, Pierpoint was one of the first Black Loyalists to come to the Niagara region. During the American War of Independence, he escaped his bondage and fought with Butler's Rangers. Later, he was part of the Colored Corps in the War of 1812–14. See Pat Mestern, *Fergus, A Scottish Town by Birthright,* (Toronto: Natural Heritage, 1995) 16–20. For more information, see P. Meyler and D. Meyler, *A Stolen Life: Searching for Richard Pierpoint* (Toronto: Natural Heritage, 1999). For information on the escape routes used by the fugitive slaves and free Blacks who got to Upper Canada, see Adrienne Shadd, Afua Cooper and Karolyn Smartz Frost, *The Underground Railroad: Next Stop Toronto!* (Toronto: Natural Heritage, 2002).

91 Meyler & Meyler, *A Stolen Life*, 116–17.

92 Harper, *Emigration from North East Scotland*, 216–7.

93 Bon Accord was comprised of concessions XI, XII and XIII.

94 "Bon Accord" was used as a password by Aberdonian supporters of King Robert Bruce when they attacked a garrison in the castle under the control of the English during the Wars of Independence (1306–28). The password was apparently then conferred on the city as its motto.

95 "George Elmslie's Diary" in John R. Connon, *Elora* (Waterloo, ON: Wilfred Laurier University Press, 1975) 82. The diary is held by the Wellington County Museum.

96 Ibid, 85. For example, a group of 14 sailed on the *Sir William Wallace* of Aberdeen in 1834, and another group of 20 sailed on the *Brilliant* of Aberdeen in 1835. Harper, *Emigration from North East Scotland*, 215–7.

97 However, numbers declined sharply in 1837 following the rebellion in Upper Canada. Although the uprisings were a manifestation of widespread discontent, dissent was quickly suppressed and emigration levels recovered their earlier fervour from 1841.

98 *AH,* March 26, 1836.

99 Wright, *Pioneer Days in Nichol,* 51–5.

100 A.E. Byerly, *Fergus or the Ferguson-Webster Settlement with an Extensive history of North East Nichol* (Elora, ON: Elora Express, 1932–34) 54, 262.

101 Elmslie worked as a teacher for some 35 years at Ancaster, Hamilton, Guelph, Elora and Alma. Connon, *Elora,* 167.

102 Ibid, 103.

103 Ibid, 103–4; Byerly, *Fergus,* 50.

104 Harper, *Emigration North East Scotland,* 215–24. Alexander Dingwall-Fordyce produced many early sketches of Fergus.

105 Wright, *Pioneer Days in Nichol,* 46. Although suffering less than most other parts of Scotland, Aberdeenshire did experience a severe enough depression by 1848 to cause large-scale unemployment. Harper, *Emigration from North East Scotland,* 130–50.

106 *Smith's Canadian Gazetteer,* 130. New Aberdeen, located near Berlin (later Kitchener) which was settled from 1824, may also have attracted Aberdeenshire settlers. See A.E. Byerly, *The Beginning of things in Wellington and Waterloo Counties with particular reference to Guelph, Galt and Kitchener* (Guelph, ON: Guelph Publish Co., 1935) 35.

107   For example, *PP* w/e May 16, 1840; *PP* w/e July 11, Sept. 23, 1843.

108   PP 1850(173)XL. They had sailed on the *Charlotte* (333 passengers) and the *Barlow* (246 passengers).

109   Cameron, "Scottish Emigration to Upper Canada," 341–2. Many of the emigrants became ill with cholera on their arrival in Hamilton. In addition to Fergus, they were intending to settle also at Hamilton and at Owen Sound on Georgian Bay.

110   Jean F. Hutchinson, *The History of Wellington County* (Grand Valley, ON: Landsborough, 1997) 271–3. However, by the early 1850s they were apparently regarded as an embarrassment and were persuaded to move to the Lake Erie area – presumably to the Talbot townships. See Ted Cowan, "The Myth of Scotch Canada," in Harper and Vance, *Migration and the Making of Memory*, 59.

111   Anon, *Satisfactory results which have attended emigration,* 1.

112   For background on the formation of the Columbian Agricultural Society of London and for details of the Scottish colony at Caracas, see Marjory Harper, *Adventurers & Exiles, The Great Scottish Exodus* (London: Profile Books, 2003) 257–8.

113   *GH,* Jan. 22, 1827.

114   Hutchison, *History of Wellington County,* 10, 28–9. Lee, *The Canada Company,* 59, 61.

115   Galt was criticized for using company funds in this way, even though the money was being used to alleviate great hardship and suffering.

116   Hutchison, *History of Wellington County,* 31–3. Cameron, "Scottish Emigration to Upper Canada," 440.

117   Biographical data of families living in Wellington County, published in 1906, reveals striking concentrations of emigrant Scots in particular townships. Biographies of 1,166 families were examined, representing about 20% of the families living on farms in Wellington County. The survey shows that Guelph Township had particular appeal to Scots from Roxburghshire, Renfrewshire and Ayrshire. See K.J. Duncan, "Aspects of Scottish Settlement in Wellington County," *Scottish Colloquium Proceedings, University of Guelph,* Vol. 3, 1970, 15–20. Also see Cameron, ibid, 440 for a summary of the survey results.

118   *Report from the Scottish Poor Law Commission,* 87. Between 1840 and 1842, a total of 157 people emigrated from Castleton parish in Roxburghshire to Upper Canada. Ian Levitt and Christopher Smout, *The State of the Scottish Working Class in 1843: a statistical and spatial enquiry based on data from the poor law commission report of 1844* (Edinburgh: Scottish Academic Press, 1979) 241.

119   *Smith's Canadian Gazetteer,* 141.

120   Hutchison, *History of Wellington County,* 124.

121   Crieff was initially named Fraserville. Ibid, 113, 125. Some of the initial Puslinch settlers had originated from Mull and Skye, see Cameron, "Scottish Emigration to Upper Canada," 440.

122   A frame church, with a seating capacity of 400 was built on the site of the present Crieff Church in 1854. It was replaced in 1882 by a white brick building which was named Knox Church. The two churches were served by a single minister again from 1890.

123   Cameron, "Scottish Emigration to Upper Canada," 440.

124   Cowan, "From the Southern Uplands to Southern Ontario," 67–68; Rolph, *Emigration and Colonization,* 291.

125 Hutchison, *History of Wellington County*, 142–3. A stone library was built in the 1850s.

126 Cameron, 440.

127 For the Garafraxa Road see Paul White, *Owen Sound, The Port City* (Toronto: Natural Heritage, 2000) 15–6; for the Durham Road see Elliott, *Irish Migrants in the Canadas*, 172.

128 William MacEnery Brown, *The Queen's Bush, A tale of the early days of Bruce County* (London: J. Bale & Co., 1932) 86–93.

129 Most of the Lewis families who went to Lower Canada settled in Compton County in the Eastern Townships. See Bill Lawson, *A Register of Emigrant Families from the Western Isles of Scotland to the Eastern Townships of Quebec* (Quebec: self-published, 1988).

130 These tenants were among those who sailed on the *Urgent* and *Wolfville* of Ardrossan which landed in late July. PP 1852(1474)xxxiii. Matheson spent £10,000 in assisting them. See Richards, *Highland Clearances*, 246.

131 John Munro MacKenzie, *Diary, 1851, John Munro MacKenzie, Chamberlain of the Lews* (Inverness: Acair Ltd., 1994). The diary was published by MacKenzie's great-grandson.

132 The 18 families sailed on the *Blanche* of Liverpool. PP1852–53(1650)lxviii; *QM*, July 31, 1852.

133 A full list of the Lewis emigrants who settled in Bruce County is given in Norman Robertson, *The History of the County of Bruce and of the minor municipalities therein, Province of Ontario, Canada*, 2nd edition (Bruce County Historical Soc., 1960) 418–21. Also see, Campbell, *Scotsman in Canada*, 231–45.

134 Robertson, Ibid, 420.

135 PP 1856(325)xxiv. Some 74 Lewis settlers who had travelled on the *Melissa* settled in the Goderich area.

136 MacKay, "Tiree Migrants," 49–51.

137 W.M. Brown, *Queen's Bush, Grey and Bruce Counties, 1840–1880*, as reported in Cameron, "Scottish Emigration to Upper Canada," 445.

138 PP 18152(1474)xxxiii.

139 Ibid.

140 PP 1856(325)xxiv.

141 In 1861, 44% of Bruce County's population had Presbyterian affiliations. Brown, *Queen's Bush*, 86–93.

142 PRO CO 384/74: Letter dated March 24, 1843, from the Governor General.

143 MacLeod, "Scottish Settlements in Nineteenth Century Ontario," 98–9. McVicar, *Letters on Emigration,* Robert McVicar to A.N. Morin, Jan. 16 and Sept. 12, 1843. In 1873, Balacava was also known as Glenlyon (see *Lovell's Gazetteer*).

144 E.L. Marsh, *A History of the County of Grey* (Owen Sound: Fleming Pub. Co., 1931) 98, 104–5.

145 Lawson, *Emigration from the Western Idless,* Vol. 1 (Isle of Harris). For the Harris exodus to Cape Breton, see Campey, *After the Hector,* 107–21, 145–6, 158. For the exodus to Australia, see Cameron, "Scottish Emigration to Upper Canada," 392–3. They emigrated to Australia with financial aid provided by the Highland Emigration Society and Lady Dunmore who owned the estate.

146   Lawson, *Emigration from the Western Isles,* Vol. 2 (South Uist & Benbecula). Law-
      son lists 34 South Uist families who went to Glenelg (Grey County) four who
      went to Kincardine (Bruce County) and one who went to Culross (Bruce
      County). Harris suffered badly from the potato blight and lost large numbers
      to Cape Breton during the 1840s, and to Australia during the early 1850s.

147   During the period from 1847 to 1851, nine ships carried around 2,000 emi-
      grants, who were mainly from Mull and Tiree, to Quebec. The *Eliza* of Cardiff,
      Jamaica of Glasgow and the *Charlotte Harrison* of Greenock sailed in 1847, the
      Barlow and *Charlotte* in 1849, the *Conrad* of Greenock in 1850, the *Birman* of
      Greenock and *Conrad* of Greenock in 1851 and the *Alan Kerr* in 1853. See PP
      1847–48(964)xlvii, 1850(173)xl, 1851(348)xl, 1852(1474)xxxiii 1852–53(1650)lxviii
      and Devine, *Highland Famine,* 326. The Iona emigrants, who were much small
      in number than the Mull and Tiree contingents, sailed on the *Jamaica* in 1847
      and the *Barlow* in 1849. Some also sailed on the *Britannia* of Newcastle in 1847.
      See MacArthur, *Iona Living Memory*, 236.

148   The Duke of Argyll spent a total of £6,500 of his own money in funding their
      transport.

149   See Glenelg (John Frost), *Broken Shackles: Old Man Henson from Slavery to Free-
      dom* (Toronto: Natural Heritage, 2000)

150   Marsh, *A History of the County of Grey*, 193.

151   MacKay, "Tiree Migrants," 51–2.

152   See Chapter 6.

153   MacArthur, *Iona Living Memory,* 102–4.

154   Brunger, *Distribution of Scots and Irish in Upper Canada*, 250–8.

155   Ibid.

Nine – Emigrant Ships and Atlantic Crossings

1   NLS MS 9656ff.101–02: Murray Correspondence, letter to Capt. Murray from
    Ewan Cameron, on board ship, Saturday, Apr. 7, 1841.

2   McDonald, *Narrative of a Voyage to Quebec,* 36.

3   Ralph Davis, *The Industrial Revolution and British Overseas Trade,* (Leicester:
    Leicester University Press, 1979) 48–49. Between 1814 and 1843, Baltic timber
    was sometimes shipped to North America and then back to Britain, as the sav-
    ing of duty more than compensated for the double freight.

4   Bell, *Hints to Emigrants*, Letter I, 1–9.

5   *Lloyd's List,* 1817; E. 504/22/76, *QM*, June 3, 1817.

6   Skelton, *Man Austere,* 65–87. Emigrants did what they could at this time to
    counter the offensive taste of the water supply on ships by adding vinegar, but
    this was not always effective.

7   Ibid, 68.

8   *Lloyd's Shipping Register.* See Appendix III for a further explanation of the
    Lloyd's Shipping codes.

9   The *Lloyd's Shipping Register* is available as a regular series from 1775, apart
    from the years 1785, 1788 and 1817.

10 Run by a Classification Society with a world-wide network of offices and admin-
    istrative staff, the *Lloyd's Register* continues to provide standard classifications
    of quality for ship building and maintenance.

11   The number of years that a ship could hold the highest code varied according to where it was built. In time, rivalries developed between shipowners and underwriters and this led to the publication of two Registers between 1800 and 1833 – the Ship Owners Register (Red Book) and the Underwriters Register (Green Book). Their coverage was similar but not identical. By 1834, with bankruptcies facing both sides, the two Registers joined forces to become the *Lloyd's Register of British and Foreign Shipping.*

12   To locate a ship's code from the *Register,* it is usually necessary to have the vessel name, the tonnage and/or captain's name. Such data is not always available and is highly problematic to locate. Some vessels may not have been offered for inspection. The lack of a survey might arouse suspicions, but it is not necessarily conclusive proof of a poor quality ship.

13   A – first class condition, kept in the highest state of repair and efficiency and within a prescribed age limit at the time of sailing; AE – "the second description of the first class," fit, no defects but may be over a prescribed age limit; E – second class, although unfit for carrying dry cargoes was suitable for long distance sea voyages.

14   Entries in *Lloyds List* show that each vessel returned to the Clyde with a cargo of timber.

15   Oliver Macdonagh, *A pattern of government growth 1800–1860, The Passenger Acts and their enforcement* (London: Macgibbon & Kee, 1961) 54–62.

16   Edwin C. Guillet, *The Great Migration, The Atlantic crossing by sailing ships since 1770* (Toronto: University of Toronto Press, 1963) 13–19.

17   Typical steerage fares throughout the 1820s were around £3. 10s. They fell to £2 10s. in the 1830s, and rose again in the 1840s to £3 10s. (fares assume passenger supplied own food). See *Glasgow Herald* shipping advertisements and Cameron, "Scottish Emigration to Upper Canada," 516–7. Steerage rates for the 1830s are to be found in NAS GD 46/13/184: Information published by His Majesty's Commissioners for Emigration respecting the British colonies in North America (London, Feb. 1832). For the 1840s, see Anon., *Information for Emigrants to British North America* (1842) 7–8.

18   The physical characteristics of a vessel greatly affected sailing performance as well as passenger comfort and safety. For an analysis of the different types of Aberdeen-registered vessels which were used to take emigrants to British North America, see Campey, *Fast Sailing,* 80–98.

19   Only 1,152 out of 86,598 passengers, known to have travelled to Quebec from Scotland between 1831 and 1855 travelled in cabins.

20   For example, the *Brilliant* had a depth of 19.3 feet and could offer six feet between decks. The others also had relatively deep hulls. The names of their captains are to be found in Appendix II.

21   Initially, Greenock was the more important port, but Glasgow overtook it from the late 1830s once the River Clyde was opened up to large sailing ships.

22   A history of the Allan Line is provided in Thomas E. Appleton, *Ravenscrag, The Allan Royal Mail Line* (Toronto: McClelland & Stewart, 1974). Also see Gerald Tulchinsky, *The River Barons: Montreal business and growth of industry and transport 1837–53* (Toronto: University of Toronto Press, 1977) 79–80.

23   Alan Kerr and Co. advertisement quoted in Appleton, Ibid, 35.

24 Hugh Allan obtained his grounding in the North American shipping trade from a fellow-Scot, James Millar, a Montreal merchant and shipowner. Appleton, ibid, 46–55. The Allan Line later ran regular services from Liverpool to Quebec.

25 For example, the *Harlequin* (702 tons) took around 850 passengers in just four crossings, while the *Caledonia* of Greenock had taken a similar number in 15 crossings.

26 Official figures are available from 1831. See PP Annual Reports of the Immigration Agent at Quebec. However, because of gaps in some years these figures understate emigrant totals.

27 Cameron, "Scottish Emigration to Upper Canada," 458–74.

28 See the Glasgow and Greenock Shipping Registers (SRA, CE 59/11, CE 60/11) for ownership details and ship dimensions.

29 A passenger list for the *Portaferry's* 1833 crossing also survives. See *QM,* June 13, 1832; May 30, 1833. Both the 1832 and 1833 passenger lists appear in Appendix I.

30 Cameron, 482–6.

31 Jean Lindsay, *The Canals of Scotland* (Newton Abbot: David & Charles, 1968), 39–42,78. The Forth and Clyde Canal extended from Bowling near Dumbarton to Grangemouth. The Union Canal connected with the Forth and Clyde Canal at Port Downie near Falkirk and extended eastwards to Edinburgh.

32 Campey, *Fast Sailing,* 80–98.

33 See the Aberdeen Shipping Registers (ACA CE87/11) for ship dimensions.

34 Even by as late as 1828, the legislation still only required shippers to give their passengers at least five-and-one-half feet between decks

35 Macdonagh, *Passenger Acts,* 150–51.

36 William Duthie learned his trade as an apprentice in Alexander Hall's shipyard. He became a ship builder and large-scale timber merchant, later handing over the business to his brothers, who included Alexander, owner of the *Berbice.* Donaldson Rose first worked as a cooper, making wooden casks and barrels. Realizing the potential of the timber trade, he established himself as one of Aberdeen's principal timber merchants and shipowners by the early 1820s. Information on Donaldson Rose was kindly communicated by Mr. Michael Rose, his great-great grandson.

37 Campey, *Fast Sailing,* 95–8.

38 Dundee's linen and other exports were generally moved from Dundee to large ports like Liverpool and London for shipment overseas.

39 PP Annual Reports of the Immigration Agent at Quebec, 1831–55.

40 Cameron, "Scottish Emigrants to Upper Canada," 474–9.

41 Campey, *Fast Sailing,* 59–79.

42 NAS GD 226/15/1: Trinity House of Leith, misc. vols. 1841–1941. Account Book of John Smith for voyages in the timber trade 1826–33 with disbursements at Leith, Quebec, Waterford, Halifax, New York, Liverpool, Baltimore, Cork, Miramichi, Orkney, Burntisland, St. Petersburg, Elsinore and Dundee.

43 *JJ,* March 31, April 14, May 26, 1837; April 30, 1841.

44 NAS GD 226/15/1. A total of £180. 3s. had been collected in passenger fares. William Allan received a commission of £9. 14s. 10d. General advertising had cost £9, while advertisements in Kelso had cost £3. 18s. 5d. An additional £1. 7s. had been spent on the printing of handbills.

45 NAS CE/57/11: Leith Shipping Registers. The *Margaret Bogle* was 104.2 feet × 27 feet × 18.11 feet.

46 *IC,* April 7, 1830.

47 PRO CO 384/4, f. 29: Special Meeting of the Quebec Emigration Society, Oct. 11, 1819.

48 The proceeds of the immigrant tax were divided among the Quebec Emigrant Hospital, the Montreal General Hospital, the Quebec Emigrant Society and the Montreal Emigrant Society. Cowan, *British Emigration,* 56–7, 152–3.

49 For example, Archibald MacNiven, the emigration agent who arranged Atlantic shipping for Western Isle emigrants, complained that the tax would stop emigration entirely. PRO CO217/154 ff. 877.

50 Campey, *Fast Sailing,* 63–9.

51 For example, see their *John O'Groat Journal* advertisement (Jan. 22, 1841) which included material from *A Statement of the satisfactory results which have attended emigration to Upper Canada from the establishment of the Canada Company until the present period.*

52 PRO CO 384/77 ff. 461–69: Memorial to the Colonial Office from John Sutherland, Wick, 1846. Emigrants were also collected at Loch Laxford and Lochinver (see Appendix II).

53 *Pictou Observer,* Sept. 6, 1842.

54 *IJ,* July 1, 1842.

55 *JJ,* June 15, 1849.

56 Ibid.

57 Ibid.

58 PP 1842 (301)xxxi. Campey, *After the Hector,* 171–3.

59 NAS RH 1/2/908, *Mechanic and Farmer,* Pictou. N.S., July 28, 1841.

60 Ibid.

61 *DC,* Feb. 7, 1834. The *Fairy* carried 50 passengers whose names are listed in the commendation printed in the *Dundee Courier.*

62 Thomas Fowler, *Journal of a Tour through British North America to the Falls of Niagara containing an account of the cities, towns and villages along the route in 1831* (Aberdeen: L. Smith, 1832) 252.

63 LAC MG24 D41: Letter written by Bryce Allan in April/May, 1847.

64 Ibid.

65 Ibid.

66 PP 1847–48(964)xlvii.

67 LAC MG24 D41.

68 André Charbonneau and André Sevigny, *1847 Grosse Isle: A record of daily events* (Ottawa: Canadian Heritage, 1997) 1–32.

69 PP 1850(173)xl.

70 Ibid.

71 PP 1852(1474)xxxiii.

72 Ibid.

73 Richards, *Highland Clearances,* 207–25.

74 *QM,* Sept. 21, Sept. 24, 1821.

75 *QM,* Sept. 5, 1854.

76 Guillet, *The Great Migration,* 19, 67.

77 Arthur R.M. Lower, *Great Britain's Woodyard: British America and the timber trade 1763–1867* (Montreal: McGill-Queens University Press, 1973) 242.

Ten – Border Guards and Trailblazers

1   Sir Richard Cartwright, *Reminiscences,* (Toronto: William Briggs, 1912) 341.
    Also see (Royce MacGillivray, *The Mind of Ontario,* (Belleville, ON: Mika Pub-
    lishing Co., 1985) 34.
2   J.M. Bumsted, *The Scots in Canada*, Canada's Ethnic Group Booklet No. 1
    (Ottawa: Canadian Historical Association, 1982) 17.
3   William J. Rattray, *The Scot in British North America,* 4 vols. (Toronto: Maclear,
    1880–83) Vol. 1, 196.
4   Ibid.
5   Ibid.
6   LAC MG30-C77: H. McColl fonds.
7   LAC MG29-C29: George Sanfield McDonald fonds.
8   1841 Emigration Select Committee, A943.
9   Ibid.
10 Ibid.
11 Ibid, A2034.
12 Ibid, A222.
13 Ibid, A1561.
14 Howison, *Sketches of Upper Canada,* 188.
15 Ibid, 184.
16 *GC,* April 22, 1820.
17 1827 Emigration Select Committee, A142–145.
18 Rattray, *Scot in British North America,* 197.
19 LAC M-1352: John Robertson to Rev. David Welsh, May 14, 1828. Butler's *Anal-
    ogy of Religion* was written in 1736. Joseph Butler was an English theologian
    whose writings concentrated on moral philosophy.
20 Scotland had a national education system in place by the eighteenth century.
    Schools provided basic literacy and numeracy and a knowledge of the catechism.
21 LAC M-1352: John McIntyre to Rev. Burns, Oct. 23, 1828.
22 Hayden, *Pioneer Sketches of the District of Bathurst,* 188.
23 LAC MG24 J50: Donald Mackenzie fonds.
24 For example, at Lochiel during 1861 Gaelic services attracted 800 people while
    services spoken in English attracted a mere handful. Royce MacGillivray and
    Ewan Ross, *A History of Glengarry,* (Belleville, ON: Mika Publishing Co., 1979)
    276–7.
25 1841 Emigration Select Committee, A921. Toronto also had a Gaelic periodi-
    cal (*An Gaidheal*) which was produced for a few years from 1871, and it still
    has a Gaelic Society.
26 MacGillivray and Ross, *History of Glengarry,* 278.
27 MacLeod, "Scottish Settlements in Nineteenth Century Ontario," 209–10. The
    Highland Society of Glengarry was an offshoot of the Highland Society in Lon-
    don, founded in 1778, which did a great deal to preserve and rehabilitate these
    earlier Highland traditions. Thanks largely to its efforts, the wearing of the
    kilt, which had been banned following the Jacobite uprising of 1745–46, became
    the accepted national dress of Scotland.

28 Cowan, "The Myth of Scotch Canada," in Harper and Vance, *Migration and the Making of Memory*) 59. 49–72.

29 *North Bay Nugget,* March 1, 2004.

30 Shinty is a Gaelic word. For the connection between shinty and hockey, see Harper, *Adventurers and Exiles,* 360–1. Originating in pre-Christian times, it is western Europe's oldest team game. Played with a ball and stick, it continues to be played today, as an amateur sport, mainly in the Highlands. For further details of the history of curling in Ontario, see John A. Stevenson, *Curling in Ontario, 1846–1946* (Toronto: Ontario Curling Assoc., 1950).

31 George S. Emmerson, "The Gaelic Tradition in Gaelic Culture," in Stanford Reid, *Scottish Tradition in Canada,* 244–6.

32 Vincent Crichton, *Pioneering in Northern Ontario* (Belleville, ON: Mika Publishing Co., 1975) 199, 370–2.

33 Emmerson, "The Gaelic Tradition in Gaelic Culture," 240–1.

34. Anon., "The Scot in Canada, A Run Through the Dominion," reprinted from the *Aberdeen Daily Record,* 1907.

35. John Kenneth Galbraith, *The Scotch* (Toronto: Macmillan of Canada, 1964) 141–2. Galbraith was a leading twentieth century economist who has spent much of his life in the United States. He is a former advisor to John F. Kennedy and was a U.S. ambassador to numerous countries.

36 For instance R. Tait McKenzie built the Scottish-American War Memorial in Edinburgh. Having studied medicine at McGill University, he used his knowledge of anatomy to launch himself as a sculptor in later life.

37 Ged Martin and Jeffrey Simpson, *Canada's Heritage in Scotland* (Toronto: Dundurn, 1989) 33–4. Today the mill of Kintail is a museum.

38 For example, as Ralph Connor, Rev. Gordon wrote *The Man from Glengarry* and *Glengarry School Days.*

39 Alexander Graham Bell also spent time in Boston and thus both Brantford and Boston claim the distinction of being Bell's place of residence. Brantford today honours the man and his work with a museum, the Bell Homestead National Historic Site.

40 Martin and Simpson, *Canada's Heritage,* 81–3.

41 George Brown established his anti-establishment credentials when he founded his first paper, *The Banner,* a weekly Presbyterian journal, which advocated support for the Free Church. The widespread support which it received helped Brown to launch his political career.

42 William Lyon Mackenzie's grandson, William Lyon Mackenzie King, would become Canada's longest-serving Prime Minister.

43 Donaldson, *Scots Overseas,* 144–5.

44 Craig, *Upper Canada,* 182–5.

45 Howison, Ibid, 188.

46 Fowler, *Tour through British North America,* 152.

47 LAC MG24-I183: Letter-book, Archibald McMillan.

Bibliography

Primary Sources (Manuscripts)

Aberdeen City Archives (ACA)
CE 87/11: Aberdeen Shipping Registers

Aberdeen University (AU)
MS 2137-8: Rev. Patrick Bell, Journals or Rather Observations made in Upper Canada during the years 1834–5–6 and 37

Archives of Ontario (AO)
MU2928: Talbot Settlement Lease Book, 1824–45.

Dundee City Archives (DCA)
CE 70/11 Register of Ships
Dundee and District Shipping Local Collection, D3113.

Library and Archives Canada (LAC)
M-1352, M-1353, M-1354: Glasgow Colonial Society Correspondence, 1829–37 (microfilm reels).
M-5505: Monthly nominal returns of emigrants, 1815–1822.
MG23 HII19: Mrs. Nancy Jean Cameron to Mrs. Kenneth Macpherson, May 15, 1785.
MG24 D41: Bryce Allan, log book of sailing vessels, 1829–47.
MG24 I8: Alexander McDonell Papers.
MG24 J13: Rt. Rev. Alexander Macdonell Papers
MG24-I67: John Millar Collection.
MG24 I183: Archibald McMillan family papers.
MG24-J50: Donald McKenzie fonds.
MG25-G272: Barclay Family fonds.
MG29 C29: George Sandfield Macdonald fonds.
MG30-C77: Hugh McColl fonds.
RG1 L3: Upper Canada Land Petitions MC 21 (1837–39).
RG4 A1: Correspondence of provincial and civil secretaries (Lower Canada).

RG5 A1: Upper Canada Sundries.

RG8 Vol. 625 ff. 219–23; Passenger list *Commerce* of Greenock, June 1820.

RG19 Vol. 4447, no. 14: Victualling list, Glengarry settlers.

SP (C-13) (C-14) Selkirk Papers (microfilm reels)

National Archives of Scotland (NAS)

CE 57/11: Register of Ships, Leith.

E.504: Customs records, collectors quarterly accounts, 1776–1830/1 Aberdeen, /9 Dumfries, /12 Fort William, /15 Greenock, /22 Leith, /25 Oban, /27 Perth, /33 Stornoway, /35 Tobermory.

GD 1/814/5/3: Arthur Stocks to his brother, John Colquhoun, Dec 10, 1825.

GD 1/92/12: James Aitchison to his father William, Nov. 23, 1834.

GD 45: Dalhousie Papers.

GD 46/13/184: Information published by His Majesty's Commissioners for Emigration respecting the British Colonies in North America (London, Feb. 1832).

GD 112: Breadalbane Papers.

GD 133: Robertson of Inches Papers.

GD 202: Campbell of Dunstaffnage Papers.

GD 221: Lord MacDonald Papers.

GD 226/15/1: Trinity House of Leith, misc. vols. 1841–1941.

HD 21: Highland Destitution Board Papers.

RH1/2/612/9: Adam Hope to George Hope, Oct. 8, 1849.

RH 1/2/908, *Mechanic and Farmer,* Pictou. N.S., July 28, 1841.

RH 4/80: George and Henry Forbes to their father, Oct. 4, 1853.

RH 4/188/2: Prize essays and Transactions of the Highland Society of Scotland, Vol. iii, 1802–03.

RH9/17/237: List of letters received from applicants wishing to settle in Canada.

National Library of Scotland (NLS)

Acc 7020: Letters, Marjorie McNicol and John Mackintosh, 1831, 1853.

Adv MS 35.6.18, ff. 8–15, Melville Papers, State of Emigration from the Highlands of Scotland, its extent, causes and proposed remedy, London, March 21, 1803.

GD 46/13/184: *Information published by His Majesty's Commissioners for Emigration respecting the British Colonies in North America* (London, Feb. 1832).

MS 9646: "On Emigration from the Scottish Highlands and Islands attributed to Edward S. Fraser of Inverness-shire (1801–04)."

MS 9656ff.101–02: Murray Correspondence.

Public Record Office (PRO)

CO 42: Correspondence, Canada.

CO 217: Nova Scotia and Cape Breton Original Correspondence.

CO 226: Prince Edward Island Correspondence.

CO 384: Colonial Office Papers on emigration containing original correspondence concerning North American settlers.

CO 385: Colonial Office Papers on emigration, Entry Books of correspondence.

Strathclyde Regional Archives (SRA)
CE 59/11: Register of Ships, Glasgow.
CE 60/11: Register of Ships, Greenock.
T/CN 26: Clyde Bills of Entry.
T/CN 21: Report Books, Glasgow.

Primary Sources and Contemporary Publications (Printed)

Anon., "The Scot in Canada, A Run through the Dominion," reprinted from the *Aberdeen Daily Journal,* 1907 [by John M. Gibbon].

Anon., *A Short Account of the Emigration from the Highlands of Scotland to North America; and the Establishment of the Catholic Diocese of Upper Canada* (Kingston, ON: 1839).

Anon., *A Statement of the satisfactory results which have attended emigration to Upper Canada from the establishment of the Canada Company until the present period* (London: 1841).

Anon., *Information for Emigrants to British North America* (1842).

Baird, C.R., "Observations on the poorest class of operatives in Glasgow in 1832" in *Journal of the Statistical Society of London,* Vol. 1 (1839) 167–74.

Bell, Rev. William, *Hints to Emigrants in a series of letters from Upper Canada* (Edinburgh: Waugh & Innes, 1824).

Bouchette, Joseph, *The British Dominions in North America: a Topographical and Statistical Description of the Provinces of Lower and Upper Canada, New Brunswick, Nova Scotia, the Islands of Newfoundland, Prince Edward Island and Cape Breton,* Vols I, II (London: 1832).

Brown, Robert, *Strictures and remarks on the Earl of Selkirk's observations on the present state of the Highlands* (Edinburgh: Abernethy & Walker, 1806).

Campbell, Jessie, *Some reminiscences of the life and labours of the Rev. George Buchanan, first Presbyterian Minister of Beckwith, Lanark County, Upper Canada* (Toronto: self-published, 1900).

Browne, James, *History of the Highlands and the Highland Clans* (Glasgow: A. Fullarton & Co., 1840) Vol. iv.

Canniff, William, *History of the Settlement of Upper Canada* (Toronto: Dudley & Burns, 1869).

Cartwright, Sir Richard, *Reminiscences* (Toronto: William Briggs, 1912).

Census of Lower Canada, 1861.

Census of Upper Canada, 1851, 1861, 1871.

Colonial Records of North Carolina, Vol. ix (1772).

Ermatinger, Edward, *Life of Col. Talbot and the Talbot Settlement* (St. Thomas: A. McLachin's Home Journal Office, 1859).

Fowler, Thomas, *Journal of a Tour through British North America to the Falls of Niagara containing an account of the cities, towns and villages along the route in 1831* (Aberdeen: L. Smith, 1832).

Glasgow Colonial Society, *Seventh Annual Report of the Glasgow Colonial Society for promoting the religious interests of the Scottish settlers in British North America* (Glasgow: 1833).

Gourlay, Robert F., *Statistical Account of Upper Canada compiled with a view to a grand system of emigration* (London: Simpkin & Marshall, 1822).

Head, Sir Francis Bond, *The Emigrant,* (London: John Murray, 1846).

Historical Atlas of Huron County, Ontario (Toronto: H. Belden & Co., 1879).

Howison, John, *Sketches of Upper Canada, domestic, local and characteristic, to which are added practical details for the information of emigrants of every class* (Edinburgh: Oliver & Boyd, 1822).

Illustrated Atlas of the County of Perth County (Toronto: H. Belden & Co., 1879).

Kingdom, William, *America and the British Colonies* (London: Whittaker, 1820).

Johnston, William, *History of the County of Perth from 1825 to 1902* (Stratford, ON: W. M. O'Beirne, 1903).

Lizars, Robina, and Kathleen MacFarlane, *In the Days of the Canada Company 1825–1850: The story of a Settlement in the Huron Tract and a View of the Social Life of the Period* (Toronto: William Briggs, 1896).

Lloyd's Shipping Register 1775–1855.

Lovell's Gazetteer of British North America (Montreal: John Lovell, 1873).

MacKay, Rev. W.A., *Pioneer Life in Zorra* (Toronto: William Briggs, 1899).

MacTaggert, John, *Three Years in Canada: An account of the actual state of the country in 1826–7–8 comprehending its resources, productions, improvements and capabilities and including sketches of the state of society, advice to emigrants, etc.* Two Volumes (London: H. Colburn, 1829).

Martin, Montgomery R., *History, Statistics and Geography of Upper and Lower Canada* (London: Whittaker, 1838).

Mathison, John, *Counsel for Emigrants, and Interesting Information from Numerous Sources concerning British America, the United States and New South Wales,* Third edition with a supp. (Aberdeen: 1838).

McDonald, John, *Narrative of a Voyage to Quebec and journey from thence to New Lanark in Upper Canada, detailing the Hardships and Difficulties which an Emigrant has to Encounter, before and after his Settlement; with an account of the Country, as regards its Climate, Soil and the Actual Conditions of its Inhabitants* (Edinburgh: the author, 1823).

McLennan, William, *Spanish John: being a memoir now first published in complete form of the early life and adventures of Colonel John McDonell, known as "Spanish John" when a lieutenant in the Company of St. James of the Regiment Irlandia, in the service of the king of Spain operating in Italy* (London: Harper, 1898).

McVicar, Robert, *Letters on Emigration from the British Isles and the Settlement of the Waste Lands in the Province of Canada* (Hamilton, ON: S. Hewson, 1853).

Morgan, Lieutenant J.C., *The Emigrants Notebook and Guide with Recollections of Upper and Lower Canada during the Late War* (London: 1824)

Pope, Miss A.M., "A Scotch Catholic Settlement in Canada," in *Catholic World,* Vol. 34 (Oct. 1881).

Sinclair, Sir John, *First Statistical Account of Scotland,* 21 Vols. (Edinburgh: W. Creech, 1791–99).

Rattray, William J., *The Scot in British North America,* 4 Vols. (Toronto: Maclear, 1880–83).

Rolph, Thomas, *Emigration and Colonization; Embodying the Results of a Mission to Great Britain and Ireland during the years, 1839, 1840, 1841 and 1842* (London: J. Mortimer, 1894).

Ross, Donald *Glengarry evictions or scenes at Knoydart in Inverness-shire,* (Glasgow: W.G. Blackie & Co., 1853).

Smith, W.H., *Smith's Canadian Gazetteer: statistical and general information respecting all parts of the Upper Province or Canada West* (Toronto: H. & W. Rowsell, 1846).

Telford, Thomas, *A Survey and Report of the Coasts and Central Highlands of Scotland* (London: 1803).

Young, James, *Reminiscences of the Early History of Galt and the Settlement of Dumfries* (Toronto: Hunter Rose & Co., 1879).

Parliamentary Papers

Annual Reports of the Immigration Agent at Quebec (1831–55).

Colonial Land and Emigration Commissioners, Annual Reports (1841–55).

Emigration Returns for British North America 1830–40.

Report from the Commissioners appointed for inquiring into the Administration and Practical Operation of the Poor Laws in Scotland, 1844; Answers to Questions 30–32 in the Appendices.

Reports from the Select Committee appointed to inquire into the expediency of encouraging emigration from the United Kingdom, 1826, IV; 1826–27, V.

Report from the Select Committee appointed to enquire into the condition of the Population of the Highlands and Islands of Scotland, and into the practicability of affording the People relief by means of Emigration, 1841, VI.

Contemporary Newspapers

Aberdeen Herald

Aberdeen Journal

Dumfries and Galloway Courier

Dundee Courier

Dundee Perth and Cupar Advertiser

Dumfries Times

Dumfries Weekly Journal

Edinburgh Advertiser

Elgin Courant

Glasgow Chronicle

Glasgow Herald

Glasgow Saturday Post

Greenock Advertiser

Inverness Advertiser

Inverness Courier

Inverness Journal

John O'Groat Journal

Kelso Mail

Lloyd's List

Montreal Gazette

North Bay Nugget

Paisley Advertiser

Perthshire Courier and General Advertiser

Quebec Gazette

Quebec Mercury

Scots Magazine

Scotsman

Contemporary Material of later printing

Coyne, James H. (ed.), "The Talbot Papers, Parts I & II," *Transactions of the Royal Society of Canada,* 3rd series, 1909–10, Vol. III, Section II (Ottawa: Royal Society of Canada, 1910).

Douglas, Thomas, Fifth Earl of Selkirk, *Observations on the Present State of the Highlands of Scotland, with a view of the causes and probable consequences of emigration*, 1805 in Bumsted, J.M. (ed.), *The Collected Writings of Lord Selkirk*, Vol. I (Winnipeg: The Manitoba Record Society, 1984).

Lamond, Robert, *A Narrative of the progress of Emigration from the Counties of Lanark and Renfrew to the New Settlements in Upper Canada on Government Grant* (Ottawa, ON: Canadian Heritage Publications, 1978 [first published 1821]).

Macdonell, J.A., *Sketches illustrating the early settlement and history of Glengarry in Canada* (Belleville, ON: Mika Publishing Co., 1984 [first published 1893]).

McDougall, Elizabeth, Ann Kerr and John S. Moir (eds.), *Selected Correspondence of the Glasgow Colonial Society 1825–1840* (Champlain Society, Toronto, 1994).

Illustrated Historical Atlas, County of Simcoe, Ontario, 1881 (Port Elgin, ON: Cumming Atlas Reprints, 1975).

MacDougall, Robert, *The Emigrant's Guide to North America*, edited by Elizabeth Thompson (Toronto: Natural Heritage, 1998) (first published 1841).

Pringle, J.F., *Lunenburg or the Old Eastern District* (Belleville, ON: Mika Publishing Co., 1972 [first published 1890]).

Proudfoot Papers, *Papers and Records, Ontario Historical Society*, Vol. xxvi (1930) 566.

White, Patrick Cecil Telford (ed.), *Lord Selkirk's Diary 1803–04; A journal of his travels through British North America and the Northeastern United States* (Toronto: The Champlain Society, 1958).

Secondary Sources

Adam, Margaret I., "The Highland Emigration of 1770," in *Scottish Historical Review*, Vol. xvi (1919) 280–93.

Adams, Ian and Somerville, Meredyth, *Cargoes of Despair and Hope: Scottish Emigration to North America 1603–1803* (Edinburgh: John Donald, 1993).

Aitchison, Peter and Andrew Cassell, *The Lowland Clearances: Scotland's Silent Revolution* (East Linton: Tuckwell, 2003).

Anon., "Views of General Murray on the defence of Upper Canada, 1815," in *Canadian Historical Review*, Vol. xxxix (1953) 158–65.

Appleton, Thomas E., *Ravenscrag: The Allan Royal Mail Line* (Toronto: McClelland & Stewart, 1974).

Barrett, Clark, "The Glengarry Indian Lands," *Ontario Genealogical Society Bulletin*, Vol. 8 (1969) 5–6.

Beaton, Duncan, "Clan Mackellar, The Mackellars in Glassary Parish – Emigration to Canada," in *Scottish Genealogist*, Vol. L (3) Sept., 2003, 114–21.

Bennett, Carol, *In Search of Lanark* (Renfrew, ON: Juniper Books, 1980).

Bennett, Carol, *The Lanark Society Settlers, 1820–1821* (Renfrew, ON: Juniper Books, 1991).

Berton, Pierre, *The Invasion of Canada, 1812–1813* (Toronto: Anchor Canada, 2001).

Binnington, Rev. R.F., "The Glasgow Colonial Society and its work in the development of the Presbyterian Church in British North America 1825–1840" (unpublished Th.D., thesis, University of Toronto, 1960).

Blake, George, *Lloyd's Register of Shipping 1760–1960* (London: Lloyd's, 1960).

Brander, Michael, *The Scottish Highlanders and their Regiments* (Haddington: The Gleneil Press, 1996).

Brock, William R., *Scotus Americanus: A Survey of the Sources for links between Scotland and America in the Eighteenth Century* (Edinburgh: Edinburgh University Press, 1982).

Brown, William MacEnery, *The Queen's Bush: A tale of the early days of Bruce County* (London: J. Bale & Co., 1932).

Brunger, A.G., "The Distribution of Scots and Irish in Upper Canada 1851–71," in

Canadian Geographer, Vol. 34, 1990, 250–58.

Buckner, Philip, *English Canada – The founding generations: British migration to British North America, 1815–1865.* Canada House, Lecture Series No. 54, Canadian High Commission, Grosvenor Square, London, UK.

Bumsted, J.M., *Interpreting Canada's Past,* Vol. 1 (Toronto: Oxford University Press Canada, 1993).

_____, *The Peoples of Canada: A Pre-Confederation History,* Vol. 1 (Toronto: Oxford University Press, 1992).

_____, *The People's Clearance: Highland Emigration to British North America 1770–1815* (Edinburgh: Edinburgh University Press, 1982).

_____, *The Scots in Canada,* Canada's Ethnic Group Booklet No. 1 (Ottawa: Canadian Historical Association, 1982).

Byerly, A.E., *Fergus or the Ferguson-Webster Settlement with an Extensive history of North East Nichol* (Elora, ON: Elora Express, 1932–34).

_____, *The Beginning of things in Wellington and Waterloo Counties with particular reference to Guelph, Galt and Kitchener* (Guelph, ON: Guelph Publish Co., 1935).

Cage, R.A. (ed.), *The Scots Abroad: Labour, Capital, Enterprise, 1750–1914* (London: Croom Helm, 1985).

Calder, Jenni, *Scots in Canada* (Edinburgh: Luath Press, 2003).

Cameron., J.M., "A Study of the factors that assisted and directed Scottish Emigration to Upper Canada 1815–55" (unpublished Ph.D. thesis, University of Glasgow, 1970).

_____, "An Introduction to the Scottish Settlement of Southern Ontario," in *Ontario History,* Vol. 61 (1969) 167–72.

Campbell, R.H., *Scotland Since 1707, The Rise of an Industrial Society* (Edinburgh: John Donald, 1985).

Campbell, Wilfrid, *The Scotsman in Canada,* Vols. I & II (London: Sampson Low & Co., 1911).

Campey, Lucille H., *After the Hector: The Scottish Pioneers of Nova Scotia and Cape Breton, 1773–1852* (Toronto: Natural Heritage, 2004).

_____, *Fast Sailing and Copper-Bottomed: Aberdeen Sailing Ships and the Emigrant Scots They Carried to Canada, 1774–1855* (Toronto: Natural Heritage, 2002).

_____, *The Silver Chief: Lord Selkirk and the Scottish Pioneers of Belfast, Baldoon and Red River* (Toronto: Natural Heritage, 2003).

_____, *"A Very Fine Class of Immigrants": Prince Edward Island's Scottish Pioneers, 1770–1850* (Toronto: Natural Heritage, 2001).

Carrier, N.H., and J.R. Jeffrey, *External Migration: A Study of the Available Statistics 1815–1950* (London: HMSO, 1953).

Charbonneau, Andre and Andre Sevigny, *1847 Grosse Isle: A record of daily events* (Ottawa: Canadian Heritage, 1997).

Clark, G., "North Dumfries, Ontario," in *Borders Family History Society Bulletin,* June 1996, 17–8.

Colvin, James A., "Scottish Emigration Societies 1820–1830," (unpublished M.A. thesis, University of Guelph, 1979).

Connon, John R., *Elora* (Waterloo, ON: Wilfred Laurier University Press, 1975).

Cornelius, Donna Jean, *History of Wallaceburg, Part Two* (Wallaceburg Research and Information Study, 1974).

Cowan, Edward J., "From the Southern Uplands to Southern Ontario: Nineteenth

Century Emigration from the Scottish Borders" in T.M. Devine (ed.), *Scottish Emigration and Scottish Society* (Edinburgh: John Donald, 1992) 61–83.

Cowan, Helen, *British Emigration to British North America; the first hundred years* (Toronto: University of Toronto Press, 1961).

Craig, Gerald M., *Upper Canada: The Formative Years 1784–1841* (Toronto: McClelland & Stewart, 1993 [originally published 1963]).

Crichton, Vincent, *Pioneering in Northern Ontario* (Belleville, ON: Mika Publishing Co., 1975).

Davis, Ralph, *The Industrial Revolution and British Overseas Trade* (Leicester: Leicester University Press, 1979).

Devine, T.M., and Rosalind Mitchison (eds.), *People and Society in Scotland 1760–1830*, Vol. i (Edinburgh: John Donald, 1988).

_____, "Highland Migration to Lowland Scotland 1760–1860," in *Scottish Historical Review*, Vol. lxii (1983) 137–49.

_____, *Scottish Emigration and Scottish Society* (Edinburgh: John Donald, 1992).

_____, "Temporary Migration and the Scottish Highlands in the Nineteenth Century," *Economic History Review*, Vol. 32, (1979) 344–59.

_____, *The Great Highland Famine: Hunger, Emigration and the Scottish Highlands in the Nineteenth Century* (Edinburgh: John Donald, 1988).

_____, *The Scottish Nation, 1700–2000* (London: Allen Lane, Penguin, 1999).

Dictionary of Canadian Biography, Vols. V–XIII (Toronto: University of Toronto Press, 1979–85).

Donaldson, Gordon, *The Scots Overseas* (London: Robert Hale, 1966).

Duncan, K.J., "Aspects of Scottish Settlement in Wellington County," in *Scottish Colloquium Proceedings, University of Guelph*, Vol. 3, 1970 15–20.

Duncan, K.J., "Patterns of Settlement in the East" in Stanford W. Reid (ed.), *The Scottish Tradition in Canada* (Toronto: McClelland & Stewart, 1976) 49–75.

Elliott, Bruce S., *Irish Migrants in the Canadas: A New Approach* (Kingston, ON: McGill-Queen's University Press, 1988).

Emmerson, George S., "The Gaelic Tradition in Gaelic Culture," in Stanford Reid, *Scottish Tradition in Canada* (Toronto: McClelland & Stewart, 1976) 232–47.

Fleming, Rae (ed.), *The Lochaber Emigrants to Glengarry* (Toronto: Natural Heritage, 1994).

Fraser, Marjorie J.F., "Feudalism in Upper Canada 1823–1843," in *Ontario Historical Society*, Vol. 12 (1914) 142–52.

Galbraith, John Kenneth, *The Scotch* (Toronto: Macmillan of Canada, 1964).

Gates, Lillian F., *Land Policies of Upper Canada* (Toronto: University of Toronto Press, 1968).

Gillies, Rev. William A., *In Famed Breadalbane: The story of the antiquities, lands and peoples of a Highland district* (Perth, ON: Munro Press, 1938).

Glazebrook, G.P. de T., *A History of Transportation in Canada*, Vol. 1 (Toronto: McClelland & Stewart, 1964).

Gough, Barry, *Fighting Sail on Lake Huron and Georgian Bay: The War of 1812 and its Aftermath* (St. Catharines, ON: Vanwell, 2002).

Graham, Ian Charles Cargill, *Colonists from Scotland: Emigration to North America 1707–83* (New York: Cornell University Press, 1956).

Grainger, Jennifer, *Vanished Villages of Middlesex* (Toronto: Natural Heritage, 2002).

Gray, John Morgan, *Lord Selkirk of Red River* (London: Macmillan, 1963).

Gray, Malcolm, *The Highland Economy 1750–1850* (Edinburgh: Oliver & Boyd, 1957).

_____, "The Social Impact of Agrarian Change in the Rural Lowlands" in T.M. Devine and Rosalind Mitchison (eds.), *People and Society in Scotland 1760–1830,* Vol. i (Edinburgh: John Donald, 1988) 53–69.

Gray Malcolm, "Transcript of Letter from Canada," in *Central Scotland FHS,* No. 29, Autumn, 2004.

Guillet, Edwin C., *The Great Migration: The Atlantic crossing by sailing ships since 1770* (Toronto: University of Toronto Press, 1963).

_____, *Early Life in Upper Canada* (Toronto: University of Toronto, 1963) (reprint – original written in 1933).

_____, *Pioneer Days in Upper Canada* (Toronto: 1966).

Halliday, Clarence, *John Holliday: A Forthright Man* (Cobourg, ON: C. Halliday, 1962).

Hamil, Fred Coyne, *Lake Erie Baron: The Story of Colonel Thomas Talbot* (Toronto: Macmillan of Canada, 1955).

_____, *The Valley of the Lower Thames, 1640–1850* (Toronto: University of Toronto Press, 1951).

Hamilton, Henry, *The Industrial Revolution in Scotland* (Oxford: Clarendon Press, 1932).

Harkness, John Graham, *Stormont, Dundas and Glengarry: A History 1784–1945* (Ottawa: Mutual Press, 1972).

Harper, Marjory, *Adventurers & Exiles, The Great Scottish Exodus* (London: Profile Books, 2003).

_____, *Emigration from North-East Scotland,* Vol. 1, *Willing Exiles* (Aberdeen: Aberdeen University Press, 1988).

_____, "Image and Reality in Early Emigrant Literature," *British Journal of Canadian Studies,* Vol. 7 (1992) 3–14.

_____ & Michael E. Vance (eds.), *Myth, Migration and the Making of Memory: Scotia and Nova Scotia, c. 1700–1990* (Halifax: Fernwood & Edinburgh: John Donald, 1999).

Haydon, Andrew, *Pioneer Sketches of the District of Bathurst* (Toronto: Ryerson Press, 1925).

Hayes, Geoffrey, *Waterloo County: An illustrated history* (Kitchener ON: Waterloo Historical Society, 1997).

Herman, Arthur, *The Scottish Enlightenment: The Scots Invention of the Modern World* (London: Fourth Estate, 2001).

Hunter, Andrew F., *A History of Simcoe County* (Barrie, ON: Historical Committee of Simcoe County, 1948).

Hutchinson, Jean F., *The History of Wellington County* (Grand Valley, ON: Landsborough, 1997).

Jackson, Gordon with Kate Kinnear, *The Trade and Shipping of Dundee, 1780–1850* (Dundee: Abertay Historical Society, 1991).

Johnston, H.J.M., *British Emigration Policy 1815–1830: Shovelling out paupers* (Oxford: Clarendon Press, 1972).

Johnston, H.J.M., "Immigration to the Five Eastern Townships of the Huron Tract," in *Ontario History,* Vol. liv (1962) 207–24.

Johnston, Thomas, *The history of the working classes in Scotland* (Glasgow: Forward Pub. Co., 1922).

Lawson, Bill, *A Register of Emigrants from the Western Isles of Scotland 1750–1900,* 2

Vols. (Harris: self-published, 1992).

_____, *A Register of Emigrant Families from the Western Isles of Scotland to the Eastern Townships of Quebec* (Quebec: self-published, 1988).

Lee, Robert C., *The Canada Company and the Huron Tract, 1826–1853: Personalities, Profits and Politics* (Toronto: Natural Heritage, 2004).

Lenman, Bruce, *An Economic History of Modern Scotland 1600–1976* (London: Batsford, 1977).

Levitt, Ian and Christopher Smout, *The State of the Scottish Working Class in 1843: a statistical and spatial enquiry based on data from the poor law commission report of 1844* (Edinburgh: Scottish Academic Press, 1979).

Lindsay, Jean, *The Canals of Scotland* (Newton Abbot: David & Charles, 1968).

Lindsay, Virginia Howard, "The Perth Military Settlement: Characteristics of its permanent and transitory settlers 1815–22," (unpublished M.A. thesis, Carleton University, Ottawa, 1972).

Lower, Arthur M., *Great Britain's Woodyard: British America and the timber trade 1763–1867* (Montreal: McGill-Queen's University Press, 1973).

_____, "Settlement and the Forest Frontier in Eastern Canada" in W.A. MacKintosh and W.L.G. Jaergs (eds.), *Canadian Frontiers of Settlement,* Vol. ix, (Toronto: Macmillan, 1936).

MacArthur, E. Mairi, "Iona, History Tradition and Settlement," in *Northern Studies,* Vol. xxvi (1989) 1–14.

_____, *Iona: The Living memory of a crofting community, 1750–1914* (Edinburgh: Edinburgh University Press, 1990).

Macdonagh, Oliver, *A pattern of government growth 1800–1860: The Passenger Acts and their enforcement* (London: Macgibbon & Kee, 1961).

MacDonald, Norman, *Canada: Immigration and Settlement 1763–1841* (London: Longmans & Co., 1939).

MacGillivray, Royce, *The Mind of Ontario* (Belleville, ON: Mika Publishing Co., 1985).

_____ and Ewan Ross, *A History of Glengarry* (Belleville, ON: Mika Publishing Co., 1979).

MacKay, Donald, *The Lumberjacks* (Toronto: Natural Heritage, 1998).

MacKay, Margaret, "Tiree Migrants in Canada," in *Oral History Journal,* Vol. 9 (1981) 49–60.

MacKenzie, A.E.D., *Baldoon: Lord Selkirk's settlement in Upper Canada* (London, ON: Phelps Publishing Co., 1978).

MacKenzie, George A., *From Aberdeen to Ottawa in 1845: The Diary of Alexander Muir* (Aberdeen: Aberdeen University Press, 1990).

MacKenzie, John Munro, *Diary, 1851, John Munro MacKenzie, Chamberlain of the Lews* (Inverness: Acair Ltd., 1994).

MacKintosh, W.A. and W.L.G. Jaergs (eds.), *Canadian Frontiers of Settlement,* Vol. ix (Toronto: Macmillan, 1936).

MacLeod, Peter Kenneth, "A Study of Concentrations of Scottish Settlements in Nineteenth Century Ontario," (unpublished M.A. thesis, Carleton University, Ottawa, 1972).

MacMillan, Somerled, *Bygone Lochaber, historical and traditional* (Glasgow: K. & R. Davidson, 1971).

Marsh, E.L., *A History of the County of Grey* (Owen Sound: Fleming Pub. Co., 1931).

Martell, J.S., *Immigration to and Emigration from Nova Scotia 1815–1838* (Halifax: PANS, 1942).

Martin, Chester, *Lord Selkirk's Work in Canada,* Oxford Historical and Literary Studies, Vol. 7 (Oxford: Clarendon Press, 1916).

Martin, Ged and Jeffrey Simpson, *Canada's Heritage in Scotland* (Toronto: Dundern, 1989).

McCalla, Douglas, "The Economy of Upper Canada" in J.M. Bumsted (ed.), *Interpreting Canada's Past, Before Confederation* Vol. 1 (Toronto: Oxford University Press, 1993) 352–65.

_____, "Forest Products and Upper Canadian Development in *Canadian Historical Review,* Vol. 68 (1987) 159–98.

McColl, Hugh, *Some Sketches of the Early Pioneers of the County of Middlesex* (Ottawa: Canadian Heritage Publications, 1979).

McDiarmid, Garnet, "The Original Emigrants to McNab Township Upper Canada," in *Scottish Genealogy,* Vol. xxviii (1981) 109–21.

McGill, Jean S., *A pioneer history of the County of Lanark* (Toronto: self-published, 1974).

McLean, Marianne, *The People of Glengarry: Highlanders in Transition, 1745–1820* (Montreal: McGill-Queen's University Press, 1991).

Meek, Donald E., "Evangelicalism and Emigration: Aspects of the role of dissenting evangelicalism in Highland emigration to Canada" in Gordon MacLennan (ed.), *Proceedings of the First North American Congress of Celtic Studies: Held at Ottawa From 26th–30th March, 1986,* 15–37.

Mestern, Pat, *Fergus: A Scottish Town by Birthright* (Toronto: Natural Heritage, 1995).

Meyer, D. Vane, *The Highland Scots of North Carolina, 1732–1776* (Chapel Hill, NC: University of North Carolina Press, 1961).

Moir, John S., *Enduring Witness: A History of the Presbyterian Church in Canada* (Toronto: Presbyterian Church in Canada, 1975).

_____, *The Church in the British Era, from the British Conquest to Confederation* (Toronto: McGraw-Hill Ryerson, 1972).

Morehouse, Frances, "Canadian Migration in the Forties," in *Canadian Historical Review,* Vol. ix (1928) 309–29.

Murison, Barbara C., "Poverty, Philanthropy and Emigration to British North America: Changing attitudes in Scotland in the early Nineteenth Century," in *British Journal of Canadian Studies,* Vol. 2 (1987) 263–88.

Murray, Norman, *The Scottish Handloom Weavers 1790–1850* (Edinburgh: John Donald, 1978).

Norton, William, "The Process of Rural Land Occupation in Upper Canada," in *Scottish Geographical Magazine,* Vol. 91 (1975) 145–52.

Ontario Genealogical Society, *1842 Census Records for Lanark County for the townships of Bathurst, Beckwith, Dalhousie, Darling, Drummond, Lanark and North and South Sherbrooke* (Kingston: 1992).

"Passenger List, ship *Favourite,* 1815" in *Generations,* New Brunswick Genealogical Society, 65, (1995) 22–6,

Paterson, Gilbert C., *Land Settlement in Upper Canada, 1783–1840* (Toronto: C.W. James, 1921) (Report of the Department of Archives for the Province of Ontario for the Year 1920).

Perkins, Mary Ellen, *Discover Your Heritage: A Guide to Provincial Plaques in Ontario*

(Toronto: Natural Heritage, 1989).

Prebble, John, *The Highland Clearances* (London: Penguin, 1969).

Preston, Arthur Richard (ed.), *For Friends at Home: A Scottish emigrant's letters from Canada, California and the Cariboo 1844–64* (London: McGill-Queen's University Press, 1974).

Ramsay, Freda, *John Ramsay of Kildalton: Being an account of his life in Islay and including the diary of his trip to Canada in 1870* (Toronto: Peter Martin, 1970).

Raudzens, George K., "The Military Impact on Canadian Canals, 1815–25," in *Canadian Historical Review,* Vol. liv (1973) 273–86.

Read, Colin, *The Rising in Western Upper Canada 1837–8: The Duncombe Revolt and After* (Toronto: University of Toronto Press, 1982).

Read, Donald E., "House Building in Rural Canada West" in *Families,* Vol. 43 (2004) 213–8.

Reid, W. Stanford (ed.), *The Scottish Tradition in Canada* (Toronto: McClelland & Stewart, 1976).

Reilly, Valerie, *The Illustrated History of the Paisley Shawl* (Glasgow: Richard Drew, 1996).

Richards, Eric, *The Highland Clearances, People, Landlords and Rural Turmoil* (Edinburgh: Birlinn, 2000)

Robertson, Norman, *The History of the County of Bruce and of the minor municipalities therein, 1907–1968, Province of Ontario, Canada,* 2nd edition (Southhampton, ON: Bruce County Historical Society, 1969).

Scott, James, *The Settlement of Huron County* (Toronto: Ryerson Press, 1966).

Shadd, Adrienne, Afua Cooper and Karolyn Smardz Frost, *The Underground Railroad: Next Stop, Toronto!* (Toronto: Natural Heritage, 2002).

Shortt, A. and A.G. Doughty, (eds.), *Canada and Its Provinces: A History of the Canadian People and Their Institutions, By One Hundred Associates* (Toronto: Glasgow, Brook, 1914–17).

Skelton, Isabel, *A Man Austere* (Toronto: Ryerson Press, 1947).

Smith, Donald B., "British Indian Policy in the wake of the American Revolution" in Bumsted, *Interpreting Canada's Past,* Vol. i, 290–312.

Stevenson, John A., *Curling in Ontario, 1846–1946* (Toronto: Ontario Curling Assoc., 1950).

Storrie, Margaret, *Islay: Biography of an Island*, (Port Ellen, ON: self-published, 1981).

Syrett, David, *Shipping and the American War 1775–83: A Study of British Transport Organization* (London: Athlone Press, 1970).

Taylor, Andrew W., *Our Todays and Yesterdays: A history of the township of North Dumfries and the village of Ayr, Ontario, Canada* (North Dumfries & Ayr Centennial Committee, 1969).

Tulchinsky, Gerald, *The River Barons: Montreal business and growth of industry and transport 1837–53* (Toronto: University of Toronto Press, 1977).

Turner, Larry, *Perth: Tradition and Style in Eastern Ontario* (Toronto: Natural Heritage, 1998).

Vance, M.E., "Emigration and Scottish Society: The background of government assisted emigration to Upper Canada 1815–21," (unpublished Ph.D. thesis, University of Guelph, 1990).

Wall, Joseph Frazier, *Andrew Carnegie* (Pittsburgh: University of Pittsburgh Press, 1989).

Wallace, Malcolm, "Pioneers of the Scotch Settlement on the Shore of Lake St. Clair," in *Ontario Historical Society,* Vol. xli (1949) 173–206.

Wallaceburg Old Boys' and Girls' Reunion (Wallaceburg: 1936).

White, Paul, *Owen Sound: The Port City* (Toronto: Natural Heritage, 2000).

Whitton, Charlotte, *A Hundred years a-Fellin: some passages from the timber saga of the Ottawa in the century in which the Gillies have been cutting in the valley 1842–1942* (Ottawa: self-published, 1943).

Wild, Marilyn, "Natives of Scotland who emigrated to Kent County," in *Central Scotland FHS Bulletin*, No. 9 (1994); No. 10, 11, (1995); No. 12, 13, (1996).

Wright, Arthur E., *Pioneer Days in Nichol* (Mount Forest, ON: self-published, 1932).

Index

About the Author

Dr. Lucille Campey was born in Ottawa and spent much of her child-hood in Owen Sound, Ontario. A chemistry graduate of Ottawa University, Lucille worked initially in the fields of science and computing. After marrying her English husband she moved to England and she and Geoff now live near Salisbury. Lucille has had over thirty years experience as a researcher and author. It was her father's Scottish roots and love of history which first stimulated her interest in the early exodus of people from Scotland to Canada. She is a descendant of William Thomson, who left Morayshire, Scotland, in the early 1800s to settle first near Digby then in Antigonish, Nova Scotia. Lucille was awarded a doctorate by Aberdeen University in 1998 for her research into Scottish emigration to Canada in the period 1770–1850.

The Scottish Pioneers of Upper Canada is Lucille's fifth book on the subject of Scottish emigration to Canada. Lucille's sixth book, to be published in 2006, will deal with the pioneer Scots of Lower Canada. All of Lucille's books are published by Natural Heritage.

CPSIA information can be obtained
at www.ICGtesting.com
Printed in the USA
LVHW080757040121
675641LV00020B/1059